THE ECONOMICS
OF THE
IMAGINATION

THE ECONOMICS
OF THE
IMAGINATION

Kurt Heinzelman

THE UNIVERSITY OF MASSACHUSETTS PRESS   AMHERST

Copyright © 1980 by The University of Massachusetts Press
All rights reserved
LC 79-4019   ISBN 0-87023-274-6
Printed in the United States of America
Library of Congress Cataloging in Publication Data
appear on the last printed page of this book.

Previously unpublished material, including excerpts from
letters by William Carlos Williams, copyright © 1979 by the
Estate of Florence H. Williams. Published by permission of
New Directions Publishing Corporation.
Acknowledgments for permission to reprint other copyrighted
material appear on page 327.

To my closest reader—
to Gillian,
economist par excellence

CONTENTS

Preface   ix   List of Abbreviations   xiii

PART ONE. LITERATURE AND ECONOMICS   1

Chapter I. *"The Mouth-Tale of the Giants": An Introduction to the Economics of the Imagination*   3

Chapter II. *Economics in Mammon's Cave*   35

Chapter III. *"Unreal Words": Language in Political Economy*   70

Chapter IV. *William Blake and "The Price of Experience"*   110

PART TWO. LABOR THEORY AND THE LITERARY WORK   135

Chapter V. *The Art of Labor*   137

Chapter VI. *The Psychomachia of Labor*   166

Chapter VII. *Wordsworth's Labor Theory: An Economics of Compensation*   196

Chapter VIII. *"Getting It" in* Paterson: *The Increment Defended*   234

Afterword: *The Merchant as Poet*   276

Notes   283   A Selected Bibliography   310   Index   321

"Economy" is derived from the Greek word *oikonomia* meaning the management of a household. In English usage, economy suggests both frugality and efficiency; by extension, it applies to the management of many structures, political and domestic, commercial and aesthetic. In its largest sense, the word asserts our capacity for creating intellectual structures and for imaginatively regulating them. It indicates our ability to discriminate between ends and means, and therefore, as a reflector of human choice, it represents the thoroughness of our self-consciousness.

When "economy" pertains to the management and structuring of *the* economy in the modern, Western sense, then we may understand *economics* as a system of discourse used to order this political economy, to make it consistent and workable. But as a total metaphor, "economics" remains both self-referring and expansive. Economic signifiers—words such as "labor," "price," "profit," "credit," and "cost"—necessarily point to semantic and philosophical values which are not simply or merely commercial. The use of these words further reflects the self-consciousness of our very language.

The Economics of the Imagination is a study of this notoriously flexible metaphor—of how, linguistically, "economics" is produced and of how, imaginatively, it is used. Its most immediate use, of course, is in economic theory. But when economists seek to embody political economy in a workable discursive form, a struggle occurs which engages both imaginative and commercial schemes of production. In this struggle, economists interpose new forms of metaphorical logic and of mythic interpretation in order to substantiate the imaginative validity of their own discursive formations. "The achievement of economy is an art," observes the economist A. L. Macfie. "Economics in the full sense does not just examine facts; it rationalises, indeed *creates the experience with which it deals.*"[1] In assessing the value of this experience, in composing and employing the metaphors which serve as vehicles for conveying that value, the labor of the economist becomes comparable to the poet's. More importantly, insofar as economics posits its own imaginative economy, such discursive rationalizing of events will necessarily affect, as in every other creation of the imagination, the very nature of the "facts" which it structures.

This book is a work of literary criticism, even though many of the texts examined here may seem to "belong," more properly, to the sphere of social science. In its broadest speculation, therefore, this is also a study of that sense of "belonging"; of how literacy, in its fullest significance, must evidence an understanding of the literary uses and pertinence of nonliterary discourse—in our case, of political economy. To arrive at such an understanding we will also analyze how classical economics itself is metaphorically and structurally constituted, and this analysis, it is hoped, may be of some particular interest to economists and other social scientists. Unfortunately, the method of the book may be precisely what many social scientists distrust. An "ideological" essay, discussing the verbal, philosophical, and structural relations between concepts of "value," cannot derive its method from the exhaustive, inclussive model preferred by the empirical scientist. And the social scientist's distrust of an empiricism which is not "value-neutral" may be reciprocated by the literary student's indifference or hostility to economics in either its theoretical or its raw, statistical form. In short, almost every reader of this book is likely to find one set of texts (say, the poetical ones) more familiar and less threatening than another set (the economic tracts, for instance). But through this juxtaposition of known texts with stranger ones (whichever ones they happen to be for any given reader), perhaps some small light can also be shed on the burden which is propagated by our academically specialized labors. It is, in any case, a burden whose weight is measured again and again in both the economic and the literary works discussed below. Because, as I shall argue, economics governs the reading of a book as much as the writing and publishing of it, I would urge all readers to proceed with the economics of their own imaginations attuned to its specialized computation of gain and loss.

To put it another way, this book is not merely (or even primarily) a series of essays about political economy or about its "effect" on literature. Nor is it a general, theoretical excursus on the nature of metaphor. It is, rather, an intersystemic analysis of the language and logic which poetic and economic "systems" share. More specifically, by determining how economic theory imaginatively—fictively—structures economic discourse, we may explore how the art of political economy incorporates these structures; how this art is then expressed, formulated, and reassessed in literature; and how it is also transfigured there. In my discussion of Marxian economics, for instance (see chapter six, below), it is not my intention to prove that Marx was "wrong"—or that he was "right"—but only to disentangle and unfold some of the plangent and problematic metaphors upon which his theories are grounded. This work will find its final coherence, I think, if and when it has convinced the reader that such metaphors still inform our daily speech, our social fictions, and the literature we read—that they have, in fact, been translated by literature into challenging and largely unanalyzed forms of thought which we literary and economic analysts alike, often unwittingly approximate, ignore, or repossess in our own thinking.

I am indebted to those who have read and criticized the present work in whole or in part—Gillian Adams, Thomas L. Ashton, Geoffrey Carnall, Arthur J. Carr, Evan Carton, Donald Cheney, David V. Erdman, Kathryn Graham, Arthur F. Kinney, Kieron Kramer, Sarah Lawall, Allen Mandelbaum, Walter Reed, and particularly Paul Mariani. I owe thanks to the Fulbright-Hays Commission and the University of Massachusetts for fellowships which permitted this project to be completed, and to the research librarians of the John Sawyer Library at Williams College and to the staff of the National Library of Scotland for other kinds of fellowship. Grateful acknowledgment is made to the editors of *Modern Language Quarterly* and *English Language Notes,* who originally published most of the material contained in the present chapter four. Believing firmly in the economics of the imagination, the Danforth Foundation repeatedly offered for almost nine years every kind of help and support that was requested or required. To the officers and staff of the Foundation, I wish to express my special gratitude.

Austin, Texas

ABBREVIATIONS

C   Karl Marx, *Capital: A Critique of Political Economy,* ed.
Frederick Engels, trans. Samuel Moore and Edward Aveling
from 3rd German ed., 3 vols. (New York: International
Publishers, 1967)

LEY   *Letters of William and Dorothy Wordsworth: The Early
Years,* ed. Ernest de Selincourt, rev. ed. Chester L. Shaver
(Oxford: Clarendon Press, 1967)

P   William Carlos Williams, *Paterson* (New York: New Directions, 1963)

PAME   Karl Polanyi, *Primitive, Archaic and Modern Economies,*
ed. George Dalton (Boston: Beacon Press, 1971)

PL   John Milton, *Paradise Lost,* in *Complete Poems and Major
Prose,* ed. Merritt Y. Hughes (New York: Odyssey, 1957)

WN   Adam Smith, *An Inquiry into the Nature and Causes of
the Wealth of Nations,* ed. R. H. Campbell and A. S. Skinner, textual ed. W. B. Todd, 2 vols., Glasgow Edition of
the Works and Correspondence of Adam Smith (Oxford:
Clarendon Press, 1976)

PART ONE
LITERATURE AND
ECONOMICS

*Three-fourths of the demands existing
in the world are romantic; founded
on visions, idealisms, hopes, and
affections; and the regulation of the
purse is, in its essence, regulation of
the imagination and the heart.
Hence, the right discussion of the nature of price is a very high metaphysical and psychical problem.*
—*John Ruskin,* Unto This Last

CHAPTER I

"The Mouth-Tale of the Giants"
An Introduction to the
Economics of the Imagination

In 1919, Marcel Duchamp paid his dentist, Daniel Tzanck, with an over-sized, handwritten check for $115.[1] Since the check was worthless—it was only drawn on Duchamp's sketch pad, not drafted on any bank—the value of the "payment" depended initially upon the quality of Duchamp's (and presumably Tzanck's) sense of irony. In due course, however, Duchamp repurchased the check for an amount greater than its "face value." The joke had been literally cashed in: after a certain passage of time, the value of the check had effortlessly inflated. In effect, Duchamp's signature on the check (as artist) had become more valuable than the arbitrary currency value that he had assigned to it (as economic agent). Reversing the normal business transactions of art, the artist wound up with the "unreal" artifact, whereas the consumer obtained the real money paid to him, in this case, by the artist himself. The artist, normally regarded as merely the producer in aesthetic exchanges, profited in a new way: he became both the buyer and the seller of his art. A critical inquiry might initially ask: at exactly what point in these transactions did the Tzanck check become "valuable" as a commodity of exchange?

Because the check is both an artistic imitation of a monetary draft and an economic imitation of an artistic creation, the question of "value" is thrown into hopeless confusion. To speak of "value" one must frame the inquiry in somewhat different terms: what do the signs of value in monetary exchanges (the $115 of the check) have to do with the signs of value in artistic exchanges (the marks of the artist, his signature on the check)? Surrealists such as Duchamp were less concerned with hermeneutic significance—the conceptual meaning of signs in a given context or schema—than with the semiotic process of how a thing came to be a sign, a signifier, in the first place. Duchamp's check, like the surrealists' ready-made object or *objet trouvé,* purposefully distorts the question of value by raising it in an inappropriate or surprising context. Here, economic and aesthetic signifiers cross, disrupting each other. The check is found to be a "sign" only as a given individual is willing to bestow significance upon it. Duchamp, for instance, was willing to pay more than $115 for it, although, theoretically, it was not worth even that. But whatever the transactions involving the check, the check itself was *never* the equivalent of its $115 face value, because the mark of the artist on the check had disturbed the economic matrix in which the dollar sign would possess a precise, arithmetical meaning.

The check sets in motion an infinite series of resonances—on the one side into the economic area of currency equivalences and on the other side into the artistic area of imaginative representations. The problem of "value" is the midpoint where these two areas intersect. Duchamp's ambivalent identification of that meeting place encourages us to ask a more far-reaching question: what do monetary and artistic exchanges have to do with dental work?

One may require good teeth for aesthetic reasons, but one also goes to the dentist because good teeth allow the mouth to function properly. Mediating between the object (the mouth) and its necessary and pleasureable objectives (chewing, talking, kissing, and so on), teeth are metaphorical implements of nurture. The Tzanck check reminds us that business transactions are also a *tertium quid,* expressing both an actual and a fictive value. As an art object, the check is a production of Duchamp's work, just as the dental work represents the doctor's professional labor. The check is a symbolic statement; so is the dental work for which it is exchanged. According to Duchamp's logic, it would be silly and inappropriate to exchange figurative gold in the form of money for the actual dentist's gold implanted in his teeth. So Duchamp exchanges his art instead. Duchamp compensates the dentist with a coin that is appropriate to the dentist's labor, for his check is also a *tertium quid,* created by Duchamp's labor to fill the (semiotic) gap between the gold implanted in his mouth and the symbolic gold (the dollar sign) that the dental work costs. Although the marks left in the mouth by the dentist's labor are not equivalent to the marks left on the *objet d'art* by the artist's labor, , both sets of marks, as *signs* of labor value, become equivalent in exchange.

The adage that "money talks" will not account for Duchamp's more mysterious and complex metaphor. We may read the origins of Duchamp's economics in the genesis story related by the ancient Norse saga, the *Prose Edda:*

> Then said Aegir: "It seems to me that Thjazi was a mighty man: now of what family was he?" Bragi answered: "His father was called Olvaldi, and if I tell thee of him, thou wilt think these things wonders. He was very rich in gold; but when he died and his sons came to divide the inheritance, they determined upon this measure for the gold which they divided: each should take as much as his mouth would hold, and all the same number of mouthfuls. One of them was Thjazi, the second Idi, the third Gangr. And we have it as a metaphor among us now, to call gold the mouth-tale of the giants; but we conceal it in secret terms or in poesy in this way, that we call it Speech, or Word, or Talk, of these giants.[2]

The author of the *Prose Edda* finds not that money talks but that "Speech, or Word, or Talk" is itself a concealed metaphor of an original and literal wealth. The death of the father, Olvaldi, who "was very rich in gold," creates the need for division, for measure, for sharing, for community. Representing this division, Olvaldi's three sons take from their father's original wealth only such partial measures as the mouth can hold. In "determin[ing] upon this measure for the gold which they divided," the sons create an embryonic economics. We are their heirs, profiting from their belated knowledge which is "among us now." Like Midas, we cannot have our gold and eat it too. In translating gold (what we cannot eat) into nurture (what we must eat), in parsing an original mythic abundance into finite but usable commodities, we have discovered the essential insufficiency of economy itself. We proceed to conceal this insufficiency in imprecise and ambiguous "secret terms." We descend into language, "the mouth-tale of the giants." If the mouth is the original purse of economy, then it is also the original dispenser of our "poesy" and language—a coincidence which we may observe in Duchamp's imaginative economics as well.

By a poetic logic similar to Duchamp's and to the *Prose Edda*'s, John Ruskin explained that we "conceal" an original wholeness, our mythic inheritance, in the "secret terms" of political economics. Economists would conceal our real wealth from us, according to Ruskin, by a corrupt system of "Speech, or Word, or Talk":

> There are two kinds of true production, always going on in an active State; one of seed, and one of food; or production for the Ground, and for the Mouth; both of which are by covetous persons thought to be production only for the granary; whereas the function of the granary is but intermediate and conservative, fulfilled in distribution; else it ends in nothing but mildew, and nourishment of rats and worms. And since production for the Ground is only useful with future hopes of harvest, all *essential* production is for the Mouth; and is finally measured by the mouth; hence, as I said above, consumption is the crown of production; and the wealth of a nation is only to be estimated by what it consumes.[3]

We must have a wealth that we can eat: that is Midas's true dilemma. But in Ruskin's radical grammar, the primary significance of consumption or production for the mouth means that we must also possess a form of economic discourse that we can truly speak:

> The want of any clear sight of this fact is the capital error, issuing in rich interest and revenue of error among the political economists. Their minds are continually set on money-gain,

not on mouth-gain; and they fall into every sort of net and
snare, dazzled by the coin-glitter as birds by the fowler's
glass; or rather (for there is not much else like birds in them)
they are like children trying to jump on the heads of their
own shadows; the money-gain being only the shadow of the
true gain, which is humanity. [*Works*, 17:101-2]

"Humanity" is, here and elsewhere in Ruskin, that fulfillment
which is synonymous with "well-being," the "true" and original
meaning of wealth. Ruskin's puns—"capital error," "rich interest,"
and "revenue of error"—are literally verbal tokens of the economists' "money-gain." These figures of speech—when they are seen
as *figures* of speech—reveal, for Ruskin, a "shadow" discourse, the
secret terms of economic terminology. Economists weave their
theories of economic production around such metaphorical systems, fashioning capital, revenue, and interest into food for the
mouth. More precisely, economic metaphor—what Ruskin calls
"politico-economic language" (*Works*, 17:80)—is literally a capital
error: it occurs at the *capus*, the head or beginning, of economic
theory and fills the heads of economists with Midasian delusions.
They imagine that their language has a semiotic power equivalent
to the golden touch. For, by promising that the gold we carry in
our purses will sustain us as food for the mouth, politico-economic
language sustains the fiction of poetry: that metaphors are real.

Both Ruskin and the author of the *Prose Edda* would have understood the following newspaper headline: "Words, Not Wheat
Sales, Cause Higher Prices."[4] This economic phenomenon occurs
precisely because of the complex discursive and psychological
structures of economic exchange. Baldly stated, the "supply" aspect of economic management is arithmetically computable, but
the "demand" part is arithmetically ambiguous, as elusive and resonant as the "words" we use to express our desires and fears. What
is often demanded of economic discourse is a finite expression of
our infinite potential—of our "humanity," as Ruskin said. What
the movements of the economy reflect is nothing less than the
shape of our imagination, not perhaps in its fullest but certainly
in one of its most insistent displays. We say that "money talks,"
and yet, as the *Prose Edda* suggests, we must first understand the
mythic impetus behind that metaphorical turn of speech. To the
author of the *Prose Edda*, "Speech, or Word, or Talk" is a metaphor of economic transaction, just as much as money is a meta-

phor for language. In everyday discourse, we find that vehicle and
tenor are constantly changing places: money talks and talk is a
secret coinage, concealing an "economic" meaning in "secret
terms." The economic imagination calls forth a secret economics
of the imagination. Words alter wheat prices, and prices are one
way of fixing wheat in a word that the mouth can hold. Together,
they aspire to a similar imaginative sufficiency, promising an economy in which we may live, as Wallace Stevens said, on the bread of
faithful speech.[5]

One aim of the present study is to examine how we imagine and
confront, or imagine that we confront, the realities of economic
life as these struggles take form in and inform our literature. In
this pursuit, we may take Coleridge's grand assertion to task, subjecting it to the kind of empirical substantiation (and qualification) which Coleridge himself omits: "As there are two wants connatural to man, so are there two main directions of human activity,
pervading in modern times the whole civilized world; and consti-
tuting and sustaining that nationality which yet it is their tendency, and, more or less, their *effect,* to transcend and to moderate—
Trade and Literature."[6] Coleridge's essays on "Method" seek, on
one level, to determine the "principle of progression" (*The Friend,*
1: 457) by which these two activities, trade and literature, might
be forged into an "identity and living copula" (ibid., p. 521) so as
to reveal the "economy everywhere in the irrational creation"
(ibid., p. 517). The copula which connects these two activities
may be discovered initially in the metaphor of "economics." In
order to show how economic consciousness assumes imaginative
form, we must first identify economic discourse as (in Coleridgean
terms) a "method," a systematic metaphor. By unfolding this system, we may evaluate more directly the economic process of literature, including its ability to represent social issues and perhaps to
engender social change. In searching out the semantic "effect" of
economics, we may better understand how commerce and literature attempt "to transcend and to moderate," among other things,
each other.

Harriet Martineau's nine-volume *Illustrations of Political Economy* (1832) was one effort at such an understanding—literally an
attempt to explicate economic principles by means of fictional
narratives. Martineau's premise, if not the crude literalness of her

method, has been followed by later theorists who posit artistic labor as an explanation or even a verification of the labor that produces material things, as if the former activity ought to serve and imitate the latter. But this mimetic premise immediately puts literary forms in both a derivative and a divisive relationship to economic forms. The trope of "economics," when applied to the content of literature or when extended to account for its structures, becomes merely belated, secondhand. Subsequently, literary criticism that analyzes economic issues as they arise *in* literature often ends by ascribing a certain economic or class status *to* literature (and to the artist). At best, therefore, literature seems to become merely a chronicle or *exemplum,* not a creator, of economic consciousness.

Psychoanalytic criticism attempts to break through this passivity by exploring the psychical origins of character traits which are often associated with economic desires. Even so, Freud's description of money's anal eroticism did not prevent him from using economics as a basal (and wholly honorific) metaphor throughout his work and especially in *Jokes and Their Relation to the Unconscious* (see chapter eight, below). The metaphor's imaginative force and the author's unrepressed use of it would seem to belie the psychical symbolism which Freud elsewhere attributes to it. Indirectly, then, Freud reveals the thesis of the present work: that "economics" does not issue forth in a psychologically consistent way or in a single discursive form. Or, to state the thesis positively, the economic complicity of literature is integrally connected to the discursive complexity of economics. The literature discussed below prompts us to understand economics itself as an imaginative event, forming what could be regarded as a counterpoetics, and supplying our written and oral discourse with a linguistically rich, ethically ambiguous, but mythically resonant system of metaphor.

Ferdinand de Saussure has noted (but has not analyzed) the linguistic roots of such a counterpoetics. According to Saussure, "the intervention of the factor of time" creates in the field of linguistics "two completely divergent paths": a synchronic, vertical "axis of simultaneities" which describes linguistic relations between "coexisting things," and a diachronic, horizontal "axis of successions" which takes into account the factor of language's temporal change.[7] This dualism in linguistic structures is repeated, according to Saussure, in one other science, economics:

> Here, in contrast to the other sciences, political economy and
> economic history constitute two clearly separated disciplines
> within a single science; the works that have recently appeared
> on these subjects point up the distinction. Proceeding as they
> have, economists are—without being well aware of it—obey-
> ing an inner necessity. A similar necessity obliges us to divide
> linguistics into two parts, each with its own principle. Here as
> in political economy we are confronted with the notion of
> *value;* both sciences are concerned with *a system for equating
> things of different orders*—labor and wages in one and a signi-
> fied and signifier in the other. [P. 79]

For Saussure, "value" itself is the midpoint between economics as
a historical system and "economics" as a structurally inconstant
idea; it constitutes the meeting place of the economist's and the
linguist's purposes, one point at which the axes of simultaneity
and of succession cross. By extension, "value" is the discursive
event which equates such different orders of things as signifer and
signified, wages and labor, and ultimately, the production of
words and the production of material goods. My examination will
proceed to dissect economics as a monolithic entity, unveiling a
verbal and philosophical constellation of individual signifiers, such
as labor, price, cost, and credit, whose meaning alters in relation
to one another depending upon whether they are construed as
"illustrative," "connatural," or "of different orders." In the language of Michel Foucault, we are concerned here not with the
exegetical, chicken-and-egg question of which has epistemological
priority, literature or economics, but with a broader question:
How are "words" and "things" ordered? By means of what fictive
(cultural) structuring?

If regarded as a metaphor, "economics" may assume its radical
function—the ability to transfer (as in the root meaning of *meta-
pherein*) ideational value through the medium of linguistic exchange. What Saussure says about "value" may also apply to
metaphors in particular: they are "a system for equating things
of different orders."[8] *The Economy of Literature,* a recent study
by Marc Shell, posits money as a sign of correspondence between
the linguist and the economist and diagrams how money functions
as a discrete, highly complex art form within economic systems.

Shell imagines a hermeneutical exchange between coins as economic *sema* and coins as aesthetic tokens and, by analyzing the signs that make up monetary inscriptions, illuminates what much literary criticism has conditioned us to ignore or to deprecate—that aesthetic and commercial economies emerge out of similar semiotic necessities, which lead to "the internalization of economic form" and result in "the economics of thought itself" (p. 62). In revitalizing John Ruskin's contention that there is a "political economy of literature," Shell's findings significantly expand the parameters of aesthetic theory.

Economic notation is the subject of the present study as well, but the importance of commercial economics to aesthetic economy will be seen to supersede the artifice of monetary signs. The greater and more pervasive art form—the one which has a direct effect upon literary practice as well as theory—is the metaphorical constellation of "economics" itself. Money is but one of many economic *sema* which literature appropriates, for literature must accommodate a whole system of metaphor, an entire economic language, which has become entrenched in our everyday rhetoric and thought.[9] There, the homogeneity to which economists would like to restrict the idea of "economy" is disrupted. By analyzing the economic forms of poetic discourse and the poetics of economic discourse simultaneously, as equally significant and instructive exertions of the imagination, we may see how the development of the political economy changes the idea of the imagination and how, through the further labor of the imagination—through its expression in poetry—economic discourse is forced to speak in more responsive ways. The literature examined here reorganizes "economics" as an organic metaphor of its own structural economy, an act that reasserts the political and social authority of literature at its most radical level—in language itself. The right interpretation and use of economics thus becomes a test of our literacy, as if literacy were a condition and function of our moral responsibility.[10]

We are speaking, then, of two phenomena: (1) "imaginative economics," the way in which economic systems are structured, by means of the imagination, upon what are essentially fictive concepts—including, ultimately, "the economy" itself—and (2) "poetic economics," the way in which literary writers use this fictive economic discourse, this body of systematized knowledge, as an

ordering principle in their own work. *The Economics of the Imagination* will seek to identify the coincidence and the continuity of
these two "economics" by showing how the "secret terms" of
economic discourse encroach upon moral and aesthetic issues—
indeed, upon the whole life of the imagination.

The rest of the first chapter surveys the effects of this encroach-
ment in literature; culminating in a discussion of Thoreau's "economy," it provides a capsule summary of the critical questions and
terminology to be employed in this study. Chapters two and three
chart the evolution of "the economy" as a formal, semantically
unique structure, created by a "politico-economic language"
which disrupts linguistic signifiers and fashions its own myths and
metaphors in order to prove its imaginative authenticity. We shall
see how these "secret terms" are anticipated in Spenser's sixteenth-
century depiction of Mammon, how they are played out against
competing Christian and classical myths, and how Mammon's
"art" develops, during the nineteenth century, into "political
economy," a discrete, self-enclosed, and "value-neutral" science—
a systematic discipline. That "art" will be examined in the economic writings of Adam Smith, David Ricardo, Thomas Malthus,
Karl Marx, W. Stanley Jevons, and John Stuart Mill. Subsequent
chapters will reveal how Romantic and post-Romantic writers (including Blake, Wordsworth, Ruskin, Yeats, and Frost) tried to
outwit, even as they recoiled from, this commercial system by
creating their own texts. The present study concludes by identifying in modern literature—particularly in the unique economies
of Ezra Pound and William Carlos Williams—the hope and the
nightmare of nineteenth-century aesthetics: the idea of the poet
as economist.

The literary uses of economic tropes discussed here are almost
always *overt* and not, as in much Marxist analysis, a solely (and
regrettably) unconscious expression of an author's class status or
of the forms of social production under which he lives. This poetry dramatizes the intersystemic relationship between literature and
economics, not as if one "illustrates" (in Martineau's sense) the
other but because, aesthetically and epistemologically, each crosses
and passes through the other. Initially, such poetic economics will
reveal the intellectual and imaginative burden of "the economy"
to be the proper metaphorical representation of economic thought.
Ultimately, poetry shows economics as a form of metaphorization

which partakes of the mythic force of poetry itself and which, therefore, may be used in poetry as a schematic method of defining poetry's own ontological status. In apprehending that schema, our study will need to derive a practical criticism, permitting us to see economics, when fully articulated both in and through literature, as at once a humanized product of and a transformational grammar for the imagination.

Perhaps all literature, including the literature of economists, implicitly marks itself with an exchange value and becomes (in Ruskin's words) a "commercial text" (*Works*, 17:53)—as Duchamp's check explicitly does. And perhaps, in the following analysis, this tropic awareness will comprise Duchamp's final insight, his supreme fiction.

The Dissociation of Economies

It is among the miseries of the present age that it recognizes no medium between Literal *and* Metaphorical.—*S. T. Coleridge,* The Statesman's Manual

Coleridge's "Method" is an attempt to reconcile literal and figurative, functional and metaphysical meanings by creating the "medium" of a unifying power—what he often called "the Shaping Spirit of Imagination." Without it, trade and literature remain dissociated disciplines, not "connatural" participants in one human "science." And, like T. S. Eliot after him, Coleridge viewed Renaissance writers as exemplars of a "method" which avoided our "present" misery, the dissociation of sensibility and vision.

Coleridge's sense of the past, and therefore his view of "the present age," require closer study. During the sixteenth and seventeenth centuries, the effects of rapid economic change generated a dramatic and wholesale alteration not only in the structure of English society but also in the semantics of the English language. At the beginning of the sixteenth century, economists were searching for the best monetary substance[11] as the use of trading monopolies increased dramatically.[12] In 1568 a formal market, the Royal Exchange, was instituted by Thomas Gresham. At century's end, England had become a principal participant in what economic historians tell us was the first genuinely international money market.[13] Lawrence Stone has precisely surveyed the new kinds of

capitalist finance practiced by some of the more eminent aristocratic families in Elizabethan and Jacobean Britain.[14] Although
to speak of a Renaissance rise of "capitalism" is a bit anachronistic
(the word "capitalism" did not attain its modern sense until well
into the nineteenth century[15]), one must also recognize that by
the time of Ben Jonson, for instance, a significant change in economic methods, and a significantly new reliance upon them, had
come to pass.

These developments bequeathed to the English language a revised set of linguistic signifiers using economic terms. Jonson, in
his commonplace book *Discoveries,* attempted to evaluate the disparity between the moral and the economic senses of "value":
"The price of many things is farre above, what they are bought
and sold for. *Life,* and *Health,* which are both inestimable, we
have of the *Physician:* As *Learning,* and *Knowledge,* the true tillage
of the *mind,* from our *Schoolemasters.* But the fees of the one, or
the *salary* of the other, never answer the *value* of what we received;
but serve to gratifie their labours."[16] Already, by Jonson's time,
the concept of "value" had bifurcated, so that its abstract significance in ordinary usage became circumscribed by its specific and
narrower meaning in economic discourse. Coleridge would assert
that "value" and "worth" were not at all synonymous (and Duchamp would have to create his own money form to "answer the
value" of what he received) because Jonson's remarks had become
truisms: "value" in respect to one's physical and spiritual well-
being is not the same "value" as represented by one's monetary or
economic wealth. More precisely, the latter forms of value do not
have the *means* to express the former. "Wealth," as an instrument
and aim of economic planning, would be finally dismembered
from its root meaning (weal or well-being) in the nineteenth century, but even in the seventeenth century, the "new" meanings of
economic discourse were firmly entrenched. Words which had earlier signifed the bonds of feudal loyalty lost their ethical overtones,
their invocation of an ethos. "Price" no longer meant esteem.
"Fee" no longer meant an estate held by homage, and "in fee" no
longer signified a relationship subject to feudal obligation. "Fy-
naunce" no longer meant to take as ransom, nor did "mortgage"
mean security, or "purchase" endeavor, or "thrift" luck, or "commodity" advantage.[17] These words, among others, acquired a singularly commercial, fiduciary significance. The question became, as

Jonson's notebook entry implies, whether the discourse of economic "value" had more than a metaphorical relationship to moral conduct and philosophical attitudes.

Jonson presses the point by employing economic metaphors in order to define his art: *"Custome* is the most certain Mistresse of Language, as the publicke stampe makes the current money. But wee must not be too frequent with the mint, every day coyning. Nor fetch words from the extreme and utmost ages; since the chiefe vertue of a style is perspecuitie, and nothing so vitious in it, as to need an Interpreter" (*Works,* 8:622). The vehicle of this metaphor is meliorative, not pejorative: language is a kind of money. But Jonson also implies that language may lose its perspecuity and so require (like Donne's language, as Jonson elsewhere claimed), "an Interpreter." He thus distinguishes between metaphors that serve as currency and metaphors that require interpretation. But in fact, currency itself (or "treasure," to use an acceptable Renaissance synonym) also needs to be interpreted. On the one hand, "the *Poet* must bee able by nature, and instinct, to powre out the Treasure of his minde" (*Works,* 8:637), and yet, on the other hand, this "Treasure" could be "mis-spen[t]" in the "business" of everyday life: "What a deale of cold business doth a man mis-spend the better part of life in! in scattering *complements,* tendring *visits,* gathering and venting *newes,* following *Feasts* and *Playes,* making a little winter-love in a darke corner" (*Works,* 8:565). Here, tenor and vehicle have gone their separate ways. The business of a man's life is "cold" because it is metaphorically alienated from the economics of the mind, leaving the better part of life misspent. This "economic" paradox is further complicated by Jonson's use of the term "economy" in a strictly structural, rather than a commercial, sense: "In the *Greeke* Poets, as also in *Plautus,* we shall see the Oeconomy, and disposition of *Poems,* better observed then [*sic*] in Terence, and the later: who thought the sole grace, and vertue of their Fable, the sticking in of sentences, as our doe the forcing in of jests" (*Works,* 8: 618-19). Jonson's use of "economy" as a rhetorical term is sanctioned by classical writers—this is in fact its commonest use in literary theory —but it is dismembered from the full sociopolitical import of the word.[18] If the "economy" of poetry is its transparency, which makes it a form of currency, accessible to the reader, then our daily lives, when interpreted, are of a different coinage.

What these examples, these commonplace expressions, reveal is that poetic economy itself may need mediation. The currency of language (its verbal denotations) and the grammar of the currency (the semantics of monetary business) may not be interchangeable metaphors but different and perhaps antipathetic forms of discourse. Whether Jonson himself saw this implication is unclear, for "custome," when viewed in the context of economic discourse, was in the process of fostering a brood of "unreal words," as Walter Bagehot would call them.[19] But even by "making a little winter-love in a darke corner," one finds oneself caught up in the paradox of business, as one accomplishes a little (private) profit taking in order to separate genuine tenderness from "tendring visits," as one tries to avoid dissociating literal from metaphorical well-being.

Jonson was himself, as he often said, a stickler for proper usage. He noted in *Discoveries* a sentiment garnered from Thucydides by way of Horace: "Wheresoever, manners, and fashions are corrupted, language is. It imitates the publicke riot. The excesse of Feasts, and apparell, are the notes of a sick State; and the wantonnesse of language, of a sick mind" (*Works*, 8:593). But the medium of language is most incontinent. Ironically, John Beaumont's elegy to Jonson confirms this:

> Since then, he made our language pure and good,
> To teach us speake, but what we understood;
> We owe this praise to him, that should we joyne
> To paye him, he were paid but with the coyne
> Himselfe hath minted; which we know by this
> That no words passe for currant now, but his. . . .[20]

Jonson's economic metaphor is also Beaumont's, and the ambivalence of such economic language does "passe for currant" even now. But the elegy's *topos* of praise also puts words into Jonson's mouth. Jonson metaphorically equated custom and the mint; Beaumont bestows upon Jonson his own "publicke stampe," so that he is "paid but with the coyne / Himselfe hath minted." The deeper irony of the elegy unwittingly reveals, therefore, the incongruous poetic economics of the elegy itself. In praising Jonson's "pure and good" use of language, Beaumont echoes the classical dictum that language makes the man, a sentiment which Jonson himself rephrased in *Discoveries:* "*Language* most shewes a man: speake that I may see thee" (*Works*, 8:625). That transparency or showing forth is what Jonson affirmed as "œconomy," as the disposition of language which confirms its currency, its true value. But Beaumont's likenesses partake of a different economics. They ascribe a superior "value" to Jonson's *own* coinages, and *these* proceed to outpace all other forms of currency.

If Jonson was concerned with making language "pure and good" so that it avoided the corruption to which life, manners, and language itself are susceptible, then Beaumont's language is a testimonial to the continuing need to be concerned. More specifically, what Beaumont praises Jonson's language for is not what his own language embodies. Jonson's language quest did not even survive his fellow poets' elegies for him. In Beaumont's poem, meaning accrues through the vehicle of the metaphor (coinage), not through the tenor (value). Our metaphorical debt to Jonson is repaid, then, by extending (and expending) the *metaphor*. Whereas Jonson cautioned against being "too frequent with the mint," so that we needed an interpreter, in Beaumont's elegy we find Beaumont reinterpreting the currency which "most shewes a man." He praises Jonson, therefore, by the very kind of abstruse refinement and dissociation of language which Jonson himself deprecated. So Beaumont's poetic adulation of that literary giant, Ben Jonson, reveals how easily "the mouth-tale" of economics can become an ironic counterpointing: the currency we praise in poetry becomes a fictive commodity, a trope that out-tropes the coinages which it interprets, and thus qualitatively differentiates itself from the literal world of custom, the world of fact. Poetic discourse, the language of literary fictions, acquires a "factual" status of its own. Before long, literature may be seen to stand apart, asserting, in defiance of the materialism of the "real" world, the materialism of its own self-referring discourse.

The word "fact" becomes a symptom of this defiance. It enters common English usage rather late—about the middle of the sixteenth century—although it is an almost exact rendering of *factum*, as in the postclassical construction, *factum est* (it came to pass), the commonplace, even formulaic utterance of the Vulgate. Etymologically, a "fact" is a thing which is made or done or accomplished, just as a poem is, etymologically, a thing created by a poet or maker. Almost from its beginning in both Latin and English usage, however, the word "fact" also signified the empirical phenomena of the world itself—the world of "facts."[21] A fact is also an "event" or "occurrence." "Fact" in this sense becomes *the* facts, the building blocks of reality and the true world of causal sequence.

We may observe this transformation of "fact" into a metaphor in the preface of *Robinson Crusoe,* where Daniel Defoe, as "editor," writes that he "believes the thing to be a just history of fact": there is no "appearance of fiction in it."[22] The fictive editor is supported in this belief by the fictional narrator who, at the epistemological level, does not distinguish between events that actually occurred and those that he merely fears or wishes or dreams. For Crusoe, the latter are no less factual than every other material manifestation of his self-consciousness. Thus, the fact of his father's displeasure at his going to sea is exchangeable with the fact that he (Crusoe) is disaster prone. Crusoe's provisions, both what he manages to salvage from wrecked ships and what he grows or discovers for himself, are equally "facts" of his labor. A footprint in the sand is an uncomfortable, anxious fact, and it is somehow related to other facts of anxiety, such as his stumbling, recalcitrant faith in God. His hope for rescue, his fear of finding that he is not alone, and his dreams of massacring cannibals are, like his eventual rescue, the sudden appearance of Friday, and his eventual massacre of the cannibals, all matters of fact, all a part of the ledger of his life.[23] Because all facts correspond and are equivalent, the chapter title, "I Find my Wealth all about Me," where "Wealth" is at once both literal and figurative, an actuality and a state of mind, might serve as a properly equivocal subtitle for this "just history of fact."

Moll Flanders similarly catalogues, all with the same emotional insouciance, the streets of London which she worked, the goods which she acquired, the moral choices she made, and the men with whom she made them, in order to present "this account of my life."[24] For Moll, more explicitly perhaps than for Crusoe, in the world of facts, the appurtances of material well-being (money and what money can buy, the palpable manifestations of wealth) are facts par excellence. The full title of Moll's history, *The Fortunes and Misfortunes of the Famous Moll Flanders,* retails the moral equations by which she lives: fortune equals good luck equals money, the power of securing respectable wealth, a "good" husband, an estate, moral status; misfortune equals bad luck equals no money, the lack of means to attain salvation. "For tho' my comrade would have bargain'd for me with her brother, yet when they came to the point, it was, it seems, for a mistress, and I kept true to this notion, that a woman should never be kept for a mistress that had money to make her self a wife" (p. 54). All Moll's affairs come to a similar fiduciary "point." Deducing what certain Victorian moralists would understand as dogma, Moll sees the economics of "this notion": that matrimony is an economic fact and that sexuality is circumscribed by the economic as well as by the biological "facts" of life. As critics have often noted, the reader is never quite sure how much of Moll's (or Crusoe's) rationalizing is mediated by Defoe's authorial irony, for, in the end, Moll's notions seek to implicate the reader himself: "The moral indeed of all my history is left to be gather'd by the senses and judgment of the reader" (p. 234). So, Moll has also posited the events of her story as "things"—"facts" to be collected, added up, and evaluated like coins. Instructed by Moll's dissolute life, the reader may learn the same lesson that she has learned in writing it: that the right notion of value is success.

The commonplace Protestant understanding of how the worlds of moral and economic "fact" are related prescribes the aesthetic strategy utilized by both these fictional narrators.[25] Thinking in economic terms becomes a way of narrating the noneconomic matter of a book. The factual language of economics becomes an abstract terminology of epistemological speculation. Ben Franklin's relation to God, for instance, is a strict business transaction: "And now I speak of thanking God, I desire with all humility to acknowledge that I owe the mentioned happiness of my past life to his divine providence, which led me to the means I used and gave them success."[26] The author of "The Way to Wealth" knew that Providence meant providing and that industry and "good works" were both forms of worship and "a means of obtaining wealth and distinction" (p. 73). Economic ends cross with ethical ends to produce a new aesthetic mode: "I therefore filled all the little spaces that occurred between the remarkable days in the calendar with proverbial sentences, chiefly such as inculcated industry and frugality as the means of procuring wealth *and thereby* securing virtue . . ." (p. 88; my italics). Franklin's *sententiae* may or may not have the "oeconomy" applauded by Jonson, but they have something more. As forms of practical wisdom, these proverbs possess an economic persuasiveness: waste not, want not. *Poor Richard's Almanac* demonstrates that moral virtue can be secured by monetary wealth—kept in hand, so to speak—just as verbal meaning can be inculcated in "proverbial sentences" which are easy to keep in one's mind. Like the finer literary arts, the coinages of the *Almanac* are a material increment, printed in the book of facts, the business calendar, that measures time.

Moll Flanders and Robinson Crusoe conflate the facts narrated with the fact of narration until the mere act of relating one's personal trials (and the requisite confession of one's own shortcomings) becomes an ethical quid pro quo, the exchange for which is redemption. Franklin depends upon a linguistic conflation, a metaphysical pun which equates material goods with providential goodness. Both kinds of conflation mimic Coleridge's "Method," for they seek to interpret the material disposition of one's life as, alternatively, tenor and vehicle of one's moral disposition. The aesthetic at work here is to dispense economics as a quotidian, practical manifestation of ethical sublimity and morality as a form of economy.

One might choose, of course (as D. H. Lawrence did in reading Franklin),[27] to regard this metaphorical transference as impertinent, a verbal sleight of hand that mints from metaphorical "goods" a higher metaphor—God. Or one might choose, like Tertius Lydgate (in George Eliot's *Middlemarch*), to regard economics as neither a moral nor an epistemological "fact." As a youth, for instance, Lydgate is ignorant of both the household of the animal body and the household of the political or social body: "A liberal education had of course left him free to read the indecent passages in the school classics, but beyond a general sense of secrecy and obscenity in connexion with his internal structure, had left his imagination quite unbiassed so that for anything he knew his brains lay in small bags at his temples, and he had no more thought of representing to himself how his blood circulated than how paper served instead of gold."[28] Lydgate is content to let the "secret terms" of the economy (and of sexuality) remain secret, abstracting from his naiveté the idea that the imagination is an "unbiassed" entity, a peruser of imaginary things. It has no power to apprehend "internal structure"; it has no capacity for abstracting and parsing structures and for making them intellectually palpable and consistent.

Lydgate's imaginative failure at "representing to himself" either biological or economic ideas has social ramifications as well. Although Lydgate ultimately becomes a doctor, treating medicine itself as though it were a visionary art, his ignorance of how money circulates, of how the economy operates, and of how paper serves as gold plagues him throughout his life.[29] His marriage to Rosamund is conceived in that ignorance. While his imagination remains "quite unbiassed," Lydgate, in an interlocking complex of ways, pays for his vast indifference to the knowledge which money represents. Married to a wife whose engrossing materialism he is never able to imagine, he ends up administering to sufferers of the gout, a disease of the rich. Having sold out as a physician, he permits his dream of a fever hospital to succumb to those very movements of money which he was unable to fathom.

In Lydgate's brilliant analysis of disease, of the biological economy of the human organism, he reveals the myopic economy of his own imagination:

> He went home and read far into the smallest hour, bringing a much more testing vision of details and relations into this pathological study than he had ever thought it necessary to apply to the complexities of love and marriage, these being subjects on which he felt himself amply informed by literature and that traditional wisdom which is handed down in the genial conversation of men. Whereas fever had obscure conditions and gave him that delightful labour of the imagination which is not mere arbitrariness, but the exercise of disciplined power—combining and constructing with the clearest eye for probabilities and the fullest obedience to knowledge; and then, in yet more energetic alliance with impartial Nature, standing aloof to invent tests by which to try its own work. [Chap. 16]

On the one hand, Eliot makes Lydgate's single-minded study of pathology sound like a "pathological study" in itself. On the other hand, this remarkable passage "tests" Lydgate by the same "labour of the imagination" that Lydgate himself brings to his study of fever. We may find Lydgate wanting. In Eliot's prose, but not in Lydgate's thoughts, there is no qualitative difference between the economic abstractions circumscribing love and marriage and the pathological abstractions governing the study of disease (or of labor). Each "vision" must be subjected not to "mere arbitrariness" but to "the exercise of disciplined power." Eliot intimates that such attentiveness to the seriousness of fictive structures (and to the moral web they weave) comprises the true "labour of the imagination," its realization of a "Method." But Lydgate's failure to understand the secret terms of economics when applied to "the complexities of love and marriage" means that his imaginative understanding of other economies—such as the internal structure of the human body or the informative structures of literature—will turn out to be just that: secret, imaginary. His scholarly study and his medical research become merely a complex compensation for his social and economic ineffectiveness. Under the pressure of real economic considerations, he ultimately compromises even his original interests as a physician, what he felt he lived for.

Lydgate's "labour of the imagination" ceases precisely at the point where it must imagine the economic implications of its labor. On the other hand, Franklin's economic provisions become spiritual provisos of a new moral order precisely at the point where the material world is seen as an overlay of the providential one. For Defoe's narrators, a discrepancy between the two scarcely exists. Beaumont's revisionary reading of Jonson indicates that literature may extract its own discursive economy from economic signifiers, establishing its own "commercial text" and its own "facts." The complex "trichotomy" (as Coleridge called it) of moral and economic and aesthetic "value" has become both straitened and polarized: as Jonson said, our language "imitates the publicke riot." These brief literary illustrations may indicate that "politico-economic language" is written neither as clearly nor as discretely as Ruskin's phrase would suggest. Lydgate, for instance, is both educated and thoughtful—he might even, at times, be described as an "intellectual"—but he, like the other characters discussed here, discovers the cost to the imagination of a language which is inadequate to assess the "value" of its own "labor." Although Dorothea Brooke, at the end of *Middlemarch,* heroically affirms that she "will learn what everything costs" (chap. 83), her stated intent is betrayed by the residual insufficiency of her metaphor. Does *everything* have a cost? And is it the same "cost," measured by the same metaphorical coining, each time? What metaphorical slighting (or sleighting) will one have to "learn" in order to make *cost* suffice as a reliable indicator of our psychic, cultural, sexual, and artistic predicaments? If language is to be a true currency, from what must it be minted? Such (Coleridgean) questions could, of course, be further illustrated and refined by examining in greater detail the works we have mentioned above. But these questions provoke specific answers, requiring our closest study, when Thoreau compares directly the metaphorical and functional significances of "Economy," the title of the first chapter of *Walden*.

The Method of Walden

The language of the market would be in the schools as pedantic, though it might not be reprobated by that name, as the language of the schools in the market.—S. T. Coleridge, Biographia Literaria

In *Walden*, Thoreau uses the language of economic process in order to illuminate our concepts of economy and then to dissect our preconceptions about language itself. In defining the economy of life at Walden Pond and the economy of *Walden* as an imaginative structure, Thoreau, like Duchamp, constantly plays with the fallen duplicity of language, translating its literalizing function into its metaphorical significance and back again. Initially, the economic austerity and self-sufficiency of life at Walden is a way of identifying the moral and spiritual economy by which Thoreau lived. Ultimately, such "economy" necessitates a business talent no less vigilant than John Jacob Astor's or Adam Smith's.

Consider Thoreau's own stated reason for spending almost two years in the woods near Concord, Massachusetts: "My purpose in going to Walden Pond was not to live cheaply nor to live dearly there, but to transact some private business with the fewest obstacles; to be hindered from accomplishing which for want of a little common sense, a little enterprise and business talent, appeared not so sad as foolish."[30] Thoreau disavows any economic motive for his sojourn: he did not go merely to live cheaply or dearly. Yet, at the same time, his economic metaphor explains his genuine purpose— to transact some private business. And he proceeds to say that this private transaction could be hindered by want of common sense, enterprise, and business talent. Thus, by sentence end, this apparently straightforward statement of purpose has gradually formed a metaphorical cul de sac. We are left to wonder what "business talent" Thoreau might develop so as not to be concerned with the economics of living. But this very passage is subsequently embroidered with detailed accounts—including even ledger-type entries—of how Thoreau secured his household means, of how he managed to fund the building of his cottage, of how (down to the halfpenny) he spent his money on groceries and supplies: of how, in short, he learned the particulars of living cheaply and dearly there.

What private transaction did Thoreau wish to effect, and what exactly were the obstacles he felt he had to overcome? Recent critics have approached these questions from two different directions. The economizing method of Thoreau's artistic reductions, both in condensing two years of life at Walden into the single artistic year of *Walden* and in composing *Walden* out of the disconnected observations recorded in his *Journals,* is discussed by Mutlu Blasing.[31] Blasing thus reveals that Thoreau's "economy" extends into the work of the imagination, but she does not attempt, finally, to show how this "economy" directly informs the mundane economics of Walden life as well. And yet, the failure to understand this reciprocity is precisely what Thoreau sought to remedy by sojourning at Walden in the first place. Thoreau understood that "economy" had become a merely fictive concept, a stripped metaphor. Despite the singular importance of commercial economics in everyday life, an artist's "economic" reductions were regarded as economically reductive. Thomas Werge's list of historical uses of the word "economy" previous to *Walden* complements and expands Blasing's study. Werge notes that "economy" need not mean simply materialistic austerity but also:

1. The economy of Nature
2. The economy of Nature as an expression of God
3. The economy of the Christian soteriology
4. The economy of style and truth in the Scripture and in the judicious handling of doctrine.[32]

Werge's insight is necessary, but, like Blasing, he misses the conditional tone and, therefore, the exact import of Thoreau's economically adduced imaginative economy. Thoreau insisted that one's verbal, moral, and philosophical economies must be defined by and must emerge from practical, functional concerns. If the economies of nature, God, and one's individual "style" (both personal and prosodic) are not perceived in terms of the economics of how one really lives, then both "economy" and "economics" become fictional and insubstantial terms. Thoreau, as we shall see, sought to illuminate *all* the modalities of "economy" so as to (re)integrate, not divide, them.

Walden's first chapter dramatizes the equivocation between moral and political, philosophical and functional, figurative and literal significances of language. Its later chapters turn this equivocation into a communication between visible and invisible realities. Thoreau will not isolate language's capacity for precision and matter-of-fact clarity from language's equal capacity for imprecision and for metaphorical "translation." Thus, in expressing his aesthetic disposition in terms of a commercial dispensation, Thoreau indicates the crossings at which literature represents economic realities and economic facts represent certain mythic possibilities for the imagination. If one motive for going to Walden Pond was "to front the essential facts of life" (p. 7), then *Walden* becomes an experiment in representing those facts of life to the imagination, an essential exercise demanding an economics of the imagination by which "one man has reduced a fact of the imagination to be a fact to his understanding" (p. 62).

"Economy," the title of his first chapter, becomes the first fact that Thoreau wishes to translate. Thoreau asserts right at the beginning that "economy" poses a decisive challenge for the student: "Even the *poor* student studies and is taught only *political* economy, while that economy of living which is synonymous with philosophy is not even sincerely professed in our colleges. The consequence is, that while he is reading Adam Smith, Ricardo, and Say, he runs his father in debt irretrievably" (p. 35). To some, it may seem self-evident that the scholar is fiscally impoverished; Socrates had to remind Thrasymachus of the philosopher's true riches: "You are wrong to call me ungrateful. I give in return all I can—praise; for I have no money."[33] This *topos* of the indigent scholar has an interesting and complex history of which Thoreau was doubtless aware.[34] One of Thoreau's best (and most misleading) fictions is to picture himself as a melancholic scholar, like Jaques in *As You Like It,* retreating penniless to the pastoral woods.

But the melancholic scholar is also posited by Thoreau as the

potential reader of his book. ("Perhaps," he writes on his first
page, "these pages are more particularly addressed to poor students.") Thoreau's emphatic analysis of "the *poor* student" (p. 35)
alerts us to his own design: to explain why the scholar is poor;
at the same time, to teach him how to read *Walden* as a cure for
both his intellectual poverty and his fiscal profligacy. Now, the
student is both impoverished and impoverishing—impoverished,
because he has been taught only functional economics (*political*
economy) and not that moral or existential economy "which is
synonymous with philosophy"; impoverishing, because he has not
even learned this one-sided economic lesson very well and so "runs
his father in debt irretrievably." The "consequence" of the poor
student's ineptitude is economically debilitating; the myopic vision of economy taught "in our colleges" is philosophically debilitating. When we apprehend both thematic strands of Thoreau's
argument, then we may understand how Thoreau's rhetorical
method throughout *Walden* becomes its own *exemplum*. In order
to be better students of the *economy* of living, we must understand more thoroughly the *economics* of living. And to be better
economists, we must read the literal and figurative significances of
that poverty which is our economic and moral predicament more
astutely, not by separating political economy from other economies but by keeping our attention undivided between them. Thoreau does not say that Smith, Ricardo, and Say are impertinent—
indeed, he suggests that *they* have not been "sincerely professed"
either. A new sort of professor is needed, and a new "method."
All the senses in which the student is "poor" motivate Thoreau's
unique purpose: to delineate an economics of economy, a functional definition of the moral term, so as to generate a language
which does not merely pay lip service to but which truly serves
our needs.

Thoreau is not reticent about stating his more expansive peda-
gogy in almost cavalier terms: "I will endeavor to speak a good
word for the truth" (p. 34). If undertones of levity threaten to
erupt in such bald assertions of earnestness, then these undertones
accurately expose the true difficulty of his experiment: "Economy is a subject which admits of being treated with levity, but
it cannot so be disposed of"(pp. 19–20). Thoreau's method for
"dispos[ing] of" this subject is to show how his "reduced" economy at Walden, by enacting an ideal of self-sufficiency, allows him

to tap the allegorical potential of economic language. In the parable of the native economist, Thoreau, as poetic economist, conducts his "trade" with the "Celestial Empire," the divine commonwealth, and concludes:

> —to be your own telegraph, unweariedly sweeping the horizon, speaking all passing vessels bound coastwise; to keep up a steady dispatch of commodities, for the supply of such a distant and exorbitant market; to keep yourself informed of the state of the markets, prospects of war and peace everywhere, and anticipate the tendencies of trade and civilization, . . . studying the lives of all great discoverers and navigators, great adventurers and merchants, from Hanno and the Phoenicians down to our own day; in fine, account of stock to be taken from time to time, to know how you stand. [P. 13]

The native writer must become a consummate economist-merchant whose facility for sending and receiving messages between the spiritual and the material worlds is a demonstration of his power to transform goods into the Good. The language of this passage joyfully parodies the language of economic dispatch; its string of infinitives used as imperatives are not merely commandments but commercial orders, the rushed syntax of a busy man doing important business, the grammar of Dickens's Boffin, the Golden Dustman, in his prime. The only difficulty with such a reading of this "transparent" allegory[35] is that the passage also functions in exactly the opposite way. Fine as the Celestial Empire may be in this evocation, it is not only the truth of the spiritual world which is affirmed but also the more worldly need "to know how you stand." The parable becomes inverted and self-referring. A consequence of using this series of economic metaphors is that vehicle and tenor (like the grammar) cross in midstream: mercantile economics as a metaphorical vehicle to define commerce with God turns into the metaphorical tenor, so that economics itself becomes the Celestial emporium, a divinely sanctioned methodology for helping "you" to know how you stand.

How Thoreau stands is brought home to him by his neighbor and visitor, the Canadian woodchopper, who makes Thoreau realize the original purpose of money: "When I asked him if he could do without money, he showed the convenience of money in such a way as to suggest and coincide with the most philosophical accounts of the origin of this institution, and the very derivation of the word *pecunia*" (p. 103). What Thoreau has in mind is money's original use as a condensed representation of property for convenience in economic transactions. Thus, the woodchopper thinks "it would be inconvenient and impossible soon to go on mortgaging some portion" of his only negotiable property (*peculium*), the ox (*pecus*), every time he wished to purchase "needles and thread at the store." What must be seen behind Thoreau's account of the woodsman's native philosophy is the exchange to which Thoreau himself puts the account. Thoreau's visitor provides the occasion for a visitation: Alek Therien becomes Thoreau's Paul Bunyan, the mythic folk hero, the figure of American Nature itself, who is also "there" in the Concord woods, conversing with Thoreau. Somehow Therien has acquired the ability to pronounce Greek, although he cannot read it and needs Thoreau to translate: "and now I must translate to him, while he holds the book . . ." (p. 99). This visual image of listener and speaker becomes a kind of emblem for the communication between the old and new worlds, natural and learned philosophies, text and reader—with the contemporary American sojourner-translator-pilgrim posited as interlocutor between them. But in translating *to* Therien, Thoreau also translates *him*. The lesson learned from the woodsman about the origin of *pecunia* becomes translated also into Thoreau's strategy in *Walden:* "for convenience, putting the experience of two years into one" (p. 58). *Walden* becomes a negotiable form of property, the economic equivalent of his economy of living in the woods, the symbol par excellence of the private business he wished to transact.

How private is that business? In condensing the essential facts of life at Walden into the imaginative facts of *Walden,* Thoreau encourages direct exchange with the reader. The image of Thoreau translating is emblematic of the proper relationship between reader and *Walden.* The economy of life in the woods is (further) reduced to an economics of the imagination in which the reader may apprehend more easily "where I lived and what I lived for," the title and subject of Thoreau's second chapter. As Walden is the middle ground between Concord and the American wilderness, so *Walden* is the mediator between the labor of the individual at Walden (his economics) and the labor of the imagination (the economy of the text). The goal of the book is to assess the value for the reader of both kinds of work, so that Thoreau's labor becomes both one of the "transactions" he wished to accomplish and a narrative record of that transaction.

Reduced to a fact of the reader's understanding, *Walden* thus becomes at once the ironic aftermath and the symbolic culmination of Thoreau's experience at Walden Pond. To name the book after the place of his "experiment" is to charge that place with imaginative and literary significance and, by reducing it, to memorialize it. Because the book is composed out of recollections entered already in his *Journals,* the author's exchange with his reader is synonymous with his principle of composition: to galvanize the record of memory by raising memory to an art. This art is analogous to an accountant's ledger book. It maps by means of verbal as well as mathematical figures the way in which the author "earned [his] living." A ledger book demonstrates balance (or imbalance) between earnings and expenditures, profits and losses. The ledger of *Walden* is misread as an account of "unaccommodated man" (as Lear calls himself on the heath). One of the accommodations that Thoreau provides himself consists of "the following pages, or rather the bulk of them." Thus, the first sentence of *Walden* computes the value of the Walden experience in terms of the book that came out of it: "When I wrote the following pages, or rather the bulk of them, I lived alone, in the woods, a mile from any neighbor, in a house which I built myself, on the shore of Walden Pond, in Concord, Massachusetts, and earned my living by the labor of my hands only." Syntactically, Thoreau invites us to understand that the "living" he earned pertains to the writing of these pages, that the labor put into *them* is (especially) valuable and material, literally "the labor of *my* hands *only.*" In this book, then, the laborer-artist evaluates his earnings by becoming his own accountant. *Walden* becomes both his accommodation, the account of Thoreau's literal and figurative "transactions," *and* the embodiment of his labor. Its coinages become the increment earned by the art of memory.

The economizing mode of Thoreau's composition participates in what Susanne K. Langer has called "Virtual Memory": "Memory is the great organizer of consciousness. It simplifies and composes our perceptions into units of personal knowledge. It is the real maker of history—not recorded history, but the *sense of his-*

tory itself, the recognition of *the past* as a completely established (though not completely known) fabric of events, continuous in space and time, and causally connected together."[36] Although "the present is still amorphous, unused, unfashioned" (Langer, p. 263), memory is able to compose the fabric of the past into a finished product and to testify, thereby, to its usefulness. The price of being a product (finished but not completely known) is that it speaks only of loss, of the life exhausted in its production. In the construct of memory, however, this loss need not necessarily be seen as depreciation. The power of memory to "represent" the past "in the form of distinguishable events" is the power of coinage: to mint from the bulk of experience a new fact, so that what has been lost (to memory) need not constitute a loss (in memory). Memory transforms the past into a form of currency; more importantly, it also *adds* to the past its own incremental value: "To remember an event is to experience it again, but not in the same way as the first time" (ibid.). As Marx said of money, memory is the unnatural increment. But here "unnatural" is honorific, signifying the power of imagination to relive experience, to possess it again, to profit from it. Thoreau's art transforms memory of actual events into "virtual memory"; the accounting given in bulk in the *Journals* becomes the specific account which is *Walden*, and the representational power of that imaginative coinage is precisely what enriches Thoreau's "economy."

In the end, Thoreau computes the difference between the imaginative economics of *Walden* and the economics of life at Walden in strictly business terms. a strategy that is consistent with his attempt throughout to make the complexities of "Economy" resonate in both the world of fact and the world of myth. There is a danger in using such mundane economic language to speak of economies within and beyond the economic: the "poor reader" might be misled. He might think that economy does not translate into economics.[37] "I fear chiefly," Thoreau concludes, "lest my expression may not be *extra-vagant* enough, may not wander far enough beyond the narrow limit of my daily experience, so as to be adequate to the truth of which I have been convinced" (p. 221). Even in the main clause of this sentence, before any of the qualifications which ensue, we are struck by the ambiguous nature of *this* "expression." "Extravagant" in its common usage, means excessive: "extra-vagant enough" is oxymoronic. But Thoreau wants us to regard the word "extra-vagant" neither as metaphor nor in its common usage; he means the word in its radical sense of wandering outside, of going beyond the prescribed boundaries. But as we are invited to read the word in its literal sense, we also notice that this sentence calls for a movement beyond literalness, "beyond the narrow limits of my daily experience." Indeed, all of *Walden* contains a meticulous account of daily experience but reduced for convenience so that the literal expressions of experience may be repeated in a finer tone by being exchanged according to a more imaginable economics. The sentence concludes by returning us to the idea of what is "adequate" and sufficient, the "truth" of economy, although our perception at the end of the sentence returns us to the beginning with a new perspective. Starting as the expression of Thoreau's chief "fear," the sentence, as it unwinds, enacts Thoreau's greatest conviction: that one may be extravagant enough.

How much extravagance is enough? In the beginning, the expression "extra-vagant enough" contains its own contradiction. By using such an ambiguous expression to elucidate the idea of sufficiency, and by emphasizing that ambiguity, Thoreau wishes to spring the word free of its commonplace usages while keeping it bound in them—to make us see, as if for the first time, *how* the roots of the word are grounded: "*Extra vagance:* it depends on how you are yarded." How you are yarded (i.e., bounded, limited, or "walled-in," to use Thoreau's own etymology of "Walden")—it depends on how you see yourself in that space, what language you use to describe it.

"To know how you stand" you must become aware of all the economies of space and time by which we all are yarded. Thoreau's acquaintances in Concord want to know only about the most elementary of these, as he recalls on the first page: "Some have asked what I got to eat, if I did not feel lonesome; if I was not afraid; and the like." For two hundred pages, Thoreau tells them what he ate, what friends (both human and animal) he made, what fears he experienced, and the like. Then, he tells his Concord neighbors how to remember what he has told them: "In view of the future or possible, we should live quite laxly and undefined in front, our outlines dim and misty on that side; as our shadows reveal an insensible perspiration toward the sun. The volatile truth of our words should continually betray the inadequacy of the re-

sidual statement. Their truth is instantly *translated . . .*" (p. 221).
So the residual economic facts of "Food, Shelter, Clothing" reveal
a volatile truth: the fact of language. If the act of going to Walden
in the first place is "extravagant" in all senses, then his expression
of that act must be "extravagant enough" to translate an economics of extravagance into a mode of living which is not, paradoxically uneconomical.

In *Walden,* language itself is translated so that, like true perception, it points at once to both a literal object and a metaphysical subject, to "Walden" as a literal place outside Concord and as
a metaphorical possibility, the demesne of the imagination, the
residence of the true American, or, more specifically, the ground
upon which the American "facts" of life will be discovered. Thoreau translates the residual truth of economics into a volatile
truth: the economics of the imagination. As readers, we also translate but by a reverse process, translating the economy of *Walden*
into the economics of our daily (commercial) lives. Experience becomes, by either process, a material "thing" which is both literal
and imagined. So the train, that literal instrument of commerce,
becomes Atropos, weaver of our fate. When properly seen and
identified, "a house is still but a sort of porch at the entrance
of a burrow" (p. 30). Food, shelter, and clothing become ways
of preserving animal heat, the true meaning of Concord. Because
man "not only works for the animal within him, but, for a symbol
of this, he works for the animal without him" (p. 39), Thoreau
reminds us of the symbolic essence of real estate, the "real" meaning of squatting: "I considered that I enhanced the value of the
land by squatting on it" (p. 44). Again and again, Thoreau insists
that language which means *exactly* what it says may also express
all that it intends, until action and expression, the artist's creation
of himself and the reader's creation of himself, become identified.

To this end, one must discover words of a sufficiently extravagant and volatile nature, words whose meanings can translate from
the literal to the metaphorical and back again. "Economy" is one
of them. In that particular word, Thoreau put Emerson's dictum
that "language is fossil poetry" to work; he showed that the metaphorical implications of language must charge with renewed possibility the empirical "economy" of where we live by crediting, as
equally functional, the "economy" of what we live for. When
properly understood, language is, like Thoreau, a sojourner be-

tween literal and poetic truth. In using language to open and close the distance between words' literal referents and their symbol aspirations—and in the celebration of such extravagance—we come as close as possible to realizing our "superior natures"—our Christlike capacity to be new and translated men: "The words which express our faith and piety are not definite; yet they are significant and fragrant like frankincense to superior natures" (p. 221).

Thoreau would not have us pretend that the language of economics represents one of man's "natures" while the language of philosophy or of ethics represents another and perhaps "superior" Nature. By insisting that economics both portray the economy of living and account for the imagination in its labors, Thoreau formulates the thesis of the present study as well: that "economy" expresses multiple forms of commerce between man and God, between man and man, between man and nature, and, most volatilely, between man and language. Because there is no disparity between the economics of the imagination in its labor and the economics of laboring for our daily bread—since both partake, in Thoreau's elaborate pun, of "the *spiritus*" (p. 43) or yeast of life— there is no vanity in Thoreau's claim for his book. The imaginative exertion it asks of its reader and concedes to its author is neither excessive nor trivial, neither vain nor in vain: "It is a labor to task the faculties of a man,—such problems of profit and loss, of interest, of tare and tret, and gauging of all kinds in it, as demand a universal knowledge" (p. 13-14).

Finally, the extravagances of *Walden* redefine the labor which Thoreau demanded of himself as the labor which he demands of his reader. It is no longer possible to see this book as an extravagance in the ordinary sense, to "have come to this page to spend borrowed or stolen time, robbing your creditors of an hour" (p. 3). Indeed, following the initial metaphor, Thoreau has envisioned his own *rich* student to replace the "poor student" who could not understand economy even though he read all the economists. Of this new reader is demanded "a universal knowledge," a knowledge of how the specificity of our economic lives must be universalized in terms of the imagination's life. Thus, the laboring man who "cannot afford to sustain the manliest relations to men [because] his labor would be depreciated in the market" (p. 3) is encouraged to labor here: this page holds the accrediting power; it supplies what it demands. To read it requires a little common sense, a little enterprise, and a little business talent. In short, it "tasks" *all* "the faculties of a man."

"Economy" is a pivotal term, therefore, insofar as it allows Thoreau to link the world of facts and the fact of the imagination, to find, in the coincidence of the author's and the reader's labors, what Coleridge called a "landing-place"[38] for a new unifying "Method." Using Thoreau's economics, the student may learn to live both cheaply and dearly at the same time. Or, more precisely, because there is a demonstrable economics of the imagination, it is possible for a man to return to the discordant world called Concord and, in that world of getting and spending, "to live the life which he has imagined" (p. 220).

CHAPTER II
Economics in Mammon's Cave

It is a great aggravation of the other difficulties in the science of Econo-- my, that the most metaphysical part comes first.
—*Thomas De Quincey,* The Logic of Political Economy

The foremost metaphysical claim of economic management is that man can overrule his own irrationality. As periods of economic prosperity and economic depression arise and recede in spite of the expectations and the explanations of economists, "the science of Economy" settles for its next best claim: that, in signifying the world of "facts," economic discourse expresses the only significant world.

By encouraging us to confine our imaginative speculations to the world of "facts," the economic science expresses a new meaning of "speculation." Originally denoting vision (*speculari*) and suggesting the mirror action of *speculum,* the inward reflections of contemplative thought, "speculation" yields to the economic sense of "the buying and selling of commodities or effects in order to profit by a rise or fall in their market value" (*OED* 5). The "facts" are reflected in a new mirror of thought when the commercial world of markets constitutes the metaphysical value it most profits us to imagine.

Thoreau has instructed us in the effects of this altered vision, this straitened speech. His economics of the imagination translates "economy" into a new metaphysics. But before we can discuss the further uses of such translation, we must study the older metaphysics, the philosophies from which the economic science has been derived. The "science" to which De Quincey alludes and which Thoreau takes as his text is a belated construct, a nineteenth-century discipline. Its "most metaphysical part" has a much earlier genesis, and the study of that part, as De Quincey notes, properly "comes first."[1]

Anthropologists have explained why the metaphysics of "economy" can be "a great aggravation of the other difficulties" in defining an economic science. All societies possess economies but not all economies possess an economics. More specifically, not all economies express their economic practices in terms of *the* economy. In many primitive and archaic societies, "economy" is the direct expression of cultural and spiritual, not nutritional or materialistic needs.[2] In *Gawain and the Green Knight,* for instance, Bertilak and Gawain exchange winnings, an "economic" practice which has its roots in more primitive forms of gift giving. The conventions which govern such exchanges were outlined years ago in Marcel Mauss's classic study, *The Gift.* Social and cultural, psychological and religious, these conventions may be anything but rational; often, they may evidence a metaphysics which is uneconomic, and, in some cases, they may even be directly opposed to economic survival.[3]

Karl Polanyi has distinguished between economy as an idea (or ideal) and as a structure:

> No society could, naturally, live for any length of time unless it possessed an economy of some sort; but prior to our own time no economy has ever existed that, even in principle, was controlled by markets. In spite of the chorus of academic incantations so persistent in the nineteenth century, gain and profit made on exchange never before played an important part in human economy. Though the institution of the mar-

ket was fairly common since the later Stone Age, its role was
no more than incidental to economic life. [*PAME,* p. 3]

The economy which Polanyi identifies as modern may be called
"the economy," shorthand for the contracted and institutionalized economic processes of Western civilization as embedded in
the commodity market, in all-purpose coinage, in the market mechanism of supply and demand, and in the trade markets of foreign
and domestic commerce. Adam Smith and his successors used the
phrase *homo oeconomicus* to designate one who was knowledge-
able of and sensitive to these formalized modes of expressing production and distribution. Marx used the word "capital" to describe
such instituted economic modes, the systems of production by
which we conduct, in Alfred Marshall's phrase, "the business of
life."[4] In classical political economy, there are no economic principles to describe economies which are not so instituted.

The most metaphysical part of the economic science is what has
been borrowed from those other, uninstituted economies. Political
economy, or the "body of systematized knowledge" which takes
"the economy" as its subject, is itself a discursive superstructure
constructed upon earlier, less systematic ideas of "economy." The
modern science is appropriative: it has abandoned some of these
ideas and has built over others. Thus, a discontinuity occurs,
familiar to anthropologists, in which "we must say," as Polanyi
concludes, "that there is no necessary relationship between economizing action and the empirical economy" (*PAME,* p. 117), between the metaphysical idea and its structural embodiment,
between concept and form. As we shall see in chapter three, the
economic science, in imagining the principles which will regulate
"the economy," generates its own implicit metaphysics. But what
we need to explore at present are the historical origins of economics in pre-nineteenth-century speculations.

We discover multiple economies, derived from sometimes conflicting ideas of rationality. Aristotle's "economics" is the earliest
important example. Because "the market mechanism" was "an institution that was still unknown to Aristotle," he could not imagine that his idea of economy could be codified and regulated by
something that we would call "the economy."[5] Aristotle's perspective, although not his actual principles, held sway until as
recently as the eighteenth century. The implication of this perspective must be studied carefully, for when attempts were

made, prior to the nineteenth century, to conceive a consistent economic theory, they drew upon a broader *scientia* than the simple awareness of market principles. In that *scientia* lay the roots of the later economic myth: that the discourse of "economics" could signify, through the rational structures of "the economy," man's moral and spiritual "economy."

Mammon, in book 2 of *The Faerie Queene,* will offer an instructive early example of how these signifiers could be exploited and transformed. The basis of Mammon's art is his metaphysical assumption that commerce is the only imaginative structure which explains where we live and what we live for. His art prefigures, therefore, the later metaphysical claims made for economics—as voiced in 1831, for instance, by Thomas Love Peacock's fictional economist, Mr. MacQuedy: " Metaphysics, sir; metaphysics. Logic and moral philosophy. There we are at home. The Athenians only sought the way, and we have found it; and to all this we have added political economy, the science of sciences." [6] This view of "political economy" as "the science of sciences"—the knowledge which crowns and encompasses all other knowledge—has no direct intellectual antecedent in earlier metaphysical concepts of "economy." Although Peacock's use of MacQuedy is, of course, comic, the leap from the philosophical rationalism of Aristotle to the rationalistic economics of classical nineteenth-century economists is not merely rhetorical. The gap is bridged and the transition imaginatively explained by Spenser's Mammon, whose commercial logic challenges the Aristotelian virtues of Guyon by distorting the Christian view of a divine economy. Mammon brings, as we shall see, empirical and metaphysical economies together, thus permitting "economics" to be identified in its mythic form. In Mammon's view of history, economics is the only art, the true *speculum.* For Mammon, the world of "facts" holds precedence over the worlds of Christian and classical myth, because his economic imagination has already foreshortened such myth in the discursive structures of the economy.

The Rationale for "Economy"

"Economy" originates as one branch of moral philosophy; it is part of a triad of practical arts (*praktikē*) which includes ethics and politics as well. For Aristotle, therefore, the word's radical meaning of private household (*oikos*) management or regulation (*nomos*) was not without broader public significance in the realm of political organization and statesmanship. Aristotle's *oikonomia* functions as the pivot between ethics and politics. By means of this philosophical nexus, Aristotle is able to identify his *Politics* as the necessary culmination of his *Ethics* and so to ground the self-sufficiency of the state in the self-sufficiency of the individual. Ernest Barker emphasizes that in Aristotle's *schema,*

> the *polis* included everything; and in the same way the theory of the *polis* included studies to which we should now give a separate existence—in particular the theory of economics. . . . Such economic theory, subordinated as it is to political theory, which in turn is subordinated to (or, perhaps one should rather say, is the crown of) ethics, admits of no isolation of the economic motive, and of no abstraction of economic facts as a separate branch of inquiry.[7]

Oikonomikē is to individual ethical behavior as *politikē* is to social or communal ethical organization, and Aristotle wants us to see both sides of the relationship at once. Or, in other words, to say why Aristotle begins his analysis of politics by discussing *oikonomia* is also to say why his discussion of *oikonomikē,* the study of economic practices, eventually yields to *politikē,* the study of political institutions as such.

Because Aristotle believed that the basis of any economy must be sufficiency, or having *enough* of the necessities without having too much or too little, he saw proper economic exchange as, by definition, "gainless." In exchange we share resources, not compete for them. He asserted, moreover, the absolute equivalency of commodities, "for—putting convenience on one side—it makes no difference whether you pay five beds for a house or the value of five beds."[8] All the material conditions of a man's life can be evaluated in terms of one another. For this reason, money is not evil; actually, it is to be desired as a useful measure, "a pretty constant," of the commensurability of all things:

> Everything should be rated at a fixed value in money, for that will always make exchange possible and, if exchange, association for the purpose of exchange. So money acts as a measure which, by making things commensurable, renders it possible to make them equal. . . . Strictly speaking no doubt things so widely different can never become commensurable. Still in demand we have a common measure which will be

found to work pretty well. Some one standard there must be, and it must be accepted by a general agreement or understanding. Such a standard has the effect of making all things commensurable, since they can all be measured by money. [*Ethics,* p. 154]

The problem is that values fixed in money are not fixed values. Money not only mediates between necessities and their obtainability, but also becomes desirable in itself, a signifier whose signified content is itself. For Aristotle, however, value is *prior* to exchange; it is immanent in the commodity itself. Thus, money aids exchange only as a token of convenience, as the woodcutter reminded Thoreau. It is not to be confused with the commodities themselves, bread and water, house and bed, which men actually need.

The nexus between Aristotle's sense of "exchange" and his ensuing definition of "economy" depends upon the right use of reason: speech. "Nature, as we say, does nothing without some purpose; and for the purpose of making man a political animal she has endowed him alone among the animals with the power of reasoned speech."[9] Within the smallest *polis*—the household—economy describes the political (i.e., social) relationship between the household members as well as the material means by which that relationship should be maintained. In the largest household—the *polis*—security, order, and prosperity are attained not only by successful economy but also by a shared use of "reasoned speech": "Speech . . . serves to indicate what is useful and what is harmful, and so also what is right and what is wrong. For the real difference between man and other animals is that humans alone have perception of good and evil, right and wrong, just and unjust. And it is the sharing of a common view in these matters that makes a household or a city" (*Politics,* pp. 28-29). To misjudge the management of the household is to misallocate speech from its proper end, which is to indicate "what is useful and what is harmful." Unnatural economy will misuse economic tools, just as irrational speech misuses words. Misuse is, by definition, the diverting of the means of action from their natural and final end. Thus, economy is the right regulation or description of wealth, for wealth is merely "a collection of tools for use in the administration of a household or a state" (*Politics,* p. 40).

In some classical writing, *oikonomia* came to mean the management of public *revenue* as such, and Aristotle is sensitive to but not swayed by the increasing dependence in the Athenian economy upon money as a "fact" and end in itself.[10] In the *Politics*, moneymaking is explicitly cited as a false kind of *oikonomikē*. When moneymaking alone becomes the concern of the economist, then chrematistics (the art of wealth getting, the art of securing necessities) results in an unnatural economy. Polanyi notes that Aristotle's *chrēmatistikē* "was deliberately employed . . . in the literal sense of providing for the necessities of life, instead of its usual meaning of 'money-making.' Laistner rendered it correctly as 'the art of supply,' and Ernest Barker in his commentary recalled the original sense of *chrēmata,* which he warned, was not money, but the necessities themselves, an interpretation also upheld by Defourny and by M. I. Finley" (*PAME*, p. 113). The point is that, for Aristotle, *chrēmatistikē* could *become* the art of moneymaking alone. When it does, then the very meaning of *chrēmatistikē* is changed, and the price of this money-oriented desire is a subversion of "reasoned speech" into a false teleology. Such *chrēmatistikē*—now understood as the accumulation of wealth through monetary means only—is "not productive of goods in the full sense" (*Politics*, p. 43). In generating more economic tools (but not more goods), it fosters the illusion that means can become identical with ends: "But for this kind of money-making [*chrēmatistikē*] the end provides no limit, because wealth and getting money are themselves the end. Household management [*oikonomia*] on the other hand, not being money-making, has a limit, since money-making is not its function, but only a means to an end" (*Politics*, p. 44).

Although natural economy does not permit the hoarding of money, Aristotle elsewhere allows even the good economist to use or to trade in money: "Money-making, then, . . . is of two kinds; one which is necessary and acceptable, which we may call administrative [that is, chrematistics whose end is *dikē*, the just use of necessities] ; the other, the commercial which depends on exchange [that is, chrematistics whose end is *kerdos,* the making of a profit on mercatorial exchange] . . ." (*Politics*, p. 46). One might say that for Aristotle money has *meaning* only when it is employed as a *means*, a means to self-sufficiency, whether of the household or of the state. The failure of unnatural economists, those who interpret *chrēmatistikē as moneymaking only*, is also a failure of linguistic signifiers to signify reason: "Those who are amassing wealth in the form of coin go on increasing their pile without limit, not distinguishing this kind from the other because they are so similar. For they are similar in that both are concerned with the acquisition and ownership of property; but in method they are dissimilar; in one case the end is sheer increase, in the other something different" (*Politics,* p. 44). To fail to distinguish between similarities, to fail to differentiate that which is similar from that which is "something different," is ultimately to mismanage the economy of speech. If "the good life" is an ethical model founded upon commercial and rhetorical restraint, a model reflected in Aristotle's view of *oikonomia,* then the "life" whose chief desire is money is neither economical nor good: "The reason why some people get this notion into their head [that their store of money ought to be hoarded or increased without limit] may be that they are eager for life but not for the good life; so, desire for life being unlimited, they desire also in unlimited amount what is conducive thereto" (*Politics,* p. 44). Unlimited desire alters the means by which *oikonomikē* is enacted because it alters the purpose of wealth. Like unlimited desire, unlimited wealth contradicts the reason for language, which is to indicate the limits of human sufficiency, to empower us to recognize "the good life" as necessary and desirable in itself. To imagine an "economics" *beyond* this economy—an economics whose object is not sufficiency but the management of an institutionalized and self-contained market system—would be to constitute both a metaphysics with no relationship to the *physis* and a rhetoric with no relationship to logic. It would comprise what Aristotle calls in another context an inappropriate metaphor.[11] To envision the *polis* as an economic institution and then to speak of an economics of (the) economy would be unnatural, a confusion of first causes with final causes, of vehicles with tenors.

The Greek word *oikonomia* (but not Aristotle's use of it) survives Latinization. Aristotle understood that the right use of commerce and the right use of language were inseparable. But in Latin economics is better expressed as *commercium* or retail trade,[12] and what the Greeks meant by the domestic household (*oikos*) is expressed by the politically and ethically different structure, the *familia*.[13] Moreover, "economy" in Latin merely expresses arrangement in general and loses the functional, precise meaning of the Greek. The word *oeconomia* comes to denote an idea of decorum and harmonious accord which may or may not depend on or even

utilize specifically economic considerations.[14] Its first use in
Latin seems to be Quintilian's, and by it he means rhetorical order
only.[15] Furthermore, when the French medievalists Hatzfeld and
Darmesteter traced the French *économie* through its Latin transmutations, they noted that the meaning, *gestion intérieure d'un
maison,* was obsolete, that the word signified only the *ordre avec
lequel les choses sont administrées.*[16]

Oeconomy as public administration meant ecclesiastical administration, according to Du Cange's *Glossarium* of medieval Latin.[17]
In this sense, the Church Fathers understood an elementary and
divine economy in the pastoralism of the psalmist: "The Lord is
my shepherd; I shall not want." The economics of the Lord is conditioned by his bounty, and the psalmist's praise becomes an elementary theory of production: "The earth is the Lord's and the
fulness thereof."[18] The Christian gloss of Hebraic economy also
partakes of Roman political order, so that God becomes the pater-
familias of the economy which he himself has ordained; we, being
mortals, are but stewards of his grace and *dominium* (possessions)
—as the Vulgate explains:

> Dixit autem Dominus: Quis, putas, est fidelis dispensator, et
> prudens, quem constituit Dominus supra familiam suam, ut
> det illis in tempore tritici mensuram? [Luke 12:42]

> And the Lord said, Who then is that faithful and wise steward,
> whom his lord shall make ruler over his household, to give them
> their portion of meat in due season? [King James Version]

The biblical role of the steward-economist dramatizes the ambivalent status of Christian economics. In the passage quoted above,
the steward who is both faithful and wise (*fidelis* and *prudens*) in
serving his earthly lord will also serve his heavenly Lord. But sometimes the claims of fidelity and prudence are not in accord with
one's earthly assignments. As the parable of the unjust steward reveals (Luke 16:1-12), one may be called upon to act under the
aegis of apparently conflicting commandments. "He that is faithful in that which is least is faithful also in much," Christ advises
his disciples (Luke 16:10). But being faithful "in much" also requires that the steward of the Lord abandon that which is "least"
—his earthly economics—in order to think upon the divine economy: "Ye cannot serve God and mammon" (Luke 16:13).

The apparent contradiction in the role of the steward arises because of the equivocal meaning of "service" and because the economies of God and Mammon are metaphysically of different orders. We shall examine the Christian version of economy in greater detail below when we focus directly on Mammon's economics in *The Faerie Queene.* What the secular history of "political economy" reveals, however, is that Christian and Roman dispensations combine to separate economy in its moral sense from economics in its functional sense. In theory, the political economists of the eighteenth century attempted to put them back together. Thus, at first glance, Sir James Steuart's definition of "oeconomy" (1767) reaffirms an earlier Aristotelian synthesis: "What oeconomy is in a family, political oeconomy is in a state."[19] But *political* economy, as a discrete discipline, is precisely what Aristotle did not define. For Aristotle, what economy is in the household it must *also* be in the state. For Steuart, ethical necessity is the mother of *economy;* practical political arrangement is the father of *economics.*

Steuart's division of the economist into two offices indicates the inherited Christian burden which disrupts his Aristotelian definition:

> The whole oeconomy must be directed by the head, who is both lord and steward of the family. It is however necessary, that these two offices be not confounded with one another. As lord, he establishes the laws of his oeconomy; as steward he puts them in execution. As lord, he may restrain and give his commands to all within the house as he thinks proper; as steward [the *dispensator* of the Vulgate] , he must conduct with gentleness and address, and is bound by his own regulations. [1:2]

Practical economic management is concerned essentially with means. To oversee the general good of the household is to be concerned fundamentally with ends. The Christian *Dominus,* who foresees ends which are beyond man's means, creates the need for this division, and Steuart's economic theory respects its ambivalence. Whereas Steuart's lord directs the whole "oeconomy," the steward performs a lesser service. He becomes what Steuart calls in the next sentence an "oeconomist."[20] When viewed from a Christian perspective, therefore, Steuart's economist serves a Mammon who is faithful to God.

From an Aristotelian perspective, Steuart's Christian terminology is in danger of polarizing the whole metaphysical issue of
"economy." Whereas Aristotle insisted that we view "economy"
as a metaphor which transfers significance *from* ethics *to* politics,
Steuart metonymically associates family and state for the sake of
contrasting them. Thus, the business of "economics" (what Steuart calls "government") becomes a separate work, expressing an
idea and an end which are distinct from the *a priori* metaphysics
of "economy": "Oeconomy and government, even in a private
family, present, therefore, two different ideas and have also two
different objects" (Steuart, 1:2). Whether "government" and
"oeconomy" can become commensurable and thus yoke together
their two different "objects" will depend on how one locates on-
tologically and defines metaphysically the one in the middle—the
economist, man.

Although the term "economist" derives from the Greek *oikon-
omos* and is related denotatively to the Latin *dispensator,* it was
first used in its modern sense by eighteenth-century French and
British physiocrats.[21] The ontological status of the economist is
not explained by Hellenistic, Roman, or Christian metaphysics,
because the word posits man in a new relationship to nature. The
economist charted the physiological analogue between individual
human nature and natural Law: the physiocrats "called themselves
économistes because in their opinion the health of the community
and the State rested on natural laws similar to those that regulate
the household of the animal body" (*PAME,* p. 126).[22] Here, the
household is no longer a metaphor or a metonym. It is merely a
simile, and the discursive structure of economics (*l'économie politique*) has become a description of the likenesses between man's
reason and the rational laws of nature.

In 1742, Frances Hutcheson, Adam Smith's teacher and prede-
cessor as professor of logic and moral philosophy at Glasgow, published his important "economic" study *A Short Introduction to
Moral Philosophy* in Latin, utilizing classical Greek principles.
Book 2, "Elements of the Law of Nature," deals with economic
questions of financial contracts, coinage, property, and value.
Book 3, "The Principles of Oeconomics and Politics," discusses
marriage and divorce, the duties of parent and child, master and
slave, and questions of general political management. In these
divisions, Hutcheson is imitating Aristotle and to some extent the

pseudo-Aristotelian *Economics* which posits *oikonomia* as both theoretical and practical, both a constitutive and a regulative science:

> Now in some of the arts a division is made, and it does not belong to the same art to make a thing and to use what is made, as for example, a lyre and flutes. It is however the province of the political science to constitute a city from the very first, and when constituted to turn it to a proper use; so that it is clear that it would naturally be the province of economic science both to found a house and to make use of it.[23]

Hutcheson's loosest use of "Oeconomics" survives in the school subject "home economics," but the thematic alignment of economics *and* politics becomes the basis of the later discipline, "political economy." In Hutcheson's book, the metaphysical roots of economic theory are brought to the surface, where they wither in the bright glare of ethical instruction and moral "principles." Indeed, for as long as the adjective ("political") remained an adjunct to the noun ("economy"), "economics" did not relinquish its prescriptive function as sanctioned by its inherited moral orientation.[24] Until well into the nineteenth century, economics continued to depend upon a received and still creditable sense of natural economy: that is, of wealth which betokened a man's inner well-being, his moral philosophy, whether physiologically or spiritually adduced. Polanyi observes, somewhat disapprovingly, "The science founded by the Physiocrats was the science of society, not that of economics" (*PAME*, p. 126).

In creating the science of economics, then, a new question arose which demanded a more supple rhetoric of moral choice. Would the economist—that is, the economic "scientist" and theorist—be understood to perform the office of Steuart's "lord" or of Steuart's "steward"? Appearing thirty-four years after Hutcheson's book, *The Wealth of Nations* illustrates the conflict. Smith's economist oversees, like Steuart's lord, the creation of household and national "Wealth." He does not perform the menial service of the steward. Significantly, then, Smith defines "political economy" as "a branch of the science of a statesman or legislator": "It proposes to enrich both the people and the sovereign."[25] Linking king and countryman, the Smithian economist is, in the broadest sense, a moral governor as well as a businessman. He analyzes ethical and perhaps aesthetic "Wealth," the well-being of the community, as an integral part of the commonwealth's commercial health. Smith's now notorious concept of "economic man" is derived from his view of man's ethical status as it is revealed, or in some cases betrayed, by economic factors. The Smithian economist must formulate economic rules and principles which, while making us better merchants and laborers, will also make us better men.

Marx questioned the connection between Smith's idea of "economy" and his idea of "man" by attacking its implicit assumption—that the connection between them was rational and moral. In the opening pages of the *Grundrisse,* Marx locates the economic fallacy of Smith's philosophy in its ontological naiveté, its false definition of man:

> Individuals producing in society—hence socially determined individual production—is, of course, the point of departure. The individual and isolated hunter and fisherman, with whom Smith and Ricardo begin, belongs among the unimaginative conceits of the eighteenth-century Robinsonades. . . . Smith and Ricardo still stand with both feet on the shoulders of the eighteenth-century prophets, in whose imaginations this eighteenth-century individual—the product on one side of the dissolution of the feudal forms of society, on the other side of the new forces of production developed since the sixteenth century—appears as an ideal, whose existence they project into the past.[26]

Smith arrives at a theory of individual production which offers no concomitant theory of social distribution. In Marx's analysis, Smithian economics can only constitute an entelechy, because it is innocent of a teleological view of capitalism's uses and ends. It is an analysis of wealth without an analysis of social history. Smith does, of course, offer a reading of "the different Progress of Opulence in different Nations" (*WN,* bk. 3, chap. 1), but Smith's *progress* is not the dialectical analysis of wealth *and* distribution demanded by Marx. Actually, Smith's vision of economic "progress" is *retrospective*. In Marx's eyes, Smith and his contemporaries mistook the status of economic analysis by creating "Robinsonades," individualistic projections of an economy comprising (eighteenth-century) individuals just like themselves; their subjectively conceived evaluation of ethical process caused them to misunderstand the role of the economist himself in the broader social history of economic production.

The full title of Smith's work makes his position clear: *An Inquiry into the Nature and Causes of the Wealth of Nations.* Smith's magnum opus is a demonstration, not a polemic. Because "Wealth" has an accepted and an *a priori* moral content, Smith does not need to engage, as Marx would, a *political* economics, a rhetoric of moral and social persuasion. The wealth of nations is both the conclusion he seeks to reveal and the philosophical premise from which he begins. The assumption that there is a wealth *of* —both between and for—nations does not need to be proved but merely defined. It is consistent with Smith's eighteenth-century classicism that individual well-being in the order of nature partakes of a more generic abundance in the order of nations, just as "individual man" is an acceptable metonym for "Man." Marx contended that this view of nature polarized one's definition of "Man" into those who had access to wealth and those who did not, leaving "economy" as a socially unthinkable metaphor. As we shall see in greater detail in subsequent chapters, this changing view of what the economic art could or should represent required redefinitions of the economist's own role and of the social value of *his* labor.

In the new "science" (a science created by capitalism, according to Marx), the principles of economics no longer expressed the whole complex of man's social economy. But when economics became divorced, in the nineteenth century, from what Polanyi calls "the science of society," it did not relinquish the philosophical complexity of its genesis. Despite its "reductions," political economy, as a separate discipline, may be seen as that century's most significant and intricate construct, its greatest and most problematic myth. Walter Bagehot, for one, thought so: "No other form of political philosophy has ever had one-thousandth part of the influence on us, its teachings have settled down into the commonsense of the nation, and have become irreversible."[27] Isolated as a unique "philosophy," a functional theory of economic management evolved in the secular affairs of an expanding business world and became, ironically, the epistemological equal of earlier moral theories of economy.

Ten years before the publication of *The Wealth of Nations,* Mirabeau praised Quesnay's *Tableau Oeconomique* in these terms:

Three great primary inventions have given stability to society besides the large number of others which enriched and adorned it. These three are: (1) The invention of writing, which alone gives man the power of handing down without alteration his laws, his contracts, his annals and his discoveries. (2) That of money, which binds together all relations in civilised societies. The third and last, which belongs to our age and of which our descendents will enjoy the fruit, is derived from the other two and completes each of them equally by perfecting their object: it is the discovery of the Economic Table which, becoming henceforth the universal interpreter, embraces and harmonises all the correlative fractions or proportions which should enter into every general calculation of the economic order.[28]

Mirabeau's identification of the economic art as a man-made "invention" marks a turning away from the older, morally dependent view of *oikonomia* toward the self-enclosed science which nevertheless has "universal" significance. Its universality acquires a new metaphysical importance. According to Mirabeau, the discovery of rationalistic principles for describing the movements and exchanges of the economy becomes equal in importance to the creation of written discourse itself. This perspective locates the origin of man's rational consciousness in economic discourse alone, for economics becomes concerned with more than the facts of money, with more than the facts of business transaction in general. It sees in money that "which binds together all relations in civilised societies." Because it comprises the web that joins and unites "all relations," economics becomes "the universal interpreter." In its broadest conception, economics is no longer Aristotle's philosophical nexus between ethics and the polis but the symbolic representation par excellence of the world of "facts."

Recently, some economic analysts have gone one step further and attempted to see the structuring of commercial phenomena as, in part at least, a question of aesthetics.[29] Precisely at this point in the evolution of "economics," economists have rediscovered the artfulness which we will now see embodied in Spenser's portrayal of Mammon. Their efforts serve to emphasize a more subtle and more pervasive "fact"—that in describing our material lives, economics both appropriates and alters the language and concepts we use to represent ourselves. Economics does not merely represent the world of facts, but also imaginatively structures that world according to its own imaginative needs: "it rationalises, indeed creates the experience with which it deals."[30]

The economist is, like Mammon, a poet, a maker of fictions, who must compose and order potentially conflicting facts and values. Walter Bagehot accorded this poetic status to the "abstract science" of economics in his essay "The Postulates of English Political Economy" (1880):

> All abstractions are arbitrary: they are more or less convenient fictions made by the mind for its own purposes. An abstract idea means a concrete fact or set of facts *minus* something thrown away. The fact or set of facts were made by nature; but how much you will keep for consideration you settle for yourself. There may be any number of political economies, according as the subject is divided off in one way or another. . . . [*Economic Studies*, p. 21]

But Bagehot is not belittling economists. He is attempting to define the complex and elusive relationship between abstraction and fact, a relationship made more uneasy for the simple reason that each economist parses the facts differently, each throws something different away (see ibid., p. 17). Bagehot's protostructuralist vision encourages us to understand that the discipline of economics is imaginatively constructed out of the metaphysical need to explain our idea(s) of economy and out of the psychological need to represent our economic practices to ourselves. John Ruskin puts the magnitude of these needs succinctly: "Three-fourths of the demands existing in the world are romantic; founded on visions, idealisms, hopes, and affections; and the regulation of the purse is, in its essence, regulations of the imagination and the heart. Hence, the right discussion of the nature of price is a very high metaphysical and psychical problem. . . ."[31]

Spenser's use of Mammon exposes the metaphysical and psychical problem in its imaginative form. In Spenser's Mammon, we may see the mythic potential of "economics," and we may explore how it appropriates other economies to explain its own needs. Mammon becomes the foremost worldly antagonist to confront Guyon, the knight of temperance and hero of *The Faerie Queene*'s second book. And yet, Guyon's own virtue of temperance would also seem to make him a formidable worldly protagonist. The temperate man, according to Aristotle, neither courts nor shuns the perils of experience; unlike Redcrosse Knight, the knight of holiness who is the hero of book 1, Guyon is fortified with a secular, practical resourcefulness. But Guyon is subjected to an unworldly trial as well. Mammon is, as he himself insists, God. When the master of the economy proffers "economics" itself as a mystery, holiness is thus transmuted into a new and wholly materialistic form, Mammon's cave of wealth. In this (metaphysical) reversal of book 1, Mammon's economy also contests the implicitly Christian virtue of the poet-narrator (and of Spenser's readers). At the crossings of the Aristotelian and the Christian economies, Mammon attempts to fix a fictional garden, filled with coinage that moth and rust will not corrupt. Mammon opens this underground horde to Guyon and, like Dante's guide, leads him through it, constructing in the process an "economics" which informs Guyon's personal "economy" by means of "the economy," which extrapolates from classical and Christian interpretations "the science of sciences." Ultimately, Mammon posits his economic art as "the universal interpreter" of all linguistic signs.

The Art of Mammon

Guyon appears at the beginning of book 2, canto 7, as a kind of "unaccommodated man." In the starless dark of the canto's opening stanzas, Guyon must depend for his safe passage on the naked, material condition of his own being:

> As pilot well expert in perilous wave,
> That to a stedfast starre his course hath bent,
> When foggy mistes or cloudy tempests have
> The faithfull light of that faire lampe yblent,
> And cover'd heaven with hideous dreriment,
> Upon his card and compas firmes his eye,
> The maysters of his long experiment,
> And to them does the steddy helme apply,
> Bidding his winged vessell fairely forward fly:

> So Guyon, having lost his trustie guyde,
> Late left beyond that Ydle Lake, proceedes
> Yet on his way, of none accompanyde;
> And evermore himselfe with comfort feedes
> Of his own vertues and praise-worthie deedes.[32]

The loss of that "stedfast starre" in the canto's second line has re-sounding symbolic importance for Guyon's moral trials at the hands of Mammon. To the mariner, the star is a divine sign of geographical order by which he may chart his course. But for Guyon, the act of interpretation has lost its visible landmarks in this opening epic simile. Guyon's "trustie guyde," the palmer, is also "lost," because Guyon was forced to leave him behind when he abandoned himself to Phaedria's enchanting care (canto 6). Like the mariner's star, the palmer had served as a signifier, providing Guyon's instinctive, innate "vertues" with a contemplative focus and substantiating Guyon's experimental observations with intellectual speculation.

In the palmer's stead, Guyon turns to his "card and compas," the book by which he may interpret his position. It is a book composed of stories which Guyon tells himself about his own past deeds. As a reading of his own virtues, however, Guyon's self-fulfilling art reminds us that Guyon is, throughout book 2, a notoriously shortsighted interpreter or "reader" of experience. In canto 10, Arthur is able to read the whole mythic history of England while Guyon manages, literally, to finish only a handful of stanzas in the Elfin histories. Already, in canto 2, Guyon, as a figurative "reader" of his own actions, fails to understand why water does not wash off blood. The palmer, who is accompanying Guyon at the time, responds to that amazement:

> Ye bene right hard amated, gratious lord,
> And of your ignorance great merveill make,
> Whiles cause not well conceived ye mistake. [2.2.5]

According to Aristotle, the wise man must read the meaning of those causes behind the signified content: "The wise man, you see, must not only know all that can be deduced from his first principles but he must understand their true meaning" (*Ethics*, p. 179). But Guyon will first destroy the Bower of Bliss and then ask "what meant those beastes which there did ly" (2.12.84). Throughout book 2, Guyon summons psychical sustenance from actions which, in metaphysical terms, he is unable to fathom. In the "foggy mistes" of book 2's palmer-less middle canto, Guyon's "card and compas" lead him straight to the cave of Mammon.

When, late in canto 7, Mammon takes Guyon to view Philotime, Guyon "gan inquire, / What meant that preace about that ladies throne, / And what she was that did so high aspyre" (2.7.48). Unfortunately, there is no one to answer. Or rather, in place of his "stedfast starre," Guyon has acquired Mammon. In his broadest interpretation as the Money-God (st. 39), Mammon offers Guyon neither material substance nor the world's chattel. He proffers a system of signs (money) which purports to signify need and desire. This symbolic language further challenges Christian interpretation, because Mammon implies that his set of symbols comprises the one true art, the only guide to moral well-being. For Guyon's edification, Mammon attempts to read, as plainly as he can, the ethical exchanges to which monetary values can be put:

> Loe here the worldes blis! loe here the end,
> To which al men doe ayme, rich to be made!
> Such grace now to be happy is before thee laid. [st. 32]

The emphasis on "here" and "now" is crucial to Mammon's claim of *worldly* power; his promise of "grace" is crucial to his claim of *godliness*. Mammon's presumption of moral authority is made manifest when he becomes Guyon's de facto guide, appropriating the palmer's instructional role: " 'Come thou,' quoth he, 'and see' " (st. 20). What Mammon promises to show Guyon is a new species of "stedfast starre." Mammon claims to replace the stars in the sky with those other divine lights of guidance which are nestled in darkness deep under ground. He proclaims those lights, the precious metals and stones of the earth, as his own, and thereby invites man to see in these constellations a precise correspondence to God's astral arrangements. By urging his authority in this way, Mamon extends, by inversion, his imaginative right to be regarded as an alternative divinity.[33]

The "end" of Mammon's art is to assure Guyon "that money can thy wantes at will supply" (st. 11). In the language of medieval and Renaissance metaphysics, this art aspires to be both the method of signification (*verba*) and the thing signified (*res*). Money, the object to be supplied and the commodity of exchange, acquires both metaphorical and substantive status. Both physical and metaphysical, Mammon's exchanges, like the Word of God, mediate between worlds, making the means to sufficiency literally a golden means. Anticipating the household of Alma (canto 10), Mammon's economy proffers the soul a commodious dispensation. To justify the godliness of that dispensation, Mammon asserts that fortune (economic wealth) and not Fortune (mutability) is the principal deity of this sublunar world:

> They forward passe, ne Guyon yet spoke word,
> Till that they came unto an yron dore,
> Which to them opened of his owne accord,
> And shewd of richesse such exceeding store,
> As eie of man did never see before,
> Ne ever could within one place be fownd,
> Though all the wealth, which is, or was of yore,
> Could gathered be through all the world arownd,
> And that above were added to that under grownd. [St. 31]

This supernal bounty, greater than all the natural wealth ever known, defines Mammon's mythic status as dependent upon a divine plenitude. Mammon is not simply, therefore, the allegorical type of Wealth or Luxury or an inherited stock figure, like Lady Pecunia.[34] Like book 1's Den of Error, Mammon's cave embodies the very principle of commercial error, its dispiriting, materialistic accumulation. The ethos of the cave is expressed as the economic mythos itself. Like poetry, Mammon's art has certain fictive powers, including the power to make its fictions come true in the form of monetary coinages. Like the mariner's star, Mammon has the power to guide the voyager to a restful end, "rich to be made." Like God's abundance, Mammon's riches seem the visible incarnations of an otherworldly wealth.

Guyon responds by substituting a different matrix of his own signification:

> Another blis before mine eyes I place,
> Another happines, another end. [St. 33]

Initially, in canto 7, that other bliss is centered in Guyon's own self-reliance: "And evermore himselfe with comfort feedes / Of his own vertues and praise-worthie deedes." That he *feeds* off his own virtues will become a critical irony, considering that he ultimately faints from want of food. But this concentration of Guyon's guidance into his own redoubtable powers, his own habitual virtue, and his own instinctive knowledge is consistent with the essential optimism of Aristotelian virtue—that man possesses innate powers of sufficiency by habit as well as by instruction. Aristotelian temperance is constructed upon a bodily, as much as a spiritual, efficiency. Aristotle defines temperance first in terms of the individual and then in terms of its more extensive societal application. Individual temperance and social justice are analogically related as microcosm to macrocosm. In the first book of his *Ethics,* Aristotle explains that individual moral sufficiency is not enough, although self-sufficiency is the final end of morality: "It is a generally accepted view that the final good is self-sufficient. By 'self-sufficient' is meant not what is sufficient for oneself living the life of a solitary but includes parents, wife and children, friends and fellow-citizens in general. For man is a social animal" (*Ethics,* p. 37). We do not live, as Spenser says of Guyon, "of none accompanyde." The extension of the family means that some kind of trade or exchange is necessary for the maintenance of self-sufficiency. This trade and the economic principles which govern it should be ideally an extension of the individual economics of the self.

Mammon attempts to overcome this classical view of "economy" by simultaneously extolling the sufficiency of the self and challenging the self to account for its "maystery." The root of the paradox is money itself, which Mammon represents as the form of mastery that all men recognize and "to which al men doe ayme." When mastery is economically accountable, Mammon may then propose money as the most visible and objective means to sufficiency, the only dependable signifier of "comfort." Having reminded Guyon that he is alone, Mammon intimates what Spenser's fellow Tudor poet said plainly: "Golde never starts asyde, but in dystress, / Fyndes wayes enoughe, to ease thyne hevynes."[35] So Mammon promises a new set of commercial signifiers, a new "card and compas" with the means not only to lead the unaccompanied knight through a hostile and comfortless world but to enable him to master it.

Mammon's subversion of what Aristotle calls "reasoned speech" places new demands upon Guyon's Aristotelian understanding. In responding to Mammon's commercial interpretation of individual sufficiency, Guyon at first repeats the specifically Aristotelian doctrine of economic and moral temperance:

> through fowle intemperaunce,
> Frayle men are oft captiv'd to covetize:
> But would they thinke, with how small allowaunce
> Untroubled nature doth her selfe suffise,
> Such superfluities they would despise,
> Which with sad cares empeach our native joyes. [St. 15]

In the beginning, sufficiency was available in nature, a solidly Aristotelian premise. But in trying to understand the "meaning"—that

is, the final cause—of "such superfluities," Guyon becomes less
Aristotelian, less masterful, and less temperate. He proceeds to an
Ovidian account of the origin of money, which began with the rap-
ing of Earth's womb (st. 17), a violation perpetuated by man's
minting of earth's treasures into coin. This art of coinage in turn
creates the illusion of a greater, a more abundant richness than nature actually affords. As the rape was an unnatural act, so too the
subsequent desire for money becomes unnatural in that it "gan
exceed / The measure of [nature's] meane, and natural first need"
(st. 16). Man's aspiring mind has created the idea of "surplusage"
(st. 18). Sufficiency, then, as defined by Aristotelian economics
and as exemplified in Aristotelian temperance, becomes impossible
when the *Mater* (Earth's womb) is violated by "the matter of
[man's] huge desire" (st. 17). This "matter," which is a "com-
pownd" of man's "huge desire / And pompous pride," becomes
metaphorically a new body of desire; philosophically, it becomes
a new materialism, literally embodied in Mammon.

Already, then, Guyon's account of Mammon's creation as the
Money-God has moved away from the Aristotelian concept of
money as an exchange value only. Having said that superfluity is
unnatural, Guyon also identifies it as wholly human. Thus, Guyon's
"interpretation" of Mammon lapses into a lament for the unna-
turalness of human desire itself. The creation of "surplusage," as
if suggesting a surplus-age, is the price of living in "later times"
when man "must wage / [his] workes for wealth, and life for gold
engage" (st. 18). The invention of money brings with it the concept of "usuable" time. Now money promises that it will secure
world enough and time to realize all man's desires. So usury buys
time, but at a cost. Fiduciary credit supplants goodwill; the promise of future payment projects a new, specifically commercial
faithfulness as a condition of the future. Thus, Mammon's promise
of a manageable surplus vitiates the Aristotelian assumption that
there is an exact correspondence between the commodities of the
material world and the necessities of man's material being. By en-
ticing Guyon to reimagine the worldly state of man, Mammon
posits the economic imagination as the new vehicle of moral sustenance. Guyon identifies Mammon's art of beguilement; he also
reveals that Mammon's "card and compas" comprise a book which
he does not choose to read. In uncovering the self-contradictions
of Guyon's mastery, Spenser will invite the reader to read aright
the ironic Christian mystery in Mammon's economy.

Christian instruction demands that we choose between Aristotle's natural and Mammon's unnatural economy. And the basis for making that choice requires a new semiotic structure, a new hermeneutics of "stedfast starre" and "reasoned speech." In Christain economics, service is a necessary condition of faith, and "no man can serve two masters" (Matt. 6:24). The Christian choice between serving God's economy and Mammon's economics becomes unconditional: "Ye cannot serve God and Mammon." When the spies of the priests asked Christ if they ought to pay taxes to Caesar, Jesus "perceived their craftiness and said unto them, Why tempt ye me? Shew me a penny. Whose image and superscription hath it? They answered and said, Caesar's. And he said unto them, Render therefore unto Caesar the things which be Caesar's, and unto God the things which be God's" (Luke 20: 23-25). Christ's answer permits his listeners to hear what they are able to hear: "And they could not take hold of his words before the people: and they marvelled at his answer, and held their peace" (20:26). Condemned to their own interpretation, they "of [their] ignorance great merveill make." Because they read the image on the denarius as Caesar's, they do not see the significance of Christ's question: that gold also belongs to God, after all. What Christ renders unto the Pharisees is a kind of language that seems sufficiently corroborative of their own expectations to be unthreatening. They miss the point but get what they deserve. *They* may worship the stamped face of Caesar on the precious metal, while *we* may apprehend that the "image and superscription," in their unspoken and unseen significance, reflect the King's real face, the face of the real King.

In fact, the idea of "divine economics" itself depends upon a paradox, for how does one measure in quantitative language a substance (God) which is beyond quantification? First, as the Christian parable suggests, we must see how God makes his currency known. In Alanus de Insulis's *De Planctu Naturae*, Nature explains the origins of God's art:

When God wished to bring the creation of His worldly palace out from the spiritual abode of His inner preconception into external mold, and to express, as in a material word and by its real existence, the mental word which He had conceived from the everlasting foundation of the universe . . . [,] He fashioned the marvelous form of His earthly palace, not with the laborious assistance of an exterior agency, nor by the

help of material lying there at hand, nor because of any base
need, but by the power of His sole independent will.[36]

God's creation of the world is seen here to be perfect in "His inner
preconception." Once revealed in nature, however, these conceptions became susceptible to "the round of mutual relation of birth
and death." In order to preserve the perfect image out of which
these perishable things were first conceived, God decreed that all
things should be "stamped with the seal of clear conformity" (p.
43). Thus, for Alanus, all worldly things bear His imprint, so that
an inspired reader may perceive evidences of God's will. So, all
things are equal in value in that they share a creatural equivalency.
Nature reveals herself to be the minter of God's currency, God's
deputy: "Accordingly, obeying the command of the Ruler, in my
work I stamp, so to speak, the various coins [*numismata*] of things
in the image of the original, exemplifying the figure of the example, harmoniously forming like from like, and have produced the
distinctive appearances of individual things" (p. 44). In divine
economics, the world of matter belongs to God, not Mammon; it
bears the stamp of His creation.[37] What man must understand is
that all things which are images in God's mind are contiguous with
God's will. The denominations on all God's coinages are signs,
pointing to the sole unspeakable nomination—the name of God.
But in deference to the darkness of man's fallen estate, God ac-
commodates man's partial understanding by speaking a figurative
(and here, a specifically economic) language which man can understand. Such deference betokens God's grace toward man, "for God
provides," according to Aquinas, "for everything according to the
capacity of its nature."[38] The work of God requires a special kind
of (human) interpretation in order not to abuse His works. So,
when Aquinas points to the figure of God's arm as it is described
in Scripture, "The literal sense is not that God has such a member,
but only what is signified by this member, namely, operative power."[39] Similarly, the material world signifies God's "sole independent will," and it is marked by the grace of that creation.

In greeting Redcrosse at the beginning of book 2, the palmer
distinguishes accurately between the "marke" of Redcrosse's "late
most hard atchiev'ment" and the "atchiev'ment" itself:

Joy may you have, and everlasting fame,
Of late most hard atchiev'ment by you donne,

For which enrolled is your glorious name
In heavenly regesters above the sunne,
Where you a saint with saints your seat have wonne:
But wretched we, where ye have left your marke,
Must now anew begin like race to ronne. [2.1.32]

The "atchiev'ment" of God's creatures is to make manifest their
creatureliness, to reveal the godhead by the "marke" which their
good works and heroism have left.[40] Worldly success is nothing; it
is not a thing in itself, but it bears a mark of similitude with the
good works of God. The material organization of the world reveals
most clearly, therefore, what God is *not*, in the same way that
Spenser, addressing Gloriana, admits that her glory must be poetically dressed "in covert vele, and wrap[ped] in shadowes light" or
men "would bee dazled with exceeding light" (2. Proem.5).

Such mysteries are possible only if the equivalence of all worldly goods and the ultimate correspondence of earth and heaven
are presumed to be true, not "th'abondance of an ydle braine"
(2.Proem.1). Whereas monetary signs are a self-referring system in
which the sign points to money itself as an ultimate value, in the
currency of divine economics each signification points beyond its-
self to the ultimate glory which is God. Thus, Christian signifiers
are self-consuming, vanishing into the transcendent reality of the
invisibilia. Unlike the "witlesse" reader of the proem to whom
"nothing is, but that which he hath seene" (st. 3), the Christian
interpreter must understand that God is the "nothing"—the sub-
stance-less—who appears through the substance, the things of his
creation. By his manipulation of the terms of divine economics,
Mammon attempts to reassess the ends of human "atchiev'ment."
He would make money's worldly significance seem to embody a
transcendent sufficiency. This blasphemous distortion of Christian
discourse acquires an air of credibility in book 2 because the Aristotelian ideal of economic sufficiency, as advanced by Guyon, is
not imaginatively equipped to respond to it. Whether the "great
rule of Temp'raunce" (2.Proem.5) is able to overcome or to master Mammon's blasphemous art will appear, paradoxically, through
Guyon's limitations as a reader.

Finally, all interpretations become hazardous in Mammon's
cave. His guiding lights merely allow his visitors to see what they
want to see, rather than what is. By the light of gold, Mammon's
world becomes amorphous. Mammon is first discovered, in the

narrator's account, in "a gloomy glade, / Cover'd with boughes and shrubs from heavens light" (st. 3). In the next line, this spot has become a "secret shade." Four stanzas later, Guyon wonders why Mammon "here in desert hast thine habitaunce" (st. 7). In fact, we usually refer to Mammon's habitat as a "cave," presumably because Mammon leads Guyon along

> A darkesome way, which no man could descry,
> That deep descended through the hollow grownd,
> And was with dread and horror compassed arownd. [St. 20]

But Spenser has warned us that it is a place "which no man could descry," and "none could behold / The hew." The immateriality of this place (or these places) is analogous to the insubstantiality of money, which Mammon would confuse with the divine substance itself, *insubstantiality* thus investing the *invisibilia*. Actually, the closest one comes to any mention of a cave is in the following simile, in a likeness not an identity:

> That houses forme within was rude and strong,
> Lyke an huge cave, hewne out of rocky clifte,
> From whose rough vaut the ragged breaches hong,
> Embost with massy gold of glorious guifte,
> And with rich metall loaded every rifte,
> That heavy ruine they did seem to threatt. [St. 28]

Spenser warns us repeatedly that, in Mammon's presence, vision is figurative—a beguiling thing:

> for vew of cherefull day
> Did never in that house it selfe display,
> But a faint shadow of uncertein light;
> Such as a lamp, whose life does fade away;
> Or as the moone, cloathed with clowdy night,
> Does shew to him that walkes in feare and sad affright.
> [St. 29]

Now Mammon's "cave" has become "that house." Illumination depends upon mistaking rhetoric for reality, as in confounding "a faint shadow of uncertein light" with day. The balanced adjectives, "faint" and "uncertein," lend rhetorical weight to a light which is never more than a *shadow* of a light in any case. If Mammon's domain is a cave, it is a metaphorical one—a cave *like* the mind.

Mammon's promise "that money can thy wantes at will supply" indicates the perils of reading by this cave's light. "Money" can be either the subject or the object of "supply," the grammatical ambiguity confirming the duplicity of the promise. For if "wantes" are defined as a lack of money, then ironically, it is that "lack" which money supplies. Mammon's (unintended) pun of "wantes" indicates that money creates its own scarcities, as well as feeds off its own insubstantiality. Thus, Mammon's deepest fraud is expressed in his brightest promise, for inherent in his idea of "surplusage" is the idea of necessary scarcity, just as inherent in market exchanges is the essential disparity between demand ("wantes") and supply. Liar that he is, Mammon never reveals that moneymaking is by definition a compensation for an imagined scarcity in nature of the essential means for fulfillment. Money, as Mammon's "offred grace" (st. 18), comprises his attempt to heal the breach between nature and God. This premise of a breach in natural plenitude is foreign, in fact, to Aristotelian economics, and Guyon easily resists it. It is not, however, unfamiliar to the Christian sense of fallen nature and of the inevitable disjunction between signature and object, *verba* and *res, numismata* and true images. Mammon seems to be counting on this Christian doubt of natural capacities; at least, he profits from the metaphysical uncertainty of the word. As Christian doubt becomes the basis of Mammon's art, so a post-Aristotelian *commercium* becomes the foundation of his redefined *oikonomia*.

Step by step through Mammon's cave, Guyon is forced to relinquish the economic principles of Aristotelian temperance. What he acquires in their stead is, however, less important than how he relinquishes them.[41] By stanza 7, Mammon reads Guyon as "rash and heedlesse of thy selfe." Such imprudence, if proved, would be inconsistent with Aristotle's view of the temperate man. But, by stanza 12, Guyon sounds a little like his own palmer and, for one of the few times in the book, offers his own interpretive reading of phenomena:

> "All otherwise," saide he, "I riches read,
> And deeme them roote of all disquietnesse;
> First got with guile, and then preserv'd with dread,
> And after spent with pride and lavishnesse,
> Leaving behind them griefe and heavinesse.

Infinite mischiefes of them doe arize,
Strife and debate, bloodshed and bitternesse,
Outrageous wrong and hellish covetize,
That noble heart, as great dishonour, doth despize."

Finally, however, Aristotle provides only tangential authority for such remarks. In Aristotle's view, "riches" need not be the "roote of all disquietnesse," because the virtuous economist will use money as he uses other tools—as a means of sufficiency. It is only in the Christian dispensation that love of money is the *root* of all evil. Aristotle never called coveting "hellish" but only unnatural, contrary to reason. If Guyon's indignation is intemperate, therefore, his "reading" is proto-Christian. "Ne thine be kingdomes, ne the scepters thine," Guyon exclaims to Mammon; but we, and not Guyon, hear the unwitting Christian echo: "For Thine is the Kingdom and the power and the glory. . . ."

Ironically, Guyon becomes *our* guide, an unwitting Christian economist. When Guyon tells Mammon that "realmes and rulers thou doest both confound" (st. 13), he means that Mammon's riches beguile earthly kings into a false aggrandizement of their worldly resources. In a Christian context, however, Mammon has done more: he confounds the signifiers, because he has confused earthly riches with the treasures of the heavenly kingdom which moth and rust do not corrupt. Guyon, then, does not serve Mammon; in fact, he "despize[s]" him. But this gesture of un-Aristotelian spite is the initial and ironic step toward Christian passion. By stanza 16, when Guyon recounts a genesis story, we should know where we stand, even if Guyon is still in the dark:

The antique world, in his first flowring youth,
Fownd no defect in his Creators grace,
But with glad thankes, and unreproved truth,
The guifts of soveraine bounty did embrace:
Like angels life was then mens happy cace:
But later ages pride, like corn-fed steed,
Abused her plenty and fat swolne encreace
To all licentious lust, and gan exceed
The measure of her meane, and naturall first need.

The golden mean may *allude* to Aristotle, but the golden ages of classical antiquity, whether Hesiodic or Ovidian, were not imaged "in [the] Creators *grace*." Nor were there angels in Greek and

Roman classicism. And "pride," at least in this "reading" of the world's fall from grace, is a Christian sin. As a pagan mystery, a mythographic history, this account is counterfeit. As inchoate Christian postulation, it is orthodoxy.

By stanza 33, therefore, we are prepared to hear a different hypothetical significance in Guyon's lines than we adduced at the beginning:

> Another blis before mine eyes I place,
> Another happines, another end.
> To them that list, these base regardes I lend:
> But I in armes, and in atchievements brave,
> Do rather choose my flitting houres to spend,
> And to be lord of those that riches have,
> Then them to have my selfe, and be their servile sclave.

Guyon does not tell us what that other bliss or other end will be, but it can no longer be the Aristotelian economy of his first defense. In fact, there is no immediately available *signified* for Guyon's signifiers. We may deduce, however, from Guyon's previous, unreasonable uses of Aristotelian speech, a movement toward Christian "right reason." *We,* that is, supply the signified content. And because we expand Guyon's references as we read, we may also hear in Guyon's rebuttal of Mammon the seeds of a specifically Christian pride in his choice "to be lord of those that riches have."

In Guyon's disdain for the Money-God's economics, the Aristotelian and Christian significances of his responses reveal their mutual weaknesses. In a Christian context, Guyon's Aristotelian temperance becomes Phaedrian coyness. In an Aristotelian context, Mammon's promise of material sufficiency reveals a potential weakness of the Christian economy: its single-minded, perhaps unnatural, bias against worldly things. Whereas Christian *contemptus mundi* proceeds from a wish to save the soul, Guyon's scorn for Mammon's economic offerings proceeds from a wish to save the body: "But I in armes, and in atchievements brave, / Do rather choose my flitting houres to spend." The economies of classical *virtù* and Christian virtue are brought into focus by Mammon's economics, but, lacking a reliable interpreter, they are also in danger of crossing without recognizing or instructing each other. As temperate Guyon exemplifies, one may become too contemptuous in dispersing one's self-righteous scorn, too proud of one's mastery.

By the end of the canto, Mammon's technique of enticement is to make Guyon disdain distaining—that is, to make him sit down. Like Despaire in book 1, Mammon mirrors the doubting self, and his methods are ruthlessly reductive. Without actually showing respect for Guyon's defiance, Mammon, like a chivalrous foe, seems to concede Guyon a rest after a good fight. In fact, by stanzas 63 and 64, Guyon finds himself in a position where even to refuse this concession incorrectly is to succumb. Mammon's last offer, less a proposition than a rhetorical question, discloses the strain:

> "Thou fearefull foole,
> Why takest not of that same fruite of gold,
> Ne sittest down on that same silver stoole,
> To rest they weary person in the shadow coole?" [St. 63]

The beguiler's hint of exasperation allows us to imagine Mammon as a "weary person" also. But for Guyon, the question is: how often can one say "no" before, like the fabled lady, one says "no" while reclining (like Phaedria, who abandoned "fruitlesse labors" in order to choose a kind of commerce based upon sexual exchanges wherein all trade confirmed victorious gain for both parties, and who thought Guyon "disdainfull coy")?[42] Defiance may be self-defeating. Repetition may enervate refusal insofar as it represses the original motive for temperance. The narrator interposes the crucial observation that, if Guyon at this point "inclyned had at all," he would have been at the mercy of Mammon:

> All which he did, to do him deadly fall
> In frayle intemperaunce through sinfull bayt;
> To which if he inclyned had at all,
> That dreadful feend, which did behind him wayt,
> Would him have rent in thousand peeces strayt. [St. 64]

Inclination here must refer to both inner and outer yearnings. As with Adam and Eve, the "deadly fall" would be precipitated for Guyon by the *inclination* to fall and not by the actual physical response of inclining toward the fruit (and silver stool). But Guyon has not been deceived by Mammon's attempt to proffer stool and fruit as the "sinfull bait." He knows intuitively that the real bait is not the visible object of his regard but that it dangles on a

spiritual hook which stool and fruit signify. Guyon, in short, sees
through the *visibilia* (the signifiers) to the *invisibilia* (the signified)
which, in Christian hermeneutics, is the literal thing itself. He
reads the phenomena rightly:

> But he was wary wise in all his way,
> And well perceived his deceiptfull sleight,
> Ne suffred lust his safety to betray;
> So goodly did beguile the guyler of his pray. [St. 64]

Spenser emphasizes Guyon's achievement by refusing to say exactly what Guyon *actually* did in order to beguile the beguiler of
his prey. Did he smile wryly or turn his face away? Did he pull his
visor down or just not sit down? We cannot tell, because the
"goodly" significance of his refusal is not to be read in any physical gesture he made but in the "inclination" not to fall, which is
literally nonphysical. Here, Guyon's most "praise-worthie" deed
is in not allowing "lust his safety to betray," an internal action
which requires no outward sign but which respects the spiritually
real threat behind the physical appearance.

Then why does he faint? "For want of food and sleepe," says
Spenser in stanza 65. This simple oversight is the price of Guyon's
lack of conversion. He fails to exchange completely the reasoned
speech of Aristotelian temperance for the righteous actions of
Christian temperance, even though Christ's instructions have been
literally heeded: "Ye cannot serve God and Mammon. Therefore
I say unto you, Take no thought for your life, what ye shall eat,
or what ye shall drink; nor yet for your body, what ye shall put
on. Is not the life more than the meat, and the body than the
raiment?" (Matt. 6:24–25). Guyon avoids and refuses Mammon's
blandishments, but this is all he does. To "take no thought" is, in
the dynamics of Christian economics, not an instance of mental
laxity or of spiritual scorn but an exercise in consciously choosing
a different bliss, another happiness, an alternative end. The soldier
of Christ must take no thought of economic or material life in
order to choose a superior spiritual economy. But Guyon does not
consciously make that choice. In choosing not to serve Mammon,
neither does he choose to serve God. Guyon has beguiled the beguiler; but in using Mammon's own art of guile, no matter how
righteously, Guyon cannot avoid drifting away from the original
card and compass of his strength, his bodily virtue. Ironically, he

has neglected that material "sufficaunce" which depends upon the material necessities of food and sleep, although he has thought all along that innate bodily resources were his guiding principles. Guyon does not understand his "other" bliss to be spiritual, though he has refused Mammon throughout canto 7 in the name of it.

When Guyon involuntarily partakes of "the living light" and "this vitall ayre," he suffers the repercussions of his lost guide, his formerly "stedfast starr," and his obduracy. Relinquishment, or the right refusal of certain extremes of pleasure and pain, is a distinguishing mark of Aristotelian virtue, but the demands espoused in the rarefied air of Mammon's domain have confounded Guyon's habitual temperance. Temperance has become habitual relinquishment, sustained by guile. What suffices in Mammon's cave as a defense against economic fantasies is precisely what is too fanciful a disdain outside it. Although Guyon "well perceived his [i.e., Mammon's] deceitful sleight," he does not well perceive his own. In guarding the treasure of himself, Guyon has spent his "vitall powres" (st. 65). The difference between Guyon as a sufficient Aristotelian knight and Guyon as an insufficient Christian knight is ironic, but the quality of that irony depends upon the (Christian) reader's apprehension of the essential insufficiency of relying on oneself.

Guyon is not Christianized; the reader always has been. Yet once more, Christian interpretation exorcizes its materialistic *daimon* so that the reader may see through the figurative sense to the literal meaning, through efficient to final causes, through Mammon's economics to divine economics, through human care to heavenly *caritas,* through Spenser's verses to the Word of God.

We, if not the unconscious Guyon, are embraced by the meditation that begins canto 8 as a contemplative rejoinder to the opening stanzas of canto 7:

> But O th'exceeding grace
> Of Highest God, that loves his creatures so,
> And all his workes with mercy doth embrace,
> That blessed angels he sends to and fro,
> To serve to wicked man, to serve his wicked foe!
>
> .   .   .   .
>
> They for us fight, they watch and dewly ward,
> And their bright squadrons round about us plant;

And all for love, and nothing for reward:
O why should hevenly God to men have such regard?
[2.8.1-2]

"Th'exceeding grace / Of Highest God" is the "stedfast starre" of
the Christian economist. Monetary signs, according to Mammon,
point to an essential "surplusage," assuring fulfillment of all man's
"wantes." Divine signs, such as the "blessed angels," point to an
essential abundance—indeed, if properly read, to an excess—of
grace which assures man that there is care in heaven. Divine economics possesses both superior means (God's tokens of exchange
are angels, but not those angels which were, in sixteenth-century
markets, coins) and superior ends (which are "all for love, and
nothing for reward").

In giving all and nothing, God reveals the difficulty of his gift. It
is a gift of no thing. Mammon had tried to claim that money shared
in this divine paradox by virtue of its being both a sign (a measure
of material value) and a commodity (the most valued substance).
The greater mystery, however, engages divine sufficiency. God's
grace is nothing, the unknowable spirit which may be shown
through things but which is neither in things nor a thing itself.
Furthermore, the grace of God does not depend upon the will of
the receiver to use it. Properly speaking, God does not "offer"
grace as Mammon did, but grace is there "to succour us, that succour want." Need, in other words, is answerable without petition,
even if the one in need (in this case, Guyon) does not comprehend
the conditions of Christian necessity.

In this encompassing, increasingly specific Christian context,
Spenser has explored the Aristotelian distinction between natural
and unnatural economy. At the crossing of moral and functional
economies, which is the midpoint of book 2, Spenser has graphically depicted the metaphysics of the commercial mythos. Mammon represents a household of hoarded money where the means
of production and exchange are amassed for their own artificial
grandeur, their own ends. Later, however, Guyon enters the House
of Alma, a household which is literally imagined as the Aristotelian *oikos*, whose end is self-sufficiency, whose means are "economically" organized to prevent waste and to aggrandize individual
labor, and whose center is the kitchen. The "golden mean" of this
house's architecture symbolizes Alma's economy, which trans-

forms material nature into nurture: "The frame thereof seemd partly circulare, / And part triangulare: O worke divine!"(2.9.22). The facade's illusoriness, the way it *seemed* divinely hewn, is overlooked for a moment as we go inside, where, laboring with right reason, Alma's home economists separate what is harmful from what is useful:

> Some to remove the scum, as it did rise;
> Others to beare the same away did mynd;
> And others it to use according to his kynd. [2.9.3]

These lines directly echo the description of Mammon's refinery, where the end of labor is also the need for nutriments but where gold, no matter how refined, does not answer that need:

> Some scumed the drosse, that from the metall came,
> Some stird the molten owre with ladles great;
> And every one did swincke, and every one did sweat.
> [2.8.36]

Harry Berger notes that Alma's household disposes neatly of its waste while turning its productions into nutriments. By contrast, "Mammon's refinery converts potential food into gold, the ultimate inorganic form. Furthermore, the gold which usurps the place of grain is not gold which can be exchanged for grain" (*Allegorical Temper,* p. 25). The two households of Mammon and Alma use the same tools for different ends.[43] If Mammon's domain is imaginatively the commercial world of markets, the realm of "the economy," then Alma's economics presages the literal household economy of soul or spirit (alma), created in the image of God's "worke divine."

And yet, even Alma's art, her castle, is built of mud and sand—"of thing like to that Aegyptian slime, / Whereof King Nine whilome built Babell towre" (9.21). This "slime" may be fertile, part of the *prima materia,* but in terms of the Christian dispensation, all human labor, no matter how fertile in conception, participates in the vanity of its own aspirations; all human labor imperfectly apes the work of divine creation. Thus, even Alma's economic structurings can be traced back (in the simile) to the Tower of Babel, man's attempt to reach God by means of his own devices. The reward of that aborted attempt was the fall into the babble of language, so that human discourse became removed once more from the divine Word. In particular, language's commercial signifiers now merely imitate, even in Alma's economy, the already imperfect imitations of human labor.

The language of economics, in its broadest speculation, expresses the quintessence of our humanity. It is both the core and the potential cure of our irrationality. Ernst Cassirer has lamented the lack of an adequate "metaphorical description" of language,[44] but, according to Mammon, "economics" serves as that metaphor. Guyon's trial at Mammon's hands tests his (and our) ability to read the metaphor, to apprehend economic discourse as the metaphorical process that describes the metaphysical aspirations of language.

Mammon calls himself "God of the world and wordlings," and he is, indeed, the lord of a world of gold, if not of the Golden World.[45] He is the god created by man. From a more homocentric perspective, such as evolved in the nineteenth century, Mammon is one of man's greatest creations, the one praised by Mirabeau. The Romantic poets read Spenser aptly when they interpreted Mammon's art as a human ordering, as the apotheosis of the self, and as an analogue, however ironic, to their own mythmaking.[46] But in an earlier Christian economics like Spenser's, the idea of remuneration—such as wages for one's labor, prices for one's goods, credit for one's faith—is restored to its literal significance when man is seen to be minted in God's own image. That is the basic text. The rest, as Spenser says of Mammon, is "glistering glosse" (2.7.4). As we shall now see, the burden of formal economic discourse will be to reunite text and gloss. More precisely, if the economic art is to become "the universal interpreter," then it will have to show why its rational structuring of "the economy" is less equivocal and more compelling than the older theocentric or ethically derived ideas of "economy" which it supplants.

CHAPTER III

"Unreal Words": Language in Political Economy

[Political Economy] labors under a special hardship: those who are conversant with its abstractions are usually without a true contact with its facts ; those who are in contact with its facts have usually little sympathy with and little cognizance of its abstractions. Literary men who write about it are constantly using what a great teacher calls "unreal words."
—*Walter Bagehot, "The Postulates of English Political Economy"*

Value making is a critical function of economic theory, the constitutive part of economic discourse. Thus, the economic art was long associated with moral philosophy, because ethical and economic values were seen as the corroborative expressions which Spenser's Mammon tried to exploit. The development of an economic *science* evidenced a different purpose. Since the aim of a science is to provide a consistent, systematic, and unambiguous form of discourse (a discourse which may not be especially suited to the task of ethical choice), economists in the nineteenth century set about to disengage "economics" from its noneconomic verbal signifiers by redefining such inherited terms as "production," "distri-

bution," "commodity," "price," "exchange," "utility," "credit"—
and, more broadly, "wealth," "money," "property," "labor," and
"value" itself. But even more importantly, in order to establish scientific principles, they had to develop new, less emotive definitions of their very subject and of their own labor. A dislocation
occurred between "economics," which explores the functional
operation of empirical phenomena, and "economy," which is seen
either as a moral disposition or as a philosophical orientation
toward sociological issues. Value making became a polarized activity. The man who would deal with the facts of economics was not
necessarily conversant with "economy" in the abstract.

In the present chapter, we shall examine a series of works by
economic writers to see what fictions were required in order to
reconstitute "economics" as a single, unifying, discursive formation. The best applied definition of a "discursive formation," as
we shall be using the term, is Michel Foucault's book *Madness and
Civilization.* His thesis is that "madness"—the idea, the normative
concept—is both contained in and explained out of all positive
studies of madness offered by "clinicians."[1] He summarizes the
thesis in *The Archaeology of Knowledge:*

> It would certainly be a mistake to try to discover what could
> have been said of madness at a particular time by interrogat-
> ing the being of madness itself, its secret content, its silent,
> self-enclosed truth; mental illness was constituted by all that
> was said in all the statements that named it, divided it up,
> described it, explained it, traced its developments, indicated
> its various correlations, judged it, and possibly gave it speech
> by articulating, in its name, discourses that were to be taken
> as its own. . . . It is not the same illnesses that are at issue in
> each of these cases; we are not dealing with the same mad-
> men.[2]

We confront the same difficulty in the imaginative structuring of
"economy." Aristotle's economics and Spenser's economics are
not Thoreau's: each is structured upon a different idea of economy; each deals with different kinds of economic men. Foucault's
method is to show how a subject—in his case, madness; in our
case, political economy—does not have a linear rationality or a
congruent historicity. The subject must be inflected from objective statements about it, statements that take madness (or econ-

omy) as their object. "By interrogating the being of madness it-self," a methodology which Foucault understands as consistent with the traditional history-of-ideas approach, one merely ends up with a complex representation of one's own historical orientation. Foucault has demonstrated what cruelty civilization has perpetrated upon itself in the name of rationality, through its conviction that "madness" is a rationally deducible category, and he warns that other, more general forms of thought—for us, the structure of political economy—are vulnerable to the same canonization as *rational* categories.[3] A more supple "archaeological" methodology might reveal the essentially imaginative or fictive status of these discursive formulations as well.[4]

Foucault thus cautions the intellectual historian against representing his "rational" faculties through more complex forms in one context and through less complex forms in other contexts:

> Despite appearances, we must not imagine that certain of the historical disciplines have moved from the continuous to the discontinuous, while others have moved from the tangled mass of discontinuities to the great, uninterrupted unities; we must not imagine that in the analysis of politics, institutions, or economics, we have become more and more sensitive to overall determinations, while in the analysis of ideas and of knowledge, we are paying more and more attention to the play of difference; we must not imagine that these two great forms of description have crossed without recognizing one another. [*Archaeology of Knowledge,* p. 6]

How, then, does this "crossing" occur? In this passage, Foucault's metaphor of a crossing is introduced by a metaphor which is so common that it is virtually unnoticed. He asks us to *pay* attention (*on a prêté une attention*),[5] the translator's idiomatic English admirably catching the exact (economic) import of the French idiom (*prête* is "a loan"). Such idioms are precisely what we will now want to attend, so that we may recognize their "play of difference," "the tangled mass" (*fourmillement*) of informal semantics and the systematic formulizations of economic discourse.

In everyday speech, we do not usually employ economic discourse in its singularly commercial sense, and we rarely, if ever, use it in the specific sense of economic theorists. Nor should we.

Of the language of economic science, L. M. Fraser notes, "In the first place, it makes no claim to correspond with ordinary language."[6] Fraser proceeds to explicate, with such key concepts as "price," "value," and "labor," the discontinuity of economic tropes in the commonplace, sometimes unthinking activites of our everyday lives.[7] Ruskin had previously (but less categorically) cited a similar dislocation in language, and he had gone on to note the limitations of his own insight: that simply by calling such verbal differences to our attention, we do not throw light upon or resolve them. In practice, our economic consciousness is so integral to our ordinary thought processes that we constantly think *with* economic terms when we wish to think *about* noneconomic matters which affect moral and aesthetic values. (In German, for instance, the rather common word *Schuld* means both "indebtedness" and "guilt.") The splintering of economic discourse from other types of valuation (such as the aesthetic or the moral) has created a polarized language, what Lord Lionel Robbins, the economist, sees as two separate planes of discourse.[8] We experience the phenomenon of Freud's "primal words" in reverse. Our idiomatic use of such words as "price" or "value" (or "paying attention") has confirmed their antithetical meanings.[9] From a "scientific" perspective, such words testify to the radical duplicity—the "unreality"—of language itself.

To assess the discursive consistency of political economy, we must first examine, in the language of Foucault, "the economy of the discursive constellation" which is economics itself (*Archaeology of Knowledge*, p. 66). In disclosing the relations between economic statements and other forms of discourse, economic writing meets an impasse; economists find language recalcitrant. Karl Polanyi alludes to "the semantics of economic theory" while cautioning against the use of language in an economic capacity.[10] But the complaint against language runs like a refrain throughout economic writing. "It is unfortunate," Mill stated in the nineteenth century, "that in the very outset of the subject we have to clear from our path a formidable ambiguity of language."[11] Sir James Steuart warned in the eighteenth century that "the imperfection of language engages us frequently in disputes merely verbal," which lead to "the prostitution of language."[12] And as early as the seventeenth century, William Petty appreciated the particular verbal difficulties of economics and tried to circumvent them with his arithmetical method: "The Method I take to do this, is not very usual; for instead of using only comparative and superlative Words, and intellectual Arguments, I have taken the course (as a Specimen of the Political Arithmetick I have long aimed at) to express my self in Terms of *Number, Weight,* or *Measure;* to use only Arguments of Sense, and to consider only such Causes, as have visible Foundations in Nature. . . ."[13] By implication, language itself has become impervious to "Sense." Ideally, economic speculation would free itself from "intellectual Arguments," replacing the ambiguities of verbal discourse with the cleaner arithmetical terminology of number, weight, and measure. Ironically, Petty's embryonic statistical "Method" has become not only the "usual" method but indeed the sine qua non of modern economic theory.

The great paradox of value which Adam Smith and David Ricardo, in particular, tried to resolve originates because "the word *value* . . . has two different meanings."[14] Thus, economic analysis had to evolve its own linguistics. As the French physiocrat and professional etymologist A. R. J. Turgot pointed out, "Money is a kind of language." But in the next sentence, Turgot observed that money is also the "common term which draws all languages together."[15] The meaning of "language" equivocates between those two sentences, and the sense is not secured by Polanyi's more precise and systematic observation that "there is no grammar with which all money-uses must comply." (*PAME,* p. 178). In his early work *The Theory of Moral Sentiments,* Adam Smith tried to show that "the rules of justice may be compared to the rules of grammar." Elsewhere, however, he implied that political economy alters normal diction, when he argued that "cheapness is in fact the same thing with plenty."[16] By extension, what has little utilitarian worth (such as a diamond) is often of greatest "value"—the paradox with which *A Wealth of Nations* begins its revolutionary interpretation of "price." Polanyi rounds out the chorus: "Language itself betrays us here."[17]

Smith began his lectures of 1762-63 on rhetoric and belles-lettres with the same practical mistrust of verbal ambiguity that he would later exercise in writing about political economy: "Perspicuity requires not only that the expressions we use should be free from all ambiguity proceeding from synonymous words, but that the words should be natives . . . of the language we speak in."[18] The pun is the most economical of linguistic transactions in which verbal values may be exchanged, but to the economist-grammarian, it is also the most flagrant example of a failed "perspicuity." In a later lecture, Smith deprecates those writers who spoil their gravity with verbal jokes: "When [Sir W. Temple] says, ' The *earth* of Holland is better than the air' and 'the love of interest stronger than the love of honour', it is a mere quibble on the words 'earth' and 'profit' [*sic*] , 'air' and 'honour'. Xenophon and most other writers of this sort, as well as he, abound in jokes we are surprised to find in such grave writers" (*Rhetoric,* p. 35). That the puns noted here involve economic and moral issues, two ostensibly disparate topics yoked, in Smith's mind, by violence together, is wholly appropriate, for this intrusion of the quibble severs the political economist from the bellettrist. To some literary analysts, a certain enjoyment and even honor accrue in the formation of ambiguous words: wit does not necessarily dampen gravity. But to the scientist of the economy, the end of philology is the beginning of economics; Smith's pairing off of misleading resonances from "synonymous words" marks the turning point toward a "true" science or *mathesis.* Because Smith's semantics determine his economics, one is not surprised to read, in another lecture, that what he would call in *The Wealth of Nations* "the progress of opulence" partakes of a rhetorical and stylistic progression as well: "Thus it is that poetry is cultivated in the most rude and barbarous nations, often to a considerable perfection; whereas they make no attempt towards the improvement of prose. 'Tis the introduction of commerce, or at least of the opulence that is commonly the attendant of commerce, that first brings on the improvement of prose" (*Rhetoric,* p. 131). Smith does not say that poetry becomes, under conditions of improved commerce, merely a pleasurable *divertissement,* although that may be inferred from his contention that prose is serious business. Quibbles or puns may titillate the poetic fancy but they have no place in the labors of prose: "Prose is the style in which all the common affairs of life, all business and agreements are made. No one ever made a bargain in verse" (*Rhetoric,* p. 132). Of the two kinds of linguistic "value" pertaining to these separate verbal styles, one has been silently singled out as more politically important through the grammarian's insistence that (poetic) equivocations and ambiguities have no place in pellucid rhetoric.

To say that Smith wants to take poetry out of commerce is an

overstatement, for, in one sense, Smith's *Rhetoric* merely follows
Ben Jonson's preference for the "perspecuitie" of language and for
classical economy of style over *sententiae* (see chapter one, above).
But what Smith and his successors accomplished was far more radical—namely, the creation of political economy as a fictive structure which has the creative force of poiesis. Political economy, as
a unique form of discourse, a work of the artistic imagination,
might then appeal to a higher sort of interpretation than mere
moral "economy." Economics might serve as a counterpoetics.
Consider Frank H. Knight's assertion: "The cost of living, even in
the narrowest sense of the term 'cost,' always depends on the
'standard' of living, which is chiefly an aesthetic category, and in
a sense in which aesthetics includes all values. . . ." But, Knight
concludes, "discussion of these problems is not the task of economics."[19] Most modern economists would agree, strictly speaking.
But in order to speak with such strictness, economists have found
themselves posing another sense of "aesthetics" in which even aesthetic worth itself may be categorized, priced, and interpreted by
means of economic "values." Prose itself is thus implicitly valued
in commercial terms by Smith. How strictly speech will allow us
to contrast "value" as defined in economics and "value" as defined in other forms of discourse is the question which we must
now address. When nineteenth-century economic theory, needing
to purify its own semantics, codified its own "unreal words" into
a separate "science," then it confronted the verbal predicament
identified in my epigraph from Bagehot. If "political economy" is
not to become itself an "unreal word," then those who are "conversant with its abstractions" must also be "in contact with its
facts." J. S. Mill, who was both a literary man and an economist,
will provide an initial *exemplum,* for he attempted that difficult,
post-Aristotelian task of combining (in Bagehot's words) "sympathy" with "cognizance" and of making "a true contact" between
the economic facts of how we live and the ethical abstractions we
say we live for.

John Stuart Mill and the Making of a Reader

The full title of Mill's study is a clue to his design: *Principles of
Political Economy with some of their Applications to Social Philosophy.* By appending philosophical applications to his economic
principles, Mill seeks to unite the traditional humanist perspective

of the economist as moral philosopher with the professional, scientific perspective of the academic and analytic economist. An encyclopedic compendium of the assumptions, postulates, and conclusions of classical political economy, from Adam Smith to Mill's own father, *Political Economy* is also itself an exercise in original economic theory by a brilliant and avid student of the science. On his first page, Mill properly describes the structural history of "economics" as a belated science:

> In every department of human affairs, Practice long precedes Science: systematic enquiry into the modes of action of the powers of nature, is the tardy product of a long course of efforts to use those powers for practical ends. The conception, accordingly, of Political Economy as a branch of science is extremely modern; but the subject with which its enquiries are conversant has in all ages necessarily constituted one of the chief practical interests of mankind, and, in some, a most unduly engrossing one. [*Works*, 2:3]

Mill's purpose is twofold: to examine the "extremely modern" concept of economics as a distinct and separate department of human affairs, while guiding us toward that larger vision of human affairs in which economics would be seen as one of many methods of attaining social understanding. Thus, he addresses our "unduly engrossing" interest in the subject—our ethically usurious fondness for it—by teaching us both how much profit we ought to take from the study of economics and how we should discharge that instruction into other forms of knowledge. Within the field of economics as such, the double thrust of Mill's *Principles* has come to be seen as two distinct methodologies, the "deductive" and the "inductive." The first has been called the formalist view of the economy, or microeconomics—the study of the supply-demand mechanism which controls prices and which determines a market situation, self-regulating or otherwise. The second has been called the substantive view of the economy, or macroeconomics—the study of how human wants are expressed and fulfilled in terms of an individual's or a society's material existence.[20] Mill's thesis is that the two kinds of economics are both pertinent and must be studied together.[21] By insisting upon their conjunction, Mill becomes the last in the great tradition of British philosopher-economists which, if the word "economist" is allowed the denotative latitude that it was permitted in the late eighteenth and early nineteenth centuries, might extend from Locke and Hume through Coleridge and De Quincey.

If Mill's pluralistic approach to economics has been lost to more specialized modes of economic inquiry, then what makes Mill seem dated—historically interesting but of little use in the field—is precisely what makes him critical to our exposition of the structural complexity of "economics." For Mill, the economic "imagination" was still an operative, discernible, and believable concept. In Mill's hands, economics, that belated art, had not yet become a wholly dismal science because its mode of creation was still seen as imaginative: economics remained, in the last analysis, a structurally integral part of man's social philosophy. Mill could use the language *of* economics in order to talk *about* economic structuring itself, because "economy" retained, for him, its twofold definition as functional dispensation and moral disposition. His discussion reveals the process of economic thought as the object of his economic analysis; he presumes that the language and concepts of economic theory ought to be applicable to everyday language of fact, that there should be a structural connection between these two kinds of discourse, the semantics of economic theory and the semantics of ordinary language.

To prove the validity of this principle, Mill tacitly at first and then explicitly posited the reader's imagination as an active and necessary labor in the social philosophy of his *Principles.* Mill's pluralism extended to involve his reader as overt witness to the social validity of the author's economic inquiry. Thus, Mill's initial definition of economics must be considered carefully, for it is less a truism than it sounds. His definition of his subject, "economics," depends upon what he construes to be the object of "economy": "That subject is Wealth. Writers on Political Economy profess to teach, or to investigate, the nature of Wealth, and the laws of its production and distribution: including, directly or remotely, the operation of all the causes by which the condition of mankind, or of any society of human beings, in respect to this universal object of desire, is made prosperous or the reverse" (*Works,* 2:3). This definition depends upon a solidly Western, European, capitalist, and (as Max Weber has claimed) Protestant perspective. But it is not necessarily Mill's own definition. Mill has silently distanced himself from other "Writers on Political Economy" by using this sweeping definition less as an axiom than as a screen or matrix upon which to focus his own more deliberate questions. Can one really study, either directly or remotely, *all* the causes by which mankind is made prosperous or the reverse? Is wealth *always* "this universal object of desire"? Mill's apposite construction, "to teach, or to investigate," is instructive of his own purposes. Whereas other economic writers "profess" to do either one or the other, Mill intimates that economists ought not to relinquish the burden of moral suasion merely in order to investigate what he later calls the "economical facts." For Mill, to teach *is* to investigate, because the economist is not an object of universal knowledge, even if his subject is the "universal object of desire." Indeed, by the end of the sentence just quoted, one suspects that the meaning of "wealth" equivocates between the realm of material prosperity as such and the realm of spiritual and intellectual well-being, embracing the whole "condition of mankind." In leaving "the reverse" of prosperity to the reader's educable imagination, Mill has quietly assumed the voice of the lay preacher.

The role that Mill posits for himself is underscored a few lines later when he challenges the reader to define "wealth" in light of the author's own refusal to define it for him: "Every one has a notion, sufficiently correct for common purposes, of what is meant by wealth. The enquiries which relate to it are in no danger of being confounded with those relating to any other of the great human interests" (*Works,* 2:3). "Common" is tonally ambiguous, and the last sentence is potentially sarcastic. Ruskin did not hear it this way, though, and he was not pleased. He felt that Mill, by capitulating to the sorts of common definitions which "every one has," was playing fast and loose with "false verbal definitions."[22] What keeps Mill from succumbing to the intellectual reductiveness which Ruskin lamented, however, is the challenge posed by the repeated word "relate." How does one relate not only to Mill's complex tone but also to the larger question of whether our "sufficiently correct" notions of economic wealth are connected to "any other of the great human interests"? "It was not a book," Mill wrote of *Political Economy* in his *Autobiography,* "merely of abstract science, but also of application, and treated Political Economy not as a thing by itself, but as a fragment of a greater whole; a branch of Social Philosophy, so interlinked with all the other branches, that its conclusions, even in its own peculiar province, are only true conditionally, subject to interference and coun-

teraction from causes not directly within its scope. . . ."[23] What
relations are we able to imagine, then, between the practical business, the science of political economy, and the abstract principles,
the art, by which economics becomes a significant fragment of our
moral lives?

Ruskin misunderstood Mill's *Principles* because, as a type of
Bagehot's "literary man," Ruskin wanted to dissect the second
part of the question, the *art* of abstract "economy," by subtract-
ing moral importance from the first part of the question, the *science* of economic "facts." Having chastised Mill for slighting the
"comparative estimate of the moralist," Ruskin reveals, in the
next breath, a deeper ambivalence and a clue to how we must read
Mill's work: Mill "deserves honour among economists by inadvertently disclaiming the principles which he states, and tacitly intro-
ducing the moral considerations with which he declares his science
has no connection" (*Works,* 18:79). Mill's disclaimer, however, is
not inadvertent but pervasive. The difficulty in "relating" to Mill's
complex authorial demands arises because Mill's method of investigation is inductive, whereas the reader's means of educating himself in light of the book is deductive. We start from general notions,
sufficiently correct in our everyday lives, and we move toward
specific economic and managerial principles: that is our burden as
readers. The author himself, however, assumes a different starting
point. Mill begins with the particulars of economic theory and
moves inductively toward the larger application of these principles
to ethical behavior. But the end of these two processes is the same
for both reader and author: to understand how and why we are in
the greatest actual "danger" if we do *not* "confound" economic
inquiry with the other of the great human activities.[24] We are
asked, finally, to compound our knowledge so as not to become
confused about the importance of economic inquiry "as a thing
by itself." What Ruskin apprehended in his reading as an inadvertent disclaimer is, in fact, the dynamics of reading as prescribed
by Mill, a process of active "interference and counteraction from
causes not directly within [political economy's] scope."

Mill's rhetorical strategy is an expository version of Spenser's
poetic structuring as discussed in the preceding chapter, where the
reader is encouraged to surmount the poetic protagonist's (Guyon's) ambiguous Aristotelian perception and to anticipate the
poem's Christian vision by means of the intermediate economics

of Mammon. In Mill's work, such mediated vision makes the author himself the protagonist and the reader, the poetic antagonist. Our perception becomes an active participant in the book's *agon*. We must read *through* economics to a larger social philosophy. It is only by the utility of such reading that we grasp the utilitarian values of political economy itself.

This strategy further recapitulates the dynamics of reading as described in Mill's own youthful encounter with Wordsworth. The account, as given in the *Autobiography*, came in the wake of Mill's mental crisis and severe depression of 1826-27:

> What made Wordsworth's poems a medicine for my state of mind, was that they expressed, not mere outward beauty, but states of feeling, and of thought coloured by feeling, under the excitement of beauty. They seemed to be the very culture of the feelings, which I was in quest of. In them I seemed to draw from a source of inward joy, of sympathetic and imaginative pleasure, which could be shared in by all human beings; which had no connexion with struggle or imperfection, but would be made richer by every improvement in the physical or social condition of man. . . . And I felt myself at once better and happier as I came under their influence. [*Autobiography*, p. 89]

Mill read Wordsworth for what the poems could do for him rather than for what they were in themselves: "I long continued to value Wordsworth less according to his intrinsic merits, than by the measure of what he had done for me" (ibid., p. 90). In the course of affirming this development, the intrinsic merit of poiesis yields to the utilitarian value of reading. The hero of this passage is not Wordsworth, but Mill; not the poet, but the creative reader.

The "culture of the feelings" becomes a dynamic complement to the static culture of critical taste by which the value of poetry is usually judged. Mill, of course, recognizes and appreciates the "principles" of the latter when he remarks that "there have certainly been, even in our own age, greater poets than Wordsworth" (ibid., p. 89). What Wordsworth provides Mill is not an escape from analysis into feelings but a confirmation of analytic habits by genuine emotion: "And the delight which these poems gave me, proved that with culture of this sort, there was nothing to dread from the most confirmed habit of analysis" (ibid., pp. 89-

90). The delight is personal and "inward" but is grounded in a
further confidence that it "could be shared in by all human beings." That further step is decisive as well for the future reader
imagined in *Political Economy*. In proclaiming the poiesis exercised by himself as a reader of Wordsworth, Mill hints at the larger
connection between literary interpretation and the "improvement
in the physical or social condition of mankind." This improved
state would be literally a "state of mind," "made richer" by the
addition of social feelings, and the realization of that state of mind
becomes the target, twenty years later, of his *Political Economy*.

Mill's first intimation that the target could be hit and that his
book could therefore attain "that general tone by which it is distinguished from all previous expositions of Political Economy"
(*Autobiography*, p. 148) comes in his appreciation of Harriet Taylor's role in the making of the book: "What was abstract and purely scientific was generally mine; . . . in all that concerned the
application of philosophy to the exigencies of human society and
progress, I was her pupil" (ibid., p. 149). Whether Mill's self-efface-
ment here is ultimately justified need not concern us, for, in the
context of the present discussion, his wife becomes yet another
image of the creative reader. She functions in relation to Mill's
work on political economy in the same way that Mill himself had
functioned earlier in respect to Wordsworth's poetry and turns his
thoughts into "a living principle":

> The economic generalisations which depend, not on necessi-
> ties of nature but on those combined with the existing ar-
> rangements of society, it [*Political Economy*] deals with
> only as provisional, and as liable to be much altered by the
> progress of social improvement. I had indeed partially learnt
> this view of things from the thoughts awakened in me by the
> speculations of the Saint-Simonians; but it was made a living
> principle pervading and animating the book by my wife's
> promptings. [Ibid., p. 149]

What pervades and animates the composition of the book becomes
in turn the challenge which the book presents to its own prospective reader: to break through "the scientific appreciation of the
action of these [economic] causes" by "set[ting] the example of
not treating those conditions as final." The "provisional" —that is,
the "living"—mode of the book's argument depends, then, on the

instructive interaction of the reader's imagination, prefigured by Taylor's original expenditure, her imaginative investment. Without this sharing, the book would succumb to static, scientific analysis; with it, one might hope for an improved alteration in the progress of society, a movement toward "the very culture of the feelings."

Because Mill insists that we adduce our economic principles in the context of man's actual economizing practices and in the light of "the existing arrangements of society," he may then reveal that the "dynamics" of proper economic behavior derive from other, noneconomic experiences, such as the reading of literature. Reading is, for Mill, a vital process in the formulation of thought, and literature, in its broadest sense, embraces even non-"literary," expository texts like Mill's. The creative reader also becomes, *in parvo*, the ideal economist.

Mill's point is that "political economy" both is and is not subject to formal economic analysis: "Political Economy, in truth, has never pretended to give advice to mankind with no lights but its own; though people who knew nothing *but* political economy (and therefore knew that ill) have taken upon themselves to advise, and could only do so by such lights as they had" (ibid., p. 141). This warning resembles Bagehot's description of the dangers besetting literary men and economists who attempt to cross-pollinate each other's fields, and in *Principles of Political Economy,* Mill tried to do something about those dangers. He accounts for the necessary twofold orientation of his subject by dividing the economist's labor into its "Statics" and its "Dynamics." The "Statics" are "the field of economical facts"; to investigate them is to determine how wealth is created and defined. Surveying them, one will have "obtained a collective view of the economical phenomena of society" (*Works,* 3:707). But the "Dynamics" are the field of economical fictions; to investigate them is to determine how wealth is implemented and the means by which literal riches can be metaphorically exchanged for a larger social well-being. After assessing the statics, as Mill notes, "we have still to consider the economical condition of mankind as liable to change, and indeed . . . as at all times undergoing progressive changes. We have to consider what these changes are, what are their laws, and what their ultimate tendencies; thereby adding a theory of motion to our theory of equilibrium—the Dynamics of political economy to the Statics" (*Works,* 3:707). Precisely at this point, Mill's *Political Economy* turns its analysis of economic production into a prolegomenon for his study of social and utilitarian distribution. But Mill has argued all along that seemingly objective economic laws must be derived from a subjective awareness of social and cultural and moral arrangements—has, in fact, challenged the reader to provide this awareness implicitly from the very start. That subjective awareness is precisely what permitted Mill, in reading Wordsworth, to galvanize his self-conscious despair into a compensatory principle of cultural improvement. That same awareness on the part of his wife is what permitted the composition of *Political Economy* in its final form. Thus imagined, economics reveals its true "relations" to society: it must be simultaneously derived from and constitutive of our moral disposition.

The "progressive changes" from the statics to the dynamics of political economy have already been prefigured, therefore, in the rhetorical strategy of Mill's composition.[25] Near the beginning of the book, Mill implores economists to recognize the "utilities fixed and embodied in human beings" (*Works,* 2:48); indeed, the utilitarian value of the reader to Mill's own moral judgments is precisely what suggests that the "moral qualities of the labourers are fully as important to the efficiency and worth of their labours, as the intellectual" (*Works,* 2:109). Mill may be as revolutionary and as "activist" an author as Marx, for these "moral qualities" eventually provide the grounds for one-half of Mill's economic theory:

> The laws and conditions of the production of wealth partake of the character of physical truths. There is nothing optional or arbitrary in them.
> It is not so with the Distribution of Wealth. That is a matter of human institution solely. The things once there, mankind, individually or collectively, can do with them as they like. They can place them at the disposal of whomsoever they please, and on whatever terms. . . . The distribution of wealth, therefore, depends on the laws and customs of society.
> [*Works,* 2:199–200]

The final difficulty, of course, is that "the laws and customs of society" depend not on "physical truth" but on metaphysical ambivalences and on the vagaries of human will. Mill concludes in the

Autobiography that his greatest achievement "consisted chiefly in making the proper distinction between the laws of the Production of Wealth, which are real laws of nature, dependent on the properties of objects, and modes of its Distribution, which, subject to certain conditions, depend on human will" (p. 148). If, to the economist, the "laws of nature" are *real,* then the laws which affect human will must be *unreal* in the special sense that they express themselves by means of the imagination and manifest themselves in those fictive arrangements we call culture and society, arrangements which both are and are not subject to economic logic. If we began with wealth posited as "the universal object of desire," then we have progressed to the point where "desire" itself must become the object of economic analysis. The dilemma of political economy is that laws of nature do not apply exactly to questions of human will, and yet, if economists exclude the latter from discussion, they do so at a terrible cost to the human imagination itself. Mill addresses *directly* the question of the imagination's place in economics by appealing to the reader's imagination as a dynamic part of the "scientific" investigation. Of course, as we shall see, economists, as well as literary men like Ruskin, would counter by calling Mill's strategy a circumvention of the question of economics using "unreal words."

In 1871, Mill issued the seventh and final edition of his book. W. S. Jevons's *The Theory of Political Economy* appeared in the same year, with an utterly different definition of "economics" and, therefore, of the economist as well. What was, for Mill, the integral thematic connection between political economy and social philosophy became, for Jevons, merely "the relation of economics to moral science."[26] In the closing paragraphs of his introduction, Jevons finally discusses this "relation," as if he were obliged to say something, after all. He concludes that "it is the lowest rank of feelings which we here treat." Here, economics is solely a practical, even a pragmatic, science, more appropriate to the methods of the new calculus than to the reasoned discourse of philosophy. Although philosophy, according to Jevons, still has a place in negotiating ethical conduct, it is not needed in discussions of economic theory, because economics is actually *beneath* philosophy.

Jevons's concluding remarks, must be given in full, for the logical sleight of hand depends on his having made us take our eyes off the ball:

It is the lowest rank of feelings which we here treat. The calculus of utility aims at supplying the ordinary wants of man
at the least cost of labour. Each labourer, in the absence of
other motives, is supposed to devote his energy to the accumulation of wealth. A higher calculus of moral right and wrong
would be needed to show how he may best employ that
wealth for the good of others as well as himself. But when
that higher calculus gives no prohibition, we need the lower
calculus to gain us the utmost good in matters of moral indifference. There is no rule of morals to forbid our making two
blades of grass grow instead of one, if, by the wise expenditure of labour, we can do so. And we may certainly say, with
Francis Bacon, "while philosophers are disputing whether virtue or pleasure be the proper aim of life, do you provide
yourself with the instruments of either." [P. 93]

Unlike Mill's imaginatively expansive "principles," Jevons's strategy is to take away with one hand what he gives with the other.
Philosophy is thus "higher" than economics, but it is a "higher *calculus.*" In the same breath, then, philosophy is both removed from
and imagined in terms of the scientific methodology of economic
analysis. Indeed, Jevons insists upon having it both ways at once.
The "higher" calculus involves the employment of wealth once
gained, whereas the "lower" calculus—the matter of gaining wealth
—is morally indifferent. Mill makes the same distinction but argues
that *how* wealth is gained and how it is "read" are very important
matters for the economic imagination—ones which cannot be
treated wholly scientifically or mathematically. For Jevons, however, morality itself may be an "unreal word." Since the gaining of
wealth pertains to "matters of moral indifference," the principles
of economic progress may be, in fact, unprincipled. Labor can
be mercilessly exploited (by what Jevons calls, without irony, "the
wise expenditure of labour") to make two blades of grass grow
where there was only one. In Baconian terms, we must stop talking and provide ourselves with the instruments of pleasure and virtue. But the instruments of virtue are not accountable to the same
calculus as virtue itself. Jevons finalizes his break with Mill when
he argues that the *lower* calculus is, in fact, a *higher* form of knowledge, that philosophical discussion of virtue is secondary to economic fulfillment. Thus, at paragraph's end, the instruments of
virtue are no longer morally indifferent, although they embody a

virtue which philosophy, unaided by economics, could not hope
to understand. By revaluing the "lowest rank of feelings" as the
common denominator of our day-to-day survival, Jevons effectually raises it above all other ranks.

In trying to separate economics from ethics, Jevons has simply,
and probably inadvertently, strained language to the breaking
point. In retrospect, the idea of "value" has become almost meaningless. Broadly speaking, language itself has become morally indifferent, a set of "factual" ciphers ranking what is "higher" and
"lower" with the emotional insouciance of statistics. A few paragraphs earlier, Jevons confronts the whole "utilitarian doctrine"
by attributing a certain disutility to language: "The acceptance or
non-acceptance of the basis of the utilitarian doctrine depends, in
my mind, on the exact interpretation of the language used" (p. 92).
Just so. For Jevons, the exact interpretation of the utilitarian doctrine means utilizing that doctrine for the greater good of one's
own argument. This sleight is the price, literally, of divorcing
philosophy from economics.

This divorce settles on language a certain exchange value of its
own, a certain disposableness. Under conditions such as these,
Marx observed, "*Logic* [is] mind's *coin of the realm,* the speculative or *thought-value* of man and nature."[27] Marx's point is that
our economic status is the basis of all our epistemological, metaphysical, and ethical formulations. The premise may be disputed,
but not by pretending that our economic status has *no* fundamental relationship to epistemology, metaphysics, and morals—or to
the imagination—as Jevons does.

The pretence is further exposed in Mrs. Gaskell's *North and
South* (1854-55). Mr. Hale has moved his family from Helstone to
the northern manufacturing town of Milton (i.e., Manchester,
where Jevons was to become a professor of logic at Owens College), and Hale concedes: "I hardly know as yet how to compare
one of these houses with our Helstone cottages. I see furniture
here which our labourers would never have thought of buying, and
food commonly used which they would consider luxuries. . . . One
had need to learn a different language, and measure by a different
standard, up here in Milton."[28] The advent of a new economics
eventually dispenses with one kind of language altogether, as when
Hale's daughter, Margaret, asks the manufacturer, John Thornton,
if a certain colleague of his is a "gentleman." Thornton (who, it

turns out, is actually the son of a "gentleman") replies, "I don't quite understand your application of the word. But I should say that this Morison is no true man." Margaret answers, "I suspect my 'gentleman' includes your 'true man,' " and Thornton corrects her: "A man is to me a higher and a completer being than a gentleman." Margaret's conclusion is also one of Mrs. Gaskell's deepest insights into the differences between "North" and "South": " 'What do you mean?' asked Margaret. 'We must understand the words differently' " (pp. 217–18). But Thornton does not understand the word *differently;* he deliberately does not understand at all. Like the Manchester theorist, Jevons, the Manchester manufacturer, Thornton, simply disposes here of one set of verbal counters in order to explain a new set of economic exigencies, a new social man. In *The Way We Live Now* (1874–75), Trollope made a further connection: "As for many years past we have exchanged paper instead of actual money for our commodities, so now it seemed that, under the new Melmotte regime, an exchange of words was to suffice."[29] The point is not merely that money is a kind of language, but that social arrangements participate in multiple economies. And in Trollope's book, a kind of fictive/verbal economics determines social arrangements as well, since Melmotte is, in fact, a bankrupt; his wealth (but not his "regime") is totally imaginary. Thus, economic discourse helps to formulate—indeed, it becomes— the "exchange of words" which we credit. "*Credit,*" Marx concluded, "is the *economic* judgment of man's morality."[30]

Considered from a structuralist perspective, Jevons's argument attempts to posit economics as both self-disclosing and self-enclosed by demoting to the status of "sociology" the ethical problem of how men actually behave in economic situations. Thus, "economics" can descant upon the structure of "the economy" without needing to address the equally elusive concept of "economy." In the end, a self-sufficing theory, with all its unreal words, defines "the way we live now."

The premise of Jevons's method originated half a century earlier with David Ricardo, who attempted to define economics in terms of a self-referring system. If economics appropriates nonspecialized everyday language, it then turns around and uses this language in specialized ways which are often incompatible with common understanding and usage. Ricardo argues *contra* Smith and J. B. Say that "riches" or mere material abundance do not necessarily have economic "value." In fact, our ordinary sense of "riches" may obstruct the formation of economic (that is, exchange) values. In discussing "the vague ideas which are attached to the word value," Ricardo locates the true economic significance of the word in the idea of scarcity: "Value, then, essentially differs from riches, for value depends not on abundance, but on the difficulty or facility of production."[31] The effect of this definition is to divorce "wealth" from its everyday use, and it is this point which is also at issue in Ricardo's ensuing generalization: "Many of the errors in political economy have arisen from errors on this subject, from considering an increase of riches, and an increase of value, as meaning the same thing, and from unfounded notions as to what constituted a standard measure of value." (p. 183). These "unfounded notions" are, however, the products of ordinary semantic use.

Thomas De Quincey's objection to Ricardo extends the meaning of "unreal words." De Quincey noted that Ricardo had not invented new words but had hypostatized normal semantics, forcing a customarily ambivalent word such as "value" to have one and only one economic signification. The following passage is spoken with fine dramatic irony by Mr. X. Y. Z., one of the participants in "Dialogues of Three Templars":

> I believe that the very ground of his [Ricardo's] perspicuity to me is the ground of his apparent obscurity to some others and *that* is—his inexorable consistency in the use of words: . . . for wherever men have been accustomed to use a word in two senses, and have yet supposed themselves to use it but in one, a writer, who corrects this lax usage, and forces them to maintain the unity of the meaning, will always appear obscure; because he will oblige them to deny or to affirm consequences from which they were hitherto accustomed to escape under a constant though unconscious equivocation between the two senses. . . . Hence it is not surprising to find Mr. Malthus complaining . . . of "the *unusual* application of common terms" as having made Mr. Ricardo's work "difficult to be understood by many people:" though, in fact, there is nothing at all unusual in his application of any term whatever, but only in the steadiness with which he keeps to the same application of it.[32]

Ricardo is so precise as to seem obscure to many people. But in seeming to praise Ricardo through the speech of X. Y. Z., De Quincey actually attacks all economists at what seemed their point of safest shelter—in their claims for the immaterial "value" of language itself. De Quincey insists that we see the (Ricardian) shift in verbal counters not as "a mere dispute about words" but as an alteration in the intellectual "ground" of the argument. When Ricardo inverted Say's Law and contended that value in exchange preceded in importance value in use, his verbal exchange marked, according to De Quincey, a substantial redistribution of economic logic.

De Quincey's contention must be given in full, because it deftly summarizes what we will hear as the battle cry of Blake, the premise of Wordsworth. In De Quincey's "Dialogues," Phaedrus suggests that the Ricardian controversy is only verbal, and X. Y. Z. again replies:

> "A mere dispute about words" is a phrase which we hear daily: and why? Is it a case of such daily occurrence to hear men disputing about mere verbal differences? So far from it, I can truly say that I never happened to witness such a dispute in my whole life—either in books or in conversation; and indeed, considering the small number of absolute synonymes [*sic*] which any language contains, it is scarcely possible that a dispute on words should arise which would not also be a dispute about ideas (*i.e.,* about realities). Why, then, is the phrase in every man's mouth, when the actual occurrence must be so very uncommon? The reason is this, Phaedrus: such a plea is a "sophisma pigri intellectû," which seeks to escape from the effort of mind necessary for the comprehending and solving of any difficulty under the colourable pretext that it is a question about shadows and not about substances, and one therefore which it is creditable to a man's good sense to decline: a pleasant sophism this, which at the same time flatters a man's indolence and his vanity! [Pp. 491–92]

A dispute about words is not a question of shadows but of substances, because, in spite of Adam Smith, language contains very few true synonyms. A new word indicates a new idea, a new way of structuring or even of judging reality. (That "ideas" are "realities" ought not to shock, De Quincey implies, even hardened pragmatists who exchange symbolic coinage in the form of money for

material and immaterial objects in the form of goods and labor.)
Indeed, because language is as "real" as money, it too can be depreciated. More specifically, a change in economic wording realigns
the parameters of *all* other economies that we choose to imagine.
Regrettably, words are both real and unreal at the same time.

By solidifying "value" into value in exchange and by deempha-
sizing the importance of "riches," Ricardo has altered the meaning
of "wealth." Wealth is now founded on scarcity; therefore, value is
increased in direct proportion to material paucity. Mill's humanist
analysis, his belief in the goodwill and imaginative optimism of a
well-instructed economist, is directly belied and ultimately refuted
by the nature of economic reality—that is, by the new inflections
of economic discourse. If economic wealth is centered in a scarcity
of means, then its value will be created out of the sheer difficulty
of production, out of what Foucault calls a *fundamental* scarcity.
Foucault's conclusion merely takes De Quincey's insight to its
logical and drastic finale:

> What makes economics possible, and necessary, then, is a per-
> petual and fundamental situation of scarcity: confronted by
> a nature that in itself is inert and save for one very small part,
> barren, man risks his life. It is no longer in the interplay of
> representation [between the tokens of "wealth," money, and
> those objects that wealth can buy] that economics finds its
> principle, but near that perilous region where life is in con-
> frontation with death. [*The Order of Things*, pp. 256-57]

Foucault reveals the most pressing reason why we need to imagine
economics accurately: the means and ends which economics mediates are matters of life and death. De Quincey's analysis of verbal
disputes only touches the surface of economics as a fictive structure. At heart, Foucault goes on to observe, "The analysis of
thought is always *allegorical* in relation to the discourse that it employs." (*Archaeology of Knowledge*, p. 27). Whereas De Quincey
reveals that verbal changes in economics are also cognitive changes,
we may now see that economics itself is not a verbal means to a
cognitive end but is a kind of embattled middle ground between
language and cognition, its discourse testifying to the fundamental
insufficiency of the knowledge which it expresses. And whereas
the confrontation between life and death is "real," its urgency is
brought home by "unreal" means. What makes economics possible

and necessary, then, is its allegorical thoroughness, the authenticity of its imaginative excursus into that "perilous region."

Our analysis of "unreal words" has brought us to the point at which we may witness Spenser's allegorical portrayal of economics turning into "economics," an intellectual construction which is itself a form of allegory. Mammon's symbolic domain, conceived in terms of scarcity and abundance, yields to Foucault's "perilous region" where life confronts death. We have reached, therefore, a point beyond Bagehot at which the economic allegory seems to supplant the abstractions of literature with a more profound fiction of its own. At this point, the roles of literary man and of economist are, in effect, combined. Henceforth, fact and allegory, real and unreal words, are not merely "related," but are intricately joined—and they must be studied together.

Historically, the catalyst is Malthus. His greatly disturbing treatise, *An Essay on the Principle of Population* (1798), demonstrated how "the economy," when made to reflect ethical values, would bring the fiction of a humanistic commerce to a moral crisis. This work, more than any other, earned economics its epithet as "the dismal science," precisely because its allegory demonstrated what some took to be the wrong allegory. The Malthusian "iron law of wages," often paraphrased as the diminishing returns of prosperity, was difficult at first to disprove, but it was clear that Malthus's economic "law" went against other, stronger moral imperatives and cultural myths.

For Malthus, the economic laws of commercial production have an allegorical relation to the economy of human (sexual) production. In discussing the latter, we must alter our fictive understanding of the former. The representational art of the economist, according to Malthus, demands a new model as well as a new vocabulary.[33] If we are to "consider man as he really is, inert, sluggish, and averse from labour, unless compelled by necessity (and it is surely the height of folly to talk of man, according to our crude fancies of what he might be), we may pronounce with certainty that the world would not have been peopled, but for the superiority of the power of population to the means of subsistence" (*Principle of Population*, p. 205). The labor of sexual conception outpaces the labor bestowed in more strictly economic work: "The perpetual tendency in the race of man to increase beyond the means of subsistence is one of the general laws of ani-

mated nature which we can have no reason to expect will change"
(ibid., p. 199). The prosperity expressed by the biblical injunction,
"Be fruitful and multiply," belies and ultimately impoverishes any
economic prosperity man can attain by commercial means. Greater material abundance, the promise of all political economy, generates an unequal increase in population, so that, paradoxically,
there exists an overabundance of people who cannot subsist on
even the increased efficiency of economic production. Malthus
raises the Smithian paradox of value to cosmic terms. Man labors
blindly toward his own extinction. In the Malthusian formulation,
political economy ought to mediate between the unseen economies of sexual production and the more observable economies of
commercial production. But the allegory of Malthusian economics
reveals with crushing irony how the welfare of the state or *polis* is
grounded in the (overwhelming) prosperity of the domestic household or *oikos* and how this latter economy would ultimately destroy larger economic structuring.

The original debate between Malthus and William Godwin and
the ensuing controversy arises over a linguistic equivocation which
deepens into an ideological incompatibility.[34] Godwin, in asserting
the principle of political justice, postulated the perfectibility of
human intention and found that the Poor Law was an inadequate
expression of it. He lobbied for a more expansive Poor Law, because poverty was, in terms of his larger social vision, a disutility.
Malthus argued in virtually the same terms for a diametrically opposed end. For him, man would, if left to his natural intentions,
perfect himself out of existence. He lobbied, therefore, for a less
expansive Poor Law. Also asserting that poverty was a disutility,
Malthus redefined disutility. Mindless economic production would
ultimately render all questions of utility senseless. Malthus did not
want to starve out the poor by denying them relief, but neither
did he see the charitable provisions of the Poor Law in the way in
which some conservative economists view modern welfare systems,
as an inducement to unemployment and idleness. Malthus simply
pointed out that the Poor Law then in effect was conceived as part
of an overall view of unchecked economic production. A sufficiently utilitarian Poor Law could never be conceived without first apprehending the inherent disutility of wealth itself.

In Malthus, then, we may see the broadest reformulation of
"economics" and "economy," of explicitly economic and implicit-

ly moral statements, and of the play of difference between them.
For Malthus, economics, as the science of the accumulation of
wealth, is, at heart, uneconomical. This writer brings our keywords
to an almost Manichean impasse by noting that there is an "economy" of human response, rooted in our very ontological status as
reproductive creatures, which is unalterably opposed to our best
rational formulations of our economic status: "It seems highly
probable that moral evil is absolutely necessary to the production
of moral excellence."[35]

John Ruskin and the Mythos of the Text

"The purpose of a myth," Lévi-Strauss has contended, "is to provide a logical model capable of overcoming a contradiction."[36] The
Renaissance understood the mythic thrust of economics as an attempt to substitute an age of gold for the lost Golden Age, as
Spenser's Mammon tried unsuccessfully to do. Significantly, Mammon's mythic domain is not destroyed (as is the Bower of Bliss,
for instance) in *The Faerie Queene*. Nor do the contradictions we
have seen embodied in Mammon vanish because a "science" is spun
around them. Imaginatively, Mammon's mythic purpose survives
in the "logical model" proffered by classical economic theory.

Because economic thought attempts to reveal a rational and
harmonizing view of material life, it must necessarily overcome
that which seems irrational. Often, however, this means glossing
over underlying cultural conflicts. The common view was that
Malthus (for one) had not done this. In fact, by identifying a conflict between methods of reproduction and methods of economic
production, Malthus implicated the mythic status of economics in
a new way. He uncovered a new contradiction in economic logic.
As Frank H. Knight writes, "Economics deals with the form of
conduct rather than [with] its substance or content,"[37] but with
Malthus it became necessary to confess that the proper structuring
of these economic forms would disrupt even the most intimate
details of our lives—the dispositions of our families and of our
sexuality. Production and reproduction contradicted each other.
W. A. Weisskopf has further contended that by regulating the form
of conduct, economics must *necessarily* impose imaginative models upon its substance and content.[38] Malthus took his metaphysical authority for believing in the "sufficient-evil" theory of eco-

nomic progress from Scripture: "Sufficient unto the day is the evil thereof." Not all economists have Reverend Malthus's biblical resourcefulness in the face of economic "evil," but Weisskopf has been able to show that economic thinking generates its own myths because all economic structures promote "unconscious value systems."

Relying initially on Max Weber's delineation of the Protestant work ethic, Weisskopf demonstrates the psychological contradiction between the antichrematistic ethic taught by religious training and the "purely individual aims" of classical political economy (which are, incidentally, sanctioned by other aspects of religious belief): "As a psychocultural heritage of the anti-chrematistic ethic, the pursuit of economic self-interest was considered morally reprehensible. Thus it had to be shown that it does lead to the general welfare; that, although it was felt to be immoral for the individual, it is 'moral' from the viewpoint of the whole" (p. 46). In the case of Adam Smith, Weisskopf argues that "the fiction of the invisible hand and the natural harmony of interests" were used to blend the individualistic and subjective ethics of classical economics into "a rigid adherence to the value system, which stressed as ultimate goals such objective factors" as "labor" (p. 162). Out of religious contradiction evolves a "psychocultural" myth, and, in explaining post-Smithian (or, in Marx's joke, post-Adamic) economics, Weisskopf makes the crucial argument that economic systems have subsumed other mythologies into their own: "Economic thought served not only the purpose of explaining and interpreting the economic system. The importance of economic activity in the new society moved economic thought into the centre of the ideological system of the times. It became a sort of surreptitious cosmology, including some of the ideas which have been manifest in ancient mythology" (p. 145).

The central contradiction which Weisskopf reads in classical economic thought is sexual: "The primeval conflict between the active and passive, and male and the female, is expressed in the conceptions of labour and land, at least in the Malthusian and Ricardian systems of thought" (p. 145). Weisskopf expands this thesis beyond the Malthus-Ricardo nexus to include Renaissance economists such as William Petty (who called labor the father or active principle of wealth and the land the mother) and Enlightenment economists such as John Locke (who spoke of "property"

as the offspring of man's impregnation of nature with his labor—
"he has mixed his labour with it, and joined it to something that
is his own and thereby makes it his property") and postclassical
economists such as Marx. Economic myth strives to overcome the
sexual contradiction between land and labor. Marx, for instance,
centered all value in self-generating (i.e., self-reproducing) male
labor, mythically analogous to Zeus's giving birth to Athena. In
the masculinity of labor, Weisskopf locates Marx's primal fear that
the capitalist's creation of surplus value symbolically castrates the
worker by depriving him of the value of his labor:

> In the Marxian system the role of the father is played by the
> capitalist. He owns the means of production, as the father
> "owns" the mother. As the father prevents the son from hav-
> ing access to the mother and the female, so the capitalist pre-
> vents the worker from having access to the means of produc-
> tion. And as the father deprives the son of his penis, so the
> capitalist deprives the worker of the surplus value. . . .
> In Marxian thought [castration] means the taking-away of
> the surplus value. Marx symbolizes surplus value by the sign
> prime. In the formula which describes the capitalist process
> of circulation, $M\text{-}C\text{-}M'$, the prime after the second M repre-
> sents the surplus value. This is an obvious penis symbol. And
> this is exactly what the worker is deprived of by the capital-
> ist. It would be difficult to find a clearer case in which the
> Freudian theories are borne out and his symbols found in
> socioeconomic thought. [Pp. 156–57]

In Weisskopf's extended view, economics becomes a symbolic
structure which is, in Lévi-Strauss's sense, a mythic structure as
well.

Lévi-Strauss's "logical model" is also, of course, a fiction: the
myth behind the myth. We may now proceed from Weisskopf's
findings to observe this supreme fiction: the way in which the fictive power of individual words in political economy depends upon
a "logic" which is itself an imaginative synthesis, a mythic grammar. For instance, in setting up a prototypical market system,
classical economic theory posited a market-value/real-value dichotomy. The classical economists somehow had to explain what
real value meant in an economic context in which the only economically significant value of a commodity was its nominal value,

its agreed-upon market price. Ricardo, as we have seen, differentiated "value" from "riches" and so was forced to devolve a new standard or measure for defining value. But how could a commodity's value in exchange, which is, by definition, always fluctuating in respect to its supply and demand and the psychological vagaries of a market situation, be construed as a real and constant "measure"? Ricardo solved the question poetically by positing exchange value as a fiction which has the force of reality. Thus, after conceding that "there is no commodity which is not itself exposed to the same variations as the things the value of which is to be ascertained" (p. 27), Ricardo asserts: "To facilitate, then, the object of this inquiry, although I fully allow that money made of gold is subject to most of the variations of other things, *I shall suppose it to be invariable,* and therefore all alterations in price to be occasioned by some alteration in the value of the commodity of which I may be speaking" (p. 29; my italics). Money, Ricardo's "standard measure of value," is offered then as an imaginative concept which exists in the fictive realm of *as if.*

But the most dramatic and most pervasive example of the fictive mode of economic theory and the imaginative status of "price" occurs in the writings of Adam Smith. Smith's knottiest passages are those in which he must try to explain the dichotomy of real (natural) and market (nominal or money) value. Real value, Smith asserts, is the natural price of labor—that is, the amount of labor bestowed in production (*WN,* bk. 1, chap. 5). Market value, which is always computed in terms of money, is the amount of labor which labor bestowed can command in "the market." Market price "may either be above, or below, or exactly the same with [*sic*] its natural price" (*WN,* bk. 1, chap. 7). Natural price, for Smith, cannot vary, for it expresses amounts of labor invested and returned. Still, it *seems* to vary. Hence, the apparitional mode of Smithian analysis:

> Though equal quantities of labour are always of equal value to the labourer, yet to the person who employs him they *appear* sometimes to be of greater and sometimes of smaller value. He purchases them sometimes with a greater and sometimes with a smaller quantity of goods, and to him the price of labour *seems* to vary like that of all other things. It *appears* to him dear in the one case, and cheap in the other. *In*

reality, however, it is the goods which are cheap in the one case, and dear in the other.[39]

Despite the alleged difference between appearance and reality, ultimately appearance is economically significant. Although Smith insists upon the reality of real or natural value, his analysis proceeds as if market value were the only valid subject. His deadpan acceptance of this metaphysical paradox is as astonishing now as it was for his contemporaries: "As it is the nominal or money price of goods, therefore, which finally determines the prudence or imprudence of all purchases and sales, and thereby regulates almost the whole business of common life in which price is concerned, we cannot wonder that it should have been so much more attended to than the real price" (*WN,* bk. 1, chap. 5). In effect, then, the money price, with all its fictive fluctuations, its apparitional embodiment of nominal value, is the "reality" upon which economic theory is grounded. Inversely, (economic) reality requires the mediation of mythic fictions to explain its "unreal" foundations in words. In the world of Smithian economics, we live and prosper—literally—by the force of imagination. But not even poetry places such a singular value on the accrediting value of the unmediated imagination.[40]

The crisis of meaning generated by Smith's supererogatory use of the imagination was verbal, because, in this analysis, language has the rhetorical impact of real "fact." Engels, whose own imagination can be justly described as wintery, could barely conceal his rage:

> The difference between real value and exchange value is based on the fact, namely, that the value of a thing differs from the so-called equivalent given for it in trade; i.e., that this equivalent is not an equivalent. This so-called equivalent is the *price* of the thing, and if the economist were honest, he would employ this term for trade value. But he has still to keep up some sort of pretense that price is somehow bound up with value, lest the immorality of trade become too obvious.[41]

Engels's critique encapsulates Weisskopf's embryonic thesis and expands it. For Engels, the question of "fact" has been concealed by a verbal apparition: "price" is not the true synonym of "value." The nonequivalency of the two terms means that henceforth a commodity would become, in Marx's words, "a mysterious thing, simply because in it the social character of men's labour appears to them as an objective character stamped upon the product of that labour." Commodities thus assume the characteristics of religious icons or idols, "social things whose qualities are at the same time perceptible and imperceptible by the senses."[42] What began as the apparitional mode of classical economic logic resulted in a quasi-religious model in which the imagination was confirmed in the rightness of its belief that what was "imperceptible" was most to be valued. When measured against Weisskopf's reading of Marx, Marx's reading of capitalist production reveals the essential circularity of economic logic: out of verbal contradictions, a religious model evolved; out of this supernumerary religion, classical economics established its mythic purpose.

Polanyi has attempted to locate the roots of this circularity. He contends that classical economic theorists, including Marx, employed in their economics the very imaginative contradictions they condemned as illogical in the economy. Without Weisskopf's psychoanalytic vocabulary but on strictly economic terms, Polanyi describes "the extreme artificiality of market economy" (*PAME*, p. 33), a fictive entity comparable to some kinds of imaginative literature. Classical economics had to define, for instance, labor, land, and money as commodities in order to conceptualize "the market" as a *place* where *things* were bought and sold. The psychological need was also epistemological: like Midas, classical economists needed what was golden to be gold in fact; they needed to ground their theories in a certain physicality, so that, as Aristotle avers in terms of his rhetorical studies, "Fact also confirms our theory."[43] But labor, land, and money are obviously *not* commodities, Polanyi concludes, and when economists speak of markets they do not mean the *agora* but the mechanism or verbal nexus by which we may *say* that supply and demand coincide:

> Labor is only another name for a human activity that goes with life itself, which in its turn is not produced for sale but for entirely different reasons, nor can that activity be detached from the rest of life, be stored or mobilized; land is only another name for nature, which is not produced by man; actual money, finally, is merely a token of purchasing power which, as a rule, is not produced at all, but comes into

being through the mechanism of banking or state finance. None of them is produced for sale. The commodity description of labor, land, and money is entirely fictitious. [*PAME*, p. 32]

The metaphorical "token" of money becomes a "thing"; the actual activity of labor becomes an abstraction. Polanyi proceeds to show that economic logic has spun a structurally consistent system around these artificial concepts. Although Polanyi is never quite comfortable with the fictive elements which he detects in economic theory, his very disclaimer of economic artifice carries with it a more fertile understanding of the intellectual and emotional authority of such fictions:

> Nevertheless, it is with the help of this fiction that the actual markets for labor, land, and money are organized. . . . The commodity fiction, therefore, supplies a vital organizing principle in regard to the whole of society affecting almost all its institutions in the most varied way, namely, the principle according to which no arrangement or behavior should be allowed to exist that might prevent the actual functioning of the market mechanism on the lines of the commodity fiction. [Ibid.]

The tension in this passage illustrates the dilemma at the heart of economic logic. On the one hand, the market fictions are prohibitive and prescriptive, sanctioning only such arrangements and behavior as are consistent with the ongoing operation of those fictions. On the other hand, they evidence "a vital organizing principle." Fictions such as these are the only means we have of imagining and presenting abstract ideas in palpable forms. Similarly, the unreal "semantics of economic theory" allows us to speak conceptually about phenomena for which we might otherwise have no language. Polanyi's suggestion that fictions have the power of fact, a power which permeates not only the economy but "almost all [of society's other] institutions as well," becomes the thesis of his major work, *The Great Transformation:* "The origins of the cataclysm [of the Great Depression and the two world wars] lay in the utopian endeavor of economic liberalism to set up a self-regulating market system. Such a thesis seems to invest that system with almost mythical powers. . . ."[44] Polanyi's use of "mythical" is sardonic here, but he can expose that "utopian en-

deavor" only by adventuring upon a far more ambivalent "thesis"
—namely, that we derive a certain benefit from such fictions, including the power to unify a heterogeneous society under a workable set of institutions.

Although Polanyi, like most modern economists, doubts whether *any* fictive mode of thought *ought* to have such authority, he
must also confirm that such fictive discourse carries a remarkable,
perhaps irrational capacity for belief. The economic myth is based
upon the noble lie of poetry: that fictions *work,* even when they
are recognized as fictions. The pervasive significance, then, of the
economic myth is borne out by Lord Robbins, who also explains
why a literary study of the economic imagination might be desirable: "It is no exaggeration to say that it is impossible to understand the evolution and meaning of Western liberal civilization
without some understanding of Classical Political Economy."[45]
Polanyi reveals why Robbins is right. Without resolving the "predicament" set down by Bagehot, Polanyi identifies the "unreal"
aspects of economic logic as necessary conditions for it. But given
that difficulty, Polanyi also charges economists with the task of
understanding the implications of their own fictions. Literary
men, John Ruskin argued, could help them. The subsequent "evolution" of Western civilization would depend, according to Ruskin, upon learning to read more closely the "meaning" of those
mythical powers.

In Ruskin's eyes, to explore the mythic purpose and the logical
model of economics was to become educated to "moral culture"
(*Works,* 17:147), the fiction by which all society's institutions are
constituted. For Ruskin, the initial task of this education was to
defamiliarize economic discourse by dismembering the plain
"facts" of language from their "false verbal definitions." Ruskin
claimed that economists had confused "political economy (the
economy of a state or of citizens)" with "mercantile economy,
the economy of 'merces' or of 'pay' " (*Works,* 17: 44–45). Their
"economics" told us nothing of the household (*oikos*), because
their mercantile wealth getting revealed nothing of the welfare of
the *polis*. Ruskin therefore coined a new word, "illth," as the true
antonym of "wealth," in order to demonstrate the narrow-minded
poverty of economic discourse. Furthermore, "value" ought to
pertain to the valorous, and "utility," or the proper *use* of things,
meant, conversely, freedom from *ab-use*.[46] His most dramatic ex-

ample of economic misapprehension is the word "labor." By contrasting childbearing labor with the manual labor that men think they can buy and sell, Ruskin reassessed the *thanatos* principle of post-Malthusian economics: "Nearly all labour may be shortly divided into positive and negative labour: positive, that which produces life; negative, that which produces death; the most directly negative labour being murder, and the most directly positive, the bearing of children" (*Works,* 17:97). Malthusian economics teaches us that these two kinds of labor operate by an inverse ratio: the more productive our forms of positive labor, the more negative will be the results of the other kind. Ruskin did not escape Malthusian pessimism altogether, but in rejecting its simple mathematical despair, he cleared a solider ground for hope. For him, all labor became a contest with its opposite: "Labour is the *suffering* in effort. It is the negative quantity, or quantity of de-feat, which has to be counted against every Feat, and of de-fect, which has to be counted against every Fact, or Deed of men. In brief, it is 'that quantity of our toil which we die in' " (*Works,* 17:183).

This passage constitutes an ex post facto illustration of Ruskin's own working method in his economic treatises. The labor of the economic writer is to construe a new text for commercial economy and to show, for instance, "that the true veins of wealth are purple—and not in Rock, but in Flesh" (*Works,* 17:55-56). To do this, he must first deconstruct the economists' use of language, placing it in a new matrix where the nurturing of life holds priority over the nursing of a profit. In such a matrix, the "true" meaning of "profit"—"that is to say a 'making in advance' or 'making in favour of' (from proficio)"—would accrue to the improvement of the human condition itself (*Works,* 17:90). Profit must advance and favor procreation, the bountifulness of *human* production: "The final outcome and consummation of all wealth is in the producing as many as possible full-breathed, bright-eyed, and happy-hearted human creatures. Our modern wealth, I think, has rather a tendency the other way;—most political economists appearing to consider multitudes of human creatures not conducive to wealth, or at best conducive to it only by remaining in a dim-eyed and narrow-chested state of being" (*Works,* 17:56). A true *political* economy may emerge out of its opposite, *mercantile* economy, just as the positive labor of childbirth negates, in some sense, the negative labor of murder by the prolixity of its own example, and just as the labor of interpretive deconstruction ultimately fashions a new form of economic address. Such invention on Ruskin's part becomes the *inventum* which is, in its root sense, the coming-into or the discovery of old "facts" as well as the creation of new ones. Language becomes at once the medium of this reformation and the thing to be found, the substantive proof that Ruskin's new "commercial text" is inevitable (*Works,* 17:58).

One last example—a literary one—may suffice. Historically, Ruskin asserts, "the word 'Cher,' or 'Dear,' passes from Shylock's sense of it (to buy cheap and sell dear) into Antonio's sense of it: emphasized with the final *i* in tender 'Cheri,' and hushed to English calmness in our noble 'Cherish.' "[47] Here, according to Ruskin, the progress of language itself effectively belies the reductions and misrepresentations of the economists. To profit from this example, however, we must learn to read differently.

Ruskin's radical (and sometimes fanciful) etymologies of "politico-economic language" (*Works,* 17:80), remind us that economics, like other intellectual structures, is not a divinely mandated discipline but an act of *a priori* human interpretation. The interpreter assumes prime importance in the mapping out of those structures. Behind every demythified text is a mythic reader or, at least, a reader with mythic capacities. In taking economics as his "commercial text," Ruskin illustrates the same act of reading which is mandated in *Sesame and Lilies:* "And, therefore, first of all, I tell you earnestly and authoritatively (I *know* I am right in this), you must first get into the habit of looking intensely at words, and assuring yourself of their meaning, syllable by syllable —nay, letter by letter."[48] This Talmudic intensity illuminates the degraded economy of letters. The economists' habitual inattention to the precise meanings of words is but one symptom of a general ill regard for the printed medium as such. On a strictly commercial or merchandizing level, the physical quality of books has degenerated, a point on which the separate brands of socialism practiced by Ruskin and William Morris would concur. In a sense, one *is* able to judge a book by its cover, its text by its letters, for the genesis of printing confirms Ruskin's suspicions about the immediate and lasting complicity of economics and art. To draw an example that Ruskin himself does not use, consider the world's second printed book, after Gutenberg's Bible: Gutenberg's *Catholicon.* Its type is "a third smaller than that of the 42-line Bible," making it "more economical" to produce and "mark[ing] an important step towards varying as well as cheapening book-production by the careful choice of type."[49] The step toward economy, it will be noted, was taken immediately, almost simultaneously with the invention of printing itself; it was a step toward an imaginative economy as well, for the *Catholicon* is also an imaginative economizing of the Bible, substituting for the original text an encyclopedia of popularized stories *about* the original book. The improved economy of Gutenberg's second work goes hand in hand with its intellectual reduction of the first work—a coincidence repeatedly observed by Ruskin in that "politico-economic language" which reduced the "original" meanings of words and works to their commercially communicable senses.

In educating the public to read "letter by letter," Ruskin's work further recalls the etymology of the word "literature" itself from the Latin *littera,* a letter of the alphabet. The original meaning of the word signified, as Raymond Williams has recently put it, "a condition of reading," the state "of being able to read or of having read."[50] Literature begins, then, as "a category of use and condition rather than of production."[51] Ruskin insists that in reading by the letter we may be able to return literature to its primal utility, the condition of being read. Economists have failed to realize this category of use and condition in respect to their own writing; their literature, therefore, has lost its precision and its literalness. The effect of unlettered economists and of equally undemanding readers is noted by De Quincey as well as Ruskin:

> In an age of hasty reading, and of contempt for the whole machinery of scholastic distinctions, it cannot be expected that authors will spend much energy upon qualities which have ceased to be meritorious, upon nicety of distinction which perishes to the flying reader, or upon a jealous maintenance of consistency which, unless it were appreciated by severe study, could not benefit the writer. In this way, there arises at once a natural explanation of that carelessness in the mode of exposition which has every where disfigured the modern science of political economy.[52]

The crucial aspect of Ruskin's economic education is to restore this "flying reader" to the power and literal authority of Mill's creative reader (although Ruskin, as we have seen, did not himself read Mill in this way). The bad reader misses in language its life-sustaining economy because he cannot penetrate the corrupt mercantile texts. By the same token, writing has become corrupt because authors are not habitually interpreted with a "letter by letter" intensity. This vicious circle requires a radical re-education in which the initial act must be deconstructive, a breaking of habits of verbal inattention. Both De Quincey and Ruskin contend that intellectual slackness, like mercantile narrow-mindedness, is an *acquired* incapacity, a further (economic) manifestation of that negative value which is blind and dying labor.

The Political Economy of Art (1857), Ruskin's distych of lectures originally delivered to the merchants of Manchester, makes the point most dramatically. Sometimes combative, sometimes patronizing in tone, Ruskin's thesis is not that there *ought* to be an economics of art, but that there already *is*. What prevents us from developing a less false economy of artistic production is the fact that commercial economics is already a singular and overbearing grammar for judging social, political, and aesthetic merit. Ruskin went beyond Marx to apprehend the art *of* political economy and the *overt* relationship between economic discourse and other kinds of discourse. By insisting that political economy, like any other kind of art, must be "read," he offered the penetrating interpretation that the art of political economy actually depended upon the political economy of art.

When he reissued these lectures in 1880, he deliberately forced the point by changing the title to *"A Joy For Ever" (And Its Price in the Market)*. Ruskin explained this change in his preface to the later edition by repeating his thesis that art must have an economic permanence if it is to have a moral and aesthetic authority. All these forms of discourse must speak to one another, as Ruskin's motto from Keats implies: "Yet the motto was chosen with uncomprehended felicity: for there never was, nor can be, any essential beauty possessed by a work of art, which is not based on the conception of its honoured permanence, and local influence" (*Works*, 16:11). We are meant, therefore, to comprehend *all* implications of the title: first, that the loveliness of a thing of beauty *increases*.[53] Art collectors understand this as an economic truism: as time passes, the individuality of a great piece of art seems to become more rare, more precious, and so its monetary value escalates. But one must also read Keats's lines with a Ruskinesque

intensity, syllable by syllable. Thus, at the same time, it is specifically the *loveliness* which increases, as opposed to the thing's scarcity or commercial worth. A thing of beauty becomes more
beautiful in time as well as more expensive. *Appreciation* of that
beauty, when grasped in both its senses at once, reveals the political economy of art. Whatever its actual "price in the market" as
a *thing* of beauty or artifact, we also pay for its loveliness as a
thing of *beauty,* a labor of the imagination. This latter price is
exacted from the labor of interpretation which we repeatedly
bestow. But this "price" works to our profit, not merely to our
cost. In art, the economics of labor carries a different "moral
sign."[54] A thing of beauty does not denigrate our interpretative
labors but honors and aggrandizes them, asks for more. Educated
by the finite work of art, we are "for ever" in its debt. We *should*
put a high price on it, an economic sign which would clearly reflect both its value to us and its ability to increase in value the
more we understand why all this is so.

Ruskin found that the language of economics was constantly
moving into more rarefied senses, so that the fictive arrangements
of economic theory did not constitute real fictions—fictions which,
like those of painting and literature, help us live. All Ruskin wished
to do was to make those fictions real again, to show that the economists' "unreal words" might have a palpable wealth of meanings
if only we would imagine them correctly, and to demonstrate
"principles which are nothing more than the literal and practical
acceptance of the saying, which is in all good men's mouths[:]
namely, that they are stewards or ministers of whatever talents are
entrusted to them" (*Works,* 16:98). In citing the biblical parable
of the talents, Ruskin bared economics's central failure of belief,
its inability to interpret itself literally:

> Only, is it not a strange thing, that while we more or less ac-
> cept the meaning of that saying, so long as it is considered
> metaphorical[,] we never accept its meaning in its own terms?
> You know the lesson is given us under the form of a story
> about money. Money was given to the servants to make use
> of: the unprofitable servant dug in the earth, and hid his
> Lord's money. Well, we, in our poetical and spiritual applica-
> tion of this, say, that of course money doesn't mean money:
> it means wit, it means intellect, it means influence in high

quarters, it means everything in the world except itself.
[*Works,* 16:98–99]

Taking "the form of a story about money" at face value, one confronts the supreme paradox of Ruskin's economics. In reading
through the story one realizes the story behind the story, the reasons why the economic vehicle of the parable is an appropriate way
of speaking about one's individual gifts or genius. The economic
significance of one's metaphorical "talent" or individual genius is
as real as the metaphorical value that one assigns to one's literal
talents or individual wealth, a manifesto that we will see refined
and embodied in Blake's radical poetics (see below, chapter four).
Ruskin believed, with Blake, that one could not have this relationship functioning both ways at once unless one believed in the literal powers of the imagination, in the imagination as a real power.
To say that money talks, one must *first* believe that language or
"talk" has a far greater authenticity and moral influence than
most economists are willing to concede.

For Ruskin, political economists were not sufficiently sensitive
to the allegorical process of their thought precisely because they
were not sufficiently sensitive to the factual status of language.
This insight led him to propose a counter-allegory or, more exactly,
to demonstrate how the symbolic, fictive mode of economic discourse had been only half-realized. By the lights of commercial
instruction, we see that material wealth ought to aspire to the condition of moral well-being. But Ruskin supplied the necessary second half of this instruction: "moral power" has its monetary value
also. In that perception, Ruskin indicated one way for the economics of the imagination to assert a finer allegory, so that political
economy would represent *both* the visible facts of the functioning
commercium and the invisible facts of a functioning moral economy:

> In this moral power, quite inscrutable and immeasurable
> though it be, there is a monetary value just as real as that
> represented by more ponderous currencies. A man's hand
> may be full of invisible gold, and the wave of it, or the grasp,
> shall do more than another's with a shower of bullion. This
> invisible gold, also, does not necessarily diminish in spending.
> Political economists will do well some day to take heed of it,
> though they cannot take measure. [*Works,* 17:54–55]

Ruskin himself turns to Shakespeare's *Merchant of Venice* in order to "take measure" of this "invisible gold." In Ruskin's reading of the play, Christian *mercy,* rightly perceived, lies at the very heart of economic *merces.* When Shylock is literally called upon to exact his pound of flesh without touching the heart, without losing a drop of blood, then, for Ruskin, radical justice answers Shylock's extravagant usury, and so Shylock is ultimately

> foiled by a literal appeal to the great moral law that flesh and
> blood cannot be weighed, enforced by "Portia" ("Portion"),
> the type of divine Fortune, found, not in gold, nor in silver,
> but in lead, that is to say, in endurance and patience, not in
> splendour; and finally taught by her lips also, declaring, in-
> stead of the law and quality of "merces," the greater law and
> quality of mercy, which is not strained, but drops as the rain,
> blessing him that gives and him that takes. [*Works,* 17:223-24]

To the economist—in this case, a metonymic epithet for Shylock— "mercy" is an unreal word. And it remains an unreal word, even for Ruskin, unless one apprehends that mercy, too, has economic and political as well as moral power. In the next chapter, we shall be able to examine this correspondence in greater detail as we see how Blake took an "unreal word" like "price" and attempted to define its "moral power." At the same time, he demonstrated that such abstract concepts as "mercy," "justice," and "blessing" had acquired a politico-economic significance which would have to be reimagined if we were to grasp their "invisible gold."[55]

By understanding economics as a discursive formation, then, we have been able to apprehend the symbolic status of economics as an imaginative structure, a temporal and temporalizing mythos. We have further seen that only in its fictive mode does classical economics embrace the idea of economy. In Mill, we have confronted the fictive modality of economics as a correlative to humanist social arrangement and moral philosophy. Within Mill's lifetime, in the work of Jevons, there was demonstrated the inevitable breakdown of this correlation and the imaginative failure of certain fictive possibilities for the economic imagination, even as others were being canonized. Ricardo's redefinition of exchange value as scarcity and Malthus's promulgation of a sufficient-evil theory of economic progress strike an inevitable polarity in economic method which it would be the burden of later nineteenth-century thinkers to disentangle and to synthesize.

Ruskin confronted all these economies rhetorically by offering a strategy of textual reconstruction and by promising that economic texts must be poetically illuminated. Through Ruskin, we have seen that economics is the least economical (in the sense of austere or frugal) form of discourse, that the economy of its own discursive constellation aspires to Aristotle's *autarkeia* or self-sufficiency, mythically encompassing its own contradictions. Because the structure of "the economy" retains its traditionally ethical foundation in the idea of "economy," empirical economics has an ingrained, imaginative authority. To speak against that authority is to become vulnerable to "unreal words." And yet, thanks to such unreal words, the language of economic theory and practice is able to mediate between literal and fictive, empirical and imaginative, functional and moral, visible and invisible worlds. Economic discourse is thus found capable of absorbing its own unreal words into a self-enclosed allegory of the human predicament, of the confrontation between life and death.

CHAPTER IV
*William Blake and "The Price
of Experience"*

Having defined economics as an imaginative structure, we may now disclose more systematically the relation between economic statements and other forms of imaginative discourse. Blake provides this systematic disclosure in two ways. First, as a working printer and professional engraver, he was intimately aware of the commercial aspects of artistic production; and secondly, as a literary man, he could attempt in his art to create his own system, a poetic economics. He found, in fact, that it was impossible to serve in one capacity without following through in the other. The course of Blake's career further discloses a fundamental evolution in his economic consciousness, and this evolution will prove instructive in our reading of subsequent Romantic poetry, such as Wordsworth's. In Blake's radical poetics, the allegorical enclosures of commercial language's "unreal words" needed to be apprehended imaginatively; they were but another manifestation of the literal acts of enclosure which had made public lands private and which had refashioned the countryside to resemble London's chartered streets. Such enclosures, Blake felt, would discredit, once and for all, the mythic potential of the imagination by condemning the imagination to follow in the restricted tracks of a fraudulent rationality and counterfeit design.

How Blake wished to transform the economic imagination by means of the poetic imagination has not been adequately explored by Blake scholars, although critical studies, notably David V. Erdman's, have amply demonstrated that the "economic side of Blake's myth" is integral to the myth's claim of authenticity.[1] Blake repeatedly attempted to portray imaginatively the political and economic events of his time.[2] Moreover, as a man directly engaged in the everyday *business* of producing and selling art, Blake was not using the term lightly when he asserted, ". . . my business is to Create."[3] Despite Erdman's authoritative work, critics have been more interested in the creation than in the commerce.[4] One critic who has not avoided discussing the artist's commercialization is Raymond Williams. He speaks specifically of Blake only briefly, but his suggestions significantly amplify Erdman's observations. Williams cites from Blake's prose a rather typical diatribe against "the Fiends of Commerce": "he is Counted the Greatest Genius who can sell a Good-for-Nothing Commodity for a Great Price." Williams comments: "But, equally, Blake's criticism goes far beyond the professional complaint: the Imagination which, for him, Art embodies is no commodity, but 'a Representation of what Eternally Exists, Really and Unchangeably.' " In speaking of art as a "representation" versus art as a "commodity," Williams cites "the new kind of social relationships" embodied in Romantic literature and the need for a more precise critical methodology to describe the reader: "When art is a commodity, taste is adequate, but when it is something more, a more active relationship is essential."[5]

To understand why art is a commodity and how it may become "something more," we must first ask: how is the imagination, which is not itself a commodity, to be understood when it is embodied in a commodity such as art? What, in the end, is the relationship between the economic process which represents labor by means of commodities (material goods) and the imaginative process which represents "what Eternally Exists" by means of artistic labor and the commodities of art? To assess the "economic side of Blake's myth," we need to know how economic terms are applicable to the work of the imagination: thus, we have already delineated economics in its visionary aspect as a kind of art, a mythic grammar, which, like Blake's poetry, aspires to define the terms by which man's labor and worth will be valued. This delineation is, in fact, what Blake himself also attempted, hoping to show by contraries how the goals of proper art could be liberated from the artist's economic means of subsistence. One of his conclusions, however, is symptomatic: "Where any view of Money exists Art cannot be carried on."[6] This is not a statement of true contraries, for true contraries, as Blake envisioned them, galvanize and illuminate each other; under the pressure of imaginative revelation, they result in dialectical "Progression." Rather, Blake's statement marks a dead end. From such a passage it is only one short step to the modern platitude that the artist must expunge all economic awareness if he is to create "real" art. Blake himself may have taken that step.[7] If so, he succumbed to the awesome alienation of economic consciousness from aesthetic consciousness only at the end, after having struggled with the problem throughout his creative life.

Before we examine the struggle more closely, it is necessary to differentiate the two aspects of economic concern vital to Blake. First, he often reflects upon the commercial potential of his own art in his letters, marginalia, and notebook entries, which frequently make what Williams calls "the professional complaint." But the letters of 1804–5, which predate the economic repercussions of his trial for sedition and treason, are an important exception to Williams's generalization. Erdman has neatly grouped the happy commercialism of these documents under the rubric "Busy, Busy, Busy I bustle along" (*Blake: Prophet against Empire*, p. 433).

The second economic aspect of Blake's art is the focal point of this chapter: namely, the figurative portrayal of economic issues in Blake's poetry itself, which represents Blake's attempt to work out an economics of the imagination, an economics for the imagination in its labors. For, although Blake was naturally concerned

with the actual price his art could obtain, he was also interested
in money's mythopoeic significance, its "Giant forms" (*Jerusalem,*
pl. 3). He might attack, as he did in his Annotations to the *Works*
of Reynolds, the notion of royal liberality: "Liberality! We want
not Liberality We want a Fair Price & Proportionate Value ⟨ & a
General Demand for Art⟩ " (*Poetry and Prose,* p. 626). But this
was merely a pragmatic outpouring of the more extensive question
of symbolic value: "What is the Price of Experience do men buy it
for a song?" (*The Four Zoas: Night the Second,* 35.11). Any poetic system of value which could be as literally applicable to one's
daily bartering for bread as it was symbolically representative of
one's inherent moral worthiness would have to confront economic
reality and its myths.

In *Milton,* for example, Blake imagined commerce in its mythic
personification as "Allamanda," "the Cultivated Land" (27.42).
Northrop Frye has noticed the analogical reasoning by which commerce, the circulation of economic exchanges in the body politic,
is identified with the circulation of blood in the individual body.[8]
More importantly, perhaps, Allamanda signifies alimentary consumption in its diseased state, a self-consuming organism: "Here
the Sons of Los labour against Death Eternal" (27.44), because
here the ingestion of commodities only cries out for more. The
condition of such cultivation is scarcity. "Science" (and this includes economic science, according to Blake) "is divided into
Bowlahoola and Allamanda" (27.63), and is always laboring against
the ultimate scarcity which, "in Time & Space" (27.57), is Death.

Allamanda is Blake's mythic extension of the Miltonic description of money's origin, itself an extension of the Ovidian myth.
For Ovid, the Golden Age was finally lost when men "delved . . .
into the very bowels of the earth; and the wealth which the creator
had hidden away and buried deep amidst the very Stygian shades,
was brought to light, wealth that pricks men on to crime."[9] In Milton's Christian interpretation, the mining of gold is envisioned as a
Satanic subversion of divine creation. As God had taken a rib from
Adam (who is, in Hebrew, *adamah,* or earth), so Satan and his
crew extract from the earth "ribs of Gold" in order to build their
palace:

> Soon had his crew
> Op'n'd into the Hill a spacious wound
> And digg'd out ribs of Gold. Let none admire

> That riches grow in Hell; that soil may best
> Deserve the precious bane.[10]

Both the Ovidian and the Miltonic myths account for the origin of money in terms of violation; they share this bleak sense of what it means to be an earth-owner (Urthona), one who has "Ransack'd the Center" (*PL,* 1.686) and fallen heir (and prey) to "materials dark and crude" from "deep under ground" (*PL,* 6.478). In Blake's version, "The Plow goes forth in tempests & lightnings & the Harrow cruel / In blights of the east; the heavy Roller follows in howlings of woe" (27.47–48). Commerce aspires to become the only means of cultivating the earth, disguising its original rapine by perpetrating its own cosmology: economics, that dismal science. Minting and the distribution of monetary currencies only perpetuate the original violation. But money values—indeed, economic values in general—are directly proportionate to scarcity, so that by urging scarcity as the ultimate denominator of value, commercial economics conditions desire to be most intense when its object is least attainable. Man has purchased his own neuroses by placing credit (belief) in a language which is founded upon promises of insufficiency. Economic tyranny is therefore verbal. In economics, desire is called "demand."

But by the time he came to compose *Jerusalem,* Blake had discovered an economics of the imagination whose dynamics had become incorporated into the "energetic exertion" of the poet's labor and talent (*Jerusalem,* pl. 3). *Jerusalem,* then, enacts Blake's new labor theory of value. In *Jerusalem* we do not find the sort of parabolical portrayal of commerce which we see in either Milton or *Milton,* for commerce has become internalized, a part of the dynamics of the work itself. To use Blake's loaded word, the reader becomes involved in a *demon*-stration of Blake's imaginative economics.[11] The cultivations of Blake's illuminated text provide an antidote for "the Cultivated Land" of Allamanda, just as Allamanda embodies those quotidian economic facts and commercial aspirations recorded often in Blake's letters. These expansions and contractions are worth considering carefully, because they reveal yet another way in which Blake's striving with systems—in this case, systems of economic thought—frees him from the entrapment of those systems.

Blake's poetic economics, as displayed in his last prophetic book, is prefigured in a notebook entry dated the same year as the finished title page of *Jerusalem:* "23 May 1810 found the Word Golden."[12] No one knows for sure what Blake intended by this passage. In the first place, the parts of the passage, short as it is, do not seem to fit together. Assuming the Word to be the Johannine Logos, what sense does it make to call it "Golden"? By definition, the Word requires no adjectival qualification. And because it is difficult to imagine a situation in which the Word might be *found,* it is difficult to understand why Blake uncharacteristically dated the occasion. Virtually our only clue to the passage's meaning is its placement on the notebook page. It is written vertically along the left-hand edge of the page. Above it and to the right—looking down on the passage—is a pencil drawing of Blake's head. The passage is flanked by two prose paragraphs in which Blake attacks those artists who are foolhardy enough to imitate nature from "Models."[13] Curiously, the passage we are considering seems to suggest its own kind of model, the Word. If irony or even a kind of Blakean contrary is intended, its precision is lost in the cryptic nature of the utterance.

But it is only a convenience to call this an "utterance" at all. Lacking a suitable context, the reader may choose to imagine a voice which might say such a thing, but one's first sense of the passage is of a gnomic voicelessness, a feeling enhanced by the missing subject of the verb, "found." The passage has the rhetorical force of an inscription or a hermetic maxim or a solution to a lost riddle or a riddling itself.[14] No reading is certain. Indeed, there is so little to go on and the passage seems so slight that virtually all scholars ignore it.[15]

What we have here, however, is a verbal emblem of Blake's technique of condensing "factual" matter. Throughout his notebook, of course, Blake demonstrates this very technique with *visual* emblems. But here he found a "verbal icon" instructive enough to put in his notebook. What Blake has given us is a one-liner, a fierce joke.[16] The initial sense of hermetic secrecy in the passage may not be entirely misleading. To get the joke, one must know what the joke is "about," and here the joke seems private. Like riddles, jokes are metaphors, forms of condensed meaning.[17] Freud spoke of the economy of jokes.[18] Because jokes condense and galvanize meaning according to an economics of linguistic and psychological energy, the auditor, in order to get the joke, must tacitly supply the context which the joke condenses. The work of the auditor, therefore, is like the interpretive labor of the psychoanalyst in retrieving the latent dream content from the manifest but disguised dream form.[19] In this case, Freud's sense of a joke's dynamics is especially apt, because Blake's "utterance" is framed in quasi-economic terms itself, if we understand that "Golden" here expresses its primary sense: "made of gold, consisting of gold" (*OED* 1.).

The passage also suggests the hermetic art of alchemy, in which gold is the perfect metal, since in gold "all the qualities [or spirits —i.e., mercury and sulphur and sometimes salt (sal ammoniac) and sometimes arsenic] were compounded in a state of equality."[20] Gold is also the sun and, by analogical reasoning, the Son, Christ: "For gold was the only perfect metal, the only one that, on the level of mineral existence, corresponded to the divine perfection."[21] In considering Blake's alchemical usages, Kathleen Raine has noted that Los is the mirror image of Sol.[22] The alchemical priests who sought to derive gold from baser substances would imitate thereby the divine miracle of imagination, the Word made flesh. When the art of making gold was combined with the other goal of alchemy, the creation of the *elixir vitae* or *aurum potabile,* human creation enacted the Resurrection as well. To find a way of making gold by the transmutation of elements was to disclose, analogically, the secret of incarnation as represented in God's science, the holy art of Christ.[23]

This alchemical background may provide a partial context for Blake's notebook entry. By dating the passage, he is marking the time of this alchemical "discovery" of the imagination: namely, that the divine Word is the alchemical perfection of human words into the language of art. But this does not explain the full significance of the passage. For Blake may have intended a further condensation of "fact," which, like the Spiritual Sword of Los, would touch the heart of his poetics.

The art of Hermes was also connected, mythologically, with the business of trade and the practice of commerce.[24] So the passage may also be read, "found the *Word* Golden," not as opposed to finding it tarnished or green but as opposed to finding something else golden. The passage indirectly specifies what that something else might have been. On 23 May 1810, one could have picked up a piece of gold—a coin, say—only to find that it was less golden than it had been, say, on 22 May 1810. The coin had not changed its weight, but the gold had changed in value. It was not the substance gold which was less golden or less valuable. But the word or words stamped on the coin to specify its value did not mean the same thing as when the coin was minted. Or, to use the familiar terminology of medieval and renaissance metaphysics, the gold had suffered nominal (accidental) and not essential (real) depreciation. This was, in fact, the very language which contemporary economists were using in May 1810 to explain the fiduciary crisis of apocalyptic proportions which had gripped England and which had resulted in the convening (on 19 February 1810) of the so-called Bullion Committee.[25] The public was kept informed of the Parliament's inquiry: indeed, the newspapers had helped to bring about the parliamentary hearings when the *Morning Chronicle* began publishing, on 6 September 1809, a series of letters by David Ricardo about the deteriorating monetary situation.[26]

The fiscal crisis developed as follows.[27] As a stopgap measure to halt plummeting cash assets, the Bank of England had "temporarily" suspended (in 1797) cash payments on paper banknotes (the suspension lasted until 1819). In effect, the period of suspended payments thrust England upon an experimental monetary system. Paper money was legal tender that was not convertible to gold, but coins, as always, were still convertible. Subsequently, there was a steady and catastrophic rise in the price of gold as bullion. The effect was that gold was more valuable as bullion than as coin. The economic issue was the high price of gold versus the low rates of exchange (i.e., the depreciated value of English currency and bills of exchange). Any layman could see, however, that gold was less golden in one form (coin) than it was in another (bullion). Because "money" had to sustain two meanings, only one of which was supported by gold, this economic crisis was also a crisis in language.

Whereas some believed that the wholesale printing of inconvertible paper money initiated the crisis, others identified the problem as governmental reluctance to convert depreciated currency back into bullion. One of these was a fellow of the Royal Society named, like the poet, William Blake. Economist Blake, following Ricardo, argued the need to restore economic health by melting down that "bad money" and thereby stopping what we would call, in modern terms, a pure increase in the monetary supply. In the fire, "the value of the currency [would be] made to correspond with that of the precious metals of which it is composed, or into which it is convertible . . ." ("Observations," p. 520). The coin ought to be "consigned to the crucible, for the purpose of removing the depreciation that it suffers" (ibid., p. 522). The alchemical transmutation of sound economic theory may be witnessed here.

The dynamics of money theory as outlined by economists such as Blake provide a curious antithesis to the economics of the imagination as practiced by a poet such as Blake. According to the economists, the conversion of a quantity of depreciated coinage into bullion would restore the true meaning of the word "golden" —as good as gold—to the remaining currency. But in the poetic imagination of Blake, the Word could be found to be golden even when other substances (such as gold coin) which were supposed to be golden had depreciated meanings. Thus the passage may be paraphrased: on this day I found the Word golden, even though the word "golden" was debased. The value of the Logos does not depreciate along with its secular counterpart, the word of economic valuation, money. In fact, having "found the Word Golden," one is better able to understand how language which reveals divinity must be grounded in its literal expression (*Milton,* 42.14). The Word in Blake's passage literalizes the money signs which nominally signify gold value but which cannot justify their signification. This is the "joke": the Word is incarnate meaning; money is merely a metaphor. Money exemplifies the process of reasoning and comparing, measuring relative price in terms of relative quantities. But the Word creates meaning and is the fulfillment of meaning; the Word expresses abundance, not the ratios of political economics. Movements of money only reflect this process and this end; they do not embody it.

Thus money belongs to the lower world of "generation" and betokens the kind of riches which moths and rust and economic language may corrupt. Those who have found the Word golden, however, have discovered not only true wealth but also the imaginative dynamics by which true language engenders belief. The date on the notebook passage bestows upon this revelation the power of witness similar to the personal testament at the beginning of the last book of the Bible, where John, "who bare record of the word of God" (Rev. 1:2), is instructed, "What thou seest, write in a book . . ." (Rev. 1:11). Blake's sentence fragment becomes a kind of amulet or assurance of value, the kind of thing one would want to put in one's notebook. This is the true mone-

tary inscription. Unlike the dates on coins, this calendrical date
assures the temporal validity of *imaginative* revelation—"23 May
1810 found the Word Golden"—and guarantees that the Word of
the "Human Imagination Divine" is made of a gold which resists
the metaphysical uncertainties actual gold was at that moment
suffering in the commercial markets of the commonwealth.

Ultimately, then, the Word which is golden evidences not only
a different economics but also a different kind of art. It is the
"Model" for the imagination, although it is opposed to that mod-
eling which painters use to imitate nature. "Men think," wrote
Blake, "they can Copy Nature as Correctly as I copy Imagination"
(*Notebook,* p. [N59]). In order to copy the imagination, Blake
added to his notebook a suitably minted coin of words which, like
the proper kind of prophetic art, was modeled not from any precious metal but from the Word itself.

The Bullion Committee of 1810 did not solve the money controversy.[28] But the very convening of a parliamentary committee
to study the fluctuations of currency did dramatize the special
significance of monetary economics as a discrete aspect of political
economy in general.[29] As it became apparent that a more sophisticated theory of money was required, it also became apparent that
the simplistic poetic economics of an earlier time would no longer
suffice. Blake's notebook poem of almost two decades earlier
(dated 1793 by both Erdman and Keynes) shows Blake evoking in
a single quatrain both material wealth and spiritual health through
an unambiguous metaphor of exchange:

> The countless gold of a merry heart,
> The rubies & pearls of a loving eye,
> The indolent never can bring to the mart,
> Nor the secret hoard up in his treasury.[30]

These precious metals of heart and eye betoken man's *real* estate
and resist conversion to lesser forms of exchange. Merry and loving,
they are proof against indolence and the calculations of political
economics.

If we assume that "the secret" may refer not only to a character
type (such as "The indolent") but also to the secret of wealth,
then the secret is that wealth must be spent, not hoarded. True
spiritual health in the "mart" of human exchange comes from the
giving of one's gifts and from the active receiving of those gifts.

Hoarded, the "countless gold" becomes counted and finite—it acquires a price—whereas in the "merry heart" it is infinite. If the "merry heart" and the "loving eye" speak of desire, then the paradox beautifully conceived in terms of the exchange of precious materials in the marketplace, is that desire must be spent in order to be inexhaustible. Only then is desire "Enough! or Too much" (as in the conclusive proverb from *The Marriage of Heaven and Hell*). The secret of material health and spiritual wealth is that they are interchangeable when they are identified in the body as specie of energy, as forms of desire.

This simple substitution of monetary exchanges for the physical transaction of joy would become untenable by 1810.[31] For one thing, the policy of the Bank changed the meaning of money from specie to nonconvertible paper.[32] In the notebook entry of 22 May 1810 and, more broadly, in *A Vision of the Last Judgment* (another work circa 1810), we find Blake confronting directly the "new" meaning of money and exchange. "The Last Judgment begins," according to Blake, when "only Contention remains to Man" (*Prose and Poetry,* p. 544). Near the end of the work, Blake implicates money as a form of contention: "What it will be Questioned When the Sun Rises do you not see a round Disk of fire somewhat like a Guinea O no no I see an Innumerable company of the Heavenly host crying Holy Holy Holy is the Lord God Almighty" (p. 555). Behind the peremptory tone of the questioner (What! Do you not see?) one may hear the self-assured slogan of the physiocrats, the economists of natural law: *Laissez faire et laissez passer, le monde va de lui-même.* In physiocrat economics, the world is indeed run by a guinea-sun. The haziness of the questioner's perception (the sun is *somewhat like* a guinea) reveals the palliatives of natural religion, its tone of weary rationalism—*laissez faire et laissez passer.* Opposing this "is the Lord God Almighty." The Lord God *is* almighty as the sun rises, when the imagination can see that the Son also rises. The (concealed) pun is regenerative: this language acts out its vitality. Divinity depends upon the almighty art of the human imagination which reveals it.

In fact, the visionary's language makes the dependent relationship between God and the imagination manifest. What the perceiver of the guinea-sun cannot see is that his vision, too, is an act of imagination: he wants what is golden (like the sun) to be gold in fact (like a coin). But because the observer does not see this as an imaginative attitude, his hope that all that glitters may be gold merely evidences a Midas-like fear of losing the physicality of his perceptions and desires. Such anxiety derives from and has been conditioned by the realities of economic life and secures for itself an ultimate parsimony: one sun, one guinea—which are "somewhat like." The principles of abundance and certainty, which sight of the innumerable company of the Heavenly Host affirms, are unimaginable. Where scarcity and economic calculation are the rule, assurances of abundance must be merely fictions. And so they are, concedes the Blakean visionary, when other acts of the imagination (such as seeing the sun as a guinea) are not believed to be *imaginative* acts as well.

For Blake, the imagination cannot be priced by other measures than itself. It cannot be taught to believe a lie because it is the accrediting (the believing) principle itself. The point of Blake's parable, then, is that the wish to see the sun as a guinea is wrong not because it expresses desire, but because guinea-suns obstruct desire's true end, its fulfillment. Unlike the depreciating value which fulfillment has, say, in Ricardian economics, desire, in Blake's usage, improves by being fulfilled. Each kind of true fulfillment repeats every other kind in its capacity for belief, and this constitutes an "improvement of sensual enjoyment" (*The Marriage of Heaven and Hell,* pl. 14). The business of art is to create this improvement by making it current among all men and women. The commerce of art (of the imagination) occurs explicitly within the nature of desire itself, just as moneymaking is implicitly concerned with the nature of consumer desire. But art clarifies desire's wishes and ends, thus restoring them to a pristine clarity which the invention of money muddied. This kind of exchange satisfies, because it can be fully understood *by* the human imagination as an achievement *of* the human imagination in its undivided labors.

In retrospect, then, "the secret" of the 1793 quatrain is that in the beginning the language of economics misnames "the moment of desire" (*Visions of the Daughters of Albion,* 7.3). It subverts love of the embodied Word, the human imagination divine, into love of money. And love of money alters the ways in which desire can be expressed because it transforms the means by which love can be fulfilled. The imagination, on the other hand, engenders love, because it replaces the false products of money worship with a direct apprehension of labor value. Whereas the imagination values the ues the *moment* of desire, the economic sensibility, embodied in the secular forms of "mart" and "treasury," either stores up desire or exchanges it for something else. Thus, the "secret" of imaginative economics is that the moment of desire occurs in the physical body and is a secret only to the mind. To the body, all desires which can be attained and can produce satisfaction are bodily desires. Desire is immortal in the body because it is fulfilled there. Psychologically, the expense of spirit becomes a waste of shame only when desire is bought and sold; that is, when it is made into a commodity. When desire is exchangeable in the manner of other commodities, then to speak of it is to curse it for its scarcity or its surplus, its intransigence or its lasciviousness, its virginity or its incontinence. This is "the youthful Harlots curse" ("London," l. 14), and it is the curse upon "the Great Code of Art" which Blake felt the Bible, when not misnamed, represented: "Christianity is Art & not Money. Money is its Curse" (*Poetry and Prose,* p. 271).

In *A Vision of the Last Judgment,* Blake was thinking in economic terms (the gold and the golden, the guinea and the sun) in order to demonstrate the imaginative fallacy of economic value. True art, like Blake's radical Christianity, must be liberated from the money curse. In his notebook essay, called "Public Address" by his editors (*Poetry and Prose,* pp. 560–71), Blake measured the possibilities for art by dissecting the contentions and limitations imposed by "Commerce." With equal animosity, the shotgun logic of "Public Address" attacks the public's misplaced demand for "Great & Expensive Works ⟨of Engraving⟩ " (p. 565), the public's hazy perception of artistic labor, and the ensuing economic competition among fellow artists. The public fails to understand that artistic execution is the mother of inspiration:

> I have heard many People say Give me the Ideas. It is no matter what Words you put them into & others say Give me the Design it is no matter for the Execution. These People know ⟨Enough of Artifice but⟩ Nothing of Art. Ideas cannot be Given but in their minutely Appropriate Words nor Can a Design be made without its minutely Appropriate Execution[.]
> . . . He who copies does not Execute he only Imitates what is

already Executed Execution is only the result of Invention.
[P. 565]

Thus the public treats all art the same because it thinks that every
artist is essentially the same, that nature, for instance, is a singular
"Idea" which is interchangeable from one artistic production to
another. Ironically, what the public does not see is literally what is
staring it in the face, namely, the difference in accomplishment,
the fineness of the line (whether the line be the painter's, the engraver's, or the poet's).[33] The economic imagination belies the economics of the imagination in its labors, "for Commerce Cannot
endure Individual Merit its insatiable Maw must be fed by What all
can do Equally well at least it is so in England as I have found to
my Cost these Forty Years"(p. 562). The public's "insatiable
Maw" clamors for more of the same because it does not know
what nourishment from art is, and this "taste" in turn generates an
unnatural appetite—one might almost say, a cannibalism—among
artists: "I do not know whether Homer is a Liar & that there is no
such thing as Generous Contention[.] I know that all those with
whom I have Contended in Art have strove not to Excell but to
Starve me out by Calumny & the Arts of Trading Combination"
(p. 566). The metaphorical underpinnings of Blake's lament
emerge with ascerbic literalness: either one suits the public's taste
or one starves. If the former, then one may eat. In any case, one
is consumed.

One might say that here the metaphor of consumption consumes itself. Before the imagination can posit its own economics,
it must cleanse language of its economic banality; it must let the
Word which is the imagination itself become visible through the
haze of guinea-suns. Only by first revealing the poverty of economic concepts can the alimentary processes of Allamanda, the
laws of commercial science, be transformed into a "right reason"
which sustains and nurtures both the physical and spiritual man.

In *A Vision of the Last Judgment,* then, Blake's imagination begins to turn economic terminology on its head. Blake suggests that
the aim of his work is to reveal what everyone, including (especially) the observer of the guinea-sun really wants—a Golden Age.
"The Nature of my Work is Visionary or Imaginative it is an Endeavour to Restore ⟨what the Ancients calld⟩ the Golden Age"
(p. 545). Blake knew, of course, that what characterized the myth-

ological Golden Age (Ovid is one of the "Ancients" to whom Blake alludes throughout *A Vision*) was that it had no gold. The Golden Age was a misnomer. And because there was no mining of gold, there was no wicked love of possession (the Ovidian *amor sceleratus habendi*). If the Golden Age is to be restored, the meaning of "Golden" has to be reimagined, for its present meaning is based upon an Iron Age awareness, which makes the simple innocence of the Ovidian Golden Age literally irretrievable. And the value of the poet's restorative "Work" also must be reassessed in terms of an imaginative theory of labor value. As Blake suggests in one of his most beautiful lyrics, Enion's song from *The Four Zoas: Night the Second*, the price of our fallen state can be measured by the idea of "price" itself:

> What is the price of Experience do men buy it for a song
> Or wisdom for a dance in the street? No it is bought with
>   the price
> Of all that a man hath his house his wife his children.
> [35.11-13]

Poignant as this lament may be, the speaker fails to see "*all* that a man hath" by seeing only what may be bought and sold. That these things include one's dependents—one's wife and children—reveals a bitter irony beneath the pathos. Blake firmly identifies such concepts as price, cost, and dependency with the world of experience. Wars and "Contention" mark the final departure of the Golden Age and are the price of experience; experience itself (the awareness of mutual dependence and vulnerability) is the price of lost innocence. "Price," therefore, always indicates a labor lost. In the realm of experience, to record the cost of a thing is to lament an absence. Like the failed beholder of the sun, this speaker has succumbed to experience by seeing "all that a man hath" as "somewhat like a Guinea." In effect, the word "price" has become synonymous with "all"; "the price / Of all that a man hath" is all that he has. As an indicator of loss, money has become the only word of value.

When money becomes the sacred word of value in the commonwealth, when money is the only means of reckoning individual merit and the wealth of nations, then indeed "only Contention remains to Man." Love becomes *amor habendi* and is priced as gain and loss. Desire depends upon depriving others (illustrated,

Blake knew, in J. G. Stedman's *Narrative*).[34] The very concepts of love and desire become examples of reprobate language. Taught by economic expectations, men are led to believe this lie: that the Golden Age is at hand when one has plenty of gold at hand. They are taught to price experience, not to ask what the price is of pricing it. They do not imagine when they use the word "price" that they depend on economic terms to reveal to them noneconomic values.

The imagination, therefore, posits its own economics. It cannot wish away either gold or the economic knowledge which it breeds, nor can it pretend that experience, the knowledge of loss, is a fiction. What the imagination can do, within its own economics, is to cleanse language of impossible hopes, the expression of unfulfillable desires. In the economics of the imagination, surplus will be understood not as an accident of overproduction or as a miscalculation of demand, but as proverbial—"Enough! Or Too much"—so that belief in oneself is not purchased at another's cost or impoverishment "Till pity is become a trade, and generosity a science, / That men get rich by" (*America,* 11.10-11).

In *Visions of the Daughters of Albion*, Oothoon's questions, echoed by her sisters, take us to the heart of Blake's poetic economics:

> Does he who contemns poverty, and he who turns with
>   abhorrence
> From usury: feel the same passion or are they moved alike?
> How can the giver of gifts experience the delights of the
>   merchant? [5.10-12]

Not only are these labors different: for Blake, the re-imagining of political economics necessitated, as it did for such other innovators as Adam Smith, David Ricardo, and Karl Marx, a new evaluation of the significance of labor.

In classical economics, the labor theory of value supposes that the value of a commodity is determined by the quantity of labor bestowed in its production. Similarly, its market value is the quantity of labor it can command in exchange. In a pre-monetary or barter economy, quantities of labor are exchanged directly, so that, as Adam Smith asserts, "the produce of labour constitutes the natural recompense or wages of labour."[35] But money deters this direct recompense; it represents, in later Marxian language, the unnatural increment. In a money economy, where money has become the exchange equivalent, value is most often understood to mean money value rather than labor value. Thus, money not only replaces labor as the immediate measure of value, but it also becomes an equivalent of labor. None of the classical economists, from Smith to Marx, ever doubted that money price *ought* to represent the value of labor. They each agreed that finding a fair price for labor was a prime economic task. Blake shared this subsistence theory of wages; he derived it in fact from the same biblical authority to which Smith alludes: "A man must always live by his work, and his wages must at least be sufficient to maintain him."[36] Smith argues that man's innate "trucking disposition," his love of exchanging, was the psychological origin of all trade and has resulted not only in a natural division of labor but also in a difference of talents (*WN*, bk. 1, chaps. 1-4). Smith's picture of divided, dependent, self-interested economic man speaks directly (by contraries) to Blake:

> But man has almost constant occasion for the help of his brethren, and it is in vain for him to expect it from their benevolence only. He will be more likely to prevail if he can interest their self-love in his favour, and show them that it is for their own advantage to do for him what he requires of them. Whoever offers to another a bargain of any kind, proposes to do this. Give me that which I want, and you shall have this which you want, is the meaning of every such offer. . . . [*WN*, bk. 1, chap. 2]

From a Blakean perspective, one may see that Smith is actually affirming the specialization of desire. But "the meaning" of human exchange need not be reduced to this language. In Blake's "theory" of labor value, a man can do one thing well *and* credit the exertions of others' talents *and* entertain a hope not merely for subsistence but for abundant recompense as well.

Blake wrote, "If it were not for the Poetic or Prophetic character, the Philosophic & Experimental would soon be at the ratio of all things . . . " (*Poetry and Prose*, p. 1). The economist thrives by telling us "the meaning" of such ratios. While economic philosophy was enchained by the mythic burden of Adam's curse—that we must labor for our rewards and live by the sweat of our brows

—Blake's radical poetics created its own myth and identified the primal economic fact to be the divine labor by which the Word is embodied and made flesh. Jesus is the embodiment of God in man just as a commodity is the embodiment of human labor in things. Depreciation occurs, however, in the process of the commodity's being exchanged for something other than its direct equivalent. In political economy that something is money; in moral economy, that something is "Natural Religion." When commodities are bought and sold for money, one is encouraged to forget how the commodities were invested with value in the first place, what their original labor price was. Industrialized manufacture only speeds up the process of forgetting, because it promises more of a given commodity than unassisted human work could provide. Pre-Smithian economists demonically called such manufacture "art" or "ingenious labor."[37] This artistic illusion of plenitude becomes Satanic when commerce ultimately creates a less obtainable object than before. To support the cost of manufacture, the price of goods must represent other factors than simple labor value. In classical economics, price divides from labor in order to reflect rent (the cost of property) and profit (the cost of capital), just as labor invested divides from its natural product by the intercession of money as the ultimate measure of value. This, for Blake, was the real "division of labor"—the division of labor from the commodities which would truly represent its worth, a division promoted and sustained by monetary exchanges. Price becomes a displacer of value, then, and not a true representation. The same crisis of representation occurs in "Natural Religion" when nature becomes a metaphor for the godhead, a figurative representative of divine plenitude, not the direct presentation of divinity. Metaphor, in this sense, becomes the figural "Emanation" of a language that persists in remaining "Spectral."

The key to the correspondences between the labor value of the poet's word and the economic health of the commonwealth occurs in the last stanza of the lyric which concludes *Jerusalem*'s first chapter. There, Blake puts himself squarely in the breach between the mythic systems of economic policy and the mythic systems of poetic process. In lieu of the Royal Exchange and the bills of exchange which pass for money in the import-export mercantile transactions of the economy, Blake asserts his own methodology for creating a wealth of nations:

> In my Exchanges every land
> Shall walk, & mine in every Land,
>   Mutual shall build Jerusalem:
> Both heart in heart & hand in hand. [27.85–88]

Jerusalem, when mutually built as the sacred center of man's spiritual life, will replace the Royal Exchanges which are the sacred centers of man's economic life, the places where persons literally do "walk" and where "every Land" figuratively walks in mutually competitive trading. The new Golgotha will become the type of a new spiritual identity through commerce between man's bodily death and resurrection, achieved by the imagination's exertion of its genius so that it is used and valued as a continually current manifestation of the Holy Ghost (*Jerusalem*, pl. 91). Such an imaginative transaction replaces the bills of exchange which represent "every Land['s] " profit and loss, consumption and production, because here labor bestowed is computed directly in terms of labor commanded: "Both heart in heart & hand in hand."[38]

In the beginning, these bodily exchanges are nominally "mine," the creative exertions of the poet's heart and hand alone. As these acquire universal currency through mutual acceptance of the labor, the word of individual achievement ("mine," "*my* Exchanges") becomes a gift of universal possession ("mine in every Land"). The poet's "Exchanges" replace money as the circulating medium of the commonwealth, because in the poet's work the circulating medium becomes the Word. The poet's gift contains its own predicate for action—what is "mine" shall also "mine"—so that mining mutually for the golden Jerusalem, these labors turn up the resurrected body, the Word made flesh. By the end of chapter one, however, this is merely the prophet's promise of a profit.[39] It remains to be seen how the poet's labor can become mutually accredited.

The Word that is Jesus and the word of the human imagination divine become identical at the end of *Jerusalem*, but only to those who have seen where these exchanges are grounded. In the words of the prophet, "Look unto the rock when ye are hewn, and to the hole of pit whence ye are digged" (Isa. 51:1). The precious metal of true humanity is what Los, in the broadest interpretation of his labors, refines in his furnaces so as to reveal the true coin of man's genius. This precious metal is literally what would be "mine in every Land" if, in the political and economic spheres, mines of precious metals were not a cause of contention and a source of oppression. The price of moneymaking can be counted in "the sighs & tears & bitter groans" of the poor. Los takes those human cries into his furnaces in order to reverse the process of moneymaking:

> I saw terrified; I took the sighs & tears & bitter groans:
> I lifted them into my Furnaces; to form the spiritual sword.
> That lays open the hidden heart. [9.17-19]

This is not the sword of oppression but "the Sword of the Spirit, which is the Word of God" (Eph. 6:17). In Los's furnaces, the raw ore of "the hidden heart" is unearthed from its spectral body, so that it may be "melted into the gold, the silver, the liquid ruby / The crysolite, the topaz, the jacinth, & every precious stone" (9.23-24). Out of this true metal of human feeling, the engraver-poet prints his own forms of exchange, his own paper notes, in "well contrived words, firm fixing, never forgotten" (12.35). In the exchanges of *Jerusalem* the precious material, the "gold" of "the hidden heart," may become a blessing, a promise of the regenerated Golden Age:

> When Jerusalem was thy hearts desire in times of youth
>   & love.
> Thy Sons came to Jerusalem with gifts, she sent them away
> With blessings on their hands & on their feet, blessings
>   of gold,
> And pearl & diamond: thy Daughters sang in her Courts:
> They came up to Jerusalem; they walked before Albion
> In the Exchanges of London every Nation walkd
> And London walkd in every Nation mutual in love & harmony
> Albion coverd the whole Earth, England encompassed the
>   Nations,
> Mutual each within others bosom in Visions of Regeneration.
>   [24.37-45]

Marx would argue repeatedly that the cash nexus turns words into things, into commodities which may be bought and sold, but the "blessings" which Blake imagines here are both things *and* words, "blessings of gold."[40] They are benedictions which bestow psychic and moral worth, because here the language of social, political, and economic evaluation can be identified as the language of individual moral value. These "blessings" are as good as gold, because the attributes of the "blessings" are identical with their substance. If the Word is found to be golden, money talks without danger of depreciation, here.

Finally, this regenerative power, identified in words as things (the poem as coin) and things as words (coins as blessings) depends upon the desire of individuals to believe it. Belief, in *Jerusalem,* is an active force: it is a way of bestowing credit. It is, in fact, the real meaning of credit. In the imagination there is no disparity between consumption and production and the value of one's labor, because the primal act of imagination is not for one's own sake but for the sake of another—the precise opposite of Smithian economics. It is Los's original belief in Albion which makes *Jerusalem* possible. His initial exertion on Albion's behalf inaugurates an exchange of talents. Urging the old meaning of *talent* as coin, Blake declares that talent constitutes a spiritual gift, in which "gift" carries the triple sense of what one is gifted with and what one freely gives away and what one freely accepts from others: "I never made friends but by spiritual gifts" (91.16). In the parable of the talents, the "reasonable" man hoarded his own gift, which, in Milton's words, "is death to hide" ("When I Consider How My Light Is Spent," l. 3). This is also the predicament of Albion, who is hidden behind the Doors of Death which Los enters with his greater gift, laying down his life for his friend. The men who knew the meaning of their gifts (in the parable) spent their talents and were promised the kingdom of heaven. In Max Weber's thesis, this promise constitutes the religious pretext for the Protestant success of capitalism.[41] But Blake goes beyond Weber to anticipate Ruskin's literal reading of the parable as the economic foundation of "moral culture." For Blake, the secret of political economics is that its labor theory of value mediates between life and death. The secret of Blake's poetic economics is that this is no secret, that no "universal interpreter," other than the imagination, is required. Blake's own exchanges perform the mediation precisely, by emancipating the Word which is golden from the economic encumbrances of gold. *Jerusalem* would be, literally, the currency of exchange which redeems those other exchanges of coin for which Christ was betrayed, if only it were believed.

The crisis of belief is the last obstacle to Los's labor. In the poet's exchanges, the spending of one's talent and the exertion of

one's labor result literally in giving oneself away, as Jesus says to
Albion: "Unless I die thou canst not live" (96.14). The natural
recompense of Los's labor is that he achieves a vision of mutual
dependence in which dependence does not presuppose weakness,
although "every kindness to another is a little Death" (96.27). The
"Divine Vision" which Los "kept . . . in time of trouble" (95.20)
is, after all, a vision of men mutually laboring, as Albion reveals by

> Compelling Urizen to his Furrow; & Tharmas to his
> Sheepfold;
> And Luvah to his Loom: Urthona he beheld mighty
> labouring at
> His Anvil, in the Great Spectre Los unwearied labouring
> & weeping. [95.16-18]

But the value of the labor which Los bestows cannot be understood until it is commanded. There is no pricing at the end of
Jerusalem but merely an exchange of (labor) equivalents in which
mutual dependence is both "clearly seen / And seeing" (98.39-40).
When Jesus enters the world at the end of *Jerusalem* as "the likeness & similitude of Los" (96.7), then Los may be beheld in his
ultimate dependence as the Spectre of Urthona, and Albion may
behold his dependence upon Jesus as a form of his dependence
upon Los: "I see thee in the likeness & similitude of Los my
Friend" (96.22). In Albion's eyes (and in ours), these resem-
blances between Los and Jesus culminate in grammatical equivalences: naming (by apposition) Los as "my Friend," he names
(by direct address) Jesus as "my Friend." In short, there is no
further need for grammatical divisions: apposition and direct
address are equivalent; nominal resemblance equals real identity.
Albion becomes not just "England who is Brittania" (95.22),
but all being.

Furthermore, the grammar of economic equivalences between
the means and the end of labor is also deconstructed. In the pres-
ently supererogated language of political economy, there is no
longer a need for an exchange equivalent (money) to intercede
between labor bestowed and labor commanded. For here, market
price equals real price; labor bestowed and labor commanded correspond and are equivalent. Thus economic exchanges become as
certain as meaning. Being geniuses together, all men labor toward
the same end, a mutual dependence ("for Man is Love: / As God

is Love" [96.26–27]), in which the effect of no man's labor is
slighted or discredited.

If this vision, adduced through the fictive and mythic discourse
of the poem itself, is achieved through one man's art, it is not attained at the cost of other men's labor. Art impoverishes no one—
except the artist himself ("as I have found," Blake said, "to my
Cost these Forty Years"). The *cost* is the measure of labor dis-
placed and devalued "in the desolate market where none come to
buy" (*The Four Zoas: Night the Second,* 35.14). In *Jerusalem,*
however, Blake brought his work to participate in a larger economy which extends beyond its self-enclosed fictions to include its
potential readers as well. By the end of the poem, there is no audience in the sense of a public for whom the poet-engraver produces
in hope of making a living. Rather, the "Reader" whom Blake
addresses in the first plates of *Jerusalem* has been subsumed into
the production of the poem itself. Erdman's description of the
penultimate plate 99, in which Jesus-Albion embraces Jerusalem,
is half right: "These two persons must now symbolize all the divided persons in the now whole Song. . . . "[42] But the symbols embrace more than this. The stanza directly above the embrace insists
that "*All* Human Forms" are "identified," not simply all the persons in the poem. In *Jerusalem,* Blake's "Reader" is ultimately
"identified" by the poem as one of the persons of the poem. The
kind of return which the economics of the imagination allows for
itself is portrayed in the last plate (100), where Los-Blake is pic-
tured looking back on this work of final representation:

> All Human Forms identified even Tree Metal Earth & Stone,
>   all
> Human Forms identified, living going forth & returning
>   wearied
> Into the Planetary lives of Years Months Days & Hours
>   reposing
> And then Awaking into his Bosom in the Life of Immortality.
>   [99.1–4]

All things become commodities of value—"even Tree metal Earth
& Stone"—because they may be identified with "All Human
Forms," just as all human forms may be identified in the one depicted embrace. The economic exchanges may be read in the aesthetic exchanges between the engraved figures and the engraved

verse. In the direct imaginative apprehension of labor value, there is no need for money and its alienated expression of labor production to mediate between commodity and representation, because labor imaginatively exchanged does not exhaust itself by being spent, by going forth and returning wearied. Blake could have shown, in the closing plates, that multitude of the blessed "convers[ing] together in Visionary forms dramatic" (99.28) which he describes in the verse. Instead, his representations dramatize and so repeat those pulsations of "the hidden heart," the "invisible gold" by which Los's labor is bestowed on Albion and on all of us.

Jerusalem is the last commodity. On one fictive level, it is all the work of Los. On another level, the whole artifact is William Blake's. Similarly, the way in which we represent ourselves at the end of *Jerusalem* in terms of the worth of these fictions will determine how all human forms will be identified. It is this critical labor on our part which makes visionary forms *dramatic,* turning labor bestowed (by Blake, on Los) into labor commanded (through Los, of us). How we envision that drama is how we represent our own (critical) imagination at work. In the process of becoming a commodity, then, *Jerusalem* endeavors to end one kind of economic process by creating a new one. When literally believed and credited, economic discourse in *Jerusalem* is realized and is therefore terminated. The poem's "business" is to secure a human economy without economic valorization—that is, to create an exchange between poet-seer and see-er-reader which, quite simply, requires no commercial representation beyond that which the artistic product, in its finally identified achievement, embodies.

Blake's momentary triumph over economic discourse places artistic labor in a new economic position. If the artist is to create value and not merely catalogue or rationalize it, then he needs to envision as well a form of labor, ancillary to his own, which will command and credit it. In the second part of this study, we will examine the idea of "labor" as it is conceived in both literature and economics and will define in greater detail how the alien labor of the reader may complement and contradict the poet's own.

PART TWO
LABOR THEORY AND
THE LITERARY WORK

We have more moral, political, and historical wisdom, than we know how to reduce into practise; we have more scientific and oeconomical knowledge than can be accommodated to the just distribution of the produce which it multiplies. The poetry in these systems of thought, is concealed by the accumulation of facts and calculating processes.
—Shelley, A Defence of Poetry

CHAPTER V
The Art of Labor

*Tum variae venere artes. Labor
omnia vicit....*
−*Vergil,* Georgics

The final four chapters of this study will examine how one theoretical concept—labor—evolves simultaneously in economic and imaginative writing. What this evolution signifies in terms of the author-reader relationship has already been suggested in the economic writings of Mill and of Ruskin and in Blake's *Jerusalem.* But who exactly is this "reader"? Is "reader" itself an "unreal word" by which literary men—critics and scholars, if not poets—seek to posit a fictive, and, in this case, economically plausible audience for literary productions?

Raymond Williams's recent observation on the status of the reader does not necessarily answer these queries, but it may lead to more accurate, specific questions: "What emerged in bourgeois economics as the 'consumer'—the abstract figure corresponding to the abstraction of (market and commodity) 'production'—emerged in cultural theory as 'aesthetics' and 'the aesthetic response.' "[1] Williams's suggestion of a correspondence between economic and literary abstractions implies that the fictive relationships within one activity may also correspond to the fictive relationships within the other. He then proceeds to define, in Marxist terms, the "absolute abstraction" of the reading processes described in aesthetic theory "from the social processes within which they are still contained": "Aesthetic theory . . . represents the division of labour in consumption corresponding to the abstraction of art as the division of labour in production" (*Marxism and Literature,* p. 154). Williams's laudable perception of the reader as an aesthetic abstraction is still projected, however, upon a Marxist grid. That is, his judgment of the reading process derives from a Marxist perception of "the social processes" within which aesthetic practices are "contained." He has not judged economic theory as itself an abstraction of "production" and "consumption" corresponding to the abstractions of aesthetic theory. He has identified "reader" and "aesthetic response" as "unreal" terms but has not made the same effort with, say, "division of labor."

On the basis of our findings in the first part of this study, we must reformulate Williams's observation: abstract systems of market and commodity production require a fictive consumer just as artistic productions imply a respondent, a reader. In respect to *this* correspondence, the next four chapters will insist that we not gloss over a codetermining factor: namely, that "the abstraction of art as the division of labour in production" is as much a consequence of economic theory as it is of aesthetic theory. The operative concept, which simultaneously draws together and divides the relationship between producer-artist and consumer-reader, is "labor."

How one assesses "division of labor" as a concept linking economic and aesthetic theory will depend initially upon how one divides economic and aesthetic theory as abstract systems of thought. Both Marxist and structuralist analysts would agree that these systems, viewed as discursive formations, are functionally dependent on each other, but they would disagree over which one, if either, has priority. Following a seminal passage in Marx's *Critique of Political Economy,* Marxist analysis posits economics as the core, the basal structure from which all psychical and social activities are fashioned: "The mode of production in material life determines the general character of the social, political and spiritual processes of life. It is not the consciousness of men that determines their existence, but, on the contrary, their social existence determines their consciousness."[2] When seen as an imaginative structure, however, economics has no defensible claim to priority, but merely takes its place, as an abstract system of thought, among a configuration of similarly *structured* forms of knowledge, such as architecture, biology, literature, and so on. The impartiality of the structuralist perspective is stated by Lévi-Strauss: "The laws of thought, primitive or civilized, are the same as those which find expression in physical reality and in social reality, which is simply one of their aspects."[3] Structuralist analysis is not concerned with determination, with the cause-and-effect relationship between consciousness and social existence. It merely examines theories of cognition as such. Thus, structuralist analysis becomes vulnerable to Marxist counterattack for the simple reason that it often remains—indeed, is predicated upon—a disinterested view of social progress and its modes of consumption. "There is no progress in languages, only change"—this is the cornerstone of structural linguistics (Scholes, p. 18). Moreover, "*laws* of thought" become deducible only on the assumption that *forms* of intellection are structurally homogeneous, aesthetically indifferent. Structuralist criticism tells us nothing about how thought is received in physical and in social reality as *ideas* but only how it is structurally and discursively formulated, once it is received. Marxist criticism, on the other hand, attempts to show how social existence turns thought into political consciousness and then into cultural action, but this attempt depends upon supposing that all cognitive structures can be hierarchically classified as ideological (i.e., as *a posteriori*) expressions of the political economy.

Thus, Marxism presses beyond the theoretical neutrality of structuralism by contending that any analysis which does *not* tell us about the optative aspects of thought—how it is socially realized —has omitted a vital step in the cognitive process; it has, indeed, aestheticized the formation of consciousness. In *The German Ideology*, Marx deprecated the division of labor which abstracts "thought" from the social processes which would render cognition existentially "real":

Division of labour only becomes truly such from the moment
when a division of material and mental labour appears. From
this moment onwards consciousness *can* really flatter itself
that it is something other than consciousness of existing practice, that it *really* represents something without representing
something real; from now on consciousness is in a position to
emancipate itself from the world and to proceed to the formation of "pure" theory, theology, philosophy, ethics, etc.[4]

But here, Marx creates his own ideological abstractions. The difficulty lies in the concealed—that is, the unrecognized—metaphor,
"labor." The exertions of the mind become "mental labor" (which
can therefore be compared to "material labor") only if the idea of
labor itself is metaphorically extended beyond the sphere of economic work to the sphere of imagination. The metaphorical extension is possible because Marx assumes the economic significance of
labor to be primary, economics determining all acts of consciousness. Actually, Marx is making the sociological observation that,
under capitalism, abstract thinkers are separated from those more
"active" members of society (i.e., workers) who "have less time to
make up illusions and ideas about themselves" (*Feuerbach,* p. 52).
But in fact, by speaking of this political process in cognitive terms,
Marx has himself abstracted a secondary sense of labor and applied
it, *mutatis mutandis,* to the primary physical meaning. (And it is
this further abstraction *by the economist* to which Williams's discussion also subscribes.)

What Marx does not tell us is how economics, as a process of
cognition, is itself *re-cognized,* how "labor" as a conceptual term
in economic discourse is extended to other forms of abstract discourse (to literature or to aesthetics, for instance). One notes that
Marx himself has artificially, and perhaps unfairly, divided labor
by measuring mental work against economic principles which it
can only metaphorically approximate. Having taken this metaphysical leap, Marx then condemns ideologists for creating, from
a materialist viewpoint, spurious metaphysical structures—philosophy, theology, ethics, and so on. But nothing indicates Marx's
bias more plainly than his omission of "economics" from this list
of theoretical sciences.

In effect, Marx has regarded the distinction between "material"
and "mental" (like the classical distinction between "object" and
"subject" or between "fact" and "fiction") as the basal polarity

while ignoring the complexity of the term which carries his argument—"labor." His fictive use of "labor" subsequently colors his view of literary production. From the Marxian perspective, one must ask if the literary work of art is regulative or constitutive of a society's collective labors. Does a given piece of literature function merely as a metonymic episode that fictionally represents a society's actual labor practices? Or, is the artist's labor metaphorically constitutive of a society's economic structure and its modes of production? Is literature a superstructural by-product of the economy or may it also embody and prescribe new forms of enlightened labor? Does literature merely play at labor? Are its fictive models ultimately fictitious? Or does literature incorporate socially conscious labor? In respect to society, is the artist a producer?[5]

Most Marxist views of literature are ultimately author-oriented. The application of "labor" to literary activity seeks to determine if imaginative writing is socially useful work (an idea which is bureaucratically perpetuated by such organizations as the Soviet Writers' Union) but that application ceases when the writer's productive status in terms of other socialized labors has been defined. As a result, the importance of the literary *reader* is depreciated when the nonsocialist concept of an economic *consumer* is rejected. What we have lost, in any case, is a "real" sense (to use Marx's own qualification) of the *kind* of labor which a piece of literature expresses and the kind it demands from us as readers. Are they related? Or the same? If so, how? At this point, Marx's terminology simply does not help us to understand what "mental labor" *could* mean when applied to nonmaterialistic work such as reading a text. When one seeks to interpret Marx's own abstract writings, for instance, does a "division" reappear between material and mental labor? As we shall see, Marx himself became increasingly concerned with this question, which we may radically rephrase: how is economics itself a meaningful form of labor? In order to answer these questions, we must seek to understand "labor" as it applies both to the productions of the artist and to the "consumer" role of the reader. By emphasizing the subjective actions of the reader in making a text an object of labor, we may get beyond the rather constrictive question of whether the writer is a worker and address the more significant topic: how does literature itself *work*?

Following Raymond Williams's postulation, therefore, in order to speak of a "consumer" from an abstract economic viewpoint, one must be prepared to speak of a "reader" from an abstract aesthetic or literary viewpoint. Whereas literature is surely "consumed," the economy is just as surely "read." *Labor* is the term by which these activities become commensurable. In trying to delimit labor as an economic concept, a usefully "unreal word," economists have confronted a unique resistance. They have tried to abstract "labor" in its commercial sense from its more general meaning of "work," but, unlike the other unreal words which we have examined, "labor" will not be so easily quantified. The difficulty in applying labor to a work of art is the very difficulty which economists encounter in assessing labor as an aspect of economic production. (Historically, as this chapter will disclose, the economic use of "art" as a synonym for "labor" mirrors the poetic use of "labor" as a synonym for "the aesthetic response.") "Labor" has an emotive charge which will not be straitened by scientific objectivity. The word retains its experiential subjectivity, whether we are speaking of the work of men's hands, childbearing, or the mental exertions occasioned by the imagination; it has a phenomenological urgency and integrity which other ("unreal") economic concepts do not always share.

John Dewey has explained how our response to a work of art partakes of this experiential dimension of labor:

> For to perceive, a beholder must *create* his own experience. And his creation must include relations comparable to those which the original producer underwent. They are not the same in any literal sense. But with the perceiver, as with the artist, there must be an ordering of the elements of the whole that is in form, although not in details, the same as the process of organization the creator of the work consciously experienced. Without an act of recreation the object is not perceived as a work of art.[6]

In examining how labor emerges as a cognitive term in economic discourse, we will also see how "labor" may become a useful critical term for speaking about our cognition of the work of art, about the reader's act of "recreation," and about that "process of organization" which the reader must experience in the same formal way as the artist himself.[7] Wordsworth, for instance, sought to reassess the poet-reader relationship by regarding the text as an occasion and meeting place for multiple labors. He attempted to formulate poetry itself as an economic vocation, to raise the reader to the status of cooperating producer, and so to offer the text as a "contract" between creator and beholder. Finally, in chapter eight, we shall see how William Carlos Williams tried to measure the reader's labor as the exact complement of the artist's own and to define (in *Paterson*) that poetic measure as equivalent to the thing itself, the "real" forms of economic exchange.

The first postulate of classical economics maintains that all theories of labor production must be grounded in a theory of subsistence: "A man must always live by his work, and his wages must at least be sufficient to maintain him."[8] Adam Smith's assertion is the economic equivalent of the biblical dictum that man lives by the sweat of his brow (such is Adam's curse) and that he earns his living by means of his labor only (such is Adam's hope): "For thou shalt eat the labour of thine hands: happy shalt thou be, and it shall be well with thee. Thy wife shall be as a fruitful vine by the sides of thine house: thy children like olive plants round about thy table" (Psalms 128:2–3). But Smith cautions that the sufficient-wages theory of subsistence may not be sufficient—adding that a man's wages "must even upon most occasions be somewhat more [than sufficient to maintain him] ; otherwise it would be impossible for him to bring up a family, and the race of such workmen could not last beyond the first generation" (*WN*, bk. 1, chap. 8).

Karl Marx made Smith's theory axiomatic: a man's wages must *always* be more than sufficient to maintain him, because only through such "excess" can the labor supply be refurbished:

> The labour-power withdrawn from the market by wear and tear and death, must be continually replaced by, at the very least, an equal amount of fresh labour-power. Hence the sum of the means of subsistence necessary for the production of labour-power must include the means necessary for the labourer's substitutes, *i.e.,* his children, in order that this race of peculiar commodity-owners may perpetuate its appearance in the market.[9]

Although both Smith and Marx abandon the biblical condition

that labor must be circumscribed by service to God, they retain the ethical imperative that "the labor of thine hands" is the sole measure of "generation." Smith repeatedly uses the word "must" to describe the moral directive behind labor and subsistence theory, and Marx concludes, "In contradiction therefore to the case of other commodities, there enters into the determination of the value of labour-power a historical and moral element" (*Capital*, 1:171). Having given up the biblical sense of sufficiency, then, economic theory is obliged to develop a definition of subsistence based on economic principles alone. Indeed, the subsistence theory of wages presumes that economic regulation alone can effect the same just rewards for labor as promised by God, but by means of the wage-price mechanism rather than by means of divine mercy and grace.

Max Weber argued (in *The Protestant Ethic*) that European economic theory was sanctioned by a religiously conditioned "work ethic." Certain aspects of labor theory, such as its residual "moral element," would seem to confirm Weber's thesis. But labor theory also provides one way in which theoretical economics can ground its often abstract investigation of production in that which is both palpable and, at the same time, charged with subjective meaning—namely, in the reality of work. The economists' desire to keep economic questions of price and wages rooted in the palpable reality of human industry as well as in the equally palpable reality of technological and mechanical industrialization often distorts logic. In *Economics of Industry* (1879), Alfred Marshall surprisingly asserts: "But at any time and place [wages] are determined by the social and economic condition of the people, and they may be said to *measure* the efforts involved in the work." This is patently untrue, for, as one critic has remarked, "What they measure is the value of the work done, not the effort involved."[10] Even Marshall seems to know that he is on thin ice, for he hedges his assertion with the conditional "may be said to" (and he does not repeat this misjudgment in his later work, *Principles of Economics*). What is significant, here, is the economist's desire to relate economic remuneration to effort, to compute the wages of labor in terms of a measurable quantity of human industry, to keep *work* and *labor* commensurate.

Economic theory has, in effect, weaned the valorization of "labor" away from the psychosocial phenomenon of "work."

Before Marx and Engels, economists rarely differentiated between
the two terms. Smith, like his predecessors, used "work" and
"labor" interchangeably, the way they often are used in everyday
speech (and the way they are used in the King James Bible). For
Smith, labor is nothing but productive work: that is, work that
creates permanent objects of utility. In its generation of useful
commodities, productive work becomes a way of securing national
wealth, and wealth, when properly produced, is a way of securing
psychic and sexual well-being:

> The liberal reward of labour, as it encourages the propagation,
> so it increases the industry of the common people. The wages
> of labour are the encouragement of industry, which, like ev-
> ery other human quality, improves in proportion to the en-
> couragement it receives. A plentiful subsistence increases the
> bodily strength of the labourer, and the comfortable hope of
> bettering his condition, and of ending his days perhaps in
> ease and plenty, animates him to exert that strength to the
> utmost. Where wages are high, accordingly, we shall always
> find the workmen more active, diligent, and expeditious than
> where they are low. . . .[*WN*, bk. 1, chap. 8]

Nothing indicates Smith's premise more clearly than his identification of "industry" as a "human *quality*," so that labor, when
animated and encouraged, aspires to "the comfortable hope of
bettering" the laborer's "condition." When labor is properly rewarded, then labor not only betters the qualitative conditions of
life, but it also propagates life. In this context, labor is both economically and sexually potent. In economic discourse, labor always
means masculine or "male labor" to distinguish it from childbearing, or female labor, but, for Smith, male labor is literally connected to the business of generating and supporting life. The wages of
the laborer must maintain not only him but also his family, even
beyond the first generation. If labor is the basis of economic production, then it must ultimately bear adequate fruit to sustain
economic consumption. Labor is, in the end, the economic expression of manhood: "The property which every man has in his own
labour, as it is the original foundation of all other property, so it
is the most sacred and inviolable. The patrimony of a poor man
lies in the strength and dexterity of his hands: and to hinder him
from employing this strength and dexterity in what manner he

thinks proper without injury to his neighbour is a plain violation of this most sacred property."[11] In identifying labor as "sacred," economic discourse declares the moral authority behind its own theoretical principles.

It was Locke who had first asserted that the work of a man's hands is "the unquestionable property of the laborer," that the investment of such work is the investment of himself, and that, so invested, the laborer has a right (a *divine* right, in Locke's view) to be compensated or rewarded for it:

> Though the earth and all inferior creatures be common to all men, yet every man has a "property" in his own "person". This nobody has any right to but himself. The "labour" of his own body and the "work" of his own hands, we may say, are properly his. Whatsoever, then, he removes out of the state that Nature hath provided and left it in, he has mixed his labour with it, and joined it to something that is his own and thereby makes it his property. It being by him removed from the common state Nature placed it in, it hath by this labour something annexed to it that excludes the common right of other men. . . .[12]

Normally, Locke uses the words "labor" and "work," as he uses the words "Property" (land) and "property" (attributes or characteristics), as if they were interchangeable. In this passage, however, "labor" comes to have a more specific meaning precisely because the properties of work come to have a proprietary significance in respect to nature. "Labor" has become something more difficult, more laborious than "work"; it is the representation or embodiment of work, work realized in property. Thus, labor is work objectively embodied and quantitatively represented as a commodity or thing.

David Hume's understanding of what labor adds to work to make it economically significant is consistent with Locke's view: "Every thing in the world is purchased by labour; and our passions are the only causes of labour."[13] Hume's sentence is actually an enthymeme: passions are the causes of labor; labor purchases "every thing" in the world; therefore, labor expresses man's passions as objective and real *things*. For Locke, the fact of labor "provides the moral and philosophical justification for the institution of private property," as W. A. Weisskopf has explained.[14]

But, metaphysically, labor is clearly more than this: labor not only, as Weisskopf says, "makes things economically valuable," but labor also becomes a thing in itself. Labor is both process and product: it is the process by which man participates with nature in the discovery of use value, and it is the product of that participation, an economically valuable commodity of exchange extracted from nature. In Hume's terms, labor is the *fact* of passion.

In economic terms, labor becomes "factual" when it can be priced. The value of labor is measured economically not by work done but by the cost of commodities. Thus, Marx concluded that "the relation of the producers to the sum total of their own labour is presented to them as a social relation, existing not between themselves, but between the products of their labour" (*Capital*, 1:72). Simply put, under the conditions of capitalist production, "a social relation" develops which depends upon the nonequivalency of labor and commodities, the discontinuity between wages and prices. Marx thought, with some justification, that he was the first to understand the distinction: "I was the first to point out and to examine critically this two-fold nature of the labour contained in commodities" (ibid., 1:41). Engels, footnoting Marx, further clarified this "two-fold nature": "The English language has two different expressions for these two different aspects of labour: in the Simple Labour-process, the process of producing Use-Values, it is *Work:* in the process of creation [*sic*] of Value, it is Labour, taking the term in its strictly economic sense" (ibid., 1:186). But the "strictly economic sense" has strained the meaning of "value," for here "work" is the qualitative, "labor" the quantitative, term. The difference between simple commodity production and value production is the difference between an economy based upon the direct exchange of commodities and an economy based upon monetary exchange. To use the terms developed in part one of this study, "work" is a factor in all economies, however primitive. But "labor" is a factor only in economics—that is, in the institutionalized process of "the economy." In such structured economies, in fact, labor and work are not semantically cognate. Often, they are antithetical.

Marx was certainly, as he claims, the first "to examine critically" labor's double role as economic process and economic product. But he was not the first to point it out. In fact, by reconstructing with greater accuracy the discursive event which is "labor," one may observe, once again and in more detail, how the economic imagination generates its own art, an economics of the imagination.

From the beginnings of economic theory, the creation of labor value was connected with the idea of "art." Pre-Smithian theorists called "work," when described in terms of its economic productiveness, "art" or "ingenious labor." E. A. J. Johnson, in his pioneering study of these two terms, has noted that economic writers did not always use these words precisely or clearly.[15] For an economic historian such as Johnson, this ambiguity is symptomatic of the improvisational methodology of economics before Adam Smith. For the student of the imagination, however, this ambiguity is symptomatic of, and perhaps crucial to, all discursive economies, whether the system under discussion is "economics" or "poetry."

Sir William Petty, the seventeenth-century political economist, sometimes used "art" as a kind of antonym for "simple labour," and he sometimes suggested that "art" was one of the four factors of production, along with "land," "labour," and "stock." At times, Petty seems to mean that art is craftiness, the ability to use one's labor more efficiently. At other times, he seems to mean that art is the ability to save labor. In one passage, he puts all these meanings together:

> If by simple labour I could dig and prepare for seed a hundred acres in a thousand days; suppose I spend a hundred days in studying a more compendious way, and in contriving tools for the same purpose; but in all that hundred days dig nothing, but in the remaining nine hundred days I dig two hundred acres of ground; then I say that the said art which cost but one hundred days' invention is worth one man's labour for ever; because the new art and one man performed as much as two men could have done without it.[16]

One notes that this "art" improves what Marx called "material labor" *by means of* "mental labor." The art of Petty's "political arithmetic" further enhances the work of simple arithmetic, for "art" is able here to save work by creating a new species of productive labor. The cost of "art's" invention may be measured temporally (it has cost one hundred days of labor) but the "worth" of this invention transcends temporal measurement. Once realized, its value is "for ever."

Elaborating upon Petty, Malachy Postlethwayt in the eighteenth century defined "Manufacture or ingenious labour" as "the art of working up the productions of Nature."[17] Thus, the complex Renaissance use of "art" carried over into later economic discourse. For Postlethwayt, art was the doing over by hand (*manu-facture*) of natural—that is, agricultural—products. What man adds to natural production is his own ingenuity; "ingenious labor," therefore, becomes the addition of wit or imagination (*ingenium*) to labor so that man's industry can become more industrious. We might henceforth speak of "the art of ingenious labor," for such art creates "the arts"—"useful arts" which ingeniously make labor both more productive and more pleasureable, less like labor. Not only are the works of man's hands improved and the works of nature enhanced, but "ingenious labor" also constitutes a means of mental enrichment: "by giving real existence to [the workers'] ideas," the manufactural art "has a greater tendency to polish and humanize mankind . . . than any ideal contemplation could do."[18] Thus, labor effects both a quantitative and a qualitative improvement; the utility of this "art" encompasses both intellectual and material advancement.

Finally, one of the "useful arts" which arises from labor is posited as the economic art itself, the "mental labor" which addresses itself directly to the means and ends of "material labor." Sir James Steuart's *Principles of Political Oeconomy* (1767) identifies economics as an art in the same way and for the same reasons that earlier writers identified labor as an art: each expands the usefulness of man's enterprise. "The great art therefore of political oeconomy is, first to adapt the different operations of it to the spirit, manners, habits, and customs of the people, and afterwards to model these circumstances so, as to be able to introduce a set of new and more useful institutions."[19] Closer to our own day, John Neville Keynes maintains this sense of the word "art" in his essay "On the Scope of Political Economy Considered as an Art."[20] "Art" provides a supple connective, then, between economically productive labor and the labor of the economist's own imagination in "adapt[ing] " and "model[ing] " economic circumstances in order "to introduce a set of new and more useful institutions." "Art," too, is a "useful" word which, in its specialized economic sense, allows the economist to postulate a productive value for his own labor, even as he assesses the value of "labor" in strictly commercial transactions.

Thus, when Thomas Mun, writing in 1664, differentiates be-

tween natural and artificial wealth, he notes that to understand
the importance of the difference requires the art of the economist.
Natural wealth arises simply from the bounty of nature. (The
Americas possess, in Mun's view, such natural wealth in the form
of gold.) Artificial wealth on the other hand is created by human
labor. (The Italians, in Mun's example, have excelled at such industry by using the "raw Silks" of "Cicilia" in multiple forms of
employment.) Mun concludes: "And forasmuch as the people
which live by the Arts are far more in number than they who are
masters of the fruits, we ought the more carefully to maintain
those endeavours of the multitude, in whom doth consist the
greatest strength and riches both of King and Kingdom: for where
the people are many, and the arts good, there the traffique must
be great, and the Countrey rich."[21] Raw materials are turned by
art into useful manufactures; this process is itself turned, by the
economist's art, into an improved form of functional economic
knowledge. By chapter's end, Mun thinks about his own art, in
which he intends to be persuasive by virtue of "brevity and plainness." In a compound closing sentence, Mun's description of the
economic arts is interlaced with a description of his own labor:

> Compare our Fleece-wools with our Cloth, which requires
> shearing, washing, carding, spinning, [w]eaving, fulling, dying,
> dressing and other trimmings, and we shall find these Arts
> more profitable than the natural wealth, whereof I might in-
> stance other examples, but I will not be more tedious, for if
> I would amplify upon this and the other particulars before
> written, I might find matter sufficient to make a large volume,
> but my desire in all is only to prove what I propound with
> brevity and plainness. [P. 13]

In disclaiming a larger design and fuller amplication for his volume, Mun extends the comparison which he invites us to make.
Like the mechanic "Arts," Mun's economic art also participates in
the country's artifical wealth. What Mun adds to the economy of
manufacture is a knowledge of how the economy functions to en-
hance "England's Treasure," to make it "more profitable." Thus,
the stylistic avoidance of "tedious" amplification is also an economic virture. Like the arts which he praises in the commercial
sphere, his art aspires to be accessible (to the reader) and therefore
useful, capable of being applied. Brevity and plainness do prove

what he propounds insofar as the literary virtue of economy
is also here an economic *exemplum* of a labor well done.

By considering the function of wealth, Mun also considers the
function of the economist. Wealth is dependent upon foreign
trade: "For so much Treasure only will be brought in or carried
out of a Commonwealth, as the Forraign Trade doth over or under
ballance in value. And this must come to pass by a Necessity, beyond all resistance" (p. 87). A favorable balance of trade necessarily generates more wealth, and this means that the merchant's art
is a primary necessity. All other labors must be formed in its
image, making one useful and praiseworthy *"School of our Arts."*
Mun lets us "behold," therefore, "the true form and worth of for-
rayn Trade" (p. 88). Mun's discursive industry, his explication of
the mercantile economy, does more than illuminate England's artificial wealth; it helps to school the diverse arts into a unified treasure: "I write the more of these excesses, because they do so greatly
wast[e] our wealth, which is the main subject of this whole Books
discourse: and indeed our wealth might be a rare discourse for all
Christendome to admire and fear, if we would but add *Art* to *Nature,* our *labour* to our *natural means*" (p. 73). Mun's equivocation
here on the word "discourse" is scarcely noticeable, since, throughout his treatise, the book's "discourse" has aspired to be identified
with the discourse of "our wealth."[22] If wealth is improved by
adding art to nature and labor to natural means, then merchants
gain wealth by their arts, and economists maintain that treasure by
theirs. In Marvell's "Horatian Ode," Mun's contemporary urged
upon Cromwell a similar instruction in the whole school of the
arts: "The same *Arts* that did *gain* / A *Pow'r* must it *maintain.*"[23]

The arts of military and civil government (as invoked by Marvell) and the arts of economic management (as evoked by Mun)
would become, in Bishop Sprat's view, the basis of a new kind of
literary "art" as well. In his *History of the Royal Society*, published three years after Mun's tract, Sprat noted that "the trials
of art have been . . . little united with the plain labours of mens
hands," and argued that the new practical arts might furnish a
new subject for the poetic imagination as well:

> The *Wit* that is founded on the Arts of mens hands is mascu-
> line and durable: It consists of *Images* that are generally ob-
> serv'd, and such visible things which are familiar to mens
> minds. This therefore I will reckon as the first sort [of *Wit* in

writing] , which is still improvable by the advancement of
Experiments.

And to this I will add the *Works of Nature,* which are one
of the best and most fruitful soils for the growth of *Wit.* It is
apparent that the defect of the *Antients* in *Natural Knowledge*
did also steighten their Fancies: Those few things which they
knew, they us'd so much, and appli'd so often, that they even
almost wore them away by their using. . . .

It is now therefore seasonable for *Natural Knowledge* to
come forth, and to give us the *understanding* of new *Virtues*
and *Qualities* of things: which may relieve their fellow-creatures, that have long born the burden alone, and have long
bin vex'd by the imagination of *Poets.* This charitable assistance *Experiments* will soon bestow.[24]

Practical knowledge and "experiments" improve poetic wit while
improving the social well-being of "fellow-creatures." The case of
Thomas Mun's self-reflective economic writing, coupled with
Sprat's contemporary view of the aims of the Royal Society in
dealing with both imaginative and experimental questions, gives us
a direct and explicit example of "labor" considered as a subject
with both an economic and a literary significance. The practical
work of economics will create a new work for the poetic imagination, and all will coalesce to form, as Mun had intimated, a single
"School of our Arts"—the explicit purpose of the Royal Society.
The mid-seventeenth century was, it will be remembered, the time
of a great revival of the georgic tradition in English literature, a
genre devoted to the interdependence of poetry and labor.[25] Significantly, it is the period, too, of the first great flowering of English economic theory in which "labor" was specifically seen as an
"art."[26] Vergil's *labor omnia vicit* was in the process of acquiring
a direct commercial meaning and was coming to have a history of
theoretical economic interpretation as well. The next step would
be to show how labor as imaginative work and labor as the work
of men's hands were philosophically connected.

David Hume took that step by noting that "in times when industry and the arts flourish, men are kept in perpetual occupation,
and enjoy, as their reward, the occupation itself, as well as those
pleasures which are the fruit of their labour" (p. 21). The rewards
of such art may even transcend the usual Christian prohibition
against profiting from service to Mammon. Aquinas and other

medieval scholastics had noted that if a merchant or laborer improved a product through his own labor, then he could charge a
higher price for it. By such a price, the laborer "would seem to receive the reward of his labour" and, incidentally, to avoid the stig-
ma of usury.[27] Hume's argument is a secular version of the same
economy: by proper use of "the arts," according to Hume, "the
minds of men, being once roused from their lethargy, and put into
a fermentation, turn themselves on all sides, and carry improvements into every art and science" (p. 22). Such "improvements,"
he concludes, cement human society and make it more productive
and more humane. "Thus, *industry, knowledge,* and *humanity,* are
linked together by the indissoluable chain" (p. 23).

In Hume's epistemological chain, the useful arts constitute
unique factors of production and "an additional means of growing
rich" (as they did for Petty also). But they further sponsor, in
Hume's view, an improvement in the refined arts and so lead directly to that art whose mode of production is the imagination—
the art of poets, painters, belle-lettrists, and so on. Improvements
in the liberal arts refine, therefore, the meaning of "riches."

But Hume is virtually alone among classical economic philosophers in thinking so. The more typical view is that held by Adam
Smith, who classified most imaginative labors as unproductive because they rendered only a momentary service, not a palpable and
usable commodity. Among these "most frivolous professions"
Smith numbered "churchmen, lawyers, physicians, men of letters
of all kinds; players, buffoons, musicians, opera-singers, opera-
dancers, etc." These laborers do not "put into motion a quantity
of labour equal to that which had originally produced it." Thus,
their labor does not result in a permanent object, permanence being equated in Smith's mind with that which is vendible: "Like the
declamation of the actor, the harangue of the orator, or the tune
of the musician, the work of all of them perishes in the very instant of its production" (*WN*, bk. 2, chap. 3). Apparently, Smith
would have exempted economists from the category "men of letters of all kinds." (Does this beautifully constructed sentence of
Smith's also perish in the very instant of its production?) Smith
defined "labor" more systematically than did Hume, Mun, or
Petty but only by excluding artistic "work" from significant consideration in the wealth of nations. His failure to discuss *this* type
of "service" in light of commodity production would create, in its

wake, an unwarranted dilemma. For Smith implies that in order
to be taken seriously from an economic point of view, literary
work would have to demonstrate that its aesthetic permanence was
also vendible, that it could sell. Or conversely, art might "prove"
its resistance to commerce by affirming the instantaneousness of
its happening, by aggrandizing its ability to perish, by turning the
temporal fate of Shelley's Ozymandias into an aesthetic manifesto.
From an economic viewpoint, however, we may see that artistic
labor which aspires to either condition or which relies on either
premise is, in the exact sense of the word, reactionary; it becomes
a further concession to a Smithian theory of artistic value, not a
refutation of it.

Smith, we should remember, is not deprecating art as such, only
its *economic* status. Ricardo focuses Smith's conclusions. Ricardo
noted that imaginative work does have value, but its value is un-
related to the investment of labor:

> There are some commodities, the value of which is deter-
> mined by their scarcity alone. No labour can increase the
> quantity of such goods, and therefore their value cannot be
> lowered by an increased supply. Some rare statues and pic-
> tures, scarce books and coins, wines of a peculiar quality . . .
> are all of this description. Their value is wholly independent
> of the quantity of labour originally necessary to produce
> them, and varies with the varying wealth and inclinations of
> those who are desirous to possess them.[28]

Ricardo is content to regard artistic *productions* (such as statues,
coins, and books) as economic commodities, but he denies to artistic *process* a similar economic identity. That is, the "value" of
these artifacts "is wholly independent of the quantity of labour
originally necessary to produce them," whereas the value of other
commodities is wholly dependent, according to Ricardian theory,
upon their labor investment. Thus, the work of the imagination is
not ultimately "labor," economically speaking. Unlike other commodities, the economic value of art objects exists beyond and
apart from the artist's work and merely "varies with the varying
wealth and inclinations of those who are desirous to possess them."
Ricardo tacitly assumes not only that the painter's brush consumes his dream, but that it consumes in every economically significant sense his labor as well. Ruskin noted the same phenom-

enon in the work of living artists: "For remember always, that the price of a picture by a living artist never represents, never *can* represent, the quantity of labour or value in it" (*Works*, 16:86). As commodity, the artifact represents instead the displacement of the artist's labor.

Crudely put, the artist himself is economically disenfranchised, even as his productions, his artistic accomplishments, become economically aggrandized. This is the irony that Ruskin's "political economy of art" sought to make more understandable, perhaps to redress. Precisely at this point, the "art" of labor and the value of the art that such labor produces become divisive concepts; indeed, the useful ambivalence of the word "art" is now polarized—it becomes a paradox.

An excerpt from one of Hart Crane's letters to his sometime benefactor, Otto Kahn, will serve to exemplify this familiar predicament: "There is no monetary standard of evaluation for works of art, I know, but I cannot help feeling that a great poem may well be worth at least the expenditure necessary for merely the scenery and costumes of many a flashy and ephemeral play, or for a motor car."[29] Often relegated to this style of complaint, such lamentations about art's commodity-poor productiveness only confuse the issue further. Crane is here speaking of the need to secure some form of acceptable employment for himself so that he will have both money enough and time to write his "great poem." The economically discrete question of his labor's value is first juxtaposed with the extraneous concession that "there is no monetary standard of evaluation for works of art." He thus conflates the labor process with its products and is then reduced to speaking of the "worth" of "a great poem," urging his correspondent (and patron) to understand "worth" in its economic sense while pretending that a "monetary standard" for art is meaningless, an affront to the artist's labors. Conceding the clash between what he "knows" and what he "cannot help feeling," he attacks at last the paradoxical injustice of his situation by affirming a further paradox, the value of "a great poem" in contrast to "the expenditure necessary" for "flashy and ephemeral" commodities. And with this stroke, he asks funding for both his labor and his art. One must admire the intellectual contortions of this argument, even as one sympathizes with the frustration and humiliation which underlie and provoke them. But the equivocal status of the artist as defined by classical economic theory has not been resolved here, only manipulated and leavened with a mixture of self-pity, futility, and pride.

The tension between aesthetic and economic processes erupts whenever the artist attempts to describe the dynamics of his own labor, but the modern (i.e., post-eighteenth-century) artist has acquired a singularly pressing need to resolve that tension. Crane seems to offer poiesis not merely as the aesthetic equivalent of economic labor, but also as its paradigm. And yet, this very aestheticism complicates the economic issues that we have seen raised through the economists' definition of artistic "labor." But the artist's status is complicated for another reason. Although he shares Adam's curse, he also bears an extra-Adamic burden: to create *in the artifact* the illusion and aura of non-work:

> A line will take us hours maybe;
> Yet if it does not seem a moment's thought,
> Our stitching and unstitching has been naught.[30]

In Yeats's view, the labor of the poem is to conceal and to understate the poet's creative labor and not, as in the "real world" of economic process, to aggrandize or even to inflate that labor's worth. For Yeats as for Crane, aesthetic needs only confirm the economic disregard of a poet's work:

> For to articulate sweet sounds together
> Is to work harder than all these, and yet
> Be thought an idler by the noisy set
> Of bankers, schoolmasters, and clergymen
> The martyrs call the world. ["Adam's Curse," ll. 10-14]

Though we may like, and even value, sweet sounds, we distrust as economically idle any "labor" that articulates, as its primary product, only pleasure.

In his *Autobiography,* Yeats wrote, "I did not read economics."[31] But he had read William Morris, in whose revisionist, visionary Marxism "Art" was posited as an antidote for "Labour": "The aim of art [is] to destroy the curse of labour by making work the pleasurable satisfaction of our impulse towards energy, and giving to that energy hope of producing something worth the exercise."[32] Morris's terms are a simple inversion of Adam Smith's: labor has become unproductive of moral, social, and cultural good; therefore, only art is productive. Morris's dichotomy remains the same as Smith's but with the adjectives "productive" and "unproductive" silently reversed. In that (artful) reversal, "labor" is stripped of its economic meaning. Assisted by art, it comes to signify not work devoted to economic ends but work consecrated to societal fulfillment and individual satisfaction. For Morris, art will remove labor from the onus of economic valorization by treating economics as if it had no claim to man's moral and intellectual energies. Thus, Morris "solves" the economic depreciation of art by using art to supplant economics: "One day we shall win back Art, that is to say the pleasure of life; win back Art again to our daily labour" (p. 635).

To define art in terms of labor is actually a belated attempt to win back art from the definitions of labor offered by economists.[33] For Morris, profit making "is of its very nature destructive of Art" (p. 637). But art produces another sort of "nature," a social view of "profit." It provides an imaginative economics capable of assessing the true "worth" of labor, for the aim of art is "to make man's work happy and his rest fruitful" (p. 591). Morris reconstitutes a somewhat unexpected utilitarian argument for the "socialism" of Art based upon its utility for others and its power to elicit contemplative ease. Art, therefore, is to be "done *for* some one" who is, in turn, "to be made happier by it . . . , so that the vacancy which is the besetting evil of [the idle or restful] mood might give place to pleased contemplation, dreaming, or what you will" (p. 589). We shall win back the utilitarian value of art, then, when we are able to accept it as the reward and end of labor.

Now art and labor seem adversaries. But, when art triumphs against capitalist systems of commerce, labor will defy its economic reductiveness and reassert its "natural" origins not in property or wages but in play. Like Thomas Jefferson, who, in the Declaration of Independence, dropped the economic topic of property from the Lockean equation which included life and liberty, so Morris has proposed a new *trivium* founded not upon art, labor, and commerce, but upon art, labor, and the pursuit of happiness. Whereas the modern world has "exalted Commerce into a sacred religion," Morris proposes a humanist religion of "Art, the divine solace of human labour" (pp. 626–27). Yeats completes the anthropomorphic theology in the personified allegory of "Among School Children": "Labour is blossoming or dancing where / The body is not bruised to pleasure soul" (ll. 57–58).

Both Morris and Yeats complicate the issue raised in this chapter by simultaneously expanding and qualifying the context in which we must speak of "the art of labor." In Yeats's poem, the "or" which separates "blossoming" and "dancing" quivers with imaginative potentiality: it seems to function as the connective "and," linking natural and artistic process. But Yeats's suggestiveness was doctrinaire in Morris; labor acquired its natural potency (as a blossoming thing) precisely at the moment when it became aesthetisized (as a dancing thing). Morris made art seem to be a refinement of labor, its truest and fullest expression. The "aesthetic response" which is now the provenance of a consumer ought to become, according to Morris, the inevitable culmination of the labor process. Labor will remain disembodied in the work of art as long as labor itself is psychically unproductive—as it is under current systems of commerce. Morris would thus transform Hart Crane's self-defeating lament into a self-affirming rhapsody, a prologomenon for Morris's view of socialism. Art enriches the work of the laborer because, in art, the body is not bruised to pleasure soul. In breaking down the difference between process and product, Morris sees "Labor" as both the dancer and the dance at the same time—that is, as an economically "pure" commodity. To paraphrase the motto of General Electric, process should be labor's most important product. Psychologically, art assures labor of its processive value when it provides the laborer with the means of transforming his daily toil into a "pleased contemplation" of his own "impulse towards energy."

For Yeats, the poem becomes an "Image" of this "impulse"; thus it symbolizes its *own* labor value. Previous criticism of Yeats's work has offered to explain how this Image comes about, how it is symbolically realized through the images of a given poem.[34] But a poem such as "Among School Children" raises another question: how is this value to be *recognized*? The question is asked directly by the school inspector: "How can we know the dancer from the dance?" Despite the economic metaphor of labor in this poem, the poem's labor value to the poet is not economic but cognitive; in Morris's terms, the ability to ask the question is, in terms of the growth in the speaker's consciousness, its own reward. And indeed, the closing question is framed in a celebratory mode: "O body swayed to music! O brightening glance!"

But the "we" invoked at the end of "Among School Children"

engages another question, which we must move beyond this particular poem to answer. How exactly does the relationship between
poet and reader define the labor *in* the poem—that is, the way in
which the poem itself *works* as a cognitive process? What began as
the solitary meditation of a "smiling public man" who, in the
course of his daily work, finds himself "walk[ing] through the
long schoolroom questioning," turns at the end into a meditative
question which concerns the implied reader as well—how can *we*
know? The mental labor of the schoolchildren at their studies has
been mediated by the inspector-poet into the larger issue of the
cognitive value of poiesis as such.

How we answer these issues is crucial to Morris's and to Yeats's
view of the aesthetic response. If art is to improve labor, then we
must know how to tell the cognitive process of reading from the
economic process by which the poem becomes a consumable commodity. We must be able to recognize the value of the poet's labor
as distinct from the poem's status as product or commodity. By
viewing the poem as a symbolic form, Yeats was able to incorporate the labor of the imagination into a self-realizing poetic. The
painter's brush (or the poet's pen) might then consume the dream,
but it would not body forth a consumer. Rather, consummation
(achievement) would become synonymous with consumption (exhaustion), because the end of such imaginative production would
be synonymous with its means. The mystery which Marx attrib-
uted to commodities is thus mediated by a Keatsian mystery of
negative capability: the ability to function in uncertainty and
doubt. When labor is finally bodied forth—realized as the poem—
then the laborer-poet also becomes the principal consumer of it.
In this (imperfect) product he recognizes not merely the cost of
the imagination's exertions but also the pricelessness of his original dream.

Yeats rightly understood this poetic economy as a Romantic
legacy. What has not been adequately perceived is how Yeats's
division of labor goes back to the economists of the Romantic
period as well. In "Coole Park and Ballylee, 1931," Yeats called
himself one of the "last romantics," and he originally intended
to use the following stanza, later published separately as "The
Choice" in *The Winding Stair* (1933), in that poem:

> The intellect of man is forced to choose
> Perfection of the life, or of the work,

And if it take the second must refuse
A heavenly mansion, raging in the dark.
When all that story's finished, what's the news?
In luck or out the toil has left its mark:
That old perplexity an empty purse,
Or the day's vanity, the night's remorse.[35]

The poem initially tasks the reader's power simply to paraphrase
it. Certain crucial explanations have been omitted, such as why the
life and the work are antipathetic in the first place, why "the intellect of man" is forced to make such a choice at all. But, we are
told, if man chooses perfection of the work, then he "must refuse"
the image of heaven which "perfection of the life" traditionally
promises. "Raging in the dark," therefore, defines the existential
state of the intellect which has not chosen to perfect the "life."
The last four lines explain two equally dismaying effects of this
rage: either "the work" will fail economically to sustain the life or
it will fail to sustain "the intellect." In the first case, the man is
left with the perplexity of an empty purse; in the second, with imaginative futility, a "rage" squandered in remorse for the day's
vain labor. The poem also suggests, in retrospect, that all labor is
vain which seeks to measure its dream of perfection against any
worldly, economic equivalent.

Having spoken, then, of raging, the speaker seems to rescind
that rage, discarding it as a kind of pose: "When all that story's
finished, what's the news?" Well, we are told, "the toil has left its
mark." Although this "toil" must initially refer to the "work" of
line 2, it simultaneously implies the toil of the choice itself. This
latter toil—the work of choosing—has left its mark in the oddly
perfected despair of lines 7 and 8 in which the near rhymes remind
the speaker (and us) that his toil cannot succeed either way—either
by working for economic gain or by rejecting it. Psychologically,
therefore, the poem occurs in reverse order: having already found
that the toil of choosing *has* left its mark, the poem's opening lines
recapitulate the circumstances of a choice which has been already
determined and made. No choice occurs in the poem. As merely
the dramatization of a life already spent in living out its optative
possibilities, the poem reveals that the poet's "rage" (l. 4) has
been already chastened and subdued by the perplexities it has
learned to live with.

In a basic sense, the "mark" which the "toil" has left is invisible, an internal, psychic wound in the speaker-poet. In a more provocative sense, its mark is left in the figure of the poem itself. The choice described *in* the poem is realized *as* the poem, a kind of self-fulfilling prophesy. Unable to fill an empty purse, unable to surmount its remorse-ridden vanity, the poet's "toil" realizes a material equivalent for itself only in the perfected stanzaic form of the poem. The lone stanza ironically betokens the divided life. Completed, the "work" betrays its own defect, its lack of context. Indeed, in the absence of any palpable economic measure of its value, the poem materializes as the symbol of the economic significance which it lacks.

In recalling the old "perplexity" of whether consummation is consumption, Yeats's "choice" dramatizes what Ruskin called "negative labor": "Literally, [labour] is the quantity of "Lapse," loss, or failure of human life caused by any effort. . . . It is the negative quantity, or quantity of de-feat, which has to be counted against every Feat, and of de-fect, which has to be counted against every Fact, or Deed of men" (*Works,* 17:183). "The Choice" illuminates the effects of this principle. Yeats's view of the poet's toil alters Smith's postulate that "the produce of labour constitutes the natural recompense or wages of labour." Yeats's labor cannot, by definition, produce any "natural recompense" beyond itself. If successful, the product of his labor will only point up how the poet's life is defeated, consumed by what he has made. When we are *not* able to tell the dancer from the dance, then the work has triumphed—but at a cost. Its triumph is measured by the "loss, or failure of human life caused by any effort." On the other hand, when we *are* able to distinguish the poet from his labor, then the art is imperfectly divided. The dream of "perfection" betrays itself, in both cases, as an imperfect imagining which no stitching, however felicitous, can make whole. Ultimately, poiesis will end in "perplexity" to the extent that the poem is forced to quantify a labor which its own embodiment as a poem must serve to defeat. That Yeats needed to sever a stanza originally written as part of another work and to set it off as a separate *oeuvre* only confirms how persistently labor itself remains a "negative quantity," divided into disconnected "toils," discrete "choices," and expressed, ultimately, in broken symbols—a winding stair or a single stanza in lieu of the whole mansion.

Yeats's poetic economics confronts an aesthetic perplexity

which has become a recognizably modern poetic strategy. A prejudice is established against anything that would reduce a poem to commodity status. Thus, a poem should not mean, but be—as if it possessed no ulterior metaphysical purpose or economic pertinence. It would then be invulnerable to metaphorical transference, the process of exchange. In exchange, a poem's meanings might become vendible and so, it is feared, could be exhausted. To restrict meaning to "being," however, is to displace the complexities of possession from poetics, to throw out the perplexity with the purse. A poem that simply *is* has an exclusive commodity as well as hermeneutic status, and the poet is freed from all hint of "labor" pertaining to his enterprise. He is simply a mediator in a process of pure coinage. In Archibald MacLeish's "Ars Poetica" (to which I have been alluding), the reader is invited to make what he will of the poem's "mute," "dumb," "silent," and "wordless" images, but what he makes of them pertains strictly and exclusively to the reader-poem relationship.[36] The poet is not involved, is perhaps not even present. In such a poetics (revived in much of W. S. Merwin's poetry), the poet has become the disembodied product of the poem's labor, as if the poem, like Frankenstein's monster, were self-sufficient, could speak and reason for itself, might generate its own labor and its own consumer, and thus no longer needed its creator. Like money, the poem comes to symbolize itself: a pure commodity. It has what Marx called "an objective character stamped upon" it. The poet's individual "toil" leaves *no* mark. The poem seems not a moment's thought but nobody's thought. Existentially autonomous, the poem gives the impression of having been created *ex nihilo,* and the poet, insofar as he is "present," gives us the impression that he is just another (implied) reader, like us.

If this poetics has evolved partly from Yeats, then W. H. Auden's elegy for Yeats may be seen to refute as well as to eulogize him.[37] In praising Yeats, Auden brings the reader's labor to bear on the poetic exchanges of the poem in a way that Yeats himself did not permit. Ironically, Yeats does not suffer (in Auden's view) by this reasserted and redefined labor process; in fact, Yeats is ultimately and surprisingly invoked as an ally in answering Ricardo's deadly contention that an artistic product derives no intrinsic value from the original labor invested in it.

In the first section of the elegy, Auden repeats Yeats's own premise that poetic labor occurs on a self-sufficient symbolic level removed from "the noisy set / Of bankers, schoolmasters, and clergymen / The martyrs call the world." Conceding to poetic labor a potential disutility and impotence, Auden's speaker observes a further "fact," that "it survives":

> Poetry makes nothing happen: it survives
> In the valley of its saying where executives
> Would never want to tamper. . . .

The remainder of the elegy attempts to chart the reasons for this survival. If poetry is only "A way of happening, a mouth," then, as a mouth, it does not perish in the very instant of its production. It goes on speaking. Like the mouths we have to feed, it requires nourishment; by metaphorical extension, the labor of response. On a literal level, Auden's elegy answers Yeats's poetry with a poetry of its own. But by illustrating the way in which poetry "happens," it does more: Auden's responsiveness as a reader provides the occasion for affirming the productiveness of poetic labor on the economists' own terms. Adam Smith had said that productive labor "fixes and realizes itself in some particular subject or vendible commodity, which lasts for some time at least after that labour is past. It is, as it were, a certain quantity of labour stocked and stored up to be employed, if necessary, upon some other occasion. That subject . . . can afterwards, if necessary, put into motion a quantity of labour equal to that which had originally produced it." (*WN*, bk. 2, chap. 3). Yeats's poems had already, by the time of the elegy, "last[ed] for some time" after the events which occasioned the original labor: the political difficulties of Ireland, the love affairs, the esoteric mysticism, and so on. They have made nothing happen; they did not win the beautiful woman, Maud Gonne, nor did they bring the peace to Ireland. And yet, they have fixed a quantity of labor in them, realized in a form which can be "stored up to be employed, if necessary, upon some other occasion." How one reanimates that body of artistic realization will depend upon how one perceives the conditions of necessity. Poignantly, for Auden, the necessary "occasion" becomes the moment of elegiac memory for Yeats, in which Auden appropriates Yeats's verse forms in order to pay him homage, just as Yeats himself appropriated other poets' products into his own labor. In section three of the elegy, Auden's quatrains echo Yeats's echoing of Blake ("Follow, poet, follow right / To the bottom of the night" invokes "Tyger Tyger burning bright / In the forests of the night"): thus, they remind us not only of Yeats's lifelong debt to the earlier visionary's labor but also of the continuity of poetic production, the infinite consanguinity which it bears.

Finally, Auden has created, in Adam Smith's words, "a quantity of labour equal to that which had originally produced it." Auden's own poetic production closes with yet another invitation to the next poet-laborer, an invitation which recapitulates Yeats's (sometimes equally didactic) labor, puts it into motion, and names its value to its successors:

> In the deserts of the heart
> Let the healing fountains start,
> In the prison of his days
> Teach the free man how to praise.

Auden's last stanza resolves his poem by teaching us how to read it. The prison of the poet's days had been defined exactly in Yeats's "The Choice," and had been identified there as the vacillation between vanity and remorse, the old perplexity of an empty purse. Auden reevaluates Yeats's choice by showing the process of choosing to be more significant and affirmative than any choice made. Man becomes "free" insofar as he posits his own "toil" as liberating, insofar as he chooses to be free. For Auden, the healing fountains start precisely at the moment that man chooses the choice to choose. It is Auden who, in praising Yeats, has taught us *how* to praise by affirming the act of interpretation as essentially productive: "The words of a dead man / Are modified in the guts of the living." Auden thus reaffirms the value of the reader as quantifier, as re-creator who, in his labors of interpretive choice, produces a labor equal to that which originally set it in motion. "With the farming of a verse," both poet and reader "make a vineyard of the curse."

Auden's elegy instructs the reader in the choice available to *him:* to posit himself either as an executive who would never want to tamper with poetry or as someone who might become part of its productive process, part of its harvest. The poem ends, therefore, by answering its own doubts that poetry makes nothing happen. Although Yeats's death caused not so much as a flutter on the exchange boards of the Bourse, Auden does not indulge in any simplistic outrage over poetry's economic disregard. Instead, by viewing poetry as a labor process he reveals that poetry may transcend its economic status. He retrieves a useful and affirmative sense of poetry's own self-affirming and self-sustaining productiveness: in the valley of its saying, it teaches man that economics too might be transmuted into a means of praise. "Saying" is the labor of speech. If we praise that labor, we may affirm a freedom—if only the freedom to praise—in the very heart of the day's prison. Moreover, even those labors which now seem used up will also partake of this freedom. Paul Claudel's work will survive, according to Auden, because "Time . . . / Pardons him for writing well." "Writing well" secures its own pardon, then; freedom is implicit in every labor which is done "well."

Auden brings economic and mental labor together into one "saying." He shows that in "writing"—in Yeats's poetry especially—we may, if we choose, recognize a substantive image of the labor process. In poetry, "labor" may be judged in the singularity of its achievement—as the intellect of man "forced" to make its own unaided choices. This (poetic) logic negates negation. Precisely because the poem is *not* an economic object—because it has, in Hart Crane's words, no monetary equivalent—its accomplishment and its realization as a commodity can be judged dispassionately—in the imagination. At the same time, Auden demonstrates with *his* poem that the economic concept of productive labor has profound meaning in terms of the exchange value of poetry—its capacity to exchange values. Yeats's labor is commanded by the elegy and is transformed through the elegy into a new poetic transaction which praises both the original product and the process thus set in motion. Acting as a creative reader of Yeats, Auden in his own labor has "stored up" an expendable image of productive labor, a functional poetic economics that continues even as we respond to and participate in it. Thus, by meeting the economics of labor on its own terms, Auden does all, perhaps, that he can or needs to do. In the scholastic language of Milton, he "saves the appearances" by intimating that the art of labor and the labor of art, the reader and the poet, society and the artist, need not depreciate one another but can operate, if not in harmony exactly, then at least to one another's mutual sufficiency and (perhaps) credit.

CHAPTER VI
The Psychomachia of Labor

Here it is that the true struggle takes place, that unavoidable combat between principles originally hostile, which into every subsequent section carries forward its consequences, and which, upon every system past or to come, impresses that determinate character, exposes that determinate tendency or clinamen, *eventually decisive of its pretensions.*
—*Thomas DeQuincey,* The Logic of Political Economy

In orthodox theology, the Fall is a fall from grace into the need to labor. In orthodox political economy, the Fall is a fall from the promise of natural recompense for the products of one's labor into an existential predicament in which one's labor may not receive a just return for its productions. In economics, the prelapsarian state is one in which the products of labor can be exchanged for other commodities of use: those which would meet the laborer's needs and desires. The postlapsarian state is one in which labor is exchanged for money (wages) and this money form may or may not purchase the laborer's needs or fulfill his desires. The psychomachia of labor—its conflict of soul—occurs precisely at the moment when labor has to price itself, to account for itself as productive work, and to represent itself in its money form, as an exchange value. Labor's determinate tendency or *clinamen* is enacted when money adds a new "fact" to "the art of labor."

As we have seen, economic discourse effectually strips artistic "work" of a viable economic identity. "Mental labor" is first derived from "material labor" by metaphorically extending the word "labor" and is then severed from it by metaphorically dissociating the meaning of "art." In respect to the material world, "mental labor" becomes a perilous, perhaps a contrived, trope. In pursuing Marx's claim that this division of labor permeates the whole of capitalist society, including the imaginations of its economists, we must keep in mind that the workings of literature as economic phenomena (in this case, as subjects of labor) are irrevocably connected to the metaphorical workings of economic discourse (in this case, of labor theories). Indeed, to see the continuity between that (economic) art which is ingenious labor and that (literary) labor which is the art of *ingenium* or the imagination, we will have to examine more closely the discontinuity of labor value in systems of capitalist production, the transformation of labor into its money form.

John Locke attempted to unite life, liberty, and *property* and to compute their value in terms of one another, thus delaying the necessity of pricing *labor*. "Nature" becomes "property," according to Locke, when man "hath bestowed his labour upon it."[1] The exchange between man and nature is both the origin of economic value and the object of human labor, "for it is labour indeed that puts the difference of value on everything" (p. 136). But this direct exchange existed, as Locke emphasizes everywhere, only "in the beginning." Individual labor appropriated what was useful from nature's bounty only as long as natural bounty remained bountiful: "Nor was this appropriation of any parcel of land, by improving it, any prejudice to any other man, since there was still enough and as good left, and more than the yet unprovided could use" (p. 132). But the invention of money altered the meaning of "use" because, where money existed, excess was conceived to be private "profit," not natural abundance. As a commodity, money remained valuable even if it was not used: "And thus came in the use of money; some lasting thing that men might keep without spoiling, and that, by mutual consent, men would take in exchange for the truly useful but perishable supports of life" (pp. 139-40). Money changed the image of labor as God had originally commanded it; "now," even nature's original bounty became tainted: "Thus, in the beginning, all the world was America, *and more so than that is now;* for no such thing as money was anywhere known" (p. 140; my italics). Knowledge of money disfigured ideal nature (Locke's "America"), turned it into an exploitable "thing."

One of Locke's complexly qualified sentences reenacts this "Fall":

> This is certain, that in the beginning, before the desire of having more than men needed had altered the intrinsic value of things, which depends only on their usefulness to the life of man, or had agreed that a little piece of yellow metal, which would keep without wasting or decay, should be worth a great piece of flesh or a whole heap of corn, though men had a right to appropriate by their labour, each one to himself, as much of the things of Nature as he could use, yet this could not be much, nor to the prejudice of others, where the same plenty was still left, to those who would use the same industry. [Pp. 134-35]

As in the biblical Fall, the economic fall irrevocably altered the relationship between man and nature. Originally, the property of man's labor, when added to "the spontaneous products of Nature," "did thereby acquire a propriety in them" (p. 135). Locke's own pun shows, on all levels, the effect of the Fall. For the Fall changed the propriety as well as the proprietary aspects of human labor. Instead of appropriating bountiful nature into property by means of labor, man was now forced to labor against a growing scarcity of resources, "to the prejudice of others." In acquiring what was more than useful, man's "labor" confronted a new economy redefined by the presence of money. Labor was no longer an exercise in economic appropriation but in economizing. More specifically, money now presents man with a different form of appropriation: the need to *price* the objects of utility. The economics of labor (whose end is "property") becomes the economics of money (whose end is catallactics—"the science of price" or "the economics of the price system").[2] Finally, property is understood as a less productive expression of man's labor when money must mediate the value of possessing it—when money, that is, displaces nature as an object of economic value.

Theories of labor displacement are derived from Adam Smith. In the space of two paragraphs, Smith makes the following assertions concerning labor:

> 1. The value of any commodity, therefore, to the person who possesses it, and who means not to use or consume it himself, but to exchange it for other commodities, is equal to the quantity of labour which it enables him to purchase or command.
> 2. Labour, therefore, is the real measure of the exchangeable value of all commodities.
> 3. Labour was the first price, the original purchase-money that was paid for all things.[3]

Smith's three definitions posit labor as value, measure, and price. Unfortunately, these terms are not, in economics, synonyms—as Smith knew. He thus declares that he is speaking of labor in an earlier, preindustrialized, essentially agrarian (and, historically, wholly imaginary) economy of barter rather than of monetary exchange and commercial markets. In this "original state of things, which precedes both the appropriation of land and the accumulation of stock" (*WN*, bk. 1, chap. 8)—in the time, as Locke says, when America was more "America" than it is now—labor was price, value, and measure all at once. Because in this original state there was no rent on property and no profit paid on capital, the *value* of any commodity was equal to the amount of labor bestowed on its production. Therefore, "the produce of labour constitute[d] the natural recompense or wages of labour" (ibid.). When one commodity was traded for another, the *purchase price* was the amount of labor the original commodity could command. Here, neither price nor wage is counted in money but in labor only, for Smith's labor theory of value is founded upon the original homogeneity of production and exchange, of labor bestowed and labor commanded. In this original equivalence of value and price, the effort of a man's work was directly equivalent to the economic effect of his labor. In short, labor possessed economic "power": "The power which that possession [of one's own labor] immediately and directly conveys to him, is the power of purchasing a certain command over all the labour, or over all the produce of labour, which is then in the market. . . . The exchangeable value of everything must always be precisely equal to the extent of this power which it conveys to the owner" (ibid, chap. 5).

The Wealth of Nations describes the social genesis of labor by imagining trade as having originated in what the eighteenth century called a "natural law" of human conduct: namely, in man's innate "trucking disposition," in his desire to trade, and in the pleasure he takes when exchanging one thing for another. The division of labor "is the necessary, though very slow and gradual consequence of a certain propensity in human nature which has in view no such extensive utility; the propensity to truck, barter, and exchange one thing for another" (bk. 1, chap. 2). This "natural" propensity, Smith felt, was positively self-serving: "Whoever offers to another a bargain of any kind, proposes to do this. Give me that which I want, and you shall have this which you want . . . ; it is in this manner that we obtain from one another the far greater part of those good offices which we stand in need of" (ibid.). But out of the "power of exchanging"—the power, that is, of getting more of what one wants—utility is effected. Although exchange is socially privative, it effects economic improvement not only for the individual but indirectly for the entire commonwealth as well.

How this social improvement comes about comprises one of Smith's most curious principles: the doctrine of differing talents. On the one hand, Smith claims that a man who bakes bread all his life will become naturally adept at baking bread and not so adept at, say, weaving textiles. On the other hand, Smith also advances this as a general principle regulating human character development. Working for their own self-interest, men find that their economic practices create a new, previously unimaginable, society, a community comprised of heterogeneous talents. At the social level, the trucking disposition now renders specialization useful, because now man *must* trade for his necessities and luxuries. In the beginning, the trucking disposition creates a difference of talents, and, in the end, these difffering talents depend for their economic value upon each other. Utility is the product of that process. Smith did not state the logical conclusion: that dependence is the bedrock of economic harmony. Instead, Marx stated it for him.

In fact, that sense of dependence was not Smith's own conclusion. Smith thought men would truck and barter more vigorously to avoid any such dependence, if only they were allowed to compete freely and fairly. Or rather, in realizing a material sufficiency from an activity (trucking) whose original motive was self-interest, men would come to understand dependence upon others as useful, a positive expression of community. Thus, out of labor's economic specialization a new concept of labor community is realized. Like Mandeville before him, Smith saw a system of public virtue arising directly from man's private vice of self-interest. Smith explained this transformation by means of a metaphor. In *The Wealth of Nations* he attempted to deduce "the rules which men naturally observe in exchanging [goods of all kinds] either for money or for one another" (bk. 1, chap. 4), but in *The Theory of Moral Sentiments,* he intimated the presence of these rules by means of "the Invisible Hand." The Invisible Hand is essentially a metaphor of psychological management as ordained by the laws of nature. Its invisibility is due to the innate sense of dependence which men do not want to see and which they labor to avoid. The metaphor is, therefore, a fictive representation of a moral process which man cannot or does not himself imagine while he is engaged in economic process.[4]

Although the Invisible Hand governs simple labor production and mediates the effects of barter, it does not wholly explain the catallactics of those more sophisticated economies founded upon the circulation of money as embodied labor units. With barter, there is no middle term between the quantity of labor bestowed in commodity A and the quantity of labor bestowed in commodity B. Exchange occurs on the basis of unmediated equivalences, as Gary Snyder exhibits in his poem "The Market," a meditation which occurs while the speaker is bartering at an open market in India. Noting the exchanges which take place in this market, the poet asks, "How much / is our change?"

> seventy-five feet hoed rows equals
> one hour explaining power steering
> equals two big crayfish =
>   all the buttermilk you can drink
> = twelve pounds of cauliflower
> = five cartons greek olives = hitch-hiking
>   from Ogden Utah to Burns Oregon
> = aspirin, iodine, and bandages

```
= a lay in Naples = beef
= lamb ribs       = Patna
              long grain rice, eight pounds
equals two kilogram soybeans = a boxwood
                          geisha comb.⁵
```

And the list goes on, an infinitely expandable equation that never yields a sum. In a barter economy, "change" is not the product of exchange but its essence, rendering commodities equivalent. Thus, "change" is also the number of metamorphoses through which labor passes. But "the intervention of money" (*WN,* bk. 3, chap. 1) changes the nature of the catallactics: ". . . though labour be the real measure of the exchangeable value of all commodities, it is not that by which their value is commonly estimated" (bk. 1, chap. 5). In the post-barter world of modern economy (which is the subject of *The Wealth of Nations*), money becomes the actual measure of value. Smith can therefore drop the fiction of the Invisible Hand because its regulative function is already contained in the visible increment, money: "But when barter ceases, and money has become the common instrument of commerce, every particular commodity is more frequently exchanged for money than for any other commodity" (ibid.). To follow Snyder's suggestive terms: in the transference to a money market, a new kind of "change" is created in "exchange." Money, as Marx graphically declared, "congeals into the sole form of value."⁶ In Snyder's poem, the equal sign signifies direct exchange of products in lieu of other signs of indirect equivalence, such as $ and ¢. The burden of classical economics is to prove that the money sign also inherits the equivalence function of the equal sign through the moral intervention of the Invisible Hand.

In Smithian economics, the function of money is to represent quantities of "labor bestowed" in terms other than "labor commanded." If the *value* of a commodity reflects the quantity of labor bestowed on its production, then such value may or may not be truly represented in its market *price,* because the price must also represent other "real" values such as rent (from property) and profit (from capital investment). Not only is the word "real" sorely tried, but labor bestowed and labor commanded also diverge from each other. The two concepts no longer express a homogeneous process. Labor bestowed becomes a measure of *wages;* labor commanded becomes a measure of commodities' *prices.* Catallactics again preempts the labor process. If labor originally equaled a quantity of work, then with the intervention of money, labor becomes just another factor in production, merely a sign of value, and not even the primary one. In the process of exchange, labor becomes a fiction.

Whereas Smith contended that economic community arose out of a utility in man's trucking disposition that man himself was unable to imagine while blinkered by the reality of work, Ricardo argued that we have only to *imagine* money as a measure of value, "the medium in which *price* is always expressed,"[7] in order to resolve the psychomachia of labor. In order to distinguish value from price, labor bestowed from labor commanded, Ricardo proposed to regard the former series (value; labor bestowed) as absolute, prior to exchange, and the latter series (price; labor commanded) as variable, dependent upon exchange. Thus, he could separate the creation of *value* from the fluctuations of economic *values* in the marketplace. The original investment of labor in commodity production created a value not necessarily represented by the monetary values actually exchanged: "It is the comparative quantity of commodities which labor will produce that determines their present or past relative value, and not the comparative quantities of commodities which are given to the labourer in exchange for his labour" (p. 9). Ricardo is speaking, finally, of two things at once: (1) "labor" as labor production, the process by which value is created; and (2) "labor" as a representative commodity which "like all other things . . . has its natural and its market price" (p. 52). Ricardo is ultimately not concerned, as Marx would be, with the question of labor's value but only with the labor theory of value, the theory of how labor creates value in the commodities which it has produced. As a regulative agent of price, then, labor is used both literally and fictively by the economist. But the metaphor loosens beyond recognition when Ricardo (and following him, McCulloch) uses "labor" to describe as well "the implements, tools, and buildings, with which such labor is assisted."[8]

Marx recognized this metaphorical displacement of labor from the social context in which work occurs. When "labor" can refer to implements, then it is not long before laborers themselves are understood as tools or pawns. When represented through commodities, labor takes on a new *imaginative* form. In exchange, labor becomes a form of money. Marx contended that the classical economists (such as Smith and Ricardo) spoke of "labor" only in its alienated form, as the capitalist's "surplus-value." Rhetorically, labor became the vehicle of a metaphor whose tenor was not "work" but "capital."

Marx wished to apprehend the seminal value of labor itself, not its mediated money form. Properly speaking, the labor process ought to be regarded as precommercial and considered "independently of the particular [economic] form it assumes under given social conditions": "It is the everlasting Nature-imposed condition of human existence . . ."(*C*, 1:177, 184). With Locke, Marx posited labor as man's capacity to participate with and to control nature: "Labour is, in the first place, a process in which both man and Nature participate, and in which man of his own accord starts, regulates, and controls the material re-actions between himself and Nature" (*C*, 1:177).

The first effect of labor is cognitive. Man learns how to act not only "of his own accord" but, "by thus acting on the external world and changing it, he at the same time changes his own nature" (ibid.). What the seventeenth-century economists called "art" Marx called "labour-power": "By labour-power or capacity for labour is to be understood the aggregate of those mental and physical capabilities existing in a human being, which he exercises whenever he produces a use-value of any description" (*C*, 1:167). Labor produces commodities of use which, by being produced, exhaust the labor that went into them. Use value arises out of labor, and labor is redefined accordingly as what is lost in the creation of utility: "While the labourer is at work, his labour constantly undergoes a transformation: from being motion, it becomes an object without motion; from being the labourer working, it becomes the thing produced" (*C*, 1:189). As a commodity, labor is what the laborer sells. The *price* of his labor may be measured in wages, but not its emotional and psychological *cost*. The laborer "must constantly look upon his labour-power as his own property, his own commodity, and this he can only do by placing it at the disposal of the buyer temporarily, for a definite period of time. By this means alone can he avoid renouncing his rights of ownership over it" (*C*, 1:168). Thus, the laborer must sell his labor in order to possess it. "Labour-power . . . becomes a reality only by its exercise; it sets itself in action only by working" (*C*, 1:171). But, in being expressed, this power can also be exhausted. Ultimately, the laborer "owns" only his capacity for depletion, according to Marx, because the capitalist has purchased his capacity for production. The wages paid to the laborer reflect the productiveness which he no longer possesses, the participation with nature which he no longer controls. Quite simply, money replaces nature as the "condition of human existence." Whereas the original purpose of labor was "to appropriate Nature's productions in a form adapted to [the laborer's] own wants" (*C,* 1:177), now the capitalist presents the laborer with the prospect of wages and forces him to adapt instead that money form to meet his wants and needs as best he can.

At the beginning of part 3 of *Capital,* however, Marx attempts to describe the labor process in "a form that stamps it as exclusively human" (*C,* 1:178)—a form which is prior to exchange. Unlike "those primitive instinctive forms of labour that remind us of the mere animal" (ibid.), the process of human work inaugurates a transformation of consciousness. Man "develops his slumbering powers and compels them to act in obedience to his sway"—that is, to the necessities of his working life (*C,* 1:177). What further distinguishes human from animal labor is the element of imagination embodied in the effort exerted. Whereas both architects and bees construct dwellings,

> what distinguishes the worst architect from the best of bees is this, that the architect raises his structure in imagination before he erects it in reality. At the end of every labour-process, we get a result that already existed in the imagination of the labourer at its commencement. He not only effects a change of form in the material on which he works, but he also realizes a purpose of his own that gives the law to his modus operandi, and to which he must subordinate his will. [*C,* 1:178]

Man's imagination is indwelling, immanent in his labor. Here, Marx identifies the origin of labor's psychomachia in its internal conflict, its need for "close attention," and its imaginative exercise of willed subordination. "And this subordination," he adds, "is no mere momentary act." Labor is a dialectical progression of imagination and will, and this process renders unto labor its moral value. "Besides the exertion of the bodily organs, the process demands that, during the whole operation, the workman's will be

steadily in consonance with his purpose. This means close attention" (ibid.). Thus, both material product and mental cognition
are realized together in the physical act of labor, for the original
purpose of the work process is to bind together mind and body
into a language which is cognate with action.

The intervention of money changes the sort of "language" in
which labor will be expressed; it creates a new dialectic, and, from
a moral point of view, a paradox. Whereas labor represents, on the
one hand, man's sacred property—that is, his work—on the other
hand, the commodity which he must exchange in the marketplace,
is himself. Every man has a price and that price is his labor.[9] In
having literally to price himself, man must posit his ontological
status in a new way, according to the economically instituted
process of circulation: namely, the medium of money. Marx asserts that classical economists did not apprehend "that form under
which value becomes exchange-value," because they did not understand that the labor process itself acquires a new *form* when
embodied in monetary transactions, in systems of capitalist production (see *C,* 1:80–81, n. 2).

In the system which Marx calls "simple commodity production"
(Smith's barter economy), labor produces a product which may be
exchanged, usually by means of money, for another more useful
and necessary commodity. Marx's formula for this process is
C-M-C. In transaction, money (*M*) functions merely as an exchange
equivalent. It possesses no independent value apart from its use as
a token of exchange. It does not measure value but merely facili-
tates transference of the first and third terms. In this Newtonian,
mechanistic view of economic transaction, the three particles of
matter operate by predictable and self-contained laws. Matter is
neither created nor destroyed. The formula can be reversed, for
instance, and nothing has been lost or added. Its meaning remains
constant.

But the circulatory system of capitalist production bestows a
new significance upon money, replacing the direct exchange of
commodities: "Money is a crystal formed of necessity in the
course of the exchanges, whereby different products of labour are
practically equated to one another and thus by practice converted
into commodities" (*C,* 1:86). We are back to alchemy.[10] In economic circulation, money is no longer an exchange equivalent but
possesses the power of transformation *in itself,* "in the course of

the exhanges." Thus, "the circulation of commodities differs from the direct exchange of products [barter], not only in form, but in substance."[11] Marx proposes a new formula, different in both form and substance, to account for the transformations of capitalist production. The capitalist, by investing his resources into the production of a commodity, naturally expects to sell for more than the original investment. His return from the commodity produced must be greater: *M-C-M'*. We are no longer in the self-enclosed universe of Newtonian physics but further back, in the magical transformation of alchemical elements: "Value therefore now becomes value in process, money in process, and as such, capital" (*C*, 1:54). The commercial process (*M-M'*) is more potent than the commodity product (*C*), for in this process capital "comes out of circulation, enters into it again, preserves and multiplies itself within its own circuit, comes back out of it with expanded bulk, and begins the same round ever afresh" (*C*, 1:154–55). In this progression from *M* to *M'*, matter is created, "Money which begets money" (*C*, 1:155). Marx ultimately condemns this process as Aristotle did before him, but he also marvels at it. Sometimes he sees it as a kind of natural generation in which *M'* is related to *M* as son to father, alike but different. At other times, he insinuates that the process is onanistic:

> In simple circulation, C-M-C, the value of commodities attained at the most a form independent of their use-values, i.e., the form of money; but that same value now in the circulation [M-C-M, or the circulation] of capital, suddenly presents itself as an independent substance, endowed with a motion of its own, passing through a life-process of its own, in which money and commodities are mere forms which it assumes and casts off in turn. Nay, more: *instead of simply representing the relations of commodities, it enters now, so to say, into private relations with itself.* [*C*, 1:154; my italics]

The value of the "money-form" has a power of metamorphosis which labor does not have. The money form is "self-expanding value" (*C*, 1:153); it "expands spontaneously" (*C*, 1:154). But the laborer does not receive the *M'* value; the capitalist does, as his profit on the original outlay of *M*. The laborer receives only the value of *M minus M'*, which means that he does not even receive *C*, because the circulation of commodities through their

money form has escalated the prices of commodities beyond any
wages that can possibly be tendered. Finally, the money form of
labor is not equal to the market price of the commodity. Wages
and prices represent the "different modes of existence of value
itself" (*C*, 1:153).

In the completed capitalist system, the laborer is bound by
the simple commodity production of labor which operates by
the simple mechanistic laws of exertion and exhaustion, the
Newtonian principles of "fixed, immutable, eternal categories"
(as Marx himself describes the physics of classical economics).[12]
But the capitalist operates in a realm of almost spontaneous generation, where value "assumes an automatically active character"
and where money, as if engaged in a new kind of *metalleutikē*,
creates its own crystalline form of existence. Whereas the labor
process is a human reaction to nature—in Lockean terms, labor
appropriates nature and transforms it into property—the monetary
process creates an entirely new meaning of "property": "By possessing the *property* of buying everything, by possessing the property of appropriating all objects, *money* is thus the *object* of eminent possession. The universality of its *property* is the omnipotence of its being. It is therefore regarded as omnipotent. . . ."[13]
Money "appropriates" not only nature but labor as well by putting a price on *everything*. The different *logos* of the capitalist's
method speaks to a different *physis* in which money acquires (in
Marx's fierce pun) the *property* of omnipotence.

Marx's theory of labor value, then, takes Ricardo's emendation
of Smith to its logical conclusion. Labor, for Smith and for the
Utilitarians, was work represented in economically significant (i.e.,
quantifiable and vendible) commodities of production. Labor was
the original value, the first price, and the true measure of things,
but only in the primitive, precapitalist, essentially agrarian economy. For Ricardo, labor bestowed in production was the absolute
measure of value, although the commodities produced by that labor were subject to the same variations in price as any other commodities. For Marx, labor bestowed (the labor process) and labor
commanded (the circulation of commodities by means of capital)
were two different—dialectically different—processes. In capitalist
economics, "the consumption of labour-power is *at one and the
same time* the production of commodities and of surplus-value"
(*C*, 1:175; my italics). The attachment of a money form (surplus
value) to labor reformulates "money" as a superior fiction.

Capital remains the foremost economic examination of the fictive status of production. In Marx's terms, money generates an alternative labor process of its own. To convince us that money is a form of labor, capitalist production redefines the imagination itself; it offers money not as a token of exchange but as an object of mediation between fact and fiction, between material things and the imagination. So, "the weight of gold represented in imagination by the prices or money-names of commodities, must confront those commodities, within the circulation, in the shape of coins or pieces of gold of a given denomination" (1:124). In imagination, we represent commodities in terms of their "money-names," their prices. Money's "purely symbolical character" discloses "in imagination" that the thing which it symbolizes is itself (*C*, 1:127). The inspection of prices becomes, therefore, the introspective examination of our wishes and desires, but not of our labor.

"The inverted relationship" of money to value prescribes the labor process of the imagination itself under capitalist systems.[14] Both capitalist production and the work of the imagination become forms of "*alien mediation.*" To be exact, "the *divine* power of money" lies in its "fraternisation of impossibilities": "That which I am unable to do as a *man,* and of which therefore all my individual essential powers are incapable, I am able to do by means of *money.* Money thus turns each of these powers into something which in itself it is not—turns it, that is, into its *contrary*" (*Works,* 3:325). Money is the alienated ability of man precisely because it is a condensation of his incapacities as an individual—"that is, it converts my wishes from something in the realm of imagination, translates them from their mediated, imagined or desired existence into their *sensuous, actual* existence—from imagination to life, from imagined being into real being" (ibid.). In making man more than he is by virtue of his individual capacities, the transformational power of the medium renders up man's *other*ness, what he is *not.* "In effecting this mediation," money "is the *truly creative* power" (ibid.). Under circumstances such as these, we say that "money talks" because desires seem to be created and fulfilled "in the shape of coins." As mediator between the realm of the imagination and the realm of "facts," money's "mere symbolical existence absorbs, so to say, its material existence" (*C*, 1:129). Money's symbolic status preempts the materiality of things:

> No doubt the *demand* also exists for him who has no money, but his demand is a mere thing of the imagination without

effect or existence for me, for a third party, for the [others],
and which therefore remains even for me *unreal* and *object-
less.* The difference between effective demand based on money and ineffective demand based on my need, my passion,
my wish, etc., is the difference between *being* and *thinking,*
between the idea which merely *exists* within me and the idea
which exists as a *real object* outside of me. [*Works,* 3:325]

Money has refashioned the imagination in its own image. The
movement of money does more than merely translate thought into
reality: it renders ideology objective and as literal as coins. Thus,
what originally existed only as an idea now has objective *ex-istence*
—it literally stands outside us "as a real object." The parallelism of
Marx's grammar allows us to understand *being* as that which "exists within me" and *thinking* as that which "exists as a real object
outside of me." In bringing "a mere thing of the imagination" into
existence, money objectifies imaginative process as such and crys-
tallizes "thought" into material realities, into things to be desired.
We may call this crystallization a kind of poiesis, for, in external-
izing ideas, it also gives them shape and objective meaning "for a
third party." In a moment, we shall see how that "third party" is
also posited as Marx's own image of the reader, the alien mediator
between authorial demands and their ineffective object, the text.
Here, in the money form itself, Marx recognized, in miniature, the
basis for a (capitalist) poetic. Serving initially to depict a metaphorical relationship between object and internal idea ("demand"),
money was not, in the end, a metaphor. Its real, actualizing power
lay in de-metaphorizing metaphor, in filling the heretofore insur-
mountable gap between sign and meaning, between intention and
fact, with itself. In the capitalist economy, *we* do not represent
value; rather, it is represented *to* us by the mediation of money.
Both men and commodities acquire money names. (In *Capital,*
Marx calls the capitalist Mr. Moneybags, although the laborer remains nameless.) Money "becomes an *actual god*"; creator of our
existential predicament, it presents imaginative process (the way
in which we relate man to man and man to nature) as a function
of economic process (the way in which the production of commodities creates exchange).[15]

By translating desires into their money names, capitalism creates a new set of verbal signifiers based upon money as the signified object. "Apart from this meditation," commodities "lose

their value" (*Young Marx,* p. 266). Desire may then be conceived as unlimited, since its expression no longer depends upon natural attainability through labor but upon the mediative fluency of money alone.[16] Marx argued, therefore, that "economics" was itself a fallen trope, a capitalist ideology. "Money-values," he noted could be just as easily "produced by man or produced in economics" (*Young Marx,* p. 268). For Marx, the economists' juggling of "unreal words" was the verbal equivalent of surplus value. In order to uncover the true dialectic of the labor process, even as it touched economic writing itself, the Marxian economist needed a new poetic.[17]

As *Capital* prepares to consider the creation of surplus value (at the end of part 2), the argumentative strategy of the book changes from protoscientific exposition to a kind of imaginative *bildungsroman* involving a number of "dramatis personae" (as Marx calls them): Mr. Moneybags (the would-be capitalist), the simple laborer (Marx's protagonist), and Free-trader Vulgaris (Marx's economist-rival). These "characters" appear intermittently throughout, but as Marx's argument shifts to consider the new subject of surplus value, his fictive characters assume center stage. Marx has told us, after all, that the passage from "simple commodity production" to the circulation of capital is a change in *both* form and substance, and his discursive strategy reflects this twofold change as well. To begin with, the transformation of labor (the substance of work) into its money form (wages) is not instantaneous; labor acquires a price only after work has ceased: "The alienation of labour-power and its actual appropriation by the buyer, its employment as a use-value, are separated by an interval of time" (*C,* 1:174). In effect, Marx explains, the laborer "everywhere gives credit to the capitalist" by accepting the delay between work and wage. Marx quickly points out "that this credit is no mere fiction" (ibid.), and in order to describe the changes which such credit undergoes in capitalist production, Marx himself needs to break through the fiction of "free trade."

In capitalist production, the money owner exploits the credit which the laborer bestows upon him. Thus, the interval of time between the laborer's selling of his labor and his receiving payment for it becomes itself a hidden aspect of production. Time works to the profit of the capitalist and not of the laborer, for the means of production are the possessions of the money owner alone.[18] In describing how the capitalist "earns" his profit by gaining ownership, ultimately, of the laborer as well, Marx depicts the psychomachia of labor in its most profound and disturbing expression: the laborer, in becoming a commodity, relinquishes his individuality, his unique imagination. Precisely at this point, discursive "meaning," like economic "value," no longer "takes place on the surface" for the meaning of exchange now implicates the very humanity of its participants:

> The consumption of labour-power is completed, as in the case of every other commodity, outside the limits of the market or of the sphere of circulation. Accompanied by Mr. Moneybags and by the possessor of labour-power, we therefore take leave for a time of this noisy sphere, where everything takes place on the surface and in view of all men, and follow them both into the hidden abode of production, on whose threshold there stares us in the face "No admittance except on business." Here we shall see, not only how capital produces, but how capital is produced. We shall at last force the secret of profit making. [*C*, 1:175-76]

We are entering another cave like Mammon's, and the inscription over the threshold reminds us of the entryways to other literary versions of Hell. The mythic aspects of this descent are repeated in Marx's next paragraph: "This sphere that we are deserting, within whose boundaries the sale and purchase of labour-power goes on, is in fact a very Eden of the innate rights of man" (*C*, 1:176). The voyage that *Capital* now undertakes is, metaphorically, a recapitulation of the Fall, a tour through a postlapsarian landscape, "the hidden abode of production." (As we shall see, it is also a voyage into the fallen state of metaphor, the hidden abode of linguistic production.) In this voyage, the psychic makeup of the fictive personae undergoes a transformation, and it is this change in character which Marx's dramatic interlude allows us, initially, to perceive:

> On leaving this sphere of simple circulation or of exchange of commodities, which furnishes the "Free-trader Vulgaris" with his views and ideas, and with the standard by which he judges a society based on capital and wages, we think we can perceive a change in the physiognomy of our dramatis personae. He, who before was the money-owner, now strides in

front as capitalist; the possessor of labour-power follows as his labourer. The one with an air of importance, smirking, intent on business; the other, timid and holding back, like one who is bringing his own hide to market and has nothing to expect but—a hiding. [Ibid.]

With the descent into the realm of capitalist production, we are, in Marx's view, entering the realm of private as opposed to social production. In effect, Marx's drama allows us to look into the private psyches of his characters as the smirking capitalist now strides ahead of the timid, cowering laborer who becomes virtually a slave of Mr. Moneybags ("his" laborer). Even as he brings his labor power to market, we see that the laborer also brings himself to market as the property of the money owner. At the same time, Marx exposes the vulgar error of the mercantile economist, Free-trader Vulgaris—his blindness to the psychological subjugation which makes "free trade" possible. Now we may visualize the psychical effect of capitalist production on the human participants, which is the true cost of surplus value. We can literally perceive the effects of economic alienation by noting the changes in the features and "physiognomy" of the dramatis personae. Marx's fictive characters become externalized creations of an internal conflict—a psychomachia—the marks of which were before internal and unseen. At the same time, Marx is working to replace Free-trader Vulgaris's "views and ideas" with a more effective "economics."[19]

Marx promises that he will "at last force the secret of profit making," and, in his own writing, Marx is as good as his word. The secret of this "hidden abode" is forced into the open by Marx's own pun making: the laborer, "in bringing his own hide to market," will get "a hiding [*Gerberei*] ." In the next section of *Capital* (part 3) Marx will describe how the creation of the capitalist's surplus value gradually strips away the laborer's individual identity. The laborer disappears in the production of capital; the labor process disappears in the capitalist product (cf. *C,* 1:180–81). Economically speaking, the commodity made by the laborer replaces *him; its* money value is greater than his. The full meaning of labor as "the property of the capitalist" (*C,* 1:185) will then be clear. Not only will the laborer's wages be insufficient to clothe him, but, in this transformation of labor process into commercial product, the laborer will also relinquish his hide, his very identity:

it becomes, in fact, the capitalist's product. So, Marx's pun on "hiding" becomes a kind of metacritical revelation of the capitalist's metaphorical whip, money.

The young Marx had noted in his 1844 manuscript the process of alienation by which the laborer is divested of the private property of his labor:

> When I yield my private property to another person, it ceases being mine. It becomes something independent of me and *outside* my sphere, something *external* to me. I *externalize* my private property. So far as I am concerned, it is *externalized* private property. I see it only as something generally *externalized;* I only transcend my *personal* relationship to it; and I return it to the *elemental* forces of nature when I externalize it only in relation to myself. It only becomes externalized *private property* as it ceases being *my* private property without ceasing to be *private property* in general, that is, when it acquires the same relationship to *another* man *outside* of me, as it had to me—in a word, when it becomes the *private property* of *another* man. [*Young Marx,* p. 273]

Although the process of externalization is explicitly revealed in Marx's metaphor of "hiding" (in *Capital*), here the italicized words elaborate the significance of *Capital's* drama. They call attention to the labor process of Marx's own writing, its movement beyond the imaginative realm of his forebear, the Free-trader Vulgaris. The italics, which sometimes seem disruptive of normal syntactical sense, serve to underscore the externalization of Marx's own discourse. The inflections of this writing—which is the author's "private property"—become alienated from the prose grammar in order to be repossessed as the property of another, in order to be *heard.* Like the fictive "Fall" related in *Capital,* this passage serves as a metacritical *exemplum* of the exchanges posed by writing itself. That the entire passage is related in the first person, as if Marx were literally sounding out his argument, further suggests that the passage is self-referring. It is applicable to both economic transactions and the written transactions of the author's discourse with an implied reader.

Marx's description of labor's psychomachia, or conflict of soul, becomes itself a kind of psychomachia or play of embattled dis-

course, the discursive form of his argument reflecting and refuting
the altered metaphorical implications of capitalist production.
This play of the economic imagination in assessing the process of
both commercial and "literary" production is, for the purposes of
this study, at once the most curious and the most significant aspect
of Marx's labor theory. Insofar as economic discourse is a form of
mediation between the economic process as such and the active intelligence of the economic theorist, then, as Marx himself knew,
that discourse is subject to the very dangers of alienation which in-
fect all the other sorts of "labor-power."

Again, in the manuscript of 1844, Marx contends that "Economics—like the actual process itself—proceeds from the *relationship of man to man* and from the relationship of one *property
owner to another. (Young Marx,* p. 272). Marx implies here that
economics must posit a labor process of its own between author
(economist) and reader (the laborer, in respect to the text). In this
he differs from Adam Smith, who had instead established a *mercantilist* relationship between two producing partners in his version
of political economy: "*Society,* says Adam Smith, is a *commercial
enterprise.* Each of its members is a *merchant.* It is evident that political economy *establishes* an *alienated* form of social intercourse
as the *essential, original,* and definitive human form" (ibid.).
Smith had actually written: "Every man thus lives by exchanging,
or becomes in some measure a merchant, and society itself grows
to be what is properly a commercial society" (*WN,* bk. 1, chap. 4).
But Marx is reading through and between Smith's lines. Because
Smith represented everyone as a merchant, including his reader,
his representations could never disclose a vision of "mutual redin-
tegration toward generic and truly human life" (*Young Marx,* p.
272). The form of "social intercourse" in the writing is misrepre-
sented also. The dialectical exchange between author and reader
merely extends the alienation which Smith's economic theory describes. The discursive form participates in the same "secret of
profit making" as "the actual process itself," and Smith's discursive stratagem emerges as a mercantilist version of the phenomena
which it purports to explain. Political economy—specifically, in
this case, Smith's "economics"—deceives us as to the "definitive
human form" of both trade and literature.

In the broadest application of Marx's psychomachia, then, eco-

nomics itself assumes a money form and furthers the alienation
of imaginative process: "The essence of money is not primarily
that it externalizes property, but that the *mediating activity* or
process—the *human* and social act in which man's products recip-
rocally complement one another—becomes *alienated* and takes on
the quality of a *material thing,* money, external to man" (*Young
Marx,* p. 266). When the very activity of mediation becomes a material thing, then the way in which we imagine "the human and
social act" of exchange is also subject to reification. The means by
which we imagine forms of social intercourse, such as the author-
reader relationship, becomes a commodity as well. Economists,
too, live by exchanging; their economic writing reduces the reader
to a consumer in respect to the text, even as he must become a
merchant in "what is properly a commercial society." "Economics" becomes a fiction in which both mental labor and material labor are consumed. If the private writings of Marx's manuscripts
help to identify and sound out this problem, then *Capital,* with its
figurative journeys, figural dramas, and metaleptic puns, is his attempt to face it head on.

The attitude that the economist takes toward his own discursive
work, the way in which he represents his text to the reader, will
reflect the kind of political economy which his imaginative system
will permit. Insofar as the psychomachia of labor portrayed   ed
metaphorically *in* Marx's writings reflects the psychomachia *of*   s
his writing, the imaginative labor of his poetics, Marx directly
refutes one Marxist (i.e., post-Marxian) view of the author-reader
relationship as merely a functional by-product of a society's collective labor. Ultimately, Marx's own writings would seem to grant
writing the status of both social and individual work, when "labor" is properly understood. And whether by "Marxism" one
means a revolutionary theory of social process or a dialectical
reading of previous political economies (such as Smith's), the same
conclusion may be drawn in respect to the economics of the imagination. As Raymond Williams has aptly stated: "At the very centre of Marxism is an extraordinary emphasis on human creativity
and self-creation. . . . The notion of self-creation, extended to civil
society and to language by pre-Marxist thinkers, was radically extended by Marxism to the basic work processes and thence to a
deeply (creatively) altered physical world and a self-created hu-

manity."[20] What Marx is fighting, of course, is the reification of individual human labor as a commodity to be transformed into a monetary form by systems of capitalist production. So, an economic system which restores this labor value restores also the validity of the complete author-text-reader relationship by giving reality to the author's labor, to the text (as a material process), and to the reader (as something more than a consumer artificially created by "money" desire). For Marx, the "Fall" of economic theory into literature, into the condition of being read and of needing to be read, may be a fortunate, potentially liberating Fall.

In literature, the thing or the commodity made by labor is a text, a body of words which is the material production of an author. Classical economic analysis of art tends to stop at this point and to ponder the economic value of the book as an artifact, a commercial object (as we have seen in Smith and Ricardo). Traditional Marxist analysis, however, also stops at this point and assigns an economic value to the author's labor only in terms of its social productiveness, of its usefulness to socialist revolution. But Marx's own work as an author indicates a more radical view of the work of art: in the beginning an author may need to create the labor process by which he will be read. Thus, literature might be regarded not as a commodity but as a labor implement which is materialized in the act of reading. Marx, in his early writings, promises to transform "labor" into a more fertile concept, so that it may be understood in a way that *directly* contests the overriding abstractions and symbolic resonances of money. *Capital* promises that when labor is truly understood as an imaginative exertion—a work which originates in the imagination—that understanding will alter the laboring consciousness of the reader. Considered in these terms, "economics" could reintegrate "mental labor" with the labor now alienated by the concealing mode of capitalist production.

In literature (and we must now specifically include economic writing as one form of "literature") the metaphorical division of mental and material labor involves author and reader at the most basic social level: in the productiveness of language. How we evaluate this division will depend upon how we—authors and readers together—are able to validate the "art of labor" when applied to a literary work. Indeed, this is Marx's most difficult task: to elicit dialectically from the reader the "mental labor" which his own texts have sought to define. Moreover, perhaps the cognitive potentiality of labor, which is obscured and devalued when labor is priced and exploited by capitalist systems of production, is rescued *only* in the literary work of the text where the original, precommercial labor process may be restored to its imaginative function through the reader's cognitive re-creation of the author's art.

In the following discussion of poems by Robert Frost, Marx's psychomachia can help us to understand how the economics of labor as an imaginative process invites a more penetrating vision of the economic status (and significance) of literature. Frost has been selected here partly because he would seem, on the surface, to be one of the least likely practitioners of a poetic economics. His work reveals, however, that a more deliberate reading of "economics" may result in a more useful view of the economic imagination in poetry as it assesses its own value by dramatizing the psychomachia of its own labor. In "Mowing," a poem which describes what Marx called "simple commodity production," labor retains its cognitive potential; indeed, while portraying a man at work, the poem simultaneously permits the poet to reflect upon his own labor in the making of the poem. But the self-reflections of this early Frost poem are transformed in a later lyric, "Provide, Provide," where labor becomes an aspect of consumption, a commercial mediation between life and death. Here, economic labor, as well as the work of the poem, are seen as capitalist processes only, labors which must be bought and sold. A new relationship between speaker and listener—by extension, between text and reader—is therefore invoked. These two poetic examples thus display the economic phenomena we have been studying in this chapter: the transformation of labor into its money form and the transformation of the literary work into its economic form as a commodity of exchange.

The original publication of "Mowing" in *A Boy's Will* (1913) included a short description on the contents page: "He takes up life simply with the small tasks."[21] "He" is the boy of the volume's title, willing to discover in the quotidian "tasks" of manual labor his quest for "a boy's will." "He" is also the poet, willing to make of that quest this book of poems, *A Boy's Will:*

rhymed lines. The *personal* activity of the poetic laborer cannot be deduced from his use of a *traditional* instrument. Nor can the subject of this particular poem's labor be inferred from its literary forebears. Perhaps this is why the scythe whispers and does not speak: the poem's quietness is an assertion of the originality of its own labor, its origin in the imagination of *this* poet alone.

The penultimate line of the sonnet asserts the "purpose" of both labors, the work of the mower and the work of the poet: "The fact is the sweetest dream that labor knows." But a different set of facts will appertain depending on whether we wish to know about the labor of mowing or about the labor of making the poem. There are several dreams at work here. Besides the fact of mowing, orchises and snakes are facts. The grass left to be cut, the heat of the sun, and the hay remaining to be dried are facts. A sonnet is a fact. And so is the (rejected) "fact" of the poem's allegory, in which this field of labor recalls the postlapsarian predicament of the man who is cursed to work for his bread and destined to scare bright snakes. As we have seen, the poem cautions against what seems "more than the truth," what is "too weak" an explanation for the actual work at hand. Because the poet has posited his own labor as original, he cannot settle for less than an original response from the reader. A new poem is a new fact. The poet's "earnest love" requires the reader's earnest effort in return, as Frost explains in "The Most of It": "what it wants / Is not its own love back in copy speech, / But counter-love, original response" (*Poetry*, p. 338, ll. 6–8).

In judging these various "facts," the predicament of the reader, as he labors at the poem, becomes yet another "fact" in the poem's labor process, perhaps the poem's "sweetest dream." If the "hay" in the last line is the mower's end result, the product of his labor of mowing, then it may stand symbolically for the poet's labor of poiesis, the effort of making meaning. But just as the mower's purpose has become subsumed into the movements of his instrument, the scythe itself, so the poet's purpose has become subsumed into the movements of *his* instrument, the poem, the discursive event. The produced commodity is the only "fact" which our labor of interpretation "knows." Our field of labor is this tract of verses (with the laying of the swale in rows a further modification of those "verses" which originally denoted the furrows left by a plow). The sound of the scythe is virtually synonymous with the

sound of the poet's stylus: "My long scythe whispered and left
the hay to make." As readers, we participate in the aftermath,
bringing to what is "left" that critical making which follows the
poet's original labor. Our labor is not the same as the poet's, but
it demands the same "process of organization," as John Dewey has
said, which "the creator of the work consciously experienced."
What we are left with, in the end, is the fact of a labor completed,
a sonnet realized as a work of art even as we read. It is not yet a
usable commodity. Like the cut swale, the work of the poem has
yet to be turned into hay. There must be, John Dewey observed,
"work done on the part of the percipient as there is on the part
of the artist."[22] The process of Frost's poem demonstrates the
mystery of the labor process as described by Marx: "The process
disappears in the product. . . . Labour has incorporated itself with
its subject: the former is materialized, the latter transformed. That
which in the labourer appeared as movement, now appears in the
product as a fixed quality without motion" (*C,* 1:180). In "Mowing," the labor process of the scythe disappears in the poem. The
poem appears as the "fact" of a sonnet, a "fixed quality without
motion," until the reader's labor parses it out, energizes it again.
Only by such an act of re-creation is the poem perceived as a
work of art so that its sweetest dream may be separated from its
actual achievement, its metaphors from its facts, its originality
from its traditional vehicle, the mowing from the hay.

Frost's later poem "Provide, Provide," however, shows this
entire process of poetic economics turning into an hermeneutical
cul-de-sac, its labor power transmuted into mercatorial exchange
(*Poetry,* p. 307). The poem issues a series of prescriptions for fac-
ing an horrific future (of death, abandonment, poverty, solitude):

> Die early and avoid the fate.
> Or if predestined to die late,
> Make up your mind to die in state.
>
> Make the whole stock exchange your own!
> If need be occupy a throne,
> Where nobody can call *you* crone. [ll. 7–12]

There are tacit metaphysical assumptions in the poem's economics
which the poem's economic argument (the procuring of means
against a day of final scarcity) is at pains to conceal. The need to
provide is conditioned, for instance, by the poem's vision of time

as an insufficient mode of production: "Too many fall from great and good / For you to doubt the likelihood" (ll. 5-6). But the "likelihood" is, perhaps, precisely what we might like to doubt. Nevertheless, the poem does not provide for doubts to enter the vision of the future which it proposes. The trouble is that, before we can wonder how "great and good" we might have been in the first place, the poem's provisos have already posited us as fallen. Thus we are trapped, from the start, in the speaker's presumptions of what constitues the great and the good. We might feel uneasy that they are equated with the "picture-pride of Hollywood" (l.4). In wondering who *would* call us crone, we are reminded that the speaker is the principal crone-caller in this poem:

> The witch that came, the withered hag
> To wash the steps with pail and rag,
> Was once the beauty Abishag. [Ll. 1-3]

But what are the provisions which this reversed fairy tale offers? To die early, to die in state, to make the stock exchange one's own, to occupy a throne—all are equally impossible or undesirable or perverse.

The hortatory title urges a foresight which the provisions of the poem cannot provide. All provisions are insufficient. Indeed the urgency of the poem's advice is conditioned by the desperation of the measures which it invokes. Wordly-wise, the speaker recognizes that the labor of providing will never confront the fact which is the sweetest dream that labor knows:

> Some have relied on what they knew,
> Others on being simply true,
> What worked for them might work for you.

Given the provisions offered by the poem, however, to choose to rely on one's own knowledge and so to be "simply true" is truly to be simpleminded, as the speaker's sarcasm suggests. For, in thinking that *we* know better, we merely play the part of Guyon to the speaker's Mammon. The reader's moral vigor is precisely what the speaker trades upon. If the speaker's provisions are inadequate, then he dares us to come up with better ones: "what worked for them *might* work for you."

The only way to deny the speaker's provisions is to refute their premises. In this poem, "anything more than the truth" is precisely what is required against such a singleminded fusillade of platitudes. The speaker seems to have made the whole "stock exchange" of moral mottoes his own. More art, less matter; better fictions, less truth; something at least not so simply true—these are the provisions which seem to be called for, and these are not provided by the poem. Indeed, the poem assumes that all provisions are equally compensations, taking the Marxian description of money's "fraternisation of impossibilities" to its logical end: "That which I am unable to do as a *man,* and of which therefore all my individual essential powers are incapable, I am able to do by means of *money.* Money turns each of these powers into something which in itself it is not—turns it, that is, into its *contrary*" (*Works,* 3:325). Frost's poem, too, ends by affirming the essential power of money to turn one's incapacities into "what might work for you":

> Better to go down dignified
> With boughten friendship at your side
> Than none at all. Provide! Provide!

Again, however, what money makes "better" is compromised by the tunnel vision of the poem's metaphysics: in the end, we all "go down," both those with friends and those with none at all. Like "boughten friendship," this advice is offered to the reader in the spirit of acquisition, not exchange. If we buy it, we become "dignified" only in the sense that we accept our individual incapacities. Incapacity being our common lot, all is negotiable, including our sense of what is "great and good," including the meaning of "friendship."

Although the poem superficially resembles the proverbial *sententiae* of something like *Poor Richard's Almanac,* its moral directives seem, in the end, more like a memento mori. The last stanza has the inscriptive tone of an epitaph. Why *should* we be friendless at the end, we might ask. Because all hopes are vain, the poem replies. Including, then, these very provisions, we might respond. Yes, the poem assures us. In the poem's revelation that all knowledge will be improvident, it is not far removed from just this sort of Hardyesque dialogue between subalterans. The speaker's poetic capitalism is predicated upon its singleminded metaphysical view that the consumer will ultimately be himself consumed. The question is not whether it is better to have boughten friendship than to have none at all; the question is whether the "facts" provided by

the poem are sufficient to "keep the end from being hard." Whereas "Mowing" exacts from the reader another kind of labor, similar
to the poet's own, "Provide, Provide" merely provides the reader
with a product: itself. The poem may allow us to deny its "facts,"
but only if we call for something which is "more than the truth."
In showing that all other possibilities are mere fictions beside the
one "future shock" which the poem envisions, "Provide, Provide"
acquires, like money, the property of omnipotence. The speaker
of the poem is the cruel "god" of capitalist economics; the reader,
the laborer who brings his hide to the market.

Both of Frost's poems, by addressing the labor process of the
speaker, comment implicitly on the equivalent labor process of the
poet in making the poem. Each in turn posits the reader in a dis-
tinctly different (economic) relationship to the text. In order to
study the labor relations of poetry more systematically, we shall
now turn back to an earlier poet, Wordsworth, who explicitly engaged the labor of the reader, contracting it to his own. One way
of keeping the end from being hard, Wordsworth averred, was to
allow the reader's improvident knowledge to be improved by the
poem. Such improvement occurs, Wordsworth theorized, because
the reader participates directly in the poem's creation of value.
For Wordsworth, then, the psychomachia of the writer's labor
would recur precisely at the moment when the poem must either
command a reader or compensate for the absence of one. By re-
imagining the poet's relationship to his reader, Wordsworth hoped
that a poetic economics could be employed to mediate the commodity status (or money form) of poems themselves. Like Blake,
Wordsworth appropriated economic discourse into his own poetry
as a means of affirming the economic propriety of his own labor.
But whereas Blake had sought to transform and so terminate economic discourse (and whereas Frost's speakers would be manipulated by such discourse even as they tried to be manipulators of
it), Wordsworth sought to "naturalize" economic language, to
teach men how to live with it.

CHAPTER VII
Wordsworth's Labor Theory:
An Economics of Compensation

Wordsworth's critics, like Blake's, have tended either to deemphasize or to ignore the economic side of his poetics. There have been Marxist readings of Wordsworth, to be sure, and biographical and critical studies of Wordsworth's business career, but these have not equally illuminated the career Wordsworth created for himself —the vocation of poet—and the specific achievement of that choice.[1] Alternatively, some scholars have applied "economics" to Wordsworth's texts in strangely abstracted, dissociated ways: one sees Wordsworth's psychological dynamic of the sublime, for instance, "as an economic event";[2] another speaks of "the economy of interchange" between author and reader.[3] Although these are meritorious topics (and the present study is indebted to them), we must here again take care that criticism does not unwittingly substitute its own loose and reductive metaphors for a poet's original and precise ones. Economics, for Wordsworth, was part of the real language of men—an exact and exacting trope. Through his poems, he sought to retrieve economic discourse from its mismanaged and facile rhetorical forms and thus to construct a cogent poetics of labor value.

One aspect of Wordsworth's economic sensibility emerges with the belated tribute to his benefactor, Raisley Calvert, in the last book of *The Prelude;*

> A youth—(he bore
> The name of Calvert—it shall live, if words
> Of mine can give it life,) in firm belief
> That by endowments not from me withheld
> Good might be furthered—in his last decay
> By a bequest sufficient for my needs
> Enabled me to pause for choice, and walk
> At large and unrestrained, nor damped too soon
> By mortal cares. Himself no Poet, yet
> Far less a common follower of the world,
> He deemed that my pursuits and labours lay
> Apart from all that leads to wealth, or even
> A necessary maintenance insures,
> Without some hazard to the finer sense;
> He cleared a passage for me, and the stream
> Flowed in the bent of Nature.[4]

"Mortal cares" are precisely what Wordsworth understood economic decisions to be. His early letters relate the understandable anxieties of one who wished to choose poetry as his profession, to "seek beneath that name / My office upon earth, and nowhere else" (*Prelude*, 11. 347–48), despite his family's desire that he pursue a viable occupation. The economic resolution of his life played a more than usual part in its imaginative resolution as well. To William Mathews's proposal that he give up the search for a profession and become a wanderer, Wordsworth replied, "I should not be able to reconcile to my ideas of right, the thought of wandering about a country without a certainty of being able to maintain myself. . . ."[5] Believing that "Britons born and bred" were "early trained / To earn, by wholesome labour in the field, / The bread they eat,"[6] he had to concede that the poet's quest might be arrested by the sort of economic crisis related in the 1805 *Prelude:* "Reluctantly to England I returned, / Compelled by nothing else than absolute want / Of funds for my support. . . ."[7] If Calvert's bequest did not reconcile the idea of right and the certainty of honorable maintenance, it certainly helped allay the immediate conflict between them.

But the legacy did more, and this additional benefit is Wordsworth's real subject: Calvert's gift "enabled me," he says, "to pause for choice." The choice pertains to the interdependence of material and imaginative possibilities and recalls the burden described in book 1 of *The Prelude,* where Wordsworth attempted to justify the poet's occupation to himself, to posit poetry as a labor worthy of regard, and to find a sufficient starting point for this poem about the growth of a poet's mind. The first book's ensuing debate over the "Power of choice" (1.166) dramatizes, therefore, the economic implications of metaphysical considerations. Sometimes, the poet considers taking his work from the lost labors of earlier authors and so "will settle on some British theme, some old / Romantic tale by Milton left unsung" (1.168-69). And "sometimes it suits me better to invent / A tale from my own heart" (1.221-22). Resolution occurs when the British theme of wholesome labor becomes a tale from his own heart, when the search for the origin of his poetic work is centered in and mediated by his attempt to define poetry as *real* work, genuine "labor." When Wordsworth compares himself to "a home-bound labourer" (1.101), that trope may seek to reverse the directionless wandering of his own youth, and also that of Adam and Eve at the end of *Paradise Lost,* and so posit its author as a strong successor to Milton's labor. But the image also ought to bring home to the reader Wordsworth's equally "determined aim" (1.115): to identify his poetic task as a moral and economic equivalent of the work done in the fields.

In the last book of *The Prelude,* Wordsworth also pauses, not *for* choice but *by* choice, and realizes, in retrospect, the contiguity of moral, economic, and aesthetic cares which Calvert's enabling bequest has represented. The passage depicts Wordsworth's complex identification of economic and poetic labor. Although Calvert's inheritance alleviated one sort of care—the poet's financial tribulations—it entailed another sort. The inheritance became a passing of Calvert's life, as well as his money, into the poet's hands. Wordsworth assumes the care of Calvert's mortality and good "name"—"if words / Of mine can give it life." They do. By not withholding "endowments" from the poet, Calvert released the imaginative endowments of the poet's words, which are here specifically returned to and bestowed upon Calvert at the conclusion of *The Prelude,* as if the work as a whole were the interest on, the recompense for, Calvert's bequest. A Coleridge-like "Friend," Calvert comes to profit the poem in more ways than one, for his gift, when properly accepted and returned, has both bequeathed and acquired "life"; it has transformed the kind of "mortal cares" which connect the two men. Fully articulated as the poem, the bequest reveals, yet once more, the quality and multiplicity of our moral relations.

To an uncharitable reader, however, Wordsworth's attitude might seem self-serving: wealth becomes a "hazard to the finer sense" for those who do not have it and an instrument by which "Good might be furthered" for those who do. E. E. Bostetter's reading appears to deprecate the very economics of the imagination which, he claims, Wordsworth affirmed: "For the first time [Wordsworth] had a steady financial income, thanks to the bequest left him by Calvert. And, if he felt momentarily disillusioned, he also felt enriched and fulfilled. He was confident of his poetic powers and his ability to use them. He had almost inexhaustible emotional capital to draw on: he needed no new experiences."[8] Whereas Bostetter rightly suggests a correspondence between Wordsworth's economics and his poetics, this critique does not pursue Wordsworth's argument to its most fertile conclusion, the one that Wordsworth himself reached.[9] Wordsworth's newly confirmed sense of "profession" allowed him also to regard poetry itself as part of an economic transaction, with the poem endowing its own form of exchange (as it does in giving life to Calvert's good name). Whatever his sense of "emotional capital," Wordsworth was also probing more deeply than either his predecessors or his contemporaries into the economic status of poiesis itself, the need to produce in all readers a disposition in harmony with the author's own understanding of poetry as a socially productive, economically pertinent labor. Wordsworth found that such production required a new evaluation of those "pursuits and labors" which "lay / Apart from all that leads to wealth." It required, therefore, a new evaluation of the worth of the reader's labor.

In Wordsworth's poetic exchanges, labor bestowed and labor commanded—the relationship between systems of production and consumption, text and implied reader—could still be computed directly. In the language of such theorists as Adam Smith, poetry's labor exchanges took place in the realm of barter, in a fictively realized agrarian economy.[10] To refute, through the imagination, "the doctrines of political economy which are now prevalent"[11] meant inculcating "the economic virtues" (*Prose*, 3:245) which political economics had obscured. A man "should be versed in the knowledge of existing facts" (*Prose*, 3:253)—among which Wordsworth explicitly cites "the use of money" and "pecuniary difficulties" (*Prose*, 3:251). "Versed" is not an idle word. Poetry produces this knowledge. But "the production of poetry" (*Prose*, 3:26) also *reverses* current modes of economic production, restoring them to their origins in labor—in the mutual exertions of poet and reader. More specifically, the poetic or creative process is communal; its moral relations are incorporated in the psychomachia which the text enacts with its readers. In assessing poetry's power to affect moral choices, Wordsworth required a poetic economics that would leave the reader "versed" in the use of both the economic and the aesthetic imagination and that, by showing the connection between them, would educate the reader in the reciprocal labor demanded of him. As the rural laborer became an archetype for the poetic laborer, so the rural community became the prototype for poetry's compensatory faith, with its evocation of "the Poet, singing a song in which all human beings join him. . ." (*Prose*, 1: 141). The participatory impulse of this "song," like Blake's exchanges in *Jerusalem,* would realize its labor power when the poet's work was both bestowed and commanded, the latter action effectively dispossessing the former of any taint of vanity.

For Wordsworth, these reciprocating actions became equivalent in exchange. To show why, the initial work of the Wordsworthian poet had to be that of a teacher: "Every great Poet is a Teacher; I wish either to be considered as a Teacher, or a nothing."[12] Thus, Wordsworth sought to achieve a "dominion over the spirits of readers by which they are to be humbled and humanised." Some might agree with one critic that this "is a very odd thought. Perhaps it never occurred to any other poet."[13] And some have found that Wordsworth's avowed, didactic purpose—his sense of "profession"—is, after all, too vauntingly professorial. At best, however, it is more accurate to say that Wordsworth's instruction is meant to be passed on rather than passed down; imparted, not imposed. The "ephebe," to use Harold Bloom's Stevensian description of the reader, is not seen as a passive recipient but as a toiling co-learner whose expertise is acquired by means of the ego, by the individual labor of a conscious and reflective self.[14] Whereas the instruction transacted by Wordsworth's poetry may be seen as the logical and inevitable consequence of the instruction which the poet himself had received, usually (but not always) at the hands of nature, Wordsworth proceeds to create *through his poems* his most inclusive figure of compensation: the literary work as a form of labor to be exchanged for the reader's. In respect to the economics of poetry, the successive labor of the reader is a recompense for the original work bestowed upon the text. Thus, the importance of the *reader's* work mediates between Wordsworth's economic idea of rural labor and his poetic idea of (civilized) instruction.

Wordsworthian "instruction" participates in the architectonic soul making evoked in the opening lines of *Paradise Lost:*

And chiefly Thou O spirit, that dost prefer
Before all Temples th'upright heart and pure,
Instruct me, for Thou know'st. . . .[15]

Instruction is literally an in-forming, a building from within of the inner self, as Milton understood: "What in me is dark / Illumine, what is low raise and support" (*PL*, 1.22–23). Here, the blind Miltonic poet is also an ephebe, instructed so that he may be restructured as the divinely inspired bard, justifying the ways of God to men. In Wordsworth's case, poetry is seen as "the image of Man and nature" (*Prose*, 1:146), its exercise an attempt "to justify myself" (as the poet explains in the 1800 Preface to the *Lyrical Ballads*), "to state what I have proposed to myself to perform" (*Prose*, 1:122).[16] In Wordsworth's meditation on the connection between economics and the status of poetic consciousness (a meditation inaugurated in the Preface to the *Lyrical Ballads* and expanded in the poetry composed between Calvert's death and the acknowledgment of him in *The Prelude*), Wordsworth proposed an imaginative reworking of the economic processes which threatened, in the later view of Marx, to deprive the labor process of its imaginative powers. For Wordsworth, economic discourse was not yet a wholly alienated form of expression. To the contrary, in justifying the ways of poetry to man, it might help instruct man's labor within an economy of human sufficiency.

The original Preface to the *Lyrical Ballads* was Wordsworth's first public declaration of poetry as his profession; it spoke to men whose own language had become increasingly inflected with terms of commerce and business, accumulation and exchange. If poetic composition required "selecting from the real language of men, or which amounts to the same thing, composing accurately in the spirit of such selection" (*Prose,* 1:143), then by composing accurately in that spirit, Wordsworth would frame a poetic economics which could both expound and bear witness to the productive reality of the poet's labor. He thus distinguishes between the poet and the man of science: "The knowledge both of the Poet and the Man of Science is pleasure; but the knowledge of the one cleaves to us as a necessary part of our existence, our natural and unalienable inheritance; the other is a personal and individual acquisition, slow to come to us, and by no habitual and direct sympathy connecting us with our fellow-beings" (*Prose,* 1:40–41). Although one kind of knowledge is seen as "inheritance" and the other as "acquisition," the poet also implies that knowledge itself is a commodity, which is economically and quantitatively rendered in either case. The labors of scientist and poet merely use qualitatively different means of realizing and circulating that product.

The line drawn between capitalist inheritance and capitalist acquisition may seem, at first sight, rather too fine, but Wordsworth differentiates further between the *kinds* of pleasure yielded by each. Pleasure is directly connected to the *quality* of the self's investment in the cognitive process. Thus, the poet galvanizes "a certain quantity of immediate knowledge" into "the quality of intuitions" (*Prose,* 1:140), employing the poem so as to engender cognition as feeling. Marx would also attribute this transformational power to labor: "By thus acting on the external world and changing it, [the laborer] at the same time changes his own nature." Thus, the laborer "opposes himself to Nature as one of her own forces . . . in order to appropriate Nature's productions in a

form adapted to his own wants."[17] The laborer is himself changed
by what he adds to nature: he is himself the product of his labor.
On the one hand, the man at work acts as one of nature's own
forces, for his acts of imaginative appropriation and intellectual
adaptation merely imitate and recapitulate the natural process of
(for instance) biological evolution. On the other hand, the laborer
is also opposed to nature, for the end of his labor is ultimately internal and cognitive, a transformation of consciousness by means
of consciousness. For Wordsworth, the poet's labor also sustains
that delicate balance between opposing and appropriating nature.
On the one hand, he appropriates "natural" language, the language
really used by men. On the other hand, he transforms this language into the "unnatural" utterances of a poem. Although he then
tries to "naturalize" this language again by means of such mimetic
devices as meter, rhythm, and rhyme, the mental labor of the poet
always betrays a contest between the poet's imaginative use of language "in a form adapted to his own wants" and the "natural"
product, the real language which has been thus appropriated.

Poetry's capacity for imparting pleasure is the test of its success
in overcoming this contest. When cognition acquires the quality of
intuition, then "thought" will be both felt and understood. The
man of science instructs us in understanding only; the poet teaches
us that mental labor is necessarily pleasurable, as inevitable as our
feelings. The labor of the man of science (such as the economist)
produces "facts," but the poet's labor reproduces itself. More specifically, the poem teaches the reader how knowledge is *embodied*,
not in the commodity which the poet's labor has created (the
text) but in the pleasure which that labor imparts (through the
text, to the reader). Unfortunately, the products which men have
added to nature in the name of economic progress have taught
men to regard themselves as merely opposed to nature (and to
each other) and not as "one of [nature's] own forces" as well:

> For a multitude of causes unknown to former times are now
> acting with a combined force to blunt the discriminating pow-
> ers of the mind, and unfitting it for all voluntary exertion
> to reduce it to a state of almost savage torpor. The most ef-
> fective of these causes are the great national events which are
> daily taking place, and the increasing accumulation of men in
> cities, where the uniformity of their occupations produces a
> craving for extraordinary incident. . . . [*Prose*, 1:128]

A further comparison is implicitly drawn between the discriminating powers of the poet's labor and the occupations of the accumulating masses. But Wordsworth goes on to say that a cumulative "uniformity" has depressed his own profession. Poetic tradition has prescribed a kind of acceptable poetic diction and acceptable poetic forms; it has acquired a conventionalized, abstract language. The public's uniformity of response has created a "taste" which poets too willingly oblige. This "taste" creates a further division of labor—an effectual barrier to direct commerce between labor bestowed and labor commanded. Standard eighteenth-century poetic practice often allowed the public to "exult over the Poet as over a man ignorant of his own profession" (*Prose,* 1:132) when he did not meet its expectations and desires.

Wordsworth attacks this condition by identifying the economic predicament of modern man as a case of aesthetic torpor. The public has forgotten that "an *accurate* taste in poetry, and in all the other arts . . . is an *acquired* talent, which can only be produced by thought and a long continued intercourse with the best models of composition" (*Prose,* 1:156). Acquisition is honorific in this context because it is related to attentive, individualistic *labor,* to the productions of the reader's *talent,* and to the need for exchange ("intercourse"). But the public has forgotten what *work* is required on its part even as it demands a kind of poetic production which will confirm its own forgetfulness. "If Poetry be a subject on which much time has not been bestowed, the judgment may be erroneous . . ." (*Prose,* 1:156). This judgment of the value of time further connects the reader's response to Wordsworth's new labor theory of poetic value.

Contrary to all popular understanding of the Romantic poet as a self-centered and isolated individualist, Wordsworth's sense of poetry's social value depends upon instructing the reader in the true meaning of social production—the relevance (and dignity) of another's labor to the poet's own. He proceeds to inform the reader in two ways. The poem proposes, first of all, "to choose incidents and situations from common life, and to relate or describe them, throughout, as far as was possible in a selection of language really used by men . . ." (*Prose,* 1:123). But the task of relating confronts an immediate obstacle. When, in the "Essay Supplementary to the Preface," Wordsworth speaks of "the appropriate business of poetry, . . . her appropriate employment," he goes on to note that poetry is in danger of becoming "only an occasional recreation": "to those whose existence passes away in a course of fashionable pleasure, it is a species of luxurious amusement." Often the reader comes to poetry without the desire to be informed but only to escape the pressing business of business life itself: "The Book was probably taken up after an escape from the burden of business, and with a wish to forget the world . . ." (*Prose,* 3:63-64).

The poet must, therefore, inform his reader in a literal sense as well. He must bring his reader into form, teaching him to regard the "business" of poetry as pertinent to and not as an escape from the commercial relations of the world. His economic metaphors must strike at the heart of the reader's forgetfulness, the comatose state to which commerce has reduced him, by forcing the reader to rethink the economic reality of his life. A favorite Wordsworthian sentiment is borrowed from Coleridge: "Every author, as far as he is great and at the same time *original,* has had the task of *creating* the taste by which he is to be enjoyed . . ." (*Prose,* 3:80). If the poet is "a man speaking to men," then he must regard the public not as an autonomous mass, but as real men and women. He can overcome this temptation, Wordsworth feels, only by distinguishing himself as a man *speaking,* as an individual laboring and not as a medium of "poetic sensibility." After all, Wordsworth wryly notes: "Poems, however humble in their kind, if they be good in that kind, cannot read themselves . . ." (*Prose,* 3:29).

In economic exchange, work is transformed into labor through the medium of price. In poetic exchange, the poet's work becomes productive labor when mediated by the evaluative process of reading. For Wordsworth, the reader is the inevitable product of poetic creation. But the added burden of *in-forming* the reader is also what distinguishes the poet's task from the imaginative efforts of economists. In the penultimate book of *The Prelude* (book 13 in the 1850 version) and again in the last book of *The Excursion,* Wordsworth asserts that the value of the poet's labor supersedes economic prescriptions for a "Wealth of Nations" by virtue of its superior power to instruct. Having identified politicians and economists as "modern statists,"[18] as rulers of "the passive world," and as men whose plans are "without thought, or built on theories / Vague and unsound" (*Prelude,* 13.70-71), the poet has "brought [their] books" to what he calls the "proper test" (13.71-72):

And having thus discerned how dire a thing
Is worshipped in that idol proudly named
"The Wealth of Nations," *where* alone that wealth
Is lodged, and how increased; and having gained
A more judicious knowledge of the worth
And dignity of individual man,
No composition of the brain, but man
Of whom we read, the man whom we behold
With our own eyes—I could not but inquire—
Not with less interest than heretofore,
But greater, though in spirit more subdued—
Why is this glorious creature to be found
One only in ten thousand? [13.76-88]

Wordsworth specifically rejects the *imaginative* orientation of the
statists' books, their failure to produce the "man / Of whom we
read," *as* "the man whom we behold / With our own eyes." Books
of economics do not tell us "*where* alone that wealth / Is lodged,
and how increased," because the man whom they portray is merely a "composition of the brain." To read about him is merely to
confirm his fictitiousness. But to participate in Wordsworth's inquiry is to discover wealth's true lodging in the principle of increase
which "right reading" bestows. What the poet himself has gained,
in the act of reading (and rejecting) the statists' books, is the realization that *here,* in his own work, the reader whom he evokes and
the "individual" whose "worth and dignity" he describes are *in
fact* the same man. The individual value of the reader (and of reading) is rightly prized only in the economics of *his* book, Wordsworth implies.

Whenever Wordsworth refers to economists it is to repeat the
point that their instruction is defective. Although they possess the
means for improving life, they have failed to inform this machin-
ery with imaginative authority. The Wanderer in *The Excursion*
refers to economic planning as

                        evils that are new and chosen,
A bondage lurking under shape of good,—
Arts, in themselves beneficent and kind,
But all too fondly followed and too far. . . . [9.187-90]

The question is: how far is too far? The Wanderer's antidote to ec-

onomic malaise indicates, in effect, that literary work has not gone
far enough in reshaping the economic arts:

> O for the coming of that glorious time
> When, prizing knowledge as her noblest wealth
> And best protection, this imperial Realm,
> While she exacts allegiance, shall admit
> An obligation, on her part, to *teach*
> Them who are born to serve her and obey;
> Binding herself by statute to secure
> For all the children whom her soil maintains
> The rudiments of letters, and inform
> The mind with moral and religious truth,
> Both understood and practiced. . . . [9.293-313]

The principal *poetic* model which Wordsworth inherited for economically instructing the reader and for engendering a practical
awareness of man's "noblest wealth" was the georgic. That is: the
georgic is one literary genre which specifically attempts to bestow
practical information for nurturing and sustaining the social contract; it provides for a direct transference of economic consciousness into literature. In his notes to book 9 of *The Excursion,*
Wordsworth singled out and praised Dyer's georgic, *The Fleece,*
for "the pleasing picture . . . given of the influence of manufacturing industry upon the face of this Island" (*Poetical Works,* 5:469).
In the same breath, however, Wordsworth had to concede the difference between his task and Dyer's. For Wordsworth, the didactic
function of the georgic had become compromised by the belated,
pernicious effects of this same "manufacturing industry." In this
new economy, who would listen to the ruralizations of the georgic?
In order to restructure this older genre to meet changing economic
practices and so that it could again by used to inform new, "modern" readers, Wordsworth first needed to compare poetry's economic potential with the imaginative deficiency of economics
itself.

Thus, in the 1800 Preface, Wordsworth appropriated economic
terminology—the idea of a metrical "contract"—to describe the
sense of "allegiance," "obligation," and "statute" (in *The Excursion*'s words) which should govern the aesthetic relationship between poet and reader: "I will not take upon me to determine the
exact import of the promise which, by the act of writing in verse,

an Author, in the present day makes to his reader: but it will un-
doubtedly appear to many persons that I have not fulfilled the
terms of an engagement thus voluntarily contracted" (*Prose,* 1:
123). The contract is especially significant here because Wordsworth himself concedes that he may not have fulfilled it. By means
of his confession, however, Wordsworth was already forging a new
sense of contract in which the promise made by the author to the
reader would exact a commensurate promise from the reader in
turn. That is, the poet's effort "to relate or describe" "incidents
and situations from common life" would become valuable only
when the relation between poet and reader had been voluntarily
contracted on *both* sides. The poet's labor would be fulfilled only
in exchange with the reader's. The "terms" of this reciprocating
"engagement" are economic, but in Wordsworth's poetry, such
commercial metaphors could take on a humanistic value and purpose which economics itself often lacked. Restructuring economics
as a more vigilant fiction, Wordsworth's burden would be to show
that the poetic "contract" thus negotiated through the reciprocity
of creator and beholder had a signifying "power" equivalent to the
biblical covenant between God and man.[19]

Adam Smith asserted that wealth was power: "The exchangeable value of everything must always be precisely equal to the extent of this power which it conveys to the owner."[20] Wordsworth
understood the exchange value of poetry in precisely the same
(capitalist) terms: "Every great poet with whose writings men are
familiar, in the highest exercise of his genius, before he can be
thoroughly enjoyed, has to call forth and to communicate *power*
... " (*Prose,* 3:82). For Wordsworth, as for Smith, this power extends to the exchange practices of producer (poet) and consumer
(reader): "Therefore to create taste is to call forth and bestow
power, of which knowledge is the effect; and *there* lies the true
difficulty" (ibid.). The difficulty arises because, in the economics
of Wordsworth's imagination, the poet and the reader have a more
or less equal value. Contractually, each is a part owner of the
poem. The difficulty is increased (or perhaps merely made manifest) when one realizes what has happened to the word "taste" in
Wordsworth's new use of it. In positing the reader as a consumer,
he has also taken the idea of "taste" literally: the exchanges of
poetry become acts of appetite, facts of nurture. Like Hazlitt's
metaphor in his essay "On Gusto," Wordsworth's metaphor has

radically equated the reader's aesthetic judgment with poetry's power to sustain him. To create "taste" in this sense is to imagine poetic exchange not merely as an economic trope but as Ruskinesque "food for the Mouth" as well.

Wordsworth, then, incurs a risk which the older poets did not or could not assume. In reevaluating the trading partners, he also reassesses the nature of poetic exchange as such. In the case of an older poetic, centered upon the use of "poetic diction," "the Reader is utterly at the mercy of the Poet, respecting what imagery or diction he may choose to connect with the passion" (*Prose*, 1: 145). But in the new poetics espoused by Wordsworth, "the metre obeys certain laws, to which the Poet and Reader both willingly submit because they are certain and because no interference is made by them with the passion. . ." (ibid.). No "interference" or standard of poetic "taste" (which serves, in aesthetic theory, as the equivalent of money) will mediate between labor bestowed and labor commanded. Wordsworth's language is imagined only as a *measure* of value; it is not, like poetic diction, an interchangeable *commodity* which can become institutionalized. Nor is the reader an unproductive consumer in Wordsworth's poetics. For the test of poetry's value is the amount of *labor* that the reader is himself willing to produce for the sake of exchange: "Because without the exertion of a co-operating *power* in the mind of the Reader, there can be no adequate sympathy with either of these emotions; without this auxiliary impulse, elevated or profound passion cannot exist" (*Prose*, 3:81). This remarkable passage grounds the idea of sublimity ("elevated or profound passion") in the palpable exercise of cooperating labors. Passion, then, is the *effect* of exchange and is not prior to it. Passion depends upon the reader's sympathy; it is not the private possession of a single, deeply sensitive individual but is created, like the process of cognition itself, in the give-and-take of multiple sensibilities. No one has cornered the market on passion. In effect, passion is a form of knowledge—*felt* knowledge; Mill called it a culture of the feelings. Sublimity is not transcendent passion, therefore, but the recognition that, in being shared, passion may also be borne, lived with.

Like Marx's capitalist, Wordsworth imagines that his labor theory creates its own surplus value: "If Nature be thus cautious to preserve in a state of enjoyment a being so employed, the Poet ought to profit by the lesson held forth to him, and ought espe-

cially to take care, that, whatever passions he communicates to the
Reader, those passions, if his Reader's mind be sound and vigorous, should always be accompanied with an overbalance of pleasure" (*Prose*, 1:149–51). "Overbalance" accrues to *both* reader
and poet because their mutual "contract" forms the basis of it.
The reader's pleasure is his recognition that the poet's labor is original and not a paltry derivation from "taste" and "sensibility."
Wordsworth answers the question of whether nature really *can*
"preserve in a state of enjoyment a being so employed" by transforming it. Ultimately, the poet looks to the reader's corresponding energy, as much as to nature's, for the source of his "profit."
Poetry's surplus value is its ability to re-form the reader. Thus,
the poet's original relation to nature as a laborer alters with his
acknowledgment of labor as a form of (human) exchange. As always in Wordsworth, the breaking away from a direct relationship
to nature is seen as growth. Although the end of poetry is self-
realization, that individual purpose depends upon communicating
with another. To effect communication, the poet must transform
his imagination into a form that can be recognized by others. This
he calls "mutual sympathy." Poetry, Wordsworth implies, "over-
balances" nature, for it is the poem and not nature which *preserves*
one man's state of enjoyment by transforming it into imaginative
currency, a source of compensation for another. Ultimately, the
"business" of poetic exchange is to humanize "labor."

The so-called organic nature of Romantic poetics is posited
throughout Wordsworth's Prefaces as an exchange of labor modeled upon an economic contract. Acknowledging that this contract
sometimes fails, Wordsworth still insists on the essential validity of
his metaphor, here unfolded in all its complexity:

> The love, the admiration, the indifference, the slight, the
> aversion, and even the contempt, with which these Poems
> have been received, knowing, as I do, the source within my
> own mind, from which they have proceeded, and the labour
> and pains, which, when labour and pains appeared needful,
> have been bestowed upon them, must all, if I think consis-
> tently, be received as pledges and tokens, bearing the same
> general impression, though widely different in value; —they
> are all proofs that for the present time I have not laboured in
> vain; and afford assurances, more or less authentic, that the
> products of my industry will endure. [*Prose*, 3:80]

Syntactical positioning disrupts the grammar of this sentence, creating an initial uncertainty over which pledges what and how exactly the conflicting responses of Wordsworth's readers are related
to the poet's original effort. The uncertainty is made difficult because Wordsworth exploits it when he chooses to regard *both* his
readers' responses *and* his subsequent response to those responses
as forms of currency, as pledges and tokens that he has not labored in vain. The basis of his assurance is the precisely ambivalent
antecedent of "they" in the clause, "knowing, as I do, the source
within my own mind, from which *they* have proceeded. . . ." If
"they" refers to "these Poems," then the source of their value is
the (mental) labor and pains originally bestowed upon their production. But at this point in the sentence, "they" may also refer—
surprisingly, but equally correctly—to the range of responses elicit-
ed by "these Poems." Thus, the syntax implies that the poems and
the readers' responses to them bear the same general impression
because the poet knows the source of both in *his* mind. In effect,
the multiplicity of the readers' responses comes to reflect the multiplicity of (the poet's) emotions which went into the poems' composition in the first place.

The syntax makes reader response and poetic effort correlative,
even interchangeable. If the responses of Wordsworth's readers are
not—all of them—exactly what he desired, then this disparity
merely indicates the difficulty of fulfilling the contract which he
had proposed. If he had wished for the public's approbation, its
tasteful approval, he could have proposed a different poetic. But
what he affirms instead is the working contract; the poet, becoming in turn the reader of his readers' passions, shows how much he
himself values the reading process. "Value" is attained not when
poetry reproduces the "facts" of the common day but when it
touches the real lives of men: not only their love, but also their indifference and even their contempt. Although these responses are
"widely different in value," they are all part of the same "proof":
"that . . . I have not laboured in vain." This resolution is not a
form of vanity, however, because the *products* of Wordsworth's
industry are not merely the poems but also the whole congeries of
response which his poems have provoked. The moral relations described *by* his poems are, Wordsworth imagines, embodied *in* the
responses listed here. In exchange, as tokens of each other, they
make up one subliminal contract. The sincerity of Wordsworth's

economic logic is nowhere better illustrated than in his self-admonishing tone. He admits, after all, that the "assurances" asserted here are only "more or less authentic." But we ought not to underestimate what Wordsworth feels he can "afford" merely because the economic trope strains here to console the author. Whatever the practical difficulties of the contract that Wordsworth wished to negotiate, we need not confuse his solace with solipsism, or his self-instruction with vanity.

In "Resolution and Independence," Wordsworth tests the terms of his contract by learning how to become his own reader. The poem is a meticulously constructed dramatization of how the thinking self comes to regard the value of its own thoughts as a source of comfort. The opening description of the dove's song might be seen as an emblem of the poem's internal dynamics: "Over his own sweet voice the Stock-dove broods" (l. 5). At the beginning of the poem, the speaker broods over his own sweet carefree life until that brooding becomes a burden. At the end, the poet's prayer for himself bears witness to the power of (and his belief in) his own voice. In responding to the Leech-Gatherer's choice word and measured phrase, the poet emerges as the prototypical reader whom he sought to identify in the Prefaces. The poet's response to the Leech-Gatherer's occupation allows him to imagine his own "honest maintenance," a poetry which need not end in "despondency and madness."

At the beginning of the poem, the speaker's freedom from employment reminds him that such "joy" often turns into its opposite, and that "there may come another day to me— / Solitude, pain of heart, distress, and poverty" (ll. 34–35). Doubting the power of joy, the poet doubts his own place in "life's business":

> My whole life I have lived in pleasant thought,
> As if life's business were a summer mood;
> As if all needful things would come unsought
> To genial faith, still rich in genial good;
> But how can he expect that others should
> Build for him, sow for him, and at his call
> Love him, who for himself will take no heed at all?
> [Ll. 36–42]

"Pleasant thought" here means thought without labor, thought which effects (and requires) no action. When he thinks, however, of Burns, the laborer-poet "following his plough along the mountain-side" (l. 46), this evocation of the poet as an actual laborer reminds Wordsworth that *he* neither labors nor weeps but merely idles away his time. Despondency comes almost as retribution for too much "joy," as if the balance between them was what constituted man's "dues" (l. 98), as if "madness" and "gladness" were "homeostatic" rhymes: "We Poets in our youth begin in gladness; / But thereof come in the end despondency and madness" (ll. 48–49).[21]

"Now" (l. 50), at the very moment when he is most despondent over the fate of poets (and when his dejection seems mostly self-generated), Wordsworth unexpectedly meets a self-sufficient laborer who is also a kind of poet. Wordsworth tries to reject his previous "thoughts" as "untoward," both because they do not move toward the kind of resolution needed and because they are impropitious, self-pitying. But after his initial question to the Leech-Gatherer, "What occupation do you there pursue?" (l. 88), the old doubts return:

> My former thought returned: the fear that kills;
> And hope that is unwilling to be fed;
> Cold, pain, and labour, and all fleshly ills;
> And mighty Poets in their misery dead.
> —Perplexed, and longing to be comforted,
> My question eagerly did I renew,
> "How is it that you live, and what is it you do?"
> [Ll. 113–19]

We may understand "the fear that kills" *as* the "hope that is unwilling to be fed," because the poet's "misery" is also a form of miser-y—a hoarding of resources, a continued squandering of his "labor" in that self-inflicted perplexity which can be neither unwilled nor comforted but only "renewed."

Both gladness and despondency are seen as "untoward," however, when the Leech-Gatherer replies to these questions by explaining where he lives and what he lives for:

> He with a smile did then his words repeat;
> And said, that, gathering leeches, far and wide
> He travelled; stirring thus about his feet
> The waters of the pools where they abide.
> "Once I could meet with them on every side;

> But they have dwindled long by slow decay;
> Yet still I persevere, and find them where I may."
> [Ll. 120-26]

Except for the quotation marks in the printed text, a listener would not know who had spoken the last three lines. In effect, the two voices (of poet-speaker and poet-respondent) have become one. Indeed, it is difficult at this moment to know who is listening to whom. The old man pursues his thoughts; Wordsworth pursues his: "While I these thoughts within myself pursued, / He, having made a pause, the same discourse renewed" (ll. 132-33). We are not told what the Leech-Gatherer makes of his thoughts, but we are told what Wordsworth makes of the "pause" which the old man has given him. "Longing to be comforted," Wordsworth truly *renews* his discourse when, repeating his "genial faith" (l. 39) in a new key, he reads the Leech-Gatherer's wanderings as symbolic of his own mental vacillations—and as a cure for them:

> While he was talking thus, the lonely place,
> The old Man's shape, and speech—all troubled me:
> In my mind's eye I seemed to see him pace
> About the weary moors continually,
> Wandering about alone and silently. [Ll. 127-31]

The precise symbolic significance of the Leech-Gatherer as wanderer is less important than the process of "pursuit" by which the poet's wandering thoughts have discovered their own "discourse," finding a comfort in the configuration of the poem itself.[22] What Wordsworth affirms at last is the labor process by which thought follows consecutively from thought to yield "an honest maintenance" (l. 105): the ability to earn one's own sustenance by the dignity and worth of one's individual effort. What is curious about this poem is that the poet's individuality becomes a source of affirmation only when he confronts the individual strength of another. The poet's self-sufficiency, his power of choice, becomes manifest only when he takes the Leech-Gatherer as a "help" and "stay secure" (l. 139) for the irresolution of his own labor.

In "Resolution and Independence," the poet himself acts out the contractual agreement of the 1800 Preface by finding in the Leech-Gatherer a "practical faith" for his own enterprise.[23] Having discovered "In that decrepit Man so firm a mind" (l. 138), Wordsworth realizes almost unawares a firmness in his own mind and a

justification for his own occupation. A creative reader, Wordsworth takes "a stranger's privilege" (l. 82) and confronts the old
man with "an auxiliary impulse" and "a corresponding energy."
Wordsworth's ability to respond—literally, to talk back—is ultimately what resolves the fear that his is a wasted labor. Resolution
elicits a new increment, the accomplishment of "Resolution and
Independence."[24]

"By our own spirits," Wordsworth asserts, "are we deified"
(l. 47). As the Leech-Gatherer ministered to what was untoward
in Wordsworth's thoughts, so later, in response to Sara Hutchinson, Wordsworth tried to recall yet another reader to her own best
spirits: "You speak of [the Leech-Gatherer's] speech as tedious:
everything is tedious when one does not read with the feelings of
the Author" (*LEY*, p. 367). In this poem, however, both the
Leech-Gatherer and Wordsworth are "authors." If Sarah Hutchinson had read with the feelings of the author, then her response to
Wordsworth's poem would have been precisely what the poet himself had experienced in the encounter with the Leech-Gatherer. In
other words, Wordsworth himself, as a "reader" in the poem, acts
out the exchanges which he hopes the poem might perpetuate in
contracting the labor of *its* reader(s). Wordsworth's question to
the Leech-Gatherer—"What occupation do you there pursue?"—is,
then, the challenge he makes to himself. The poet's experience as
reader indicates that reading is in itself a productive labor process;
in reading with the feelings of the Leech-Gatherer, Wordsworth resolves to pursue his own occupation, thus becoming the author of
his own independence.

In theory, then, Wordsworth's labor theory afforded him an op-
portunity to describe in concrete terms the way a poem actually
worked, how it functioned in exchange. In practice, we have yet
to determine if the archetypal reader in "Resolution and Independence" is actually applicable to our *own* labor as readers. One remembers that Blake, commenting on the Essay Supplementary to
the Preface, with its daring poetic economics, growled, "I do not
know who wrote these Prefaces: they are very mischievous & direct
contrary to Wordsworth's own practice."[25] In "Michael," however, the poet, who is again a kind of auditor or witness, will
specifically enjoin the reader in a cooperative attempt to surmount
both the economic and moral effects of Michael's family tragedy.

The story of "Michael" describes how property is lost and how, in the prodigal wanderings of Michael's son Luke, a certain kind of communal knowledge and familial labor is also relinquished. Writing about "Michael" to Thomas Poole, Wordsworth indicated that he wished to dramatize the connection between the two by giving "a picture of a man, of strong mind and lively sensibility, agitated by two of the most powerful affections of the human heart, the parental affection, and the love of property, *landed* property, including the feelings of inheritance, home, and personal and family independence" (*LEY*, p. 322). Such a picture represents, as the poet claims in *The Excursion,* "The old domestic morals of the land" (8.236)—the connection between the economics of ownership and the economy of soul-making. And yet, though the subject is loss (as if Michael were a kind of mute, inglorious Milton), the poem is not an elegy. Wordsworth himself called it "A Pastoral." But even as a pastoral, "Michael" is a belated one, modeled on a Vergilian landowner rather than on a Theocritan shepherd. Undercutting pastoral conventions, Wordsworth intrudes into his own fiction, reminding us that the pastoral is merely a fiction—one which may also have been devalued along with Michael's intimate family economy and the labors lost upon his son. At the same time, Wordsworth calls it a "history" (l. 34). The question is: how will such a conflicted tale result in "delight" for "a few natural hearts" (l. 36)?

If we are to discover Michael's now overgrown pastoral site, we are first told to turn from the public way, taking the poet as our guide. To understand the rationale behind Wordsworth's "pastoral, " we must understand how Wordsworth came to be our guide in the first place:

> It was the first
> Of those domestic tales that spake to me
> Of Shepherds, dwellers in the valleys, men
> Whom I already loved;—not verily
> For their own sakes, but for the fields and hills
> Where was their occupation and abode. [Ll. 21–26]

Although "Michael" was one of the last poems added to the *Lyrical Ballads* (in 1802), Wordsworth here suggests that Michael's story is a kind of prototypical "lyrical ballad," "The first / Of those domestic tales that spake to me. . . ."[26] What humanized the story for Wordsworth as a boy was not, ironically, the human figures in it but the natural agency of the landscape which led him on to explore passions and feelings outside himself:

> And hence this Tale, while I was yet a Boy
> Careless of books, yet having felt the power
> Of Nature, by the gentle agency
> Of natural objects, led me on to feel
> For passions that were not my own, and think
> (At random and imperfectly indeed)
> On man, the heart of man, and human life. [Ll. 27–33]

To retell the tale (as "Michael") is to focus and to regenerate those earlier thoughts. The difference now is that the reader has changed. In making the story his own, Wordsworth himself assumes the role of nature. His story becomes "the gentle agency" which leads *us* on to passions that may not be our own:

> Therefore, although it be a history
> Homely and rude, I will relate the same
> For the delight of a few natural hearts;
> And, with yet fonder feeling, for the sake
> Of youthful poets, who among these hills
> Will be my second self when I am gone. [Ll. 34–39]

"Therefore" makes the imaginative and moral connection between poet and reader as well as the logical one between the poet's memory and his present endeavor. The "history" of the story as story is also part of the inheritance bestowed upon the reader. Such an "inheritance" is not "a personal and individual acquisition" but a communal activity, an imaginative patrimony crystallized in the act of relating stories and of relating to them.

Luke, on the other hand, relinquishes his natural inheritance by seeking private gain. His exodus to the city results in a forgetfulness, in a forfeiture of his original sympathies, and, ultimately, in a relinquishment of both his patrimonial and his imaginative rights. When Luke "reached / The public way, he put on a bold face" (ll. 426–27). This boldness is a mask against "the dissolute city" (l. 444), an inward hiding of the self, and not the boldness required to confront the mountains "face to face." In the end (and for unspecified reasons), Luke is forced "to seek a hiding-place beyond the seas" (l. 447). But the story's outward gesture toward the reader enacts a precise alternative to Luke's dissolution. Its pastoral directives command a voyage of discovery: "they / Who journey thither find themselves alone" (ll. 9-10). Journeying thither, one finds that the symbol of the son's failed labor is still visible in the unfinished sheepfold. By taking the reader directly into a landscape whose "pastoral mountains front you, face to face" (l. 5), to the very spot where this symbol may still be found, Wordsworth himself turns the sheepfold into a symbol of his own poetic "covenant" (l. 414) with his reader. The journey into the interior (of "man, the heart of man, and human life") requires the "courage" to confront "face to face" an interior landscape as well as the actual one. The poem, by its exemplary labor of sympathy, rediscovers the original impetus for both the sheepfold and the story about the sheepfold: namely, the need to forge a mutual labor—whether between father and son or between storyteller and listener. Geoffrey Hartman has aptly noted that Wordsworth is Michael's true heir (p. 266).

The poem is, thus, an act of compensation. Michael's exemplary moral life shows how the Lockean terms—life, liberty, and property—might be connected. Michael benefits from a luxurious pastoral self-sufficiency, "A pleasurable feeling of blind love, / The pleasure which there is in life itself" (ll. 76-77), because for Isabel and himself, home and labor, family and occupation, are one. Michael's property is "like a book" (l. 70) in which he could read "the certainty of honorable gain" (l. 73). And so, the family's household economy becomes "a proverb in the vale / For endless industry" (l. 94-95), and the lamp in Michael's house becomes "a public symbol of the life / That Thrifty Pair had lived" (ll. 130-31). But for the belated laborer—the poet—a different and more austere work is exacted. The truth is that Michael's virtues are only a memory; they have now been occluded by the economic conditions of what Wordsworth calls "modern life." Before constructing a poetic economics which will complete Luke's failed labor and restore the broken covenant of Michael's pastoral economy, Wordsworth must recognize the broken covenant of his own labor. Michael's agrarian economy in the poem and what Hartman calls the poet's "pastoral care for words" are both threatened.[27] When the former disappears under the complexities of economic legalisms involving entailment and inheritance, the traditional methods of the pastoral genre are similarly compromised. Because the actual pastoral narrative concerning Michael (ll. 40-466) is pre-

sented inside another narrative (the ruminations of the storyteller
as he speaks about himself and to the reader), the pastoral itself
seems distanced, just as the self-enclosed rural economy described
by the poem is distanced from modern economics. In relating
Michael's tale, the poet also reflects, through the poem, upon the
viability of pastoral fictions when confronted with the demands of
a new capitalist dispensation.

In its broadest sense, as a meditation upon the fate of poetry,
Wordsworth's poem finds its immediate literary antecedent in
Oliver Goldsmith's poem of a quarter century earlier, "The Deserted Village." Goldsmith's ostensible subject is the economic
"progress" which has led to the depopulation of the countryside,
a not uncommon concern in the eighteenth century. But Goldsmith's ultimate subject is, like Wordsworth's, the progress of poetry itself. At first, the rural virtues depart because "Luxury" has
literally left no room for them:

> The man of wealth and pride
> Takes up a space that many poor supplied;
> Space for his lake, his park's extended bounds,
> Space for his horses, equipage, and hounds. . . .[28]

And, at the end of the poem, poetry makes ready to leave England
itself, for, without the rural virtues, there is nothing further to
write about. Thus, "The Deserted Village" suggests that poetry is
also a rural virtue, vulnerable to the "rage of gain" and "trade's
proud empire," and "trade's unfeeling train":

> And thou, sweet Poetry, thou loveliest maid,
> Still first to fly where sensual joys invade;
> Unfit in these degenerate times of shame,
> To catch the heart, or strike for honest fame. . . .
> [Ll. 407–10]

Poetry's honesty—her chastity and truthfulness—is violated precisely because "Luxury" no longer makes "success" conditional
upon "Contented Toil," "hospitable Care," "Connubial Tenderness," "Piety," "steady Loyalty, and faithful Love" (ll. 405–8)—
the virtues of "Michael" as well. Thus, in Goldsmith, the poet is
seen as the last victim of wealth's paradoxical power to impoverish
what it seeks to improve:

Dear charming nymph, neglected and decried,
My shame in crowds, my solitary pride;
Thou source of all my bliss, and all my woe,
That found'st me poor at first, and keep'st me so;
Thou guide by which the nobler arts excel,
Thou nurse of every virtue, fare thee well! [Ll. 411-16]

In effect, the nymph Poetry has replaced Auburn as the "source" of all sadness and happiness, and now she suffers the same desertion as the village. Now, for Goldsmith, the dispossession of the village's pastoral economy also dispossesses the poet of his poem. Poetry's celebratory and communal function in the pastoral scheme is abandoned and finally lost, a development to which this "last" elegy for poetry must bear witness against its will.[29]

For Wordsworth, Luke's reprehensible forfeiture of his birthright is also a form of "Luxury" and creates not only an economic but also an aesthetic crisis. "Economists will tell you," Wordsworth declared in *The Excursion,* "that the State / Thrives by the forfeiture" (8.283-84)—that is, by the decision of young men to abandon an outdated agrarian and familial economy. Adam Smith, for one, saw entailment as a holdover from the more ancient law of primogeniture, and he saw the economics of primogeniture as a potential obstacle to the ongoing wealth of nations. On the other hand, Smith noted that entailments (such as the one which afflicted Michael and which prompted him to endorse his son to a salary-paying employer) were originally designed to protect the landowner from precisely the kind of choice and the kind of loss which, in Michael's case, occurred: "Entails are the natural consequences of the law of primogeniture. They were introduced to preserve a certain lineal succession, of which the law of primogeniture first gave the idea, and to hinder any part of the original estate from being carried out of the proposed line either by gift, or devise, or alienation; either by the folly, or by the misfortune of any of its successive owners" (*WN,* bk. 3, chap. 2). Such was not the case for Michael; indeed, entailment continued to threaten Michael's freeholding even after he had worked off the mortgage debt (see ll. 376-80). In his poem, however, Wordsworth was particularly interested not in the reason behind entailment or in the (considerable) legal complexities surrounding it, but in the implications of the idea of primogeniture itself.[30] The moral obligations

underlying that first idea are summed up when Michael equates
the inheritance of his father's property with the need to sustain
one's inheritance by labor: "Herein," declares Michael at his work,
"I but repay a gift which I myself / Received at others' hands . . ."
(ll. 362-64). For Wordsworth, the basis of poetic value is also a
contract which burdens the reader with the need to labor in order
to sustain that (poetic) inheritance which is a necessary part of
existence. A metaphorical law of primogeniture further entails
"Michael," insofar as Wordsworth replays, in respect to the reader,
Michael's role in respect to Luke. The labor bestowed upon Luke
prefigures the (poet's) labor bestowed upon the reader. The poem's
greatest risk is also, therefore, its greatest challenge, for it presents
the reader, symbolically, with Luke's very choice. Michael's property, which is "like a book," and Wordsworth's property, which is
this poem, become equivalent: each becomes vulnerable to a similar disregard, an equally crippling forfeiture. Wordsworth in fact
challenges the reader to help him prove that the *labor* embodied
by both of them together in the literary work is abundant recompense for the dispossession of Michael's *land*.

Wordsworth's "pastoral" is, then, an attempt to rescue the figure of poetry from the impending exile at the end of "The Deserted Village," to reconstruct a place for poetry in the "depopulated"
world. This is accomplished by turning the new economics of
capitalism into a labor theory of poetic value in which the labor
bestowed by the poet may be directly exchanged through the
auxiliary and cooperating labor of the reader—if both partners are
able to apprehend the full import of the metrical contract which
the poem proposes. In teaching the reader to see what he might
not think worthy of regard, the poem takes him back, imaginatively, to the point where the labor demanded by Michael was misunderstood by his son:

> Nor should I have made mention of this Dell
> But for one object which you might pass by,
> Might see and notice not. Beside the brook
> Appears a straggling heap of unhewn stones!
> And to that simple object appertains
> A story—unenriched with strange events,
> Yet not unfit, I deem, for the fireside,
> Or for the summer shade. [Ll. 14-21]

Wordsworth's modest parenthetical aside, "I deem," is precisely the token of his redemptive economics. The poem's value lies in its exchange, in the story's engagement of the listener who was once Wordsworth himself and who now is "you." As "history," the poem is determinedly, affirmatively revisionary: the story related by Wordsworth provides the means for transforming that "straggling heap of unhewn stones" into a new imaginative currency. The sheepfold's heap of stones symbolizes a quantity of labor which, as yet, has no qualitative value assigned to it (or whose qualitative value was lost with Luke's profligacy). It is unpriced and unmeasured until the work of author/reader valorizes and enriches it. This valorization exemplifies what Marx called "homogeneous human labor": "Value, therefore, does not stalk about with a label describing what it is. It is value, rather, that converts every product into a social hieroglyphic. Later on, we try to decipher the hieroglyphic, to get behind the secret of our own social products; for to stamp an object of utility as a value, is just as much a social product as language" (*Capital*, 1:74). Wordsworth's poem would, through *its* language, stamp the unhewn stones as a social hieroglyphic, reafffirming the mutual labor contract which binds author and reader in a new covenant. Thus, "Michael" becomes a "public symbol" to replace Michael's now redistributed ancestral property. But the poem also allows us "to get behind the secret of our social products." Behind the social hieroglyphic of the pastoral is this poetic "contract" with its new, workable art of labor, yielding an "object of utility" from what before seemed to be an outmoded poetic convention.[31]

Lore Metzger's conclusion about "Michael" summarizes traditional criticism of the poem: "The tableau of the oak and the heap of stones suggests the vanity of pastoral covenants in a rapidly changing world. . . .The old covenant has been destroyed, but there are no signs of a new dispensation" (p. 320). But this is to misapprehend the imaginative economics by which, in Metzger's view, "the poet's words can restore the pastoral covenant in an iron age" (p. 323). Wordsworth does not restore the pastoral; he creates a new georgic. Marx was to declare that the laborer "raises his structure in imagination before he erects it in reality" (*Capital*, 1:178). Even though, in reality, the sheepfold remains unfinished and abandoned, Wordsworth's poem completes the structure raised in imagination—that is, the original idea behind the sheepfold and the moral purpose symbolized by it. After laying the cornerstone of the sheepfold, Michael had said to Luke, "Now, fare thee well— / When thou return'st, thou in this place wilt see / A work which is not here . . ." (ll. 412–14). In "Michael," that work is precisely what *we* see. The reader who returns to "this place," guided by the poet, is enabled to see both what is and what is not "here" by seeing what has been made of the sheepfold in this poetic "history" and what needs to be made of the poem as a social product. Only the reader can decipher the hieroglyphic value of Michael's and Wordsworth's labor: he does so by apprehending the value of his own.

Wordsworth's most sustained celebration of his poetic contract, "Home at Grasmere," a poem written in the same year as "Michael," attempts, finally, to justify the economics of Wordsworth's imagination as an extension of his own household economy. It may therefore be read, psychically, as the successor to "Michael," as Wordsworth's attempt to consolidate the georgic mode inferred there.

First published some thirty-eight years after Wordsworth's death and the only part of *The Recluse* which he had actually composed (*The Prelude* being but a prelude to this projected work), "Home at Grasmere" has eluded the close textual and critical commentary accorded to Wordsworth's other poetry. Although a full-scale reading cannot be attempted here, the context of the present inquiry is also the subtext of "Home at Grasmere." The poem seeks to explain why Wordsworth and Dorothy acquired their secluded cottage at Town End, Grasmere, and how they read the value of their acquisition. In his explanation, Wordsworth reveals that Grasmere Vale had always seemed to him a special kind of imaginative possession ever since, as a "roving School-boy," he had accidentally come upon it in a walk. Possessed by Grasmere's natural beauty, Wordsworth in his poem celebrates not only "this individual Spot" but also his sense of feeling "at home," a celebration modulating into an extended meditation upon the economics of possession. "Home at Grasmere" becomes Wordsworth's most direct and explicit attempt to define economic, moral, and aesthetic consciousness as mutually supportive and equally constitutive of the self's well-being.

The poem has little of the economic *anxiety* of *The Prelude* and no longer questions *The Prelude*'s "Power of choice." The choice had already been made. When Wordsworth moved to Grasmere, the *Lyrical Ballads* had been published; and the poet had been enabled by Calvert's bequest to choose and to purchase his own dwelling place. Whereas the act of choosing required one kind of economics, his present situation required another and perhaps more vigilant kind. He would now have to show that his "choice of the whole heart"—Grasmere—was a sufficient choice, one that continued to bestow "Power." Among his Grasmere neighbors, Wordsworth adduces a vision of labor which confirms his own aspirations as a poet, and he appropriates their rural labors as an image of his own, just as he had earlier appropriated Grasmere Vale as a private possession of his own inner thoughts. "Home at Grasmere" proceeds to speak in unabashedly economic terms about the value of the poet's work, asserting that one's individual "gain" may be turned into a "penetrating bliss" (l. 234), "a genuine frame / Of many into one incorporate" (l. 616). In declaring the communal "profit" (l. 699) to be earned "from self-regarding interests" (l. 452), Wordsworth is able to affirm an abundant "wealth" (l. 662) which replaces the "vacant commerce" (l. 595) practiced in the world from which he and Dorothy were now removed. In its poetic economics, "Home at Grasmere" may be the greatest domestic—the greatest bourgeois—poem in the language.[32]

The celebratory mode of the poem is established at the beginning, in Wordsworth's recollection of his first sight of the Vale:

Once to the verge of yon steep barrier came
A roving School-boy; what the Adventurer's age
Hath now escaped his memory—but the hour,
One of a golden summer holiday,
He well remembers, though the year be gone.
Alone and devious from afar he came;
And, with a sudden influx overpowered
At sight of this seclusion, he forgot
His haste, for hasty had his footsteps been
As boyish his pursuits; and, sighing said,
"What happy fortune were it here to live!
And, if a thought of dying, if a thought
Of mortal separation, could intrude
With paradise before him, here to die!" [Ll. 1–14]

The boy had no "paradise within him happier far" but rather, a paradise before him, here to die. In the rhythms of the Miltonic line, and with a postlapsarian consciousness which included the prospect of death, the boy seemed able to regain Paradise unawares. In the retrospective conflation of time (the boy's *age* has been forgotten but not the *hour,* although the *year* is gone), the poet remembers only a timeless, "golden summer holiday." The laborless day is indeed holy. It seems to reverse the Miltonic eviction from Eden. Alone and devious, the boy came with wandering steps in haste and was literally stopped short by his sight. Whereas Milton's holy spirit brooded over the abyss in the first book of *Paradise Lost* and made it pregnant,[33] the schoolboy encountered, at "the verge of yon steep barrier," his own "happy fortune" in the mothering, womblike enclosures of the vale whose limits are drawn by the mounting birds (ll. 193-229) as they span the abyss between sky and lake. In the cosmology of the Wordsworthian landscape, the fortunate fall is transformed into the fells of happiness—literally, the Vale of Grasmere—thus revealing the boy's potential wealth (happy fortune) as a fortuitous and unearned beatitude.

In the second paragraph, the quasi-Miltonic "barrier" has become a "Station when he look'd . . . ," the speaker's lucky brinkmanship already giving way to a sense of this spot's sacredness. Like the stations of the cross, this spot is a resting place; like a traveler's station, it is a point of congruence between the end and the beginning of a journey. In memory, Grasmere is both beginning and end. In the present time of the third paragraph, it becomes at last the adult's property: "And now 'tis mine" (l. 56). Perceiving Grasmere "as termination and a last retreat," Wordsworth also creates of it "A centre . . . , / A whole without dependence or defect," a "Unity entire" (ll. 147-51). Remembering that his wealth appeared unearned, the speaker's conclusion raises another question: "And was the cost so great?" (l. 60).

The awareness of cost depends upon the adult's understanding that memory is the true capitalist of the Wordsworthian imagination. Circumscribing present possession with the self-consciousness which is a burden of ownership, memory repeatedly deprives the self of its comforts by recalling times and occasions (such as depicted at the beginning of "Home at Grasmere") when labor seemed uncalled-for, when thought occurred as if unbidden.

> Can the choice mislead,
> That made the calmest, fairest spot of earth,
> With all its unappropriated good,
> My own. . . . [Ll. 72-75]

If the syntax of this passage suggests a question, the rhetoric offers, at the same time, an answer. Compensation for the self-consciousness of memory and for the recollection of loss is sought in the present attempt at appropriation. Living at Grasmere, Wordsworth determines to show that its previously "unappropriated good" may indeed be appropriated, that his actual economic possession of property is also therefore appropriate. He reads his own property, "This individual Spot," as yet another "spot of time" in which he finds, to his surprise, his own individuality.

Earlier manuscript versions of this poem reveal how Wordsworth pondered the question of "cost" and then transformed it:

> This solitude is mine, the distant thought
> Is fetch'd out of the heaven in which it was.
> The unappropriated bliss hath found
> An owner, and that owner I am he.
> The Lord of this enjoyment is on Earth
> And in my breast. What wonder if I speak
> With fervour, am exalted with the thought
> Of my possessions, of my genuine wealth
> Inward and outward, what I keep, have gain'd,
> Shall gain, must gain, if sound be my belief
> From past and present, rightly understood,
> That in my day of Childhood I was less
> The mind of Nature, less, take all in all,
> Whatever may be lost, than I am now.[34]

Property is an extension of the imagination, just as Dove Cottage overlooking the vale is a figural extension of Milton's dovelike spirit brooding over the abyss; it is an impregnation of the landscape by means of the imagination's investment of itself. Thus inward wealth, the power of thought, is made outwardly manifest, so that mental power may be seen as a material possession also. Indeed, Wordsworth insists that his exaltation over all his possessions is not untoward vanity but the consequence of his greater insight now. He is *more* "the mind of Nature" now than he had been as a child. His "genuine wealth" is not the house he owns but the act of imagination which reads into the house an outward image of the imagination's need to appropriate that which will sustain it. "Rightly understood," then, he reads his actual ownership as a confirmation of his own ability to appropriate from nature all that he needs—a human sufficiency. Conceding that "I cannot take possession of the sky," he circumscribes his "fervour" with a recognition of possession's limits, affirming his own determination to live within them. Wordsworth's greater insight "now" is of man's capacity not only to gain but, in the end, to keep what will sustain him, "what ever may be lost." The cost is not so great because his insight into what *must* be gained is now, he claims, far greater. In a phrase that directly echoes Michael's "forward-looking thoughts" ("Michael," l. 148), the poet here declares himself to be "rich in onward-looking thoughts" ("Grasmere," l. 233).

Wordsworth's economic argument is, then, a secular transformation of Milton's great argument:

Theme this but little heard of among men,
The external world is fitted to the mind
And the creation, (by no lower name
Can it be call'd), which they with blended might
Accomplish: this is my great argument. . . .[35]

The great theme of "Home at Grasmere" is individual accomplishment and the "blended might" of material possession possessed by imaginative labor. It is a theme of human resolution and independence, not the theme of justifying God to man. His poetry, Wordsworth avers, will not speak of men and angels but of the self's power to appropriate what is good—to see, therefore, that the "Lord of this enjoyment is on Earth / And in my breast." Wordsworthian economics replaces Miltonic theology: in placing God on earth, Wordsworth's "And" has the rhetorical effect of also locating Him in the poet's own breast. Thus, in Wordsworth's celebratory logic, his Grasmere property becomes a divine acquisition of innocence. A propertied Leech-Gatherer, Wordsworth also becomes an unentailed Michael. His home at Grasmere is not an instance of human vanity but a transformation of Wordsworth's art into life, modulating the divine commandment into a human economics, as John Locke had explained: "God and his reason commanded [man] to subdue the earth—i.e., improve it for the benefit of life and therein lay out something upon it that was his own, his labour."[36] For Wordsworth, that possession is innocent, not the Adamic curse. His labor is bestowed imaginatively in showing, through the poem, "when and where and how he lived / With all his little realities of life" (*Poetical Works*, 5:339). Ostensibly more prosaic than Milton's great argument, Wordsworth's theme affirms its own "right reason" and testifies to the power of thought to construct a rational economics of its own:

> If e'er the acceptance of such dower was deem'd
> A condescention or a weak indulgence
> To a sick fancy, it is now an act
> Of reason that exultingly aspires. [*Poetical Works*, 5:315]

"Reason," then, is defined as aspiration which chooses to live within the limits of gain and loss, to find what Wordsworth called in *The Prelude* "full measure of content" (13.110) within "this small Abiding place" ("Grasmere," l. 146). Although the place is mythically resonant, he finds that it is an abiding place precisely because one *can* live there, because it maintains a human dimension.

In Grasmere Vale, "labor" presents Wordsworth with an image not of unremitting toil but of self-affirming sufficiency, silent poetry:[37]

> Yet is it something gained, it is in truth
> A mighty gain, that Labour here preserves
> His rosy face, a Servant only here
> Of the fire-side, or of the open field,
> A Freeman, therefore, sound and unimpaired. [Ll. 358–62]

At Grasmere, labor becomes an aspect of freedom. Here, the laborers choose to see themselves as free, even in the midst of their daily wants. Thus, in this familial society, Wordsworth finds "That they who want, are not too great a weight / For those who can relieve" (ll. 366–67). He is not deluded into the debased pastoral ideal of thinking that suffering ne'er comes here; rather, he contends that here suffering is able to be borne. Labor may not be economically sufficient (although "extreme penury is here unknown" [l. 363]), but it is imaginatively and psychologically supportive of the community's social well-being. Wordsworth's answer to the economist's "Wealth of Nations" is his assertion that this labor generates a "protection" against adversity and a mental "Power" able to imagine its own rewards:

> So here abides
> A Power and a protection for the mind,
> Dispensed indeed to other solitudes,
> Favored by noble privilege like this,
> Where kindred independence of estate
> Is prevalent, where he who tills the field,
> He, happy Man! is Master of the field,
> And treads the mountains which his Fathers trod.
> [Ll. 376–83]

Shelley chided Wordsworth for being neither a Whig nor a Tory.[38] In fact, however, Wordsworth appropriated both parties for his own ends. In his view of material labor, Wordsworth is a Whig democrat; in his view of mental labor, a Tory republican. Thus, the "Power" of the mind is "favored by noble privilege," so that even when material labor fails to sustain life, there is yet an intellectual inheritance: "the silent mind / Has her own treasures . . . (ll. 424–25).

Finally, "Home at Grasmere" appropriates the language and preoccupations of economic thought in order to celebrate completely its reversal of pastoral retreat into working georgic. The occasion for this last gesture of appropriation becomes the poet's awareness that, like the rural laborers, he must add *his* labor to the whole:

> We shall not scatter through the plains and rocks
> Of this fair Vale, and o'er its spacious heights
> Unprofitable kindliness, bestowed
> On objects unaccustomed to the gifts
> Of feeling. . . . [Ll. 430–34]

The last third of the poem catalogues the ways in which life at Grasmere has "accustomed" Wordsworth to the investment and return of mutual "kindliness." The economic metaphor has already allowed Grasmere Vale to appear as nature humanized, as property. The poet's work has also profited from the lives of his neighbors for whom thought is "a glad function natural to Man" (l. 470). In defining what has been gained at Grasmere, the poet defines the labor still required of himself, that unique possession which he must now not merely appropriate but also bestow—through the instrument of poetry itself. Possession becomes, finally, the necessary prelude to labor:

> Possessions have I that are solely mine,
> Something within which yet is shared by none,
> Not even the nearest to me and most dear,
> Something which power and effort may impart,
> I would impart it, I would spread it wide,
> Immortal in the world which is to come. [Ll. 686-91]

The tone is fiercely affirmative (I *would* impart it, *I* would spread it wide), and the imagery is insistently materialistic. Possession is the privilege of "the insatiable mind" (l. 637). It is not the *end* of labor (as in Locke and Adam Smith) but the *means*. Wordsworthian economics is, therefore, the exact obverse of political economics: here, acquisition is an act of limitation; property is a means of discovering the real meaning of labor, its source in the mind; profit does not signify one man's advantage over another but expresses the privilege of "individual man" to realize his dignity and worth unaided. No profit is private, however, because, when rightly understood, all possessions and all labors demand an act of sharing. Only then can profit make prophets, "immortal in the world which is to come." That Wordsworth can finally realize an imaginative economics using the very terms of "vacant commerce" (l. 595) is not a gratuitous metaphor but a systematic rhetoric conditioned by a more judicious knowledge of what ultimate vacancy circumscribes all forms of commerce, whether natural, human, or divine. Instead of "making a silent company in death" (l. 696), man is privileged to spend his talents and to exercise his labor; he is "privileged to speak as I have felt / Of what in man is human or divine" (ll. 701-2). "Such," Wordsworth concludes, "is our wealth" (l. 662).

In the end, "Home at Grasmere" offers a tentative answer to the question of poetic achievement raised by its own economics:

>   is there not
> An art, a music, and a strain of words
> That shall be life, the acknowledged voice of life,
> Shall speak of what is done among the fields,
> Done truly there, or felt, of solid good
> And real evil, yet be sweet withal,
> More grateful, more harmonious than the breath,
> The idle breath of softest pipe attuned
> To pastoral fancies? [Ll. 401-9]

If the answer is yes, then such art would constitute a compensation for that otherwise unstoried labor, the work which "is done
among the fields" by the likes of Michael. "More" than pastoral,
however, such poetry has needed to conceive its own economics
by which a "practical faith," both in poetry itself as "the acknowl-
edged voice of life" and in the poet as a productive laborer, would
be inculcated. We may call such poetry "georgic": it is a way of
versing the reader in the existing facts; its aim is avowedly didactic; but its practical advice is not simple or one-dimensional. Here,
the poem seems purposefully, determinedly, to "commercialize"
Wordsworth's "real" property at Grasmere so as to contract it into
an imaginative form—"Home at Grasmere"—which the sympa-
thetic reader may appropriate as he will. This is Wordsworth's bequest, an imaginative endowment which enables the reader to
pause for choice—while making its own chosen labor manifest.

The vision of human community as attained in "Grasmere" is
both grounded upon and a projection of this imaginative economics:

> Society is here
> A true Community, a genuine frame
> Of many into one incorporate.
> *That* must be looked for here, paternal sway,
> One household, under God, for high and low,
> One family, and one mansion; to themselves
> Appropriate, and divided from the world
> As if it were a cave, a multitude
> Human and brute, possessors undisturbed
> Of this Recess, their legislative Hall,
> Their Temple, and their glorious Dwelling-place.
> [Ll. 614–24]

The antecedent of "here" is both his Grasmere property and the
property which is the poem itself. Wordsworth's "genuine frame"
becomes, in its broadest speculation, the contractual structure of
this working georgic. What seemed a "cave"-like "Recess" emerges
as a metaphorical equivalent to the economic metropolis. At Grasmere, a human city is raised in the imagination, comprising temple, legislative hall, and dwelling place, and is incorporated by the
superior economics of the "incorporate" poem. In the commonwealth of the poem, then, the hieroglyphic inscription for a true

community—*e pluribus unum,* "Of many into one"—is at last disclosed and made "appropriate."

The next generation of Romantic poets would make Wordsworth accountable for both his poetic "household" and the imaginative economics by which he sought to regulate it. Intimating that Wordsworth's authorial covenant was actually a capitalist exploitation of the imagination, Byron declared of the Lake Poets:

> I would not imitate the petty thought,
>   Nor coin my self-love to so base a vice,
> For all the glory, your conversion brought,
>   Since gold alone should not have been its price.
> You have your salary; was't for that you wrought?
> And Wordsworth has his place in the Excise.[39]

Thus, the narrator of *Don Juan* satirically identified Wordsworth's self-avowed economics of compensation (a place in the Excise in exchange for the "base vice" of "self-love"). But Byron's condemnation of Wordsworth's bourgeois conversion to petty bureaucrat as a sellout of the poetic profession is a political judgment that obscures the complexity of Wordsworth's poetic achievement. In regarding reading itself as an economic act, Wordsworth implied a political economy of literature which may seem to us, after considering Wordsworth's whole achievement, both more subtle and more radical than Byron's labored pun on "coin."

In the poems we have been examining, Wordsworth maintains a delicate balance between opposing and appropriating economic thinking. Unable to convince Byron and his contemporaries of the difference, Wordsworth altered the bias of at least one economist. John Stuart Mill was to concede—against the opinions of his fellow economists—one of Wordsworth's chief contentions: that poiesis, or the skill of the artist in crafting poetry, was indeed a productive labor and possessed, by Mill's own standard, "exchangeable value."[40] But even Mill, who took so much, by his own account, from Wordsworth's poetry, deferred final judgment, contending that artistic skill could not be *ultimately* productive because the product thus created could not be (in Mill's words) "productively consumed" (*Unsettled Questions,* p. 84). This final equivocation, spoken by an economist who did not devalue either the art of reading or the literary work, brings us to the core, perhaps, of Wordsworthian instruction and of Romantic poetics as such. In

Wordsworth's economy the *reader,* the nominal "consumer," must also be a *productive* laborer. Indeed, Wordsworth's labor theory affirms that *only* in the exchanges of poetry is "productive consumption" not an oxymoron—an unreal word—but a powerful transformation and overbalancing of that getting and spending which lay waste our powers:

> Our line is turned
> Out of her course, wherever man is made
> An offering, or a sacrifice, a tool
> Or implement, a passive thing employed
> As a brute mean, without acknowledgment
> Of common right or interest in the end;
> Used or abused, as selfishness may prompt.
> [*Excursion,* 9. 113-19]

CHAPTER VIII
"Getting It" in Paterson:
The Increment Defended

*Missing was the thing Jim had found
in Marx and Veblen and Adam Smith
and Darwin—the dignified sound of
a great, calm bell tolling the morning of a new age . . . instead, the slow
complaining of a door loose on its
hinges. —William Carlos Williams,*
Paterson

Missing from modern poetry,
Louis Zukofsky has argued, is a
willingness to take Marx at his
word and to "consider the labor
process apart / From its particu-
ular form under particular social
conditions"[1] —that is, to consider the labor process as the means
by which man confronts nature
and attempts to alter it. For
Marx, the labor process is an act
of will, exacting from the laborer a kind of self-identification;
it becomes, in its most radical
conception, an act of the imagination in attempting to define
the self and its values "apart
from" the money form to
which both "self" and "value"
are reduced in economic exchange. Wordsworth's poetic
"contract" formulates that act
of the imagination as an act of

poiesis. In the work of William Carlos Williams, to be considered below, we shall see how the labor process cannot be considered apart from the workings of language.

Williams's sociolinguistic relationship between economic "labor" and the writing of poetry depends upon his idiosyncratic vision of the connection between language's implemental value (as a vehicle of communication) and its incremental value (as a vehicle of self-expression). For Williams, a poem is the product of both the poet's own voice and the actual voices of others—those who mediate his being in the world. Like a physician, a poem must listen and record before it can speak of cures, before it can declare the creative value of the poet's own imagination, of his (private) labor process. As a physician, Williams also knew that his poetic vocation was never as valuable to his patients (or to the economy) as his professional skills. This disparity is where the degradation of "economics" begins: in society's failure to credit the poet's language as one of its vital products, and in poetry's failure to make it so. Missing is a language of the labor process itself, a language for connecting the poet's care with words and the doctor's occupational cares into a less fragmented form of social process.

"Language," Saussure declared, "is speech less speaking."[2] Conversely, the act of speaking is to language what the physical exertion of labor is to its implements—that is, the addition of a material self, of voice to language. "If we are to study the origin of poetry" the neo-Marxist historian George Thomson contends, "we must study the origin of speech. . . . We must go right back to the beginning."[3] Speech originated, according to Thomson, "as a directive accompaniment to the use of tools" (p. 51). One of the earliest forms of poetry, Thomson tells us, was probably the work song. Beginning as a cry, an oral exertion corresponding to the muscular effort of labor, speech became a way of coordinating the labors of a group into a more efficient form of communal production. "Speech merged as part of the actual technique of production" (p. 50). Thomson further speculates that the rhythm or ictus of poetry is also part of the labor process and derives from "the simple, disyllabic labour cry" (p. 59), in which the two syllables denote moments of preparation and exertion or of exertion and relaxation. ("Heave-ho" is an example of the former, although here the initial cry of preparation has been articulated as a discrete word.) These disyllabic elements "can be recognized in the arsis and thesis of prosody, which denote properly the raising and lowering of the hand or foot in the dance. And so the ictus or beat of rhythm is rooted in the primitive labour process—the successive pulls at the log, or the strokes of the tool on stick or stone" (p. 59). Thomson concludes: "The labour song was developed by expanding the improvised variable between the moments of exertion" (p. 60)—as, for instance, in the traditional sea shanty, where improvised verses fill the gap between each hauling cry. From this point of view, the creative trajectory of language describes the essential labor process of its own production.

Like Thomson's study (first published in 1949) of the relationship between the rhythms of the labor process and the origins of poetry, the art of William Carlos Williams grounds its labor process in the radical element of speech. In *Paterson* (published sequentially from 1946 to 1958), Williams, too, was attempting to analyze the ictus of the traditional poetic line and to find a way of liberating a new rhythm by means of an enlightened labor process. Williams could not, of course, be the archetypal laborer-poet described by Thomson:

> The primitive poet does not work alone. His audience collaborates. Without the stimulus of a listening crowd he cannot work at all. He does not write, he recites. He does not compose, he improvises. As the inspiration comes to him, he produces in his listeners an immediate response. They surrender to the illusion immediately and wholeheartedly. In these circumstances the making of poetry is a collective social act.
> [Pp. 69–70]

But Williams sought to create a poetics in which the *values* recounted here—collective effort, the stimulation of a listening crowd, its immediacy of response, and the vital contact between speech and labor—could be rescued and utilized again by a modern poet. As we shall see, the values which Williams felt he had to overcome—the idea of the artist as individual craftsman and of the poem as chiseled object, a product of the intaglio method, forsak-

ing the "crowd" as a stimulus—were most dramatically summed up
in the work of his friend, Ezra Pound.

In striving to identify the discursive core of the labor process,
Williams hoped to expose the common origin of both poetic work
and economic labor. In a manuscript draft of *Paterson,* he proposed two complementary equations which, we may see in retrospect, form the underpinnings of *Paterson*'s poetic economics.
At the top of a page dated 3 August 1950 is written *Song: Paterson IV,* followed by an epigraphlike line, "more songs than one."
The song begins "Money:Joke" and ends, at the bottom of the
same page, "credit : the gist."[4] Williams apparently meant this
visual arrangement on a single page to link both "songs" into one
quasi-mathematical formula. When the logical equivalences are un-
scrambled, the lines might read: the phenomenon of money is to
the issuance of credit as the phenomenon of a joke is to its gist of
meaning. The phenomenology of the former things (money, jokes)
depends upon the interpretive receptiveness by which we "get"
the latter things (credit, gists). Thus, when we restore the mediated formulas to their unmediated form, we may see the gist of
Williams's own inventive equation. You cannot get the gist (the
reward) of a joke without crediting (believing in) the teller. Nor
can you get money (the means of consumer power) without credit
(the means of purchasing power). Money and the gist are what you
"get," respectively, from credit and the joke. But because we are
dealing with interrelated functions, there are more songs than one:
the joke is a credit to both teller and listener when its gist is understood as a form of exchange. Williams's poetic economics will be
either productive or unproductive, therefore, depending upon how
one gets the point of it.

To grasp the connections in this hieroglyphic "Song," we must
understand Williams's interrelated psychological and epistemological economy. Value, in Williams's etymological joke, is a function
of valence; a change in the value of the poetic idiom, like a change
in the valence of uranium, results in a new isotope. As we shall see,
the "joke" was the tropic medium that Williams needed in order
to break through the traditionalized ictus of "fine writing" and to
create anew the rhythm of the essential labor process whose origin
is in speech. By metaphorically equating jokes and commercial
transactions, Williams wished to unblock the kind of imaginative
economics that, say, Hart Crane and Yeats confronted (see chapter

five) and to engender a creative labor which would set in motion
the same immediate effect upon the listener—the same economics
of response—that the primitive poet (according to Thomson) had
enjoyed. Hence, the dynamic of "getting it" in respect to a joke's
value is also the basis of Williams's poetic gist. But it is also the
secret of money. For Williams, the artistic practice which would
link these two senses of "getting it" might become the "wedge"
(to use the title of one of his books) needed to divide the poet-
economist Pound from the monetary pound and so to permit a
fresh evaluation of economics, poetry, and the connection between them. Transposing economic process into a new key, Williams's money song became one of the variable or dissonant
elements by which (in Williams's words) the "measured dance"
of the text could be expanded. To understand how *Paterson* embodies this labor process, we must first inspect both the psychological theories of the joke and the poetic theories of the gist
which were immediate stimuli for Williams's imagination.

> *Very few treat art seriously. There are those who treat it solemnly. . . ;
> and there are those who treat it as a joke.—T. S. Eliot,* The Sacred Wood
>
> *Love goes out the door when money flies innuendo.—Groucho Marx*
>
> *Dissonance | (if you are interested) | leads to discovery
> —William Carlos Williams,* Paterson

A joke (such as Groucho Marx's one-liner cited above) may be
defined as "that which presents an intellectual and emotional complex in an instant of time."[5] The similarity between Pound's definition of the "image" (given here) and Freud's nearly contempora-
neous elucidation of the joke's relation to the unconscious depends
upon understanding precisely Pound's keywords: "complex" and
"instant." Pound himself drew attention to this relationship when
he explained, "I use the term 'complex' rather in the technical
sense employed by the newer psychologists, such as Hart, though
we might not agree absolutely in our application" (*Essays,* p. 4).
In psychoanalytic language, a "complex" is conceptual shorthand
for a set of recurring repressions—that is, it is not a causative but
a descriptive word, identifying the phenomenon of psychical *recurrence*. But in Pound's usage, "complex" refers to the psychogenesis of poetic value; it is aesthetic shorthand for the creation
of something utterly *new*—the vortex of the image. Pound's evoca-

tion of the imagistic "instant" does not mean that images are
necessarily brief or compact (although, like jokes, they often are),
but rather, that they release *in the same instant* both the poet's
and the reader's psychical response to an unspecified cathexis or
blockage. Pound's sense of "response" explicitly includes the reader as a formative agent in the image's emotional and intellectual
release: "[Imagism's] presentation of such a 'complex' instantan-
eously . . . gives that sense of sudden liberation; that sense of freedom from time limits and space limits; that sense of sudden
growth, which we experience in the presence of the greatest works
of art" (ibid.). Liberation, then, applies to a complex or folding
together (*complectus*) of both writer and reader: the poet is liberated through the expression or pressing out of unconscious
energies, and the reader experiences, through his response to that
expression, a "sudden growth." Multiple responses are conjoined
in one complex instant which is not merely the presentational
time actually taken to read (or to write) the image but also the
psychical time expended to "get it."

It was Freud who defined the psychical schema behind this dynamic. He observed in jokes two of the three necessary elements
of the dream complex: namely, "the sinking of a preconscious
thought into the unconscious and its unconscious revision."[6]
Freud used the first psychical phenomenon, "this downward-
dragging force" into the unconscious (*Jokes*, p. 177), as an index
to the difference between real jokes and those which are tenden-
tious, naive, or slight (i.e., jests). A real joke hints at a deeper
blockage. He used the second phenomenon of unconscious revision to explain a joke's frequent use of ambivalent or altered
words. When preconscious meaning is unconsciously revised, the
joke emerges, like the manifest (i.e., remembered) content of
dreams, "as a mutilated and altered transcript of certain psychical
structures [or] '*latent dream-thoughts*' " (p. 160). In this transcript, "new artificial and transient common elements are created
. . . "(p. 163). In both jokes and dreams, for instance, "there is
actually a preference for the use of words the sound of which
expresses different meanings" (p. 163). These verbal homologues
(we might call them puns or—in Groucho's case—malaprops) are
sensuous increments earned in the psychical re-creation of repressed material, and they are the effect of the joke's (or the
dream's) attempt to say two things at once, a complex of re-

pressed fear and fulfilled wish. (Groucho's joke word, "innuendo," does what it means—creates innuendo.) Jokes attempt to identify repressed material by expressing it in a disguised and mutilated form. A joke's "altered transcript" embodies, therefore, what Pound called the "sense of freedom" released by the image. In jokes, that freedom is produced as laughter: "the laughter is in fact the product of an automatic process which is only made possible by our conscious attention's being kept away from it" (p. 154).

For Freud as for Pound, the blockage released by the joke image must have occurred in both author and reader: "It is essential," Freud notes, that the hearer of the joke "should be in sufficient psychical accord with the first person to possess the same internal inhibitions, which the joke-work has overcome in the latter" (p. 151). The addition to joke work of this "third-person" listener is precisely what differentiates jokes from dreams. "A dream is a completely asocial mental product; it has nothing to communicate to anyone else" (p. 179). But a joke "is the most social of all the mental functions that aim at a yield of pleasure," and "its completion requires the participation of someone else in the mental process it starts" (p. 179). If a dream is a wish, then a joke is a wish consciously developed into play—an embryonic example of poiesis. In recognizing the public aspect of jokes, Freud revealed the sensuous purpose of the joke technique: "to guarantee the joke the greatest possible pleasurable effect on the third person" (p. 155).

In realizing this effect, jokes enact a new "complex." The dynamic of "getting it" engenders a new social process which operates, according to Freud, on economic principles. Thus, the "tendency to compression" in jokes is an attempt to save psychical expenditures of energy (p. 42). The mechanism of pleasure in jokes depends upon a "factor of economy" (p. 156) and demands that "a sum of psychical energy which has been used for cathexis [be] allowed free discharge" (p. 148). The listener or third person, who "has bought the pleasure of the joke with very small expenditure on his own part" (p. 148), need not make a psychical effort equal to that of the first person. As a "release," jokes are unencumbered by the psychical demands of analysis and evaluation. Our interest in them is related only to their immediate "yield of pleasure" (p. 169) and does not require that we price or measure them by standards of moral acceptability or by standards of rationality imposed with the conscious mind. Finally, Freud related the phenomenon of laughter to a psychical economics: "the hearer of the joke laughs with the quota of psychical energy which has become free through the lifting of the inhibitory cathexis; we might say that he laughs this quota off" (p. 149). Psychically, laughter occurs in an economy of arbitrary and artificially restrictive trade practices, but jokes themselves aspire to the uninhibited economy of laissez faire.

Freud's metaphorical description of joke economy as the compressing or economizing of repressed material into the joke image thus demonstrates socioeconomic principles with far-reaching implications. The "social process" of jokes, when analyzed psychically, expresses the political process of the commercial economy—but in "a mutilated and altered transcript." In Freud's "treatment of psychical energy as a quantity" (p. 147), jokes constantly need to be told and used up, "stimulat[ing] the constant production of new ones" (p. 154), for the supply-and-demand dynamic by which jokes operate depends upon the freshness of each psychical discharge. Unlike the classical definition of "commodity," the artifice of the joke has little or no importance as a *repository* of value. Its value lies in our getting it, in its effect being momentary and immediate (a complex instant), not cumulative and stored. If one is moved to retell a joke, it is to recover "from the impression the joke makes on a new-comer some of the possibility of enjoyment that has been lost owing to its lack to novelty" (p. 154). As in the classical economics from which Freud derived his metaphor, a consumer (i.e., listener) is mandated as "the intermediary" in the process of value exchange (p. 158).

Like Freud, Pound ascribed a larger social process to the formation of images, and, like Freud, he went on to conceptualize that process in economic terms. At first, Pound's economic metaphors were intended to express the psychological expenditures of art: "In the culture of the mind, as in the culture of the fields, there is a law of diminishing return. If a book reveal [*sic*] to us something of which we were unconscious, it feeds us with its energy; if it reveal to us nothing but the fact that its author knew something which we knew, it draws energy from us."[7] Here again, Pound's psychological evaluation bestows credit on that which is creative and "new," and it assesses the psychical increment economically.

In feeding the reader with the psychical expenditure of its own energy, intellectual "culture" (as embodied in poems) enacts a productive economic exchange between minds. T. S. Eliot, in *The Sacred Wood,* further expanded this economic vehicle to explain the prevalence of a living and active "tradition" in Renaissance drama: "We should see then just how *little* each poet had to do; only so much as would make a play his, only what was really essential to make it different from anyone else's. When there is this economy of effort it is possible to have several, even many, good poets at once. The great ages did not perhaps *produce* much more talent than ours; but less talent was wasted."[8] Like the Freudian "third person" in jokes, the Renaissance dramatist was able to buy his dramatic production with little psychical expenditure of his own. The general input of creative labor meant that each new laborer was able to draw upon and to refine previous products, so that "the labour of the intellect consisted largely in a purification" (Eliot, p. 65). No one had to start from scratch; an artistic "economy of effort" was already functional, productive, and ready to hand. Thus, the poetic economics of the Renaissance dramatist circumvented the Poundian "law of diminishing return" because its dynamic of cumulative labor was shared by authors and audiences alike. Renaissance drama was "popular" in the best Eliotic sense; drawing energy from its audience, it repaid interest on that debt by adding a little something new—the incremental effort of purification, the "tone" of fine art.

"Tone" is a keyword in Eliot and has a particular economic significance. In one sense, it betokens the individuality of labor and is earned by each new author's investment of his "talent": "Every writer who has written any blank verse worth saving has produced particular tones which his verse and no other's is capable of rendering . . ." (p. 87). Traditionally, Eliot notes, we say that Shakespeare "has more of these tones than anyone else," implying that "tones" can be accumulated and that creative intelligence is something of a commodity. Eliot proceeds to answer the often-heard belief that Shakespeare, by the sheer magnitude of his economy, exhausted the profit which could accrue to artistic labors: ". . . to say that Shakespeare expressed nearly all human emotions, implying that he left very little for anyone else, is a radical misunderstanding of art and the artist . . ." (p. 87). Implying that one labor commodity can replace or preclude all others, this view of literary history is based on the wrong economic principles, according to Eliot. Preferring a less terminal view of economics, Eliot offered a more processive view of artistic "indebtedness": "The development of blank verse may be likened to the analysis of that astonishing industrial product coal-tar. Marlowe's verse is one of the earlier derivatives, but possesses properties which are not repeated in any of the analytic or synthetic blank verses discovered somewhat later" (pp. 87–88). This likening of poetic production to industrial production further extends Eliot's analysis of the economic relationship between literature and its readers: "For some generations," he tells us, "the reputation of Jonson has been carried rather as a liability than as an asset in the balance-sheet of English literature" (p. 104). The psychological economy which molded Renaissance drama and the commercial sensibility of the twentieth-century critic merge here, allowing Eliot to speculate upon (and, indeed, in *The Sacred Wood,* to prescribe) the sort of evaluative relationship which ought to exist between text and reader.

Perhaps economic metaphor is the only viable discursive model we have for describing the "exchange" between reader and text. At least, Raymond Williams's remark seems just: "In capitalist society, the difficulty of the social thinker is to know what to say about activities that are not the production and exchange of things."[9] But Pound's analysis of cultural expenditure led him to reconsider the economic model which Eliot (and perhaps Freud) took for granted. In describing the economy of images, Pound insisted that "economy" be understood in its palpable and exact implications, not merely as a kind of abstraction: "I have, confound it, to forge pokers, to get economic good and evil into verbal manifestation, not abstract, but so that the monetary system is as concrete as fate and *not* an abstraction, etc."[10] Pressing for that verbal manifestation, Pound perceived an equally elusive issue: "The question for our time is: 'What is money?' " (*Prose,* p. 274). Although money is more than an image, Pound discovered the economic dynamics of money in the psychological economics of the image. The discovery revolutionized his poetics. Henceforth, the poet's responsibility was to show that his artistic economy was not vaguely and figuratively "economic" but was as real and concrete as monetary systems.

Inversely, Pound felt that a truly workable economic system

would also account for the exchangeable value of art and would be fashioned by the same creative energies which went into the labor of poiesis. Pound calls C. H. Douglas "the first economist to include creative art and writing in an economic scheme, and the first to give the painter or sculptor or poet a definite reason for being interested in economics; namely, that a better economic system would release more energy for invention and design" (*Prose,* p. 232). Ultimately, Pound hoped that more of this "energy" might be channeled back into the commercial economy, so that artists and poets could participate in a labor-intensive, energy-rich system of production. The curious thing, for instance, about Pound's assertion that "the history of money is yet to be written" (*Prose,* p. 272) is that he apparently believed a history of money *could* be written—one which would not merely describe or chronicle the evolution of money forms but which would elucidate the imagistic intensity of money, the concrete psychological "complex" which makes it seem "the *Anagke* [*sic*] of the modern world" (ibid.). Poundian economics would have to participate in the organizing impulse of art: "No monetary system can rise above the status of gadget if it be not in concord with some *order of thought,* with some system of moral criteria" (*Prose,* p. 274).

For Pound, poetry could help to supply this "system of moral criteria." If the subject of economics seemed "dry, dull and damned" (*Prose,* p. 238), that was because it had lost touch with the imaginative delight of "inherent activity" and with the "artist's desire to *make* something, the fun of constructing and the play of outwitting and overcoming obstruction" (*Prose,* p. 239). This delight is, in embryonic form, the psychological essence of both the joke and the image. If economics were to have, for Pound, any systematic moral meaning, then it would have to find a way of crediting all kinds of "creative art." Indeed, if it did not, then the economics of gain would be a positive detriment to the gaming or inventive qualities of art. Economics would turn poetry itself into a joke, blocking the psychical release which it was art's sole duty to discharge. Pound read the cost of that blockage in the work of his friend, Gaudier-Brzeska, and conceded that one of his own motives in forging a new economics was to seek recompense for past economic crimes: "Whatever economic passions I now have, began *ab initio* from having crimes against living art thrust under my perceptions" (*Prose,* pp. 230–31). The sentence is perhaps unwittingly revealing of how Pound compromised his own avowed search for the "moral criteria" of economics in his poetry. In his most strident and implacable diatribes about the economic denigration of art, the sense of retribution (as implied in the above passage) blocks Pound himself from recording and affirming the artist's "play," his fascination with overcoming difficulty. Pound's own commercial theories (and perhaps his own poems) become increasingly dry and dull and, in some circles, damned.

Williams argued that Pound had forgotten the immediacy of the psychological complex by which poetry works and that, therefore, his economic theories had become dissociated from the actual labor process. "Mr. Pounds [*sic*] mind," Williams told Gorham Munson in 1934, in the depths of the Depression, "is clogged with a curious sort of idealism which trips him at every step." One of the systems which the imagination had to deconstruct was, for Williams, the poetic economics of Pound with its "cryptographic language of ideas that has no sequence for the average reader."[11] Williams's own imagination could not proceed by ignoring economic ideologies or by pretending that economic crimes against art for humanity were only a joke. And yet Williams sought to restore to his economic thinking the imaginative element which is still vividly operative in Freud's analysis of the economics of dream work. Elaborating upon Freud, Williams employed jokes as a rhetorical expansion of economic phenomena, and, elaborating upon Pound, he used economic terminology in *Paterson* as a way of thinking about the new measures of poetry. Economics and poetry could be regarded, Williams was to suggest, as the "obverse" and "reverse" of the imagination, as producing "an / interpenetration, both ways" (*P.* 2). The work of the poet could not be divorced, even metaphorically, from the economic reality of labor. But to value that work properly was to relearn or to remeasure the economic costs of labor, to give one's readers "fuller and more consecutive data than ever Mr. Pound seems able to give them" (Williams to Munson, 5 March 1934). If the poet's means were defective because of poetry's pejorative economic status, then to release the imaginative value of money would be to release the labor value of poetry as well. The "joke" became for Williams a dissonant element capable of illuminating this dialectic. "It can't be," as he says in an enjambment which, interpenetrating both ways, has the effect of a joke, "otherwise" (*P.* 12).

A more systematic analysis of *Paterson's* joke work is made necessary by the inadequate critical appraisal of Williams's economics. In a generally laudatory review of *Paterson's* first two books, Randall Jarrell noted disapprovingly that Williams had borrowed Pound's monomania about usury and social credit for his own "local" argument. Jarrell went on to locate, as many others would and still do, this fascination with economics as a singularly bad—or, at best, boring—influence in modern poetry: "Book II [of *Paterson*] introduces—how one's heart sinks!—Credit and Usury, those enemies of man, God, and contemporary long poems."[12] Presumably Jarrell was not deprecating a poet's concern with economics itself, a concern voiced in his own Browningesque monologue, "Money."[13] Rather, his exasperation seems aimed at economic *theory,* at the vocabulary of systematic or doctrinaire or "ideological" economics, and at those poets who would take this type of discourse seriously in their work. To paraphrase *Paterson* itself, in the systems of Marx or Veblen or Smith, "economics" may once have had the "dignified sound of a great, calm bell tolling" (*P.* 98), but in poetry it only makes a squeaky "complaining," like a rusty hinge. Jarrell was not able to accept that this complaining could become a form of music, or that, like the medieval "complaint," it might even become a kind of love song.

For both the poet and the critic, so much depends upon pinpointing accurately the economic phenomena one ought to discuss, especially when there are "more songs than one." Jarrell's notation, for instance, of Pound's economic as well as poetic influence is not inaccurate if we are not misled by the idea of "influence." Pound's importance to Williams lay in the fact that he was the premier example of a poet whose economic consciousness was made manifest in his poetry—an artistic strategy which, on the basis of our present study, may not seem as startling, original, or "modern" as it did to Jarrell. Williams certainly did not look to Pound for the particulars of his economic (or of his poetic) sensibility. As Mike Weaver, for example, has shown, Williams was quite capable of gathering his own economic documentation from local sources: handbills, newspaper accounts, pamphlets, advertisements, treatises, local New Jersey history and legend.[14] And though Williams was, like every other socially conscious writer of the day, familiar with the economic theories embraced by Pound (through contact with A. R. Orage, Gorham Munson, Major Douglas, and

the Social Credit Movement), Williams was also perfectly capable
of drawing his own conclusions about them.

One of the few critics who has recognized that Williams's
economic rhetoric is a unique and integral part of his poetics is
Benjamin Sankey. Noting the equation of money and jokes in
Paterson 4, Sankey comments, "Money is a 'joke,' or worse than
a joke."[15] What Sankey apparently means is that we should not
take money seriously, and that, unfortunately, we are often forced
to take it seriously in spite of ourselves. Sankey's reductive sense
of what constitutes a joke forces him to slight the complex psychological, linguistic, and cultural—as well as economic—workings of
"money." More recently, Joseph Riddell, in an essay on the gaming qualities of *Paterson,* explains money as the "joke" which
"marks the game of economics, the necessary dynamics of money."[16] *Paterson,* like economics, certainly exhibits gaming qualities.
(On this point, we have at least progressed beyond the reviewer in
Time who spoke of "a humorlessness and awkwardness that make
Williams the Dreiser of U.S. poets."[17]) But the core of the gaming
impulse, the joke, with its capacity to change both psychical and
verbal elements and so to generate the dissonance which is the radical variable in Williams's imaginative labor, has yet to be adequately described. Riddell's helpful thesis that "Williams seeks a new
'measure' between things because the old measures have been exposed as interpretations, fictions of the center" (p. 14), fails him
in his own interpretation of economics, which he posits, in turn,
as the fictive *center* from which "the necessary dynamics of money" radiate. We still do not know, following the radically different
critical approaches of Sankey and Riddell, what the "necessary dynamics of money" have to do with the rhetoric of jokes or what
the psychogenesis of jokes has to do with Williams's poetics. Finally, we are somewhat misled into believing that both jokes and economics lack seriousness, or that they are—to paraphrase Sankey's
rubric—something worse than a game.

As far as Williams was concerned, of course, the most significant
misinterpreter of his work was Pound. How Pound apparently misunderstood the difference between himself and Williams is evident
as late as 1960, when Pound published what he called "Gists," a
series of maxims which purport to state the economic truth of art
and society but which leave out the "joke," and thus, from Williams's perspective, ignore the psychological, as well as the meta-

phorical origin of all "gists."[18] Pound had earlier told Williams, in
a letter which was eventually incorporated into the text of *Paterson* 1: "Your interest is in the bloody loam but what I am after is
the finished product" (*P.* 50). The commercial metaphor ("interest," "product") is essential to the criticism. Pound's premise is
that the poem ought to be a well-wrought artifact, so that its value
would arise from and be equivalent to one's esteem for its crafts-
manship. Williams was too willing (in Pound's opinion) to sacrifice
some of art's polish, veneer, or finish in order to profit from the
raw materials with which he was working. The "raw" materials
which Pound himself draws upon in the *Cantos* are almost exclusively literary (or belletristic) documents; his quotations and allus-
ions usually come from texts which are also "finished" (i.e., written or composed) products. Pound wished to show that these
ought not to be regarded as finished (i.e., terminated or forgotten)
commodities but as living and generative examples of the imagination at work. The psychical forces which composed them ("Arnaut," "Confucius," "Jefferson," and so on) would become energized again in Pound's new text: in the sense of being completed,
they would be "finished" there. Pound's poems are labor intensive,
therefore, to the extent that they become products. Technical accomplishment is the necessary conceit of poetic intelligence, a
technikē which, in Pound's *Cantos,* can transform state papers of
Martin Van Buren into poetry, for instance. In the fullest sense of
the word, Pound's work is traditional, drawing from the finished
products of the past an *auctoritée* for its own statements.

Williams's first book of poems (*Poems* [1908]) had, unwittingly
perhaps, drawn upon something similar to what Pound and Eliot
understood as "tradition." Lushly descriptive, occasionally punc-
tuated by archaic syntax and diction, heavily figurative and obviously derivative, these first poems exercised their Romantic
inheritance, especially their Keatsian origins, in a way that the
Romantics themselves (such as the young Keats imitating Spenser)
might have understood. Pound pointed out what Williams already
suspected: that his first book relied on derivative, overdone, and
obsolete products: "Individual, original it is not, great art it is not.
Poetic it is . . . but nowhere I think do you add anything to the
poets you have used as models."[19] Pound went on to prescribe for
Williams, as he would continue to do throughout his life, a "reading list" of texts which would help to inform Williams, help him to

envision how his work could add incrementally to the great tradi-
tions. Understanding poetic craft to embody a broad historical and
cultural awareness, Pound always hoped that Williams would up-
lift himself from "the bloody loam" and learn new interests. But
Williams perceived what we may not recognize in retrospect—that
Pound's attempt to make him a better reader was really a way
of making him better able to read Pound's own poetry. Pound's
ideal of the immaculately crafted artifact (an ideal originally implied in the doctrine of *imagisme,* confirmed in the formulas of
the Noh drama, and expanded in the theory of the vortex) was the
result of energies gleaned through the syncretizing sensibility of
the artist and stabilized there, brought "to point" (as Pound says
in a Confucian translation) "in this stillness" of the finished product. Even when they are fragmented (as Sappho's poems are) or
lost (as the speaking voices of Arnaut or Propertius are), their imaginative kinetics can still be captured by the disciplined and attuned ear. Thus, the three-line "Papyrus" is a crystallized, imagist
rendering of word scraps from a lost text. Malatesta's mail pouch
enriches a canto. Pound, as a "reader" of forgotten or fragmented
texts, serves as prerequisite guide for the reader of Pound's own
poetry.

In *Paterson's* fourth book, Williams reveals his answer to Pound's
finished products by speaking of a time "when gold and pound
were devalued" (*P.* 217). If the pun equates the poet with the coin
of the realm, then it is not unfair to say that Pound was never far
off when Williams's poetic thoughts turned to money. But, in perceiving that pounds can also be devalued, Williams opened a joking
wedge in Pound's traditionalist defense of the finished product:
Pound's increment might be itself devalued. And so it was, in Williams's view, when the poet lost his voice in the labyrinth of history and failed to hear the current voices, the roar of the moment,
the present's jokes. Products so removed from living speech become unproductive to their living witnesses, their readers. Williams's strategy in *Paterson* was to let Pound's "gists" become part
of the general dissonance of "Voices! / multiple and inarticulate"
(*P.* 70) whose value it would then be the New Jersey's poet's labor
to discover anew. In this community of voices, Pound's unique
poetic labor could also be judged implementally, apart from his
espousal of particular social and economic theories. (In effect,
Williams had already anticipated Jarrell's lament—and answered

it.) If economic devaluation occurs in respect to other currencies, then Williams wanted to show, poetically, what Pound's autocrat of the imagination was himself dependent upon—the likes of Williams. Thus, to devalue Pound was, like the analogous process in money markets, to strip the currency of its artificially asserted value, to destandardize it as a measure of value, and to allow it to float and circulate in an unregulated market.

The unregulated market is the new poetic grid of *Paterson*. In Williams's labor process, the poet does not work alone but remains attuned to the stimulus of the listening crowd, "the great beast" as he calls it. Although the poet draws strength from these voices of the crowd, the local reaction to the poem itself is often unlaughing, notably in Cress's letters, in Dahlberg's critiques, in Mrs. Williams's remark that she missed "the pure poem " of the first part (*P.* 202), in Mike Wallace's antagonistic questions about modern poetry, in a patient's comment ("Geeze, Doc, I guess it's all right / but what the hell does it mean?"[*P.* 138]), in Ginsberg's review of book 3 as "a labored joke at your expense" (*P.* 204), and most derisively, in the poet's own self-denigrating query ("What's your game?" [*P.* 143]). By subjecting his own work to the intrusion of others' imaginations and by not ignoring those responses which were disapproving or antagonistic, Williams wished to release a new labor process whose dialectic encompassed the dissonant, "the slow complaining of a door loose on its hinges." The poem was not a finished product but, in George Thomson's sense, an improvisational expansion linking the poet's moments of individual exertion or *self*-expression with the multiple voices of other selves. If *Paterson* is a response to these voices, then it is also an attempt to give them life in a specific social context—a double labor in which *Paterson* seems to be both participant and authenticator, both creator and listener, both mother and midwife, both the work and the capital formulation of it.

Like deregulated currency, the "value" of Williams's poem changes from moment to moment, as the voices change, as the poem's jokes are produced anew, as the reader "gets it" (or does not get it), as he credits the work (or loses interest in it), and as the poet draws power from such responses (or strives to elicit them). Williams's sense of multiple returns is the obverse of Pound's law of diminishing return; the labor which *Paterson* commands from its readers is equivalent to the purchasing power which money bestows when money is understood not merely as a thing but as an idea—credit. Now, money obscures and blocks the "direct" relationship between credit and effort (*P.* 218), between the listener and the laboring poet. At present, the meaning of economic exchange remains secret and mysterious, partly because of the obscurantism of economic terminology and partly because of the cryptographic impressionism of poets like Pound. The language of economic systems, which once may have sounded dignified and prophetic, has now broken down. The science of "economics" no longer sounds a true *scientia* or formulation of knowledge. Its *mathesis* produces only a flawed *praxis,* not the "morning of a new age" (*P.* 98).

To (re)discover the luminosity—the radiant gist—of economic discourse, there would need to be, as Williams says of *Paterson,* "a poetry / of the movements of cost, known or unknown" (*P.* 133). What centers the artistic rhythms of Williams's poem in the movements of economic cost so as to create and decreate "the center of movement, the core of gaity" (*P.* 72), is the psychological, commercial, and cognitive effort of "getting it." "It" may refer to the gist of a joke and to any of its homologues: the purpose of poetry, the meaning of America (or of a city,) what money buys. All these referents, as dissonant overlays of each other, comprise the market grid of *Paterson.* What Hugh Kenner says of Poundian economics is equally true of Williams's economic consciousness: it "frequently beat[s] most strongly in the verse when we have no explicit hint of [its] proximity."[20] Jarrell, as we shall now see by examining *Paterson* more closely, could not have described Williams's economics more accurately without describing how Williams imagines that we should read his poem.

> *America the golden!*
> *with trick and money*
> *damned*
> *like Altgeld sick*
> *and molden*
> *we love thee bitter*
> *land*
> —*William Carlos Williams,* Paterson

In *Paterson'* s broadest speculation, the labor of the poet is mandated by America's repression of a native interest in itself. Williams's individual search for a fructifying labor and for a local voice necessarily became a public and economic quest as well, as he explains in his *Autobiography:* "The falls, vocal, seasonally vociferous, associated with many of the ideas upon which our fiscal colonial policy shaped us through Alexander Hamilton, interested me profoundly—and what has resulted therefrom."[21] The *association* of economic ideas with the falls is critical to Williams's purpose; if "our fiscal colonial policy" arose out of a response to the falls, then Williams's poetry, which is itself a response to the falls, could meet the economic imagination on its own ground. Hamilton heard in the falls a commercially exploitable, even an economically programmatic voice: Paterson's manufacturing potential, with its natural waterpower, made it a possible center for a self-reliant American economy. Having envisioned Paterson as a federal city, the economic hub of America's useful manufactures, Hamilton then attempted to impose this grand design in fact. The city was to be laid out with architectual precision and efficiency by Pierre L'Enfant, a child of French neoclassicism. Self-contained and exemplary (such concentrism was ultimately enacted in the cityscape of the nation's capital), Paterson would incorporate, both culturally and economically, a "Society of Useful Manufacturies." The SUM of America's economic progress, this society would be built beside the falls, transmuting the water's roar into a single voice of economic and political solidarity. Although this was not the *polis* which materialized, we occasionally stumble across the dream's ruins as a blockage to alternative means of economic rebirth. What the twentieth-century city inherits is literally the fragments of this discarded, failed vision. "What has resulted therefrom" is not Hamilton's fictional center but the sprawled, decaying, modern city of Paterson whose individuality is almost obscured in the industrial wasteland which is northern New Jersey.

Williams does not wish to show merely the effects of Hamilton's failure but to discover why Hamilton never could have succeeded. Like the later Paterson manufacturer Lambert (see *P.* 121), Hamilton's original aperçu vanished when he imposed an economic ideal which forsook the truth of the local. For Williams, the *imposition* of the imagination (Lambert's Balmoral-like castle, Hamilton's federal city) is the cardinal sin, for such grand *idées fixes* suppress the essence of imagination, its need for "the continual and violent refreshing of the idea."[22] Hamilton's economic and aesthetic classicism was destructive, therefore, precisely to the extent that it was trite, borrowed from models of another world; his economic planning was self-defeating insofar as it refused to be refreshed by local conditions. As a refusal of the imagination, it was pernicious. Although Hamilton spoke of the need for a federal government to assume responsibility for the national debit, he himself could never "credit" the local people, "the great beast" whom this federal bureaucracy should ostensibly serve (see *P.* 84).

When the imagination's potential for informing our economic ideals is blocked, then the poem's "defective means" (*P.* 11) become even more defective. Conversely, by striking at and through the means of economic valorization, the poet necessarily seeks to improve his own means. In Williams's view, Pound's poetry retold a stale economic joke—stale, at least, to the American listener. There could be no Tempios in *Paterson* for the same reasons that the New Jersey city resisted the Hamiltonian poetics of federalization. In citing the difference between Pound's poetics and his own, Williams also locates the Hamiltonian failure of the economic imagination:

Difference between squalor of spreading slums
and splendor of renaissance cities [*P.* 218]

In Pound's letter, from which this sentence fragment is quoted in book 4 of *Paterson,* Pound is on the side of splendor, Williams of squalor. But the "difference" applies not only to the goal but also to the means utilized in each man's art. For Pound, the past is represented by the opulent, insular, oligarchical renaissance city-state and has a "splendor" of its own: "In the gloom the gold / Gathers the light about it."[23] Kore, who is the essence of female beauty, energizes the rarefied air: "Kore through the bright meadow, / with green-gray dust in the grass" (Canto 17). But Paterson's "spreading slums" have an impervious formlessness, and the "squalor" of economic, moral, and verbal desuetude all but obliterates this kind of beauty. In the environment of the North American, industrialized metropolis, Pound's evanescent Kore must assume a new, dirty, and perhaps more salacious form. The wildness of the beautiful thing resists the refining touch—as Williams discovered about America in *In the American Grain* and as he discovered about the imagination itself in the earlier experiments of *Kora in Hell.*

Williams's pursuit of Kora marks the "difference" which, in the end, infects the aesthetic as well as the commercial economics of his poem. In book 4, the poet will necessarily have to awaken from "this dream of / the whole poem" (*P.* 234), recognizing a difference between the "splendor" of the whole thing in its dreamed completeness and the spreading "squalor" of the thing in its partial but actual realizations. Form is always imperfect, a joke on our attempts consciously to articulate submerged or insensate "Thought" (*P.* 51). By means of the intellect, the imagination may be mythically embodied in its ideal female form as Kora, but to pursue her in fact is necessarily to pursue many actual women. Outside Thought's idealistic cave, the imagination is perfected and made morally chaste only in the vigorous pursuit of its imperfect, chased forms. "Getting it" in *Paterson* is the addition of physical and sexual energy to the moral and intellectual exertions by which we seek out meaning. "Getting it," therefore, is the complex instant in which we grasp abundance and apprehend multiplicity.

At times, the poet's labor is in danger of resembling merely a priapic quest, a dirty joke, as in the passage at the beginning of the poem, where, "sniffing the trees," Williams calls himself,

> just another dog
> among a lot of dogs. What
> else is there? And to do?
> The rest have run out—
> after the rabbits.
> Only the lame stands—on
> three legs. [*P.* 11]

In one sense, Williams is jockeying for position in the poetic chase against Pound, Eliot, Hart, Crane, and Wallace Stevens, who had all published their long poems before Williams appeared with his first installment in 1946. This portrait of the artist as an aging dog reveals, however, that "the lame" one, an epithet for the devil, may know better than "the rest" the Sphynxian answer to the question of what walks on three legs at evening. The poet's devilish third leg (as in the off-color joke) may indeed be the source of this writer's authority. A priapic dog, chasing rabbits (whose priapic powers are proverbial), will at least know which scent is worth sniffing, even if he is too "lame" to "run out," even if he must "stand," content to "dig / a musty bone."

"Is it a dirty book? I'll bet / it's a dirty book," an unnamed reader declares in book 3 (*P.* 132). But this wagerer will never obtain her due wages in reading it because she understands "dirty" in only one vulgar, reductive sense, not as the necessary price of all labor. Thinking she has "got it," she will never "get it" until her blocked view of sexual discovery is released from the misinformed and misinterpreted economics of her wager. Squalor is dirty only when splendor is its antonym, and sexuality is lickerish only in a world where Kore floats untouched and untouching through the bright meadow. Williams does not pursue squalor as Pound pursues splendor, but he pursues the beautiful thing—Kora, the imagination—by searching in the very place where it has been locked out or hideously disguised—in the local conditions of Paterson, in its actual women, in its life-denying economics. Discovery means getting a little dirty, Williams discovers again and again, as when, later in book 3, he descends to the cellar to administer to the raped and beaten black girl. Psychologically, money also has this taint of dirtiness. Williams would suggest that money becomes tainted only when we are imaginatively conditioned to interpret it by the same (debased) standards we use to interpret our moral and sexual lives. Williams's view of money is neither naive nor revolutionary—unless it is either naive or revolutionary to regard money as one of many "measures" whose beauty is "locked in the mind past all remonstrance" (P. 11). For Williams, the refusal to subject oneself to the world, to bring one's labors and sexual passions to fruition within it, is tantamount to treating money—like women, like one's very self—as a debased object, a "fact."

Williams reads throughout *Paterson* the potential death of his poem, as well as the death of the city, in his readers' failure to understand how their attitudes toward money, credit, labor, and sexuality are all products of the "stasis" which "the outward / masks of the special interests" "perpetuate" and make "profitable" (P. 46). Williams's poetics of dissonance seeks to unblock this cathexis by *re*-presenting the facts in a new and (in Freud's sense) mutilated transcript. Only in this disguised text (of the joke) can the poet dramatize that profits are not for the few but for anyone who is interested in "getting it." When what is at stake is knowledge, then the self-interest which an individual expresses in "getting it" is precisely what refutes and denies the economic greed and selfishness imposed by the "special interests." Even at its basal, ontic level—as a form of individual speech—poetry must become a kind of enlightened social production.

In book 4's ode to credit, the connection between individual economy (*oikos*) and the economy of the community (*polis*) will become explicit: selfishness is the only mask the self *can* wear when it has been conditioned to regard money as an impervious fact, not as a thing whose very significance depends upon the social expansiveness, of the psychic value, of credit. But in *Paterson's* third book, Williams most severely tests his own resolve to prove "the beneficent power of the imagination" (*Imaginations,* p. 19) by subjecting his own "self" to the same "factual" scrutiny given to other commodities. In seeking to break the stasis of the facts, he views himself as the center of all costs. At the end of book 2, the sexual innuendoes of "getting it" are in danger of obliterating Williams's multi-valenced labor. All his effort to this point seems to be drowned out by the inundating denunciations of Marcia Nardi's (*alias* Cress) uninterrupted nine-page letter (*P.* 105-13), which describes a woman's subjugation in a male-centered world of art and commerce and which condemns Williams's whole artistic enterprise for blocking the economic and poetic identities of others, especially women.

Accusing Williams's "type" of belittling her literary skills and freezing her out of the marketplace, Cress finds herself "blocked" both professionally and artistically. She turns the tables on Williams by putting *him* at the core of that blockage. She chastises him for being indifferent to her plight in particular and to the situation of "real" people in general. She asserts that Williams is interested in others only as they serve as fodder for his own poetry —an accusation which, on the surface at least, seems to be confirmed by Williams's use of her letter in his poem. But only on the surface. The letter is hardly self-aggrandizing. Williams's use of it verges on self-abuse. Later readers of the poem have often agreed with Jarrell's observation that the poem as such is in danger of sinking into the inert mass of Cress's letters, of letting its artistic order be mutilated by them: "What has been done to them," Jarrell asked, "to make it possible for us to respond to them as art and not as raw reality"? (Jarrell, p. 173). Ironically, Cress herself, in a postscript, wonders if she has presented her case too rawly. Fearful that Williams will not "read it all the way through, and carefully" (*P.* 113), Cress expresses a moment of doubt especially poignant because our feelings might echo it.

But to answer Jarrell's objection is also to address Cress's fears.

Williams's view of art is not as circumspect as Jarrell's and therefore not as self-enclosed as Cress contends. Art's true antithesis is
not, for Williams, raw reality but impenetrable reality. If Williams
has resolved to include all the waking voices of the "great beast"
of Paterson in his poem, then he must also himself overcome the
remaining prudish idea that a poem is a pristine and inviolable
artifact, the crafting of the poet's voice alone. In reprinting Cress's
letters, Williams may be taking his greatest poetic (and moral) risk
by including the one voice which is directly antagonistic and perhaps unassimilable to his own. But he is also exercising his most
fundamental poetic belief. So, the ending of book 2 engages more
than one challenge; it is challenging to the poet personally, to the
reader's attention, and to the internal dynamics and integrity of
the poem.

By the beginning of book 3, the poem stands in almost desper-
ate need of a new beginning. Williams responds with the locust-
tree poem, reminiscent of some of his pre-*Paterson* lyrics. This
shift from book 2 to book 3, at the exact middle of the original
four-book poem, is one of the most difficult transitions in a work
whose transitions are notoriously difficult. This shift, however, is
crucial to the poem's structure, exemplary of its method, and in-
dicative of its imaginative economics. Although the beginning of
book 3 seems remarkably "cool" and formal and apparently indifferent to Cress's rhetorical onslaught, the appearance is misleading.
The lyric transmutes the "raw reality" of Cress's economic and
artistic complaint into a complex and far-reaching meditation on
the nature of "cost." By transposing the accusatory thrust of
Cress's letter into a new key, Williams is able to discover the radiant gist of her complaint, the part of it which is creditable and
authentic and which "resists the final crystallization" (*P.* 133).

The lyric opens book 3 with unexpected simplicity and clarity:

I love the locust tree
the sweet white locust
    How much?
    How much?
How much does it cost
to love the locust tree
    in bloom?

A fortune bigger than
Avery could muster
    So much
    So much
the shelving green
    locust
whose bright small leaves
    in June
lean among flowers
sweet and white at
    heavy cost [*P.* 117]

Upon closer inspection, however, the simple tone may seem strained. One notes a tight-lipped reserve in the hard-tongued, consonant-stopped penultimate line: "sweet and white at"—a line in which the long vowels are clipped by their consonantal closures, and the discrete /a/ sounds of "and" and "at" become dissonant and muddled. Nor is the syntax, on closer inspection, as straightforward as it seems. The opening declaration of love turns, by line three, into a question. This belated inflection also changes the sense, so that the speaker no longer asks how *much* he loves the locust tree, but *if* he does, and, if so, then "*How* much." The syntax hovers between a sardonic (self-deflating) and a rhetorical (self-confirming) question: "How much does it cost"? But cost, too, is a double-edged concept, for we speak of cost in terms of effort bestowed and also in terms of sacrifice or effort withheld. How much does it cost to love the locust in terms of the effort of attention one lavishes on it, and how much does it cost to love the locust in terms of what one gives up of other loves—Cress's, for instance? How much of other loves does this love for a blooming tree cost? Does one love the tree when it is not "in bloom"? And, because it is difficult to say "locust tree" without saying "locus tree," one is reminded of the difficulty of pinpointing cost and of the multiple loci of costs that accrue in love, in economics, and in the blooming of a rather common, low-cost tree.

How much does it cost? The allusion to Avery (the nineteenth-century art dealer and founder of New York's Metropolitan Museum of Art, who made his fortune buying European paintings and selling them to Americans who wanted "culture") reminds us of the exacting and literal significances behind the word "cost." One would have to possess a fortune "so much" bigger than Avery's (and Avery's is already "so much" bigger than any we possess) in order to say how much our faith in art will cost. If the syntax turns over on itself, making a kind of riddle of monetary and psychic, aesthetic and moral costs, then so much depends on saying so. "So much," the poem abruptly reveals, is to be seen *of* the locust, beyond one's initial "love" *for* it. The poem notes these "facts" as they emerge: the locust's "shelving green," its "bright small leaves," its maturation "in June," its "flowers." And by the end of the second stanza, what was originally perceived as a "sweet white locust" *tree* becomes sweet and white, in the focusing of the discriminatory eye, by virtue of its *flowers.* The locust itself goes back to being itself, "the shelving green / locust," its name now dropped into a single-word line. At last, the flowers (and not the "locust," not the observer's "love") become "sweet and white at / heavy cost." The cost has been passed on, beyond the observer's preoccupation with the movements of his own "love," to the seasonal progression of blooming itself, to what June costs as summer passes, and to what flowers cost the tree as they sweeten and whiten. The word "white" has its own cost, as it moves from the connotatively pure and virginal sense in the opening line to the sense of aging pallor at the end.

How much does it cost to make this careful description of the locust tree, making poetic capital of it? As the lyric's economic metaphors recapitulate Cress's accusations, they strip the lyric of its self-enclosed meditation. Cress had noted that without "work and jobs of that kind"—that is, literary jobs, reviewing, "literary journalism"—she would not be able to "turn into assets what are liabilities for me in jobs of a different kind" (*P.* 107). Later in book 3, the poet agrees that getting into a position to write is "where they get you" (*P.* 137). And Cress's letter has obviously gotten Williams, for he is willing to let her castigation of his liabilities silence book 2. Now, in book 3, transmuted into an elegiac mood, these issues reemerge in the lyric. Like Cress's self-centered complaint, Williams's meditation begins with a personal assertion: "I love." But significantly, the "I" vanishes as the lyric proceeds, much as Cress's personal anger vanishes or is (literally) worked out by the letter itself. They are each shelved, as the "shelving green locust" reveals its "lean" identity, its leaves "lean among flowers." "Lean" is an extraordinarily poignant word in this context, for it suggests a spareness (a frugality and an austerity—the conditions

of Cress's economic and the locust's botanical life) as well as a
bending sense of dependence, the "lien" which is part of one's
vulnerability to "cost." One's liabilities and assets—the economic
state of "living"—are conditions of one's dependence upon others.
In retrospect, we may see that Cress's complaint requires her respondent, Williams, even as it chastises him. The letter requires a
reader as sounding board for its "blockage." Similarly, the locust
tree requires its local observer or else it may become fodder for an
Avery-like culture mill in which objects of art are purchased with
respect neither for the detail (or cost) of the artist's labor nor for
the detail (and cost) of the tree as it sweetens and whitens. To
Avery's customers, only a desire for the status of the made object
counts. But the real cost of art depends upon unblocking the static,
antagonistic relationship between the artist and the third person—
his listener, consumer, creditor.

Thus, it also becomes clear that Williams needs, in some way,
Cress's presence, as he needs (perhaps in the same way) the locust
tree. He requires that sense of alternative particularity outside
himself, so that love may avoid seeking fulfillment only in its own
likeness or giving credit only to things which add up solely to
one's personal profit. The poet needs Cress's letters as the alternative voice to his own. They betoken the physician's willingness to
hear out his patient until she can express her disease, and they represent the physician's capacity to heal himself by frankly and un-
compromisingly accepting what is alien to himself. That here both
patient and physician are writers only makes the predicament
more serious and the need more pressing. Cress's letters, like Duchamp's check, test the doctor's conception of "value" though
they transmute the question of "cost" into a tragic, rather than
a comic, mode.

For almost the whole of book 3, following the meditative pause
of the locust-tree lyric, the poet seems to be sinking beneath the
cost of his own questions. The elemental damage done to the poet
by the woman's assault on the authenticity of his imaginative power to conceive a world greater than the sphere of his own interests
has evolved in book 3 into the elemental damage done to Paterson
as recorded in the histories of the public library. There, the poet
again discloses himself as a reader. Among "a cool of books" (*P.*
118), the man of words attempts to compute the world of costs
on its own terms. He tries to beat the world's elemental inunda-

tion of the self at its own game, and he finds that he is much reduced. The joke, often as not, is on him. If "there is a poetry / of the movements of cost" (and the locust-tree lyric is certainly that kind of poetry), then he also discovers that "COSTS SPIRAL AC-CORDING TO A REBUS" (*P.* 133). "Known or unknown" costs add up to a riddle. The poetry is haunted by its own riddling inadequacy "in the Joycean mode" (*P.* 129). Williams becomes explicitly aware, perhaps for the first time, that he may have been, as Hugh Selwyn Mauberly says, "wrong from the start." The problem may not be to find an adequate language but to find a listener: "So much talk of the language—when there are no / ears" (*P.* 129). Such talk divests artistic labor of its primality by reducing it to an ersatz form of consumerism:

> What is there to say? save that
> beauty is unheeded   . tho' for sale and
> bought glibly enough [*P.* 129]

Recalling the epigraph to the poem's preface, this passage takes us right back to the locked stasis of the poem's beginning, where unheeded beauty discovers its despair in an economics of indifference.

Williams's multi-leveled puns, derived from the debased language of exchange, become most costly in book 3, lacking the movement of sense. There is no longer that erotic joy of "getting it," of finding "one phrase that will / lie married beside another for delight" (*P.* 167). The noble lies of art, so delicately charted in the locust-tree lyric, turn upon the poet and begin to inundate him like the rising waters of the Paterson flood which he has been reading about in the library. Williams finds himself reading too close to the truth to distract the conscious mind. Freud claimed that the joke work began in a "sinking" of thought, in its "downward dragging force" into the unconscious. But through much of book 3, Williams seems to be experiencing that downward pull (which is also, of course, the allure of the Falls) without the promise of release, without the "multiformity of laughter" (*P.* 142). Lacking the imaginative readiness to take pleasure in verbal joking which cuts across accepted but useless meanings, the poet realizes that the riddle of money, like the inflationary rebus, like the "marriage riddle" (*P.* 129), and like "the riddle of a man and a woman" (*P.* 130), are not jokes but mortifying puzzles. And this constitutes a loss to the imagination, not a gain. His puns, for instance, fall deadpan, generating no gist, no credit, lacking a listener. Or rather, in finding that the only listener is himself, the poet discloses all his efforts to be merely self-delighting or self-damning, masturbatory. With crushing irony, he reveals that the gist may be secret, hidden in his books.

One example may suffice. As imaginative energy wanes, the poem settles for an ascetic elegiac mode: "So be it." But this refrain, suggesting stoical resolve, soon lapses into a form of indifference—"so be it" (*P.* 120). Finally, the traditional consolation of elegiac poetry, symbolized by a line from Gray's *Elegy,* also perishes in the flood:

> —and leave the world
> > to darkness
> > > and to
> > > > me. [*P.* 167]

Williams demonstrates visually here the descent "to the bottom," where, he has said, the artist must go in search of the blockage. At the bottom of these new lines, relineated from Thomas Gray's "established writing," is "me." This line is, incidentally, the only time in Gray's poem that the first-person pronoun appears. What does it cost Gray (or Williams) to keep himself out of his poem—or to put himself in? When restructured, Gray's lines visually represent the "inverted bell" of one kind of poetic and the movements of cost of one kind of in-depth reading:

> Let us read

> and digest: the surface
> glistens, only the surface.
> Dig in—and you have

> a nothing, surrounded by
> a surface, an inverted
> bell resounding, a

> white-hot man become
> a book, the emptiness of
> a cavern resounding. [*P.* 149]

Later, Williams identifies this cavern as "the cavern of death"; here, in book 3, the self—"me"—is at the bottom of it. Later, Wil-

liams will assert that there is a hole at the bottom through which
the imagination may escape; but here, the first problem of the imagination is simply to rescue the self from its inundating despair,
to bring "me" to the surface.

In one magnificent passage, Williams finds a locus and a purpose:

The future's no answer. I must
find my meaning and lay it, white,
beside the sliding water: myself—
comb out the language—or succumb. [*P.* 173]

Combing out the syntax, one may realign "myself" as an emphatic
adjectival modifier of "I," the subject of the main clause, or as the
delayed antecedent of "it" and therefore in apposition to "meaning," the object of the main clause. The meaning of this transaction takes place on the glistening "surface" of the lines' syntax.
"Myself" is, thus, the initiator *of* the action as well as the "meaning" to be discovered *in* that action. The strained, jack-in-the-box
enjambment makes the point:

> Let
me out! [*P.* 173]

The "me" which was at the bottom of the lines from Gray is here
at the beginning of Williams's new line; a laying of meaning *in* the
line as the need to find meaning is described *by* the line, just as
"myself" is both the agent of discovery and the thing to be discovered, what is lost when you "dig in" and what slides to the surface when "let . . . out."

In charting the movements of cost to the poetic "I," Williams
comes perilously close, admittedly, to typographical trickery. He
shows the strain of the joke, in this context. Perhaps the assertion
that ends book 3, "this rhetoric / is real," is half-intended as a re-
assurance against one's fear that the "meaning" is counterfeit, a
verbal sleight of hand. There have been other such carnivallike
tricks represented in the poem, and they have resulted in failure.
But perilously close to the edge of the Falls (or to the edge of a
reader's credibility), Williams, like the heroes of *In the American
Grain,* makes his primal act of defiance. His point is, I believe, that
the imagination will do anything not to "succumb." It will release
its roar of energy against the inundation of the "facts" in any way
that it can—courting burlesque, slapstick, or outright forgery—in

order to save "me." By noticing "me" ("a supple word") as it changes places throughout book 3, moving from the bottom of Gray's old line to the start of Williams's new measure, one may hear perhaps how faint "a music of survival" can be.[24]

Begun in response to Cress's letter, acknowledging the need for a listener, book 3 ends by saving the first person, the core of all jokes. Book 3 may be read as a kind of swoon in which Williams, intent upon playing the role that Cress demanded, the role of attentive listener or reader, loses (and then rediscovers) the initial vitality of his own labor. Having dug out a corner for himself in the library reading old books, he has forgotten the original need to "BRIGHTen the corner where you are" (*P.* 154). But the brightening occurs momentarily in the *re*-cognition that the self, the "I," is the core of survival, and it allows him to meet directly, for the first time, his female antinomy, the figure of Kora in the core or basement of a house. He does not know what to make of her, any more than he knows how to respond to Cress, as this passage, straining to close the distance between "I" and "you," will testify:

> I can't be half gentle enough,
> half tender enough
>   toward you, toward you,
> inarticulate, not half loving enough. [*P.* 154]

But here at least he tries to speak. He calls the brutalized black woman a "Beautiful Thing" and notes in the "black plush, a dark flame" (*P.* 154). In sexual terms, we are introduced to the formula for "getting it," the luminous gist from the black pitchblende, which will be discovered anew in the physics of book 4. And yet, the poet here is unable to find credit for his own gist: that to be tender is to tender oneself "toward" (to accept the "lien" of) another. "Half" measures are not "enough." (Even the male gangs who raped her had to break her nose "to be credible in their deeds.") The gist is earned only in the thorough exertion of one's resources ("Three days in the same dress / up and down" [*P.* 154]). But the brutality of such sexual thoroughness has perverted the playful tenderings of language, rendered them inarticulate, deadened the productive gist. The rape, therefore, was insufferable—nor is there now any exchange. Williams's tenderness in attempting to minister to the beaten woman remains strangely ineffectual, one-sided. The book concludes with a far-reaching irony: words cannot countenance, or redress, an act which serves merely to discredit the imagination. The poet finds his own language raped.

> *And as reverie gains and*
> *your joints loosen*
> *the trick's done!*
>
> . . .
>
> *Through this hole*
> *at the bottom of the cavern*
> *of death, the imagination*
> *escapes intact.*
> —*William Carlos Williams*, Paterson

In book 4, the sexual immediacy of "getting it," the economic wish to obtain the means of purchasing power, and the need to define one's own labor as an honorable maintenance coalesce in Williams's diagrammatic effort to teach the reader how to read his text. Phyllis, the naively resourceful shepherdess-masseuse of part 1's mock pastoral "Idyll," earns her economic survival by passively accepting the sexual advances of both Corydon and Dr. P himself, a "fruitful exaggeration" (*P.* 153) of what "getting it" means. The dramatic dialogue of part 1 is crystallized in part 2 as a dramatic soliloquy which begins with the poet taking his young son to hear a lecture on atomic fission, "a first for both of us" (*P.* 201). Part 2 unfolds as the poet's retort to the chemistry lecture, an attempt to locate in this new and (for Williams) virgin knowledge a breakthrough "against all that scants our lives" (*P.* 218). But the potential both for a cure (as for cancer) and for disastrous global armament is contained in the splitting of the atom: there are more retorts than one. Williams's assessment of the sociopolitical implications of the new atomic chemistry impresses his poetic purpose with renewed immediacy and complexity, from which he issues his most explicit demonstration of his poetic economics.

In book 4, we are given directly three senses of "getting it"— first, in an anecdote: "The young conductor gets his orchestra / and leaves his patroness / with child" (*P.* 211). Its gist: acquisition of the tools for making art (the maestro's orchestra) proves the artist sexually potent; his patroness's pregnancy becomes a sign of her money's power to effect artistic realization. The suggestion of

the artist's faithlessness (if "leaves" implies "abandons") poignantly shows how much the fidelity to one kind of credit may cost
in terms of other kinds of fidelity.

This sort of parabolically compressed "joke" (merely a more
elaborate version of Groucho's innuendo) is expanded as the poet
considers Madame Curie's method of "getting it," which links sexual potency with economic yield in a more complex way:

> *Item* . with coarsened hands
> by the hour, the day, the week
> to get, after months of labor .
>
> a stain at the bottom of the retort
> without weight, a failure, a
> nothing. And then, returning in the
> night, to find it .
>
> LUMINOUS! [*P.* 209]

Here, the pregnancy of the conductor's patroness yields its further
metaphorical gist, a new physics. The radiance of the new isotope
occurs, like birth, out of the woman's labor. Curie had to bypass
all previous "knowledge" of chemical valences as the "contamin-
ant" blocking discovery (*P.* 209); she had to subject her elemental
(and womanly) knowledge—learned, for instance, from Mendelief's
periodic chart—to a new "retort."

Finally, this luminous stain is the wished-for outcome of Williams's joke technique as well. In book 4, part 2, the mathematics
of atomic chemistry are joined with the particulars of prosody to
create a language of fiduciary shorthand, an algebraic formulization of poetic and human value:

> Uranium: basic thought—leadward
> Fractured: radium: credit [*P.* 217]

The fracturing described in the first three books (as when the
Beautiful Thing had her nose "busted") did not always lead to discovery but testified merely to the "fractured" status of our lives.
Book 4 will attempt to "let credit / out" (*P.* 215), a line which is
literally an extension of credit from the lines in book 3 which
"let / me out." Before "credit" and "me" can be understood as a
"complex atom" (*P.* 209), they must first be connected in the
fractured poetic lines of *Paterson.* The old poetic line is "busted"

to let the self out—that is, to let out the individual imagination which is unique in each application, in each retort. In mathematics, a line is a series of connected points, and Williams's misplaced period (as in "valences . " [*P.* 202]) is a disarming example of punctuation that splits off from its verbal line, breaking down the orthographic and syntactical valences into a new set of periodic elements. By examining these new periodic elements closely, Williams hoped at last to chart the "atomic" identity of his work song, realizing an empirical formula for poetic "labor."

The full success of Williams's labor depends upon his unblocking the rhetorical significance of money. As a joke, money "could be wiped out / at stroke / of pen" (*P.* 217), and, as money, a joke is a vehicle of exchange (between author and reader). According to Freud, a joke is a constantly new product of the imagination. According to Williams, money may be seen as a product of the imagination when one realizes that its gist is credit and that credit stalled in money is analogous to the gist stalled in poetic exchange:

> . credit, stalled
> in money, conceals the generative
> that thwarts art or buys it (without
> understanding), out of poverty of wit, to
> win, vicariously, the blue ribbon. [*P.* 215]

Williams does not say that art should *not* be bought with money but that it should also be bought with understanding. To understand fully, we must give economic measures the same investment of the imagination as poetic measures, so that each may return an equivalent credit. Credit is stalled when its factual counterpart, money, is unengendered, unpenetrated by the imagination—when it is a locked seed. Money that becomes a self-enclosed, self-sufficient product blocks the generative force of the art which it purchases.

Williams's retort to monetary facts and economic metaphor answers the "poverty of wit" in Billy Sunday's "foot-song" (*P.* 203), itself merely an extension of the earlier evangelical "joke" perpetrated in book 2 by Klaus Ehrens. The United Factory Owners' Association had allegedly asked Sunday to hold a revival meeting in Paterson for the purpose of undermining the "radicalism" behind the labor strike of 1915. Thus, Sunday, the "ex-rightfielder," becomes a pitcher for God:

.   to "break" the strike
and put those S.O.B.s in their places, be
Geezus, by calling them to God! [*P.* 203]

For Billy, "getting it" means "getting his 27 Grand in the hotel
room / after the last supper (at the Hamilton) / on the eve of
quitting town." Although his moral message is antichrematistic,
it capitalizes on the libidinal urgency of the spirit: "All together
now, / give it everything you got!" (*P.* 203). In Williams's lines,
Sunday is portrayed as a mock-Christ (after the Last Supper) and
a mock gunslinger (quitting town with his money), but his public
renunciation of money merely perpetuates the crucifixion of bounty as espoused by Klaus Ehrens, who "made a wide motion with
both / hands as of scattering money to the winds" (*P.* 90). The
bountiful gesture is a trick, however, because neither Ehrens nor
Sunday scatters the means of purchasing power. Instead, they lecture the poor on the advisability of giving away what little they
have. Ehrens's voice does not minister to the knowledge which
money restricts although he seems to enjoy his own joke:

> He stopped to laugh, healthily, and
> his wan assistants followed him,
> forcing it out—grinning against
> the rocks with wry smiles. [*P.* 84–85]

But finally, this *illusion* of psychic health is what one of Billy
Sunday's assistants identified as the economic value of Christian
instruction: "The great gospel of Jesus Christ finding its way into
the hearts of men makes man love man, makes capital appreciate
labor and labor appreciate capital. Labor agitation disappears in
some places because of the [revival] meetings in the plants and
factories. That is its moral and economic value."[25]
 The moral depreciation necessitated by this psychoeconomics
of "appreciation" is precisely what Williams seeks to remonstrate
in his own poetics. But it would be inappropriate (a typically
Poundian confusion) to answer Ehrens's or Sunday's evangelical
song with a deliberately reasoned critique or argument. Insofar as
"moral and economic value" is being debated, the authenticity
of this value will be tested by the song's persuasiveness. If Sunday's fight song is a kind of ecclesiastical buck-and-wing ("He's
on / the table now! Both feet, singing / (a foot song) his feet
canonized" [*P.* 203]), then Williams answers this evangelical voice

by rising to his own feet. "Credit. Credit. Credit. Give them all
credit" (*P.* 217), Williams's evangelical voice rings out as if ringing
up a sum on a cash register. What we need, Williams implies, are
not more weighty and erudite ideas about the fact of money (i.e.,
more of Pound on pounds) but to break through, in poetry, to the
"thing" itself—credit, the dynamics of "getting it."

By broadening our apprehension of "economics," Williams
narrows our understanding of the labor process of poetry. When
money is seen as a "thing" fractured by the imagination, it may
then function in a radiant field of multiple associations. "Interest"
acquires resonance and becomes both the beginning and the end of
labor. Pound hated the idea of interest because, as the essence of
usury, it represented the self-perpetuating power of money. Williams celebrates interest by showing what Pound was uninterested
in—the response of others to his work. Interest, for Williams, always entails a compounding of selves, even if, as in Allen Ginsberg's letters to him, the listener's attention is still not luminous:
"I don't understand the measure [Ginsberg writes]. I haven't
worked with it much either, though, which must make the difference. But I would like to talk with you concretely on this."
(*P.* 205). The difference between Ginsberg's letters and, say,
Pound's is that Ginsberg's interest is sustained in spite of a difference between the two men. Ginsberg is interested in what he
does not understand and is willing to work with it. Here, interest
is not selfish because it does not require that one spite others'
labors, so that one man gets twenty-seven grand while his listeners
give everything they've got—the predicament that Cress thought
she was in. To recognize "difference," even disagreement, and still
"to talk . . . concretely on this" is to recognize how "the mind"
must "declare itself not / alone in dreams" (*P.* 209). Getting it, we
enter into what H. Levy calls (and Williams quotes) the spirit of
"antagonistic cooperation" (*P.* 208), which is also the celebratory
spirit of Williams's poetic economics, when properly understood.[26]

In Levy's book, *A Philosophy for a Modern Man,* Williams may
have recognized the same celebratory dispersal of credit which he
attempted to affirm in book 4. Levy wished to place economics
and art in a "field" theory of psychic, imaginative, biological, and
physical motion. Anticipating Williams's economic description of
artistic "labor," Levy suggested that "the artist . . . cannot divorce
the significant part of his work from himself," but neither can he

allow himself to become an atomistic "isolate."[27] When energized, the artist's labor must become a particle in the larger movements of economic and social interactions. Writing fifteen years before Levy's *Philosophy*, Williams had already noted in *Spring and All* that "the energizing force of imagination" liberates the artist from "the acquisitive—*progressive* force of the lump" (*Imaginations*, p. 135). The artist is opposed to "the merchant" who is "hibernating, unmagnetized" and who "tends to drop away into the isolate, inactive particles" (ibid.). The song of book 4—which is simultaneously a retort to the lecture on atomic fission, to Norman Douglas's comment on the fate of fathers, to Curie's discovery of radium, to the social credit movement, to Billy Sunday's strikebreaking, and to Pound's poetic economics—permits the poet to see that, by being "interested" in the work of one's predecessors, one can compound that interest in a new measure which creates a value that is at once both unique ("different") and a "credit" to the difference.

In the working plan for book 4, Williams noted his use of "three discoveries": "1. radium. 2. poet's discovery of modern idiom. 3. political scientist's discovery of a cure for economic ills."[28] We have seen how the splitting of the atom, the splitting of the poetic foot, and the splitting of money and credit function, in the joke/ gist formula of *Paterson*, to compound our interest. For Williams, the movements of economic cost are also an imaginative process, like the visual movements of the poem's lines, like the invisible movements of atomic elements. The dissonance between these movements becomes, in the poetic trope of the joke, the "contact" (the name of a magazine with which Williams was involved) which signals discovery. Contact—the poetics of getting it—replaces the Wordsworthian notion of a poetic contract and answers the Poundian notion of art as a finished product by disclosing a new "foot-song." When the commercial measure of money and the measure of the poetic idiom are analogous, then the labor process of poetry can be associated with all other forms of labor. The socioeconomic question of credit becomes inseparable from the sociopoetic question of the gist: they both generate interest. The whole of *Paterson* attempts to show what perversions of sense have caused us to regard "getting it" as a selfish activity. We have been taught, Williams discovers, to *suppress* the self in the name of a psychoeconomic principle—interest—which actually depends upon extending and expending the self. In Williams's joke, we credit the self most fully by being interested in others, not by "exiling one's self from one's self" (*P.* 59). The social and economic importance of the poet is not a joke, even if, owing to his defective means, the poet has had to use jokes to say so.

Marx declared that the labor process "disappears in the product," in the commodity that it has made, so that "the former is materialized, the latter transformed. That which in the labourer appeared as movement, now appears in the product as a fixed quality without motion."[29] Not so for Williams. The dynamic of "getting it" prevents the poem from lapsing back into the static, inert mass as "a fixed quality without motion" because it opens the product to the labor process of the reader *at every instant* of its production. In seeing that the literary work is not exhausted by being read but is, to appropriate Marxian innuendo, "materialized," Williams is able to describe how the valences of the text are constantly being "transformed." The end of the poet's labor is not to end labor but to embody its process. "Getting it," then, the reader does not consume a product but participates in, profits from, its embodiment of expendable credit. The labor process is, at every exertion, contrapuntal. Moving foot by foot or point against point (the radical sense of "contrapuntally" [*P.* 278]), these accumulating points yield a line (a series of points— male with female, joke with gist, poet with reader), evolving into a series of lines, a graphic body of artistic realization. "The greatest work of the twentieth century" will require, according to Williams, that "reading will become an art also" (*Imaginations,* p. 362). The addition of this factor, the reader as artist, means that Williams can incorporate *in* his poem the social process which more patently socialist writers can only allude to: "Work: value created and received" (*P.* 218).

If artistic labor realizes itself by being both created *and* received, then the recurrence of great art across the centuries is owing not to an Eliotic or Poundian incremental "tradition" but to a continual economics of expenditure, of starting over again: "again is the magic word . / turning the in out" (*P.* 162). What truly endures is not the piece of art as document or as artifact or as "finished product" but the constantly new labor that is its yield—namely, the pleasure of "getting it." Each new poem is not merely a multivalenced improvisation upon texts which preceded it, but a multivalenced improvisation upon itself. An author does not merely anxiously rewrite his predecessors so as to make room for his own interests, his own unique form of self-expression; he also rewrites his immediate past—that is, what he himself has written—in order to extract from his self-exertions that gist which would return language to its communal and collective function as an implement of knowledge, of enlightened social production: "It is dangerous to leave written that which is badly written. A chance word, upon paper, may destroy the world. Watch carefully and erase, while the power is still yours, I say to myself, for all that is put down, once it escapes, may rot its way into a thousand minds, . . . and all libraries, of necesssity, be burned to the ground as a consequence" (*P.* 155). So, what is badly written is that which does not take into account how writing elicits response, how it shapes a society, how it begins again with each new word, with each new reading. What is badly written flatters itself that the writer has created a fixed quality without motion, a finished product, an "external" artifact. For Williams, however, writing, like reading, is a process of participation and, as such, is dependent upon the exhaustibility of the gist, the need to "get it" and to create it anew.

The joke is crucial to Williams's interest, then, because it is the rubric by which this "power" of renewal remains manifest so that the vitality of the "gist" can remain central. Freud said that jokes need constantly to be told and used up. So, for Williams, does the word. Language must be constantly subjected to the variations of speech, the intervening of real voices. Constantly subjected to the intrusion of the reader, the text is always variable, like the dissonant labor process of the primitive poem as defined by Thomson. *Paterson* is not an amassing or cumulative work in the sense that it rolls up a sum at the end, to be dispersed, retroactively by means of memory, over and against the grain of our linear reading experience. Indeed, Williams satirizes the dissociated economics of the literary industry—

> Texts mount and complicate them-
> selves, lead to further texts and those
> to synopses, digests and emendations [*P.* 156]

—because *Paterson* is not offered as merely a "text," at least not in the usual academic sense of the word. That is, we may, if we like, read *Paterson* as we would read a novel (or as we read *The Prelude* or *The Faerie Queene*—no one would argue, at this late date, that

Paterson is a less structured work than these); but it is structured according to a different dynamic—one which is consistent with the labor process which underlies it and which the poem seeks to expose and to understand. An ulterior (macroeconomic) reading that searches, in retrospect, only for a critical sense of the "whole poem" will miss what Williams himself most valued—the gist of the individual parts, the "reciprocal action" (*P.* 217) of voices by which the poem's metaphorical "jokes" are created and received. This (microeconomic) work comprises Williams's version of the Poundian (and Freudian) "complex"—an elucidation by multiplicity. Gain is embodied implementally in *Paterson*—at each "instant" of the reader's experience with the poem, at each line, and at each foot—so that the reader's participatory labor of "interpretation" re-creates the particularity of the author's labor in composing the poem.

Williams issues his most direct challenge to the reader in the last part of book 4:

    —you cannot believe
  that it can begin again, again, here
  again   .   here [*P.* 234]

Each of these words is a "joke" in the rhetorical sense that Williams uses that concept. The poem literally begins again (if we can believe it) at the creation of each new word, at the placement ("here") of each new word in the line. Each word is incrementally *a gain* earned by the exertion of the poet's labor *against* the stasis of recurrence (the sense of *again*-ness). Thus, this passage goes on to assert that we must "Waken from a dream, this dream of / the whole poem" (*P.* 234), for the "real" poem lies in the particularity of its individual elements ("again here") where the labor process is made manifest. Transformed into the mutilated transcript of "work," the poem discloses, using the dynamic of the joke, that the private act of "getting it" becomes a social process.

Here, the poet's elemental labor process is embodied in its bipartite labor cry: "begin again." The movement of a new exertion (begin), measured contrapuntally against the movement of repetition (again), creates an expansion of the words themselves, so that they both mean what they say and enact what they say. These two words signify the two parts, the arsis and thesis, of one labor, the poet's. They also identify the reader's labor, *his* need to "begin again," as contiguous to it. *Paterson* would seek, in this way, to *become* the labor process, not merely to describe (or to dream) it. To embody this bipartite movement in the very lay of its lines, the poem must articulate "here" the rhythms of that "primitive labor" (as Thomson called it) which also engages the listener in a collective social act. Both reader and poet must "waken" to the "gist" of the poem's economics and learn to *hear* it as the core of *Paterson*'s language. In the following definition of the poetic labor, for instance, "this" refers to the word "this" and to its palpable sounds, as well as to "this" thrusting, hammering exertion that the lines themselves "make":

    —of this, make it of *this,* this
    this, this, this, this   . [*P.* 168]

In the contact between the poet's and the reader's acts of making —in *this* identification of language itself as the basal labor process —Williams's poetry materializes as an exhaustible and therefore renewable technique of production. Its implement, language, is also its increment—its "joke," its "gist." "*La Vertue / est toute dans l'effort*" (*P.* 221), Williams asserts, crediting another language. "No one mind / can do it all" (*P.* 224), he concludes, crediting his own—and his belief in ours.

We began this study by examining the way in which Marcel Duchamp changed the valence and thus the significance of the dollar sign by adding to it his own signature as artist. Williams's work has permitted a more thorough inspection of the effects and of the responsibility that an artist thereby assumes. For Williams, the movements of cost in economics and in poetry compete in a single, intersystemic, cultural field—in an antagonistic cooperation. Economic process is the externalization of psychic and physiological processes which underlie our efforts to define love, sexual fulfillment, and social consciousness in the self and in the *polis.* Poetry attempts to internalize these processes so that their relations may be *re*-presented, apart from the stasis which compartmentalizes them and blocks their mutual release. Our modern epistemology, with its superstructures of discrete "fields" and "specialized labors," is, in effect, a world without a center; though it may display a multitude of coherent systems, none is cohesive enough to override each one's singular, ad hoc claim to priority. "The poetry in these [political, economic, scientific, and historical] systems of thought," Shelley said, "is concealed by the accumulation of facts and calculating processes."[30] But it is precisely this "poetry" that Williams wished to unconceal, to realize in *Paterson*. Language itself, he concluded, needs to be credited. His premise is surprisingly unbiased: looked at dispassionately, there is no simple, axiomatic reason why economics should be regarded as opposed to the production of art or why poetry should be impervious to economics. To make economics (or physics or general medicine) an imaginable process, its metaphorical system of production must work to our credit and its "values" must not be exchanged for other, perhaps "higher" interests. The system must become part of the labor process of our language.

The values of labor and of language, of economics and of literature, become complementary discoveries as it were possible, in Wallace Stevens's bold postulation, "to think of the national economy as a poetico-economy."[31] We discover anew the faith of Thoreau in the poetics of Williams: that "economy" may serve as a vital metaphorical variable linking where we live and what we live for. Economics, in all its figural complexity, becomes an instrument which may unblock the myriad ways in which the instrumentality of the imagination is economically compromised. For in the more polemical language of Shelley, "the great instrument of moral good is the imagination; and poetry administers to the effect by acting upon the cause" (p. 40). The poetry *of* economics is what *Paterson* would seek to embody when it shows how an economy may function according to the same expansions and contractions—the same labor process, the same birth process—as the poem. A compounded metaphor, economics is, like prosody, a "thing" which needs to be fractured in order to discover the psychic elements which underlie it. The poet, according to Williams, must chart anew the constellations of verbal elements which might truly express it. Transposing the historical complaints of poets and economists into a dissonant modern key, Williams identifies in "economics" itself an intellectual and emotional complex which, when split, discloses that the core of all cures, for the economist as well as for the poet, lies in the dissatisfied labor of the irrepressible imagination.

The quality of mercy in *The Merchant of Venice* may be strained by a more pervasive commercial irony than Ruskin's complaint against *merces* was able to consider.[1] To what extent, we might ask, has Shakespeare, as a premier example of a literary man, succumbed to or transformed the alluring "unreal words" which Bagehot, Mill, De Quincey, and Ruskin defined? In what specific ways can *The Merchant of Venice* help us to disentangle (or merely to apprehend) the symbolic complications of economic discourse? Or does it merely play into the hands of economic myth, the drama itself becoming a casualty of the very commercial dealings which it describes? Many readers have felt after all, Ruskin to the contrary, that Shylock is not dealt with justly and that the justification for Antonio's Christian dispensation is an acquittal based on a sort of verbal trick. In stepping back from the appreciative Ruskinesque rhapsode, we might refocus upon one episode from *The Merchant of Venice* which Ruskin alludes to but does not analyze—the caskets scene. The economic subtext that underlies Bassanio's choice is also a primary subject of the present study: how does one balance the economic and the noneconomic significances of "value"? How can an "unreal word" such as "price" acquire what Ruskin calls its "moral power"?

By Shakespeare's time, the meaning of "price" itself had changed in order to accommodate economic usage. Until well into the sixteenth century, price meant merely estimation or esteem, so that what was priceless was worthless. In the new language of nascent capitalist economics, however, what was priceless came to be understood as what was beyond measure, beyond mere price. Johan Huizinga has further noticed that " 'prize,' 'price,' and 'praise' all derive more or less directly from the Latin *pretium* but develop in different directions. *Pretium* arose originally in the sphere of exchange and valuation, and presupposed a counter-value. . . . Now while *price* remains bound to the sphere of economics, *prize* moves into that of play and competition, and *praise* acquires the exclusive signification of the Latin *laus.*" He continues:

> What is equally curious is to see how the word *wage,* originally identical with *gage* in the sense of a symbol of challenge, moves in the reverse direction of *pretium*—i.e. from the play sphere to the economic sphere and becomes a synonym for "salary" or "earnings." We do not *play* for wages, we *work* for them. Finally, "gains" or "winnings" has nothing to do with any of these words etymologically, though semantically it pertains to both play and economics: the player receives his winnings, the merchant makes them.[2]

The mercantile making of a price pertains to both play and economics when Shakespeare's Bassanio claims Portia as his prize. The game at the center of *The Merchant of Venice* entails a choice between three caskets, and the right "prize" is attained by pricing the true value of the caskets properly. Two centuries later, Smith and Ricardo would proclaim the imaginative reality of price structures, but here Shakespeare locates price in both its real and fictive, its economic and noneconomic senses, and computes thereby the nonequivalency of price in terms of the nonequivalency of praise. In doing so, he indicates one way in which we must correct, or at least qualify, the mythos of economic formulation with the mythos of poetic formulation.

Gain, in the symbolic play world of choices, is not the same as gain in the equally symbolic but less playful mercantile world of choices. Indeed, the symbolizations of the two worlds seem to be particularly inappropriate to each other. Some critics, acting like the Princes of Morocco and Arragon, the unsuccessful competitors for Portia's hand, have been content to show what is inappropriate about these conflicting systems of symbols. A closer examination, using Bassanio's economics of the imagination, must tell us why they are *particularly* inappropriate.

Love has little to do with choosing the right leaden casket over the other more valuable ones, although, as it happens, the correct choice is made by Portia's lover. What Bassanio reads in the actual substances of the caskets is the substantive danger of his predicament as chooser, not the substance of his love. To choose one casket is not to choose others. Bassanio takes the cost of choosing as his economic text in this test of fidelity. He understands such cost as both the labor of thought which he must put into choosing and the displacement cost, the price that any single labor exacts in terms of what else cannot be chosen.[3] Lead speaks to this displacement cost; lead provides the text for apprehending that threatening kind of play which is the labor of choosing:

> But thou, thou meagre lead
> Which rather threaten'st than dost promise aught,
> Thy plainness moves me more than eloquence;
> And here choose I. Joy be the consequence![4]

The "consequence" is that he receives "Fair Portia's counterfeit" (l. 115), a picture. In the picture, Bassanio reads the inadequacy of representation by re-presenting the substance of his own act of choosing:

> Yet look, how far
> The substance of my praise doth wrong this shadow
> In underprizing it, so far this shadow
> Doth limp behind the substance. [Ll. 126–29]

The first "shadow" seems to refer to the picture alone; the second "shadow," because it finds an antecedent in the "substance of my praise," refers also to the language of Bassanio's praise. In one expression, then, "prize," "price," and "praise"—the verbal geode of *pretium*—suddenly converge to form the perfect counterfeit: the substance which is Portia, the commodity that winning has bestowed, the wages of his choice, the (economic) pun made flesh.[5]

By degrees, then, "fortune" has revealed itself as "consequence" (the lucky outcome) and as "substance" (the wealth which is Portia herself). In playing the game rightly, by respecting the predicament of himself as chooser, Bassanio does not confuse the substance of the caskets with the substance of Portia, and so the lesser substance ultimately unlocks the greater. Moreover, he does not confuse the rules or structure of the game with that which the game is symbol of. Because he originally respects what is fortunate or unfortunate (a matter of chance and choice) in his own predicament as contestant, he is able ultimately to read the text which contains "the continent and summary of my fortune" (l. 130).

Shakespeare's economic metaphors do more than highlight the equivocation between fortune as wealth and as chance.[6] His metaphors are, finally, self-referring, revealing the metaphorical status of economic formulization itself. Portia's caskets are not (economic) commodities until her suitors' perceptions make them so, until her suitors turn the caskets' material substance into a metaphorical valorization of Portia herself. But Bassanio never mentions Portia in debating with himself which casket to choose. He debates instead with his own fears of thought and choice, and, in that economy, the caskets become cloudy symbols of a high romance. The high romance is the test of self-evaluation which all games symbolically demand. The game signifies, through its use of economic metaphor, the predicament of having to express the choice which is most equivalent to and which most certainly represents the *paucity* of one's means of choosing. Here economic consciousness becomes self-consciousness. In Bassanio's internal debate we see the value-making process of economic discourse: how pricing becomes a mark of praise, of prizing rightly, so that labor is its own reward and the work of choosing is, in its fullest economic "consequence," the "joy" of play.

Marx lamented that a "price" stamped a commodity as "a mysterious thing."[7] Because commodities represent "qualities [which] are at the same time perceptible and imperceptible by the senses," economics relies on an imaginative (and, Weisskopf would add, unconscious) value system. Economic metaphor serves in Shakespeare's hands to express this mystery also. After receiving a kiss from the lady whom he has won by this economic or Venetian version of the courtly rites of Venus,[8] Bassanio gives his own version of his estate:

> I come by note, to give and to receive.
> Like one of two contending in a prize,
> That thinks he hath done well in people's eyes,
> Hearing applause and universal shout,
> Giddy in spirit, still gazing in a doubt
> Whether those peals of praise be his or no;
> So, thrice-fair lady, stand I even so,
> As doubtful whether what I see be true. . . . [Ll. 140–47]

We realize that the "peals of praise" which Bassanio figuratively doubts "be his or no" are, in fact, these very lines, praising the outcome of his chance and choice. The couplets comprise, in effect, a double simile, mirroring their own creation. "Like one . . . so stand I" (ll. 141–46) is the actual simile, depending on the like/ so construction; "stand I even so, / As doubtful" (ll. 146–47) is a kind of repeated simile, its so/as construction echoing the first, acting as a peal of praise. What does Bassanio possess? Giving praise to Portia as his winnings, Bassanio's lines insistently receive what they give; they both name Portia as commodity, the earnings he has won, and strip themselves of any merchandizing intent. She is "thrice-fair" because in being beautiful (fair) and just (fair), she is also the fare, the object of exchange which makes this pricing, prizing, and praising worth the labor. In one magnificent chiastic line, however, Bassanio stands, by the grace of his own words, as the commodious equal of the commodity he has attained. In pricing the text of his choice, Bassanio becomes both reader and author. He is himself the product of the production which his language has produced: "So, thrice-fair lady, stand I even so. . . ."

If this interpretation seems to press Bassanio's courtesy to the heights of the inexpressible, then this is precisely what Bassanio's "mere dispute about words" (see chapter 3) means to do:

> Madam, you have bereft me of all words.
> Only my blood speaks to you in my veins,

And there is such confusion in my powers
As, after some oration fairly spoke
By a beloved prince, there doth appear
Among the buzzing pleased multitude,
Where every something being blent together
Turns to a wild of nothing, save of joy
Expressed and not expressed. [Ll. 175-83]

Marx's mystery becomes Bassanio's Mystery. In attempting to express his "confusion" by calling this figurative wordlessness the aftermath of "some oration fairly spoke," Bassanio rhetorically dismantles his rhetoric of praise from its formal occasion. In that moment of grace, the language of commerce by which Bassanio and Portia have represented their affections becomes inflected with a new significance.

To this point, the economic metaphors have sustained an intensity of response across a field of imprecise but emotionally and sexually charged meanings—a good description of the language of the playground (and here the playground is literally the stage). At last, their allegory speaks literally, mediating between what language can and what it cannot express, playing out the labor which this particularly difficult trial of caskets has cost. Here "every something," every *thing* or commodity, including this utterance, is "*being* blent together," so that material substance is no longer alienated from the economic consciousness which prices it. Price crosses with praise: Bassanio's appraising of his choice pieces together both the language of functional economics and the language of moral economy in order to prize Portia in a way that literally rewards (in the person of Portia) and so reaffirms his own decorous formation of praise.

But Bassanio is no special case. He is no poet. His world is wholly mercantile. Indeed, his evocative use of economic discourse is merely what economic discourse ultimately strives for: a completely "factual" statement of our psychological and spiritual states, bound as they are by the *prima materia,* the commercial worlds of choice and chance. Bassanio, then, is the economist par excellence in Mill's sense because, in pricing, he simultaneously interprets and shapes the price into an economics of moral and functional authority. He is also a true economist in Ruskin's sense because he reads the story behind the story, the literal commercial significance of the figuratively economic trial which he undergoes.

Bassanio's trial prefigures Shylock's and shows why Shylock cannot win. Quite simply, when Shylock is taken at *his* word, one finds that the lovers (and not Shylock) employ the more vigilant and incontrovertible economic vocabulary. When Shylock is called upon to take *his* impossible pound of flesh, we may witness how each "merchant" in the realpolitik of this play gains only those winnings which he is able to imagine, and how each is finally sentenced by the economics of his own language.

NOTES

Footnotes contain full bibliographical information for quoted sources only when those texts are not included in the Selected Bibliography.

Preface

1. A. L. Macfie, *An Essay on Economy and Value*, p. 35; my italics.

Chapter I

1. *The Almost Complete Works of Marcel Duchamp: Catalogue of the Tate Gallery, 18 June-31 July 1966,* 2nd ed. (London: Arts Council of Great Britain, 1966), p. 61.
2. *The Prose Edda by Snorri Sturluson,* trans. Arthur Gilchrist Brodeur (New York: American-Scandinavian Foundation, 1916), p. 92.
3. *The Works of John Ruskin,* ed. E. T. Cook and Alexander Wedderburn, 17:101. References in the text are to this edition.
4. *North Adams* (Mass.) *Transcript,* 10 September 1975, p. 1, cols. 1-4. The Associated Press article by Louise Cook begins: "Higher food prices resulting from U. S. grain sales to Russia are caused by controversy and concern over the deals and not by any threat to American supplies. The problem is words, not wheat."
5. *The Collected Poems of Wallace Stevens* (New York: Alfred A. Knopf, 1965), p. 408.
6. *The Collected Works of Samuel Taylor Coleridge: The Friend,* ed. Barbara E. Rooke, 2 vols. 1:507. References in the text are to this edition.
7. Ferdinand de Saussure, *Course in General Linguistics,* ed. Charles Bally and Albert Sechehaye, trans. Wade Baskin, pp. 79-80.

8. For further discussion of metaphor in this sense, see Kurt Heinzelman, " 'Cold Consolation': The Art of Milton's Last Sonnet," in *Milton Studies X*, ed. James D. Simmonds, pp. 111–25.

9. Kenneth Burke speaks of "the monetary idiom" as almost a superstructure of rhetoric (*The Rhetoric of Motives*, p. 129). Shell metaphorically transforms this term so that he may ask where rhetorical specie are minted: "The study of economic and verbal symbolization, and of the relation between them, begins at the mint" (Shell, p. 63). But we must not underestimate the myriad ways in which literature confronts and refutes, restructures and utilizes economic symbolization. (And, in any event, is economic symbolization *not* verbal?) The danger here is that Shell's thesis tends to reduce political economy to its monetary practices while, at the same time, reducing aesthetic economy to the aesthetics of money—a double reduction which is precisely what Marx warned against (see chapter six, below). In fact, Shell rarely discusses economists as such, or their particular economic theories, and therefore he overlooks the internal symbolizations of *their* structures.

10. Appearing after the present study was completed, Avrom Fleishman's *Fiction and the Ways of Knowing* attempts to analyze, in more general terms, this same sense of "literacy" by showing how nonliterary systems of discourse are appropriated into literary texts. Fleishman, extending Derrida's idea that the *difference* between systems of discourse is a function of their "substitutive supplementation [*suppléance*]" of each other, contends that we should "consider the differences among [philosophy, literature, and other systems] as an indispensable aspect of their working" (p. 11). "Boldly reversing the direction of Hegel's dictum," Fleishman asserts "that fiction is the borderland where science passes into art" (p. 16). Unfortunately, Fleishman considers the economic science in only one brief chapter on *Little Dorritt* ("Master and Servant in *Little Dorritt*," pp. 64–73), a chapter which the reader should himself supplement with N. N. Feltes's evocative study of the actual and poetic economics in that novel—"Community and the Limits of Liability in Two Mid-Victorian Novels."

11. See George Unwin, "Commerce and Coinage" in *Shakespeare's England: An Account of the Life and Manners of his Age*, 2 vols. (Oxford: Clarendon Press, 1916), 1:311–45.

12. See L. C. Knight, *Drama and Society in the Age of Jonson*.

13. See Richard Ehrenberg, *Capital and Finance in the Age of the Renaissance*, trans. H. M. Lucas; R. H. Tawney, *The Agrarian Problem in the Sixteenth Century;* F. L. Nussbaum, *A History of the Economic Institutions of Modern Europe;* J. A. Schumpeter, *History of Economic Analysis*, ed. Elizabeth Boody Schumpeter, pp. 73–142; Eli F. Heckscher, *Mercantilism*, trans. Mendel Shapiro; William Cunningham, *The Growth of English Industry and Commerce;* and, in a more speculative vein, Max Weber, *The Protestant Ethic and the Spirit of Capitalism*, trans. Talcott Parsons.

14. Lawrence Stone, *The Crisis of the Aristocracy*. See also Stone's subsequent and more specific study, *Family and Fortune: Studies in Aris-*

tocratic Finance in the Sixteenth and Seventeenth Centuries.

15. See "Capitalism," in Raymond Williams, *Keywords*. Williams omits, unfortunately, such "keywords" as "economy," "economics," and "fact" —critical terms for the present discussion.

16. *The Works of Ben Jonson*, ed. C. H. Herford, P. Simpson, and E. M. Simpson, 8:578. References in the text are to this edition.

17. See Raymond Southall, *Literature and the Rise of Capitalism*, p. 28n.

18. See Marc Shell, "The Golden Fleece and the Voice of the Shuttle: Economy in Literary Theory," in *Economy of Literature*, pp. 89–112.

19. See Walter Bagehot, *Economic Studies*, ed. Richard Holt Hutton, p. 9. "Unreal words" are the subject of chapter three, below.

20. *The Poems of Sir John Beaumont, Bart.*, ed. Alexander Grosart (n.p., 1869), p. 327.

21. See *OED* 4, and the explanatory note on Latin derivation.

22. Daniel Defoe, *The Life and Strange Surprizing Adventures of Robinson Crusoe of York, Mariner*, ed. J. David Crowley (New York: Oxford University Press, 1972).

23. Thus, Robinson Crusoe can retail the number of cannibals killed in the ledger-book style one would use to retail a store of provisions:
    3 killed at our first shot from the tree.
    2 killed at the next shot.
    2 killed by Friday in the boat.
    2 killed by ditto, of those at first wounded.
    1 killed by ditto, in the wood.
    3 killed by the Spaniard.
    4 killed, being found dropped here and there of their wounds, or killed by Friday in his chase of them.
    4 escaped in the boat, whereof one wounded, if not dead.

    ———
    21 in all.

24. Daniel Defoe, *The Fortunes and Misfortunes of the Famous Moll Flanders*, ed. James Sutherland (Boston: Houghton Mifflin, 1959), p. 283. References in the text are to this edition.

25. A good short discussion of Moll's aesthetic use of commercial "fact" is presented by Dorothy Van Ghent, in *The English Novel: Form and Function* (1953; reprint ed., New York: Harper and Row, 1961), pp. 33–43. See also Maximillian E. Novak, *Economics and the Fiction of Daniel Defoe* (Berkeley: University of California Press, 1962). For a more comprehensive view of the place of the novel in the world of "facts," see Ian Watt, *The Rise of the Novel: Studies in Defoe, Richardson, and Fielding* (1957; reprint ed., Berkeley and Los Angeles: University of California Press, 1971).

26. Benjamin Franklin, *Autobiography and Other Writings*, ed. Russel B. Nye (Boston: Houghton Mifflin, 1958), p. 2. References in the text are to this edition.

27. D. H. Lawrence, *Studies in Classic American Literature* (1923; reprint ed., New York: Viking, 1961), pp. 9–21.

28. George Eliot, *Middlemarch: A Study of Provincial Life*, Cabinet Edition

(Edinburgh: W. Blackwood, n.d.), chap. 15. References in the text are to this edition.

29. The paucity of Lydgate's monetary imagination is also the subject of Laurence Lerner's "Literature and Money," in *Essays and Studies 1975*, ed. Robert Ellrodt, pp. 106–22.

30. Henry David Thoreau, *Walden and Civil Disobedience*, ed. Sherman Paul, p. 13. References in the text are to this edition.

31. Mutlu Blasing, "The Economies of *Walden.*"

32. Thomas Werge, "The Idea and Significance of 'Economy' before *Walden.*

33. *The Republic of Plato*, trans. F. M. Cornford, p. 18.

34. The scholar's indigence, for instance, is connected with his melancholic humor (see Bridget Gellert Lyons, *Voices of Melancholy: Studies in Literary Treatments of Melancholy in Renaissance England* [New York: W. W. Norton, 1971], pp. 26 ff.) but the *topos* recurs in modern American literature in Wallace Stevens's scholar of the imagination who takes as his text the "poverty" of our quotidian lives.

35. The adjective is Sherman Paul's, p. 14n. On closer inspection, the allegory's transparency has a *coup d'oeuil* effect.

36. Susanne K. Langer, *Feeling and Form: A Theory of Art* (New York: Charles Scribner's Sons, 1953), p. 263.

37. But see Perry Miller's observation that (for Thoreau) "these metaphors— or, as he sometimes called them, 'types'—were the rewards of an exploitation of natural resources, as self-centered, as profit-seeking, as that of any railroad builder or lumber-baron, as that of any John Jacob Astor" (*Consciousness in Concord: The Text of Thoreau's Hitherto "Lost Journal," 1840-1841* [Boston: Houghton Mifflin, 1958], p. 33). The effect of Miller's economic metaphor is lost if we do not apprehend the cause of Thoreau's. It remains to be seen *how*, in becoming a prophet, Thoreau was able to transform loss into profit. But Miller, unlike Werge and Blasing, was at least aware that Thoreau's artistic economy was founded upon his sensitivity to economics.

38. The phrase is used by Coleridge to subdivide his essays collected in the three-volume *rifacimento* of *The Friend* in 1818.

Chapter II

1. Thomas De Quincey, *The Logic of Political Economy* (1844), p. 40.

2. Melville J. Herskovits, *Economic Anthropology*, pp. 155–79. See also Harold K. Schneider, *Economic Man*, p. 1.

3. Marcel Mauss, *The Gift*, trans. Ian Cunnison, p. 45: "We may then consider that the spirit of gift-exchange is characteristic of societies which have passed the phase of 'total prestation' (between clan and clan, family and family) but have not yet reached the stage of pure individual contract, the money market, sale proper, fixed price, and weighed and coined money." In "Commerce and Comedy in *Sir Gawain*," *Philological Quarterly*, 50 (1971), 1-15, P. B. Taylor suggests that certain economic exchanges participate in Christian and divine comedies. Although the

medieval economy of the Gawain poet is not archaic or primitive in the anthropological sense, it is also not our own. Taylor accords the medieval reader an understanding of "individual contract," "price," and the "instituted process" of economics which that reader could never have entertained. Taylor's analysis of "comedy" is engaging, but his "commerce" falls into what Karl Polanyi calls "the economistic fallacy" or the "artificial identification of the economy with its market form" (*Primitive, Archaic and Modern Economies* [hereafter *PAME*] , ed. George Dalton, p. 142n).

4. Alfred Marshall, *Principles of Economics,* ed. C. W. Guillebaud, 1:1. The definition given by John Neville Keynes derives from Marshall's. He calls economics "a body of systematized knowledge" (*The Scope and Method of Political Economy,* p. 34).

5. Polanyi, *PAME,* p. 80. The entire chapter "Aristotle Discovers the Economy" (pp. 78-115) sensibly differentiates between Aristotelian "economy" and our modern notion of what "economics" should be.

6. *Crotchet Castle,* in *The Works of Thomas Love Peacock,* ed. Henry Cole, 2:195.

7. Ernest Barker, Introduction to *The Politics of Aristotle,* pp. lv-lvi. Barker concludes that "Wealth, on this basis, is a means to a moral end . . ." (p. lvi).

8. *The Ethics of Aristotle,* trans. J. A. K. Thomson, p. 154. References in the text are to this Penguin edition.

9. Aristotle, *The Politics,* trans. T. A. Sinclair, p. 28. References in the text are to this Penguin edition.

10. Polybius, for instance, would use *oikonomia* to refer specifically to state financing, but Xenophon, in addition to writing his *Oeconomicus,* had also written *On the Revenues of Athens.* For the political implications of this particular view of "economy," see A. French, *The Growth of the Athenian Economy,* pp. 51-52, 105-6. The importance of this development of a money economy per se, in terms of its impact on abstract thought and on processes of metaphorization, cannot be overemphasized. Arnold Hauser points out: "The capacity for abstract thought which leads to the autonomy of spiritual forms is developed not merely by the experience of colonization [in Asia Minor during the seventh and sixth centuries B.C.] , but also to a very great extent by the practice of trading for money" (*The Social History of Art,* trans. Stanley Godman, 1:81). When money emerges as a distinct mode of abstract thought, then its pertinence to literature becomes manifest in a new way—the thesis of Marc Shell's *The Economy of Literature.* For the sake of his larger purposes, however, Shell is willing to court what Polanyi calls "the economistic fallacy" and to identify the ancients' consciousness of money as a metaphor with a historically anachronistic view of "the economy" in its market form.

11. Aristotle, *Rhetoric,* trans. W. Rhys Roberts, in *The Rhetoric and the Poetics of Aristotle,* p. 172 [1406b] : "Metaphors like other things may be inappropriate."

12. See *commercium* in Charlton T. Lewis and Charles Short, comps., *A Latin Dictionary* (Oxford: Clarendon Press, 1951).

13. See D. R. Bender, "A Refinement of the Concept of Household"; O. Brunner, "Das 'ganze Haus' und die alteuropäische Ökonomik," in *Neue Wege der Socialgeschichte*, pp. 33–61; and Friedrich Engels, *The Origin of the Family, Private Property and the State*, ed. Eleanor Burke Leacock.

14. This is the sense that the word "economy" has come to have in literary theory. See Marc Shell, "The Golden Fleece and the Voice of the Shuttle: Economy in Literary Theory," in *Economy of Literature*, pp. 89–112.

15. *The Institutio Oratoria of Quintilian*, trans. H. E. Butler, 1.8.9. and 3.3.9. See also M. I. Finley's succinct commentary on the classical usages of "economy" (*The Ancient Economy*, pp. 17–34).

16. *Dictionnaire générale*, cited in Edwin Cannan, *A Review of Economic Theory*, pp. 38–39. Cannan's entire chapter 2, "The Name of Economic Theory" (pp. 37–44), argues that "economy" and "economics" have quite different linguistic and intellectual histories.

17. Domino Du Cange, *Glossarium mediae et infimae Latinitatis*, 10 vols. (Paris: Librairie des Sciences et des Arts, 1937-38), 6:31.

18. See E. A. J. Johnson, *Predecessors of Adam Smith*, p. 239; James Bonar, *Philosophy and Political Economy in Some of Their Historical Relations*, pp. 51–55; and Barry Gordon, *Economic Analysis Before Adam Smith*, pp. 70–110. J. A. Schumpeter's *History of Economic Analysis*, ed. Elizabeth Boody Schumpeter, gives a capsule summary of early and medieval Christian economics (pp. 71–107). As minister of the divine economy, the pastor was also a shepherd-economist, *Ecclesiae facultatum dispensator*, according to Du Cange (*Glossarium*, 6:31).

19. Sir James Steuart, *An Inquiry into the Principles of Political Oeconomy*, 1:2.

20. "The better the oeconomist, the more uniformity is perceived in all his actions, and the less liberties are taken to depart from stated rules" (Steuart, 1:2). The "rules" are "stated," however, by the "lord."

21. Du Cange defines *Economicus, pro Oeconomicus* as *Homo frugi, rei temperans* (*Glossarium*, 3:229). Cf. "Political Economy" in Sir Robert Harry Inglis Palgrave, *Dictionary of Political Economy*, ed. Henry Higgs, and in Charles Coquelin et al., eds., *Dictionnaire de l'économie politique*.

22. Polanyi, *PAME*, p. 126. Cf. "Essai Physique sur l'Economie Animale" in *Oeuvres economiques et philosophiques de F. Quesnay*, ed. Auguste Oncken, pp. 739-63.

23. *The Politics and Economics of Aristotle*, trans. Edward Walford, p. 289.

24. ". . . it cannot be said that 'Political Economy' was superseded generally by 'Economics' till Marshall brought out his *Principles of Economics*, Vol. I, in 1890" (Cannan, p. 44).

25. Smith defines "political oeconomy" in his two-paragraph introduction to book 4 of *The Wealth of Nations*, "Of Systems of Political Oeconomy": "Political oeconomy, considered as a branch of the science of a statesman or legislator, proposes two distinct objects; first, to provide

a plentiful revenue or subsistence for the people, or more properly to
enable them to provide such a revenue or subsistence for themselves; and
secondly, to supply the state or commonwealth with a revenue sufficient
for the publick services. It proposes to enrich both the people and the
sovereign" (Adam Smith, *An Inquiry into the Nature and Causes of the
Wealth of Nations* [hereafter *WN*], ed. R. H. Campbell and A. S. Skinner,
textual ed. W. B. Todd). References in the text are to this edition.

26. Karl Marx, *Grundrisse,* trans. Martin Nicolaus, p. 83.
27. Walter Bagehot, *Economic Studies,* ed. Richard Holt Hutton, p. 3.
28. Mirabeau, *Philosophie rurale,* 3 vols. (Amsterdam, 1766), 1:52-53; this
    translation from Cannan, p. 33.
29. See R. Redfield, "The Art of Social Science"; Joseph Spengler, "The
    Aesthetics of Population"; and, more generally, Sir Josiah Stamp, "Aes-
    thetics," in his *Some Economic Factors in Modern Life,* pp. 1-23. One
    might also note Alfred Marshall's clarion cry: "The economist needs the
    three great intellectual faculties, perception, imagination and reason and
    most of all he needs imagination, to put him on the track of those causes
    of visible events . . . and of those effects of visible causes which are re-
    mote or lie below the surface" (*Principles of Economics,* Variorum Edi-
    tion, p. 43).
30. A. L. Macfie, *An Essay on Economy and Value,* p. 35. Macfie notes,
    therefore, that "the scope of economy reaches through all our activities;
    it is not just a cross-section through our experience, defined by the fact
    of exchange" (p. 13).
31. *The Works of John Ruskin,* ed. E. T. Cook and Alexander Wedderburn,
    17:94.
32. *The Faerie Queene,* 2.7.1-2, in *The Complete Poetical Works of Spenser,*
    ed. R. E. N. Dodge. References in the text (to book, canto, and stanza
    numbers) are to this edition.
33. Michel Foucault extends the discussion of this reflected authority by re-
    ferring to Renaissance metaphysics in general in *The Order of Things,*
    p. 173:
    The marks of similitude, because they are a guide to knowledge, are ad-
    dressed to the perfection of heaven; the signs of exchange, because they
    satisfy desire, are sustained by the dark, dangerous, and accursed glitter
    of metal. An equivocal glitter, for it reproduces in the depths of the earth
    that other glitter that sings at the far end of the night: it resides there
    like an inverted promise of happiness, and, because metal resembles the
    stars, the knowledge of all these perilous treasures is at the same time
    knowledge of the world. And thus reflection upon wealth has its pivot in
    the broadest speculation upon the cosmos, just as inversely, profound
    knowledge of the order of the world must lead to the secret of metals
    and the possession of wealth.
    Foucault's conclusion. while apposite to this discussion of Spenser, also
    veers dangerously close to a kind of breathless and subjective "apprecia-
    tion," rather than critical analysis. Here, a practical literary criticism
    might provide a fruitful link with Foucault's theorizing: "It becomes ap-

parent how tightly knit is the network of necessities that, in the sixteenth century, links together all the elements of knowledge: how the cosmology of signs provides a duplication, and finally a foundation, for reflection upon prices and money; how it also authorizes theoretical and practical speculation upon metals; how it provides a communicating link between the promises of desire and those of knowledge, in the same way as the metals and the stars communicate with one another and are drawn together by secret affinities" (p. 173). In the end, the present study will search for that "communicating link" not in an abstractly adduced "network of necessities" but in the metaphorical exchanges transacted in written discourse, in poetic *and* economic literature.

34. Cf. Lady Pecunia, described as commanding "all this *Nether-world*," in Jonson's *The Staple of News* (1626), in *The Works of Ben Jonson*, ed. C. H. Herford, P. Simpson, and E. M. Simpson, 6:305. In nondramatic poetry, see Richard Barnfield's *The Encomion of Lady Pecunia: or the Praise of Money* (1598), in *Some Longer Elizabethan Poems*, ed. A. H. Bullen (Westminster: Archibald Constable, 1903), pp. 227–39. Mammon reappears in Jonson's *The Alchemist* as the much reduced figure of Sir Epicure Mammon and in the second book of *Paradise Lost* as the fallen archangel.

35. Barnabe Googe, *Eglogs, Epythaphes, and Sonettes (1563)*, ed. Edward Arber (London: Arber Reprints, 1871), p. 100. I have normalized the spelling of *u* and *v* and the publisher's lineations.

36. Alanus de Insulis, *The Complaint of Nature*, trans. Douglas M. Moffat, p. 43. References in the text are to the Archon edition.

37. The idea of nature as a minter and distributor of God's currency would have been available to Renaissance writers from other works as well. Jean de Meun's *The Romance of the Rose* distinguishes between the art which is nature's and the art which is counterfeit copy: "But when Nature, sweet and compassionate, sees that envious Death and Corruption come together to put to destruction whatever they find within her forge, she continues always to hammer and forge and always to renew the individuals by means of new generation. When she can bring no other counsel to her work, she cuts copies in such letters that she gives them true forms in coins of different monies. From these, Art makes her models, but she does not make her forms true" (trans. Charles Dahlberg [Princeton: Princeton University Press, 1971], p. 271). Thus, in his sermon at St. Paul's on Christmas Day 1622, John Donne imagined Christ as the new currency, minted by God to redeem all the fallen denominations:
man was made according to his Image: That Image being defaced, in a new Mint, in the wombe of the Blessed Virgin, there was new money coyned; The Image of the invisible God, the second person in the Trinity, was imprinted into the human nature. And then, that there might bee *omnis plenitudo*, all sent downe the Bullion, and the stamp, that is, God to be conceived in man, and as he provided the Mint, the womb of the Blessed Virgin, so hath he provided an Exchequer, where this money is

issued; that is his Church, where his merits should be applied to the discharge of particular consciences. So that here is one fulnesse, that in this person dwelleth all the fulnesse of the Godhead bodily [*The Sermons of John Donne*, ed. G. R. Potter and E. M. Simpson, 10 vols. (Berkeley and Los Angeles: University of California Press, 1953-62), 4:288].

38. Thomas Aquinas, *Summa Theologica*, Q. 1. Art. 9. Obj. 3, in *Introduction to Saint Thomas Aquinas*, trans. Anton C. Pegis, p. 16.

39. Ibid., 1.10, Reply obj. 3. (*Introduction*, p. 19).

40. In canto 8, Guyon will think he reads those "marke[s]" in Arthur's princely deportment:
Which when he heard, *and saw the tokens trew,*
His hart with great affection was embayd,
And to the Prince bowing with reverence dew,
As to the patrone of his life, thus sayd:
My lord, my liege . . . [2.8.55; my italics]
But the true "patrone" of Guyon's life, who is God, must not be addressed with such feudal servility, as Arthur promptly, but politely, reminds him.

41. Modern criticism remains divided over whether Guyon becomes Christianized in the course of book 2, although almost every commentator identifies Guyon's confrontation with Mammon as a turning point in his career. The position of modern criticism may be triangulated as follows: (1) Frank Kermode ("The Cave of Mammon") argues that Guyon undergoes a trial in canto 7, one he has willingly chosen in order to test the mettle of his virtue. As Kermode sees it, Guyon's permitting himself to be tempted fits him for a role like that of Christ in the wilderness. Guyon's passage through the cave of Mammon is heroic, therefore, in that it tempers physical suffering with moral sufferance in order to produce the new knight of cantos 8 through 12, who fuses classical *virtù* with Christian fortitude. (2) Arguing from Guyon's faint, Harry Berger (*The Allegorical Temper*) maintains that Guyon does reveal a kind of weakness in Mammon's cave, the peccadillo of inordinate *curiositas,* but that he remains to the end the classical knight of Aristotelian temperance, which differs in kind from the Christian temperance Arthur embodies. Berger points out that Guyon can *fail* to become Christianized only if one expected him to become Christianized in the first place. (3) Maurice Evans, in "The Fall of Guyon," observes that Berger's conception of Guyon's nondevelopment would require of book 2 a significantly different behavioral and structural pattern from that of the heroic actions in the other five books. We are led to believe, therefore, that Guyon will be Christianized, or at least changed. Wishing to reconcile Kermode and Berger, Evans argues that Guyon does allow himself, of his own free will, to be tested, but that he pushes his virtue too hard and succumbs in the end to exhaustion. Guyon, therefore, may be like Christ in some respects (in contradistinction to Berger's argument), but he is profoundly not a Christ-figure (in contradistinction to Kermode's). Indeed, Guyon's sin is Adamic, the sin of pride; and this causes his "Fall." In becoming vulner-

able to a specifically Christian temptation, Guyon becomes Christianized. Thus, Evans sees book 2 as completing the Christian story of fall, redemption, and grace which was begun in book 1. See also Carl Sonn, "Sir Guyon in the Cave of Mammon"; and Patrick Cullen, "Guyon Microchristus: The Cave of Mammon Re-examined."

42. Cf. 2.6.34, where Phaedria asserts:
Another warre, and other weapons, I
Doe love, where Love does give his sweet alarmes,
Without bloodshed, and where the enimy
Does yield unto his foe a pleasaunt victory.
Phaedria's garden suffices in just this way: it supplies a certain pleasure but cannot bear a too passionate demand. The lack of conception in Phaedria's sexual economics bespeaks its own fruitlessness, for Phaedria actually devalues the body's generative (and regenerative) powers at the same time that she aggrandizes the body. Sterility is at the heart of her garden. She nurtures a moderation which reduces the body to nothing.

43. Peter D. Stambler, "The Development of Guyon's Christian Temperance," p. 78.

44. *The Philosophy of Ernst Cassirer*, ed. Paul Arthur Schlipp, trans. Robert Walter Bretall and Paul Arthur Schlipp, p. 878.

45. The distinction is made by Spenser himself in *Mother Hubberds Tale:* "That was the golden Age of *Saturne* old, / But this might better be the world of gold: / For without golde now nothing wilbe got" (ll. 151-53). See also Ovid's *Ars Amatoria*, 2.227. Literary uses of this platitude are the subject of Harry Levin's *The Myth of the Golden Age in the Renaissance* and of Henry Kamen's "Golden Age, Iron Age."

46. As Shelley says in *A Defence of Poetry:* "Thus Poetry, and the principle of Self, of which Money is the visible incarnation, are the God and Mammon of the world" (Percy Bysshe Shelley, *A Defence of Poetry*, and Thomas Love Peacock, *The Four Ages of Poetry*, ed. John E. Jordan, Library of Liberal Arts [Indianapolis: Bobbs-Merrill, 1965], p. 69). Keats, who seems not to have deemphasized Mammon's economic status, nevertheless wrote Shelley praising the figural subtlety and semiotic potency—the self-created intensity—that Spenser's Mammon stands for: "A modern work it is said must have a purpose, which may be the God—*an artist* must serve Mammon—he must have 'self concentration' selfishness perhaps. You I am sure will forgive me for sincerely remarking that you might curb your magnanimity and be more of an artist, and 'load every rift' of your subject with ore" (*Letters of John Keats*, ed. Robert Gittings [London: Oxford University Press, 1970], pp. 389-90). The early Romantics' response to economics is examined in greater detail in chapters four and seven.

Chapter III

1. Michel Foucault, *Madness and Civilization: A History of Insanity in the Age of Reason*, trans. Richard Howard. These "clinicians" include

poets, theologians, philosophers, painters, and so on.

2. Michel Foucault, *The Archaeology of Knowledge*, trans. A. M. Sheridan Smith, p. 32.

3. The warning is repeated by the modern economist Frank H. Knight: "The term economic has come to be used in a sense which is practically synonymous with intelligent or rational" (*The Economic Organization*, p. 1).

4. This is also, of course, the thesis of Foucault's *The Order of Things*, in which "political economy" is specifically compared to other discursive formations, such as "biology" and "grammar."

5. Michel Foucault, *L'archéologie du savoir* (Paris: Gallimard, 1969).

6. L. M. Fraser, *Economic Thought and Language*, p. 33.

7. Fraser distinguishes between the "verbal" meaning of a word and its "real" significance in economics (see ibid., pp. 1-20). On the difference between "price" and "value," see pp. 42-45 and 57-58. "Labor" is dramatically different in ordinary and in economic speech (pp. 219-20), a topic to be discussed in much greater detail below (see chapters six to eight).

8. Lord Lionel Robbins, *An Essay on the Nature and Significance of Economic Science*, p. 148.

9. Sigmund Freud, "The Antithetical Meaning of Primal Words" (1910), in *The Standard Edition of the Complete Psychological Works of Sigmund Freud*, trans. and gen. ed. James Strachey with Anna Freud, 11:153-62. Freud's contention, of course, was that words with antithetical meanings (such as, in English, "cleave" and "buckle") were remnants of a primal psychical wholeness in language. In the economic terms considered above, however, we may see that the categorizing, rationalizing, and repressive work of consciousness has managed to effect a belated illusion of primality.

10. Karl Polanyi, *Primitive, Archaic and Modern Economies* (hereafter *PAME*), ed. George Dalton, p. 177.

11. John Stuart Mill, *Principles of Political Economy with Some of Their Applications to Social Philosophy*, ed. J. M. Robson, vols 2 and 3 in *Collected Works of John Stuart Mill*, gen. ed. F. E. L. Priestley, 3:508. References in the text are to this edition.

12. Sir James Steuart, *An Inquiry into the Principles of Political Oeconomy*, 1:ix.

13. William Petty, "Preface" to *Political Arithmetick*, in *The Economic Writings of William Petty*, ed. C. H. Hull, 1:224.

14. Adam Smith, *An Inquiry into the Nature and Causes of the Wealth of Nations* (hereafter *WN*), ed. R. H. Campbell and A. S. Skinner, textual ed. W. B. Todd, bk. 1, chap. 4. References in the text are to this edition.

15. A. R. J. Turgot, "Value and Money," in *Precursors of Adam Smith*, ed. Ronald L. Meek, p. 79.

16. Adam Smith, *The Theory of Moral Sentiments*, ed. D. D. Raphael and A. L. Macfie, p. 175; and *Lectures on Justice, Police, Revenue and Arms*, ed. Edwin Cannan, p. 157.

17. Polanyi, *PAME*, p. 111. For a further history of the betrayal by language, see Frank H. Knight, " 'What is Truth' in Economics?" in his *On the History and Method of Economics*, pp. 151-78; and Fritz Machlup, *Essays on Economic Semantics*, ed. Merton H. Miller, passim.

18. Adam Smith, *Lectures on Rhetoric and Belles Lettres*, ed. John M. Lothian, p. 1. References in the text are to this edition.

19. See Melville J. Herskovits, *Economic Anthropology*, p. 511. Knight's remarks on the task of economics are a rejoinder to Herskovits's anthropological view of economy. The debate between the two men, originally published in the *Journal of Political Economy* 49 (1941), was subsequently revised and reprinted in Herskovits's book, pp. 508-31.

20. I have interpolated Polanyi's definitions of "formal" and "substantive" economics (*PAME*, pp. 139 ff.) into the usual definitions of micro- and macroeconomics. See William Breit and Harold M. Hochman, eds., *Readings in Microeconomics*, p. vii: "Microeconomics is that branch of economic theory concerned with the behavior of individual households and firms in the process of constrained choice." Macroeconomics is generally understood to refer to the larger social implications of economic management, and it posits, following J. M. Keynes, an "analysis of income and employment theory." See Harold R. Williams and John D. Huffnagle, eds., *Macroeconomic Theory*, p. 1.

21. Mill did not, of course, use the words "microeconomy" or "macroeconomy," but he insisted that economic theory embrace moral and functional economies, theories of production or price *and* theories of social use. See the distinction made by Overton H. Taylor between Mill's "Political Economy" and his "Economics" in *A History of Economic Thought*, pp. 247-70.

22. *The Works of John Ruskin*, ed. E. T. Cook and Alexander Wedderburn, 17:80. References in the text are to this edition.

23. John Stuart Mill, *Autobiography*, ed. Jack Stillinger, pp. 140-41. References in the text are to this edition.

24. Mill's insistence on this point is worth noting. Cf. "On the Definition of Political Economy; and on the Method of Investigation Proper to It, " essay 5 in *Essays on Some Unsettled Questions of Political Economy*, pp. 120-64: ". . . it is vain to hope that truth can be arrived at, either in Political Economy or in any other department of the social science, while we look at the facts in the concrete, clothed in all the complexity with which nature has surrounded them, and endeavour to elicit a general law by the process of induction . . . ; there remains no other method than . . . 'abstract speculation' " (pp. 148-49).

25. For an alternative view of these terms, see Frank H. Knight's "Statics and Dynamics: Some Queries Regarding the Mechanical Analogy in Economics," in *History and Method of Economics*, pp. 179-201.

26. W. Stanley Jevons, *The Theory of Political Economy*, ed. R. D. Collison Black, p. 91. References in the text are to this edition.

27. Karl Marx, *The Economic and Philosophic Manuscripts of 1844*, ed. D. J. Struik, trans. Martin Milligan, p. 174.

28. Elizabeth Gaskell, *North and South,* ed. Martin Dodsworth (Harmonds-worth: Penguin, 1970), p. 212. References in the text are to this edition.

29. Anthony Trollope, *The Way We Live Now,* ed. Robert Tracy (Indianap-olis and New York: Bobbs-Merrill, 1974), p. 363.

30. *Writings of the Young Marx on Philosophy and Society,* ed. and trans. Loyd D. Easton and Kurt H. Guddat, p. 270.

31. David Ricardo, *The Principles of Political Economy and Taxation,* p. 182. References in the text are to the Everyman's Library edition.

32. Thomas De Quincey, "Dialogues of Three Templars on Political Econo-my," in *Letters on Self-Education, with Hints on Style and Dialogues on Political Economy,* pp. 478-79.

33. T. R. Malthus, *An Essay on the Principle of Population,* ed. Anthony Flew, p. 174. References in the text are to this edition.

    Malthus's point in respect to modeling is that the economist, like "a very young painter," often tries "to copy a highly finished and perfect picture," whereas man is neither so finished nor so perfect. The need for a new model lies at the heart of the Malthusian allegory. In a later work, he tried to define what discourse would be permissible for the practicing economist. See T. R. Malthus, *Definitions in Political Economy, preced-ed by an Inquiry into the Rules Which Ought to Guide Political Econom-ists in the Definition and Use of Their Terms.*

34. One point of difference is the double meaning of "improvement" as it applies to economic behavior (as incorporated in political institutions) and to moral attitudes (as incorporated in forms of social intercourse— a word that had one graphic significance for Malthus). Godwin argued that man and his inventions and his institutions were "susceptible of per-petual improvement" (see "Book I: Of the Powers of Man Considered in His Social Capacity," in William Godwin, *Enquiry Concerning Political Justice,* ed. K. Codell Carter, pp. 17 ff.). For Malthus, "improvement" was not necessarily susceptible to both an economic and a moral inter-pretation *at the same time* (see esp. chap. 14 in *An Essay on Population,* pp. 168-73). For an apposite reading of this controversy from a literary point of view (although it concerns the eighteenth-century novel, not Godwin and Malthus), see Raymond Williams's brilliant chapter "The Morality of Improvement," in *The Country and the City,* pp. 60-67.

35. Malthus, *Principle of Population,* p. 210. For a more detailed analysis of the historical debate surrounding Malthus, see Kenneth Smith, *The Malthusian Controversy* (London: Routledge and Kegan Paul, 1951).

36. Claude Lévi-Strauss, *Structural Anthropology,* trans. Claire Jacobson and Brooke Grundfest Schoepf, p. 229.

37. Frank H. Knight, *The Ethics of Competition and Other Essays,* p. 36.

38. Walter A. Weisskopf, *The Psychology of Economics.* References are to this edition.

39. Smith, *WN,* bk. 1, chap. 5; my italics. Ricardo argued that the natural price could fluctuate as well. Nevertheless, "the market price of labour is the price which is really paid for it" (*Principles of Political Economy,* p. 53).

40. Smith learned his apparitional economics from the physiocrats. Note Turgot's distinction between "real money" (i.e., coins) and "fictive money" (*monnaie fictive* or "numerary money") in *Precursors of Adam Smith*, ed. Meek, p. 81. Turgot further suggests that the former should be called *moneta* and the latter *pecunia* (pp. 83–84), because each usage is different and each different usage requires a separate grammar. Keats changed his goddess's name in *The Fall of Hyperion* from Mnemosyne to Moneta, and K. K. Ruthven has argued that the reasons were economic as well as euphonic: "Keats came to understand that, in the very realms of gold, financial problems had their sovran shrine" ("Keats and *Dea Moneta*," p. 456).

41. Frederick Engels, "Outlines of a Critique of Political Economy," in Marx, *Economic and Philosophic Manuscripts of 1844*, p. 207.

42. Karl Marx, *Capital*, ed. Frederick Engels, trans. Samuel Moore and Edward Aveling, 1:72.

43. Aristotle, *Poetics* (1453a), trans. Ingram Bywater, in *The Rhetoric and The Poetics of Aristotle*, p. 239. The approach is different at least from that of, say, Rousseau, who begins his *Discourse on the Origins of Inequality* with the suggestion, "Let us begin, then, by setting all the facts aside . . . [*Commencons donc par écarter tous les faits, car ils ne touchent point à la question*] " (*Discours sur l'origine et les fondements de l'inégalité parmi les hommes*, ed. Henri François Muller and Réné E. G. Vaillant, p. 4.

44. Karl Polanyi, *The Great Transformation, p.* 29.

45. Lord Lionel Robbins, *The Theory of Economic Policy in English Classical Political Economy*, p. 4.

46. See the whole of essay 4, "Ad Valorem," in *Unto This Last* (*Works*, 17: 77–114), and chapter 1, "Definitions," in *Munera Pulveris* (*Works*, 17: 147–63).

47. Ruskin, *Works*, 17:225n. Ruskin continues, "The reader must not think that any care can be misspent in tracing the connexion and power of the words. . . ."

48. Ibid., 18:64. In *Fors Clavigera*, Ruskin actually "reads" the letters and symbols inscribed on English coins. See *Fors Clavigera*, 2:8–13 (letter 25).

49. S. H. Steinberg, *Five Hundred Years of Printing*, ed. James Moran, 3rd rev. ed. (Harmondsworth: Penguin, 1974), p. 18.

50. Raymond Williams, *Marxism and Literature*, p. 46.

51. Ibid., p. 47.

52. Thomas De Quincey, *The Logic of Political Economy*, p. 13.

53. As in Keats's opening lines from *Endymion:* "A thing of beauty is a joy for ever: / Its loveliness increases . . ." (*The Poetical Works of John Keats*, ed. H. W. Garrod, 2nd ed. [Oxford: Clarendon Press, 1958] , p. 65).

54. Ruskin claims that the "real value" of wealth "depends on the moral sign attached to it . . ." (*Works*, 17:52).

55. Blake provides a more direct antecedent for Ruskin's nineteenth-century view of political and poetic economies than does Shakespeare. But one

may also feel that, as a prospective reading of *The Merchant of Venice*, Ruskin's dialectic of "mercy" and *merces* requires more substantiation. The afterword to the present study gives one example of how that prospectus might be adapted for a more systematic reading, derived from the economics of the imagination.

Chapter IV

1. David V. Erdman, *Blake: Prophet against Empire*, p. 227 and passim.
2. Like many of his contemporaries, Blake would rather speak of "Commerce" than of (political) economics. Following Erdman, we may discern a specific economic awareness in Blake's poetic myths which is distinct from a more general political consciousness. The latter has been studied by (in addition to Erdman) J. Bronowski, in *William Blake and the Age of Revolution;* Mark Shorer, in *William Blake: The Politics of Vision;* and, more expansively, Carl Woodring, in *Politics in English Romantic Poetry.*
3. *Jerusalem* 10. 21, in *The Poetry and Prose of William Blake*, ed. David V. Erdman, p. 151. References in the text to the works of Blake (to plate and line numbers or to pages) are to this edition unless otherwise noted.
4. Those who have been conscious of Blake's economic imagination have tended to undervalue the complexity of Blake's economics of the imagination. There have been two elementary attempts at a more emphatic balance: Eileen Sanzo, "William Blake and the Technological Age"; and M. E. Reisner, "The Wages of Art: Blake and His Public." Both articles are now superseded, however, by Morris Eaves's finely detailed study, "Blake and the Artistic Machine: An Essay in Decorum and Technology."
5. Raymond Williams, *Culture and Society, 1780-1950*, pp. 55, 58.
6. From Blake's engraving "The Laocoön" (*Poetry and Prose*, p. 272).
7. See Erdman's conclusion in *Blake: Prophet against Empire*, pp. 491-92.
8. Northrop Frye, *Fearful Symmetry*, pp. 339-40.
9. Ovid, *Metamorphoses*, trans. Frank Justus Miller, 1:13.
10. John Milton, *Paradise Lost* (hereafter *PL*), 1.688-92, in *Complete Poems and Major Prose*, ed. Merritt Y. Hughes. References (to book and line numbers) are to this edition.
11. We may perceive such a demonic awareness of economy in the following quatrain from Blake's notebook:
Since all the Riches of this World
May be gifts from the Devil & Earthly Kings
I should suspect I worshipd the Devil
If I thankd my God for Worldly things. [*Poetry and Prose*, p. 508]
It will be noted, however, that the conditional mode of this prayer further qualifies the speaker's suspicions.
12. *Poetry and Prose*, p. 673. See also *The Notebook of William Blake*, ed. David V. Erdman and Donald K. Moore, p. [N67].
13. Also, to the right and just below Blake's head is an indeterminate pencil drawing of one or two figures either entering or leaving a room. The

dated "Word" passage is connected by a curved line to the paragraph written horizontally along the bottom of the page. The other paragraph is written in the same fine pen as the "Word" passage itself and is centered vertically along the right-hand edge of the page. These two paragraphs are from the so-called "Public Address" (see *Poetry and Prose*, p. 566).

14. It could easily be a quotation, perhaps from a periodical of this date. Extracts bearing dates are used elsewhere in Blake's notebook (see *Notebook*, p. [N59]), and if the same practice applies here, then of course we *are* dealing with an actual fragment.

15. Erdman deftly sidesteps by calling the "evidence" of the whole passage "nicely ambiguous" (*Notebook*, p. [N67 transcript] n).

16. For the sense of Blakean humor which I find applicable here, see Harold Bloom, *The Visionary Company*, pp. 35-36: "Blake must have recited *The Tyger*, as we know Kafka read aloud to his friends from *Metamorphosis* or *The Trial*, with a laughter that seems inexplicable only to the Urizenic reader. . . . Read aloud with understanding, the tone has a fierce and ironic joy." Blake's humor, demonic and otherwise, as recollected by Alexander Gilchrist in his *Life of William Blake, "Pictor Ignotus"* (2 vols. [London and Cambridge: Macmillan, 1863]), is not always taken seriously in literary criticism of his work.

17. Cf. Aristotle's *Rhetoric* (1405b): "Good riddles do, in general, provide us with satisfactory metaphors: for metaphors imply riddles, and therefore a good riddle can furnish a good metaphor" (trans. W. Rhys Roberts, in *The Rhetoric and the Poetics of Aristotle*, p. 170).

18. "All these techniques [of word-play in particular and of wit in general] are dominated by a tendency to compression, or rather to saving. It all seems to be a question of economy." Sigmund Freud, *Jokes and Their Relation to the Unconscious*, trans. James Strachey, p. 42 and passim.

19. See chapter 6 in *Jokes and Their Relation to the Unconscious*, pp. 159-80, and chapter eight, below.

20. Robert Steele, "Alchemy," in *Shakespeare's England*, 2 vols. (Oxford: Clarendon Press, 1916), 1:464.

21. Mircea Eliade, *Rites and Symbols of Initiation*, trans. Willard R. Trask, p. 124.

22. Kathleen Raine, *Blake and Tradition*, 1:223. See also Raine's chapter "A Hermetic Myth," 1:271-89. The *Hermetica* is alluded to in "The Song of Los" (*Poetry and Prose*, p. 66).

23. Blake may have had such alchemical transmutations in mind when he spoke of creating "the Body / Of Divine Analogy" in *Jerusalem* 49.57-58 (*Poetry and Prose*, p. 197). Bernard Blackstone suggests that *Jerusalem* is Blake's "alchemical *opus*," in *English Blake*, p. 411.

24. Norman O. Brown, *Hermes the Thief*, pp. 36 ff.

25. The medieval scholastics' terminology for considering the question of universals is the *lingua franca* of classical political economics, which distinguishes between natural and market price, nominal and real value (see chapter three, above). The terms were extended to describe the opera-

tions of money itself. See W. Blake, "Observations on the Principles Which Regulate the Course of Exchange; and on the Depreciated State of the Currency," in *A Select Collection of Scarce and Valuable Tracts and Other Publications on Paper Currency and Banking,* ed. J. R. McCulloch, pp. 500–501. References in the text are to this edition. The final report of the "Bullion Committee" is also reprinted by McCulloch, pp. 403–74.

26. J. R. McCulloch, the editor of Ricardo's *Collected Works,* reprinted these letters under the collective title "The High Price of Bullion a Proof of the Depreciation of Bank Notes," in *A Select Collection,* pp. 361–401.

27. See T. S. Ashton, *The Industrial Revolution, 1760–1830,* p. 103.

28. See Frank Whitson Fetter, *Development of British Monetary Orthodoxy, 1797–1875.*

29. See Bronowski, p. 45: "Village industry was thus the base for a society of trade, paid in ready money. At bottom the changes through which Blake lived were from village to factory industry; at the top they were from a society of money to one of capital."

30. *Poetry and Prose,* p. 476. See also *The Complete Writings of William Blake,* ed. Geoffrey Keynes, p. 181.

31. Indeed, the values expressed in this quatrain are changed dramatically by Blake himself when he apportions these lines into "The Mental Traveller" (ll. 32–35).

32. The cost to poetry of this change was also computed by Peacock in *Paper Money Lyrics* (1825).

33. "Every Line is the Line of Beauty it is only fumble & Bungle which cannot draw a Line this only is Ugliness[.] That is not a Line which Doubts & Hesitates in the Midst of its Course" (*Poetry and Prose,* p. 564). Pound may have had Blake in mind when he wrote: "with usura the line grows thick / with usura is no clear demarcation" (Canto 45).

34. See Erdman, *Blake: Prophet against Empire,* pp. 230–35.

35. Adam Smith, *An Inquiry into the Nature and Causes of the Wealth of Nations* (hereafter *WN*), ed. R. H. Campbell and A. S. Skinner, textual ed. W. B. Todd, bk. 1, chap. 8. References in the text are to this edition. See also bk. 1, chap. 5: "Labour was the first price, the original purchase-money that was paid for all things. It was not by gold or by silver, but by labour, that all the wealth of the world was originally purchased. . . ."

36. Smith, *WN,* bk. 1, chap. 8. And cf. Psalms 128:2: "For thou shalt eat the labour of thine hands: happy shalt thou be, and it shall be well with thee."

37. See E. A. J. Johnson, " 'Art' and 'Ingenious Labour,' " in *Predecessors of Adam Smith,* pp. 259–77; and chapter five, below.

38. It should be added that Albion's most important son in *Jerusalem* is called Hand, and whatever else may have been intended by that nomenclature, bills of exchange (i.e., paper credit notes) were sometimes called notes of hand.

39. Thomas A. Vogler, *Preludes to Vision,* p. 52, n.10: "The regeneration of Los in bk. 1 [of *Milton*], in connection with Milton's abandonment of Selfhood in bk. 2, means that when Los becomes prophet, loss becomes

profit. There is no obvious evidence of an intended pun in the text, but the movement of the poem strongly suggests it." Later, however, Vogler raises his note into the text of his analysis where, I believe, it belongs: "[Blake and Wordsworth] were as much concerned with the problem of *how* loss becomes profit as they were with the question of *whether* loss becomes profit" (p. 119). See also Thomas R. Edwards, *Imagination and Power*, pp. 151-52.

40. Coleridge anticipated Marx's observation in his "Table Talk" (recorded by T. Allsop): "It is not uncommon for 100,000 *operatives* (mark this word, for words *in this sense* are things) to be out of employment at once in the cotton districts, and, thrown upon parochial relief, to be dependent upon hard-hearted taskmasters for food" (S. T. Coleridge, *Select Poetry and Prose*, ed. Stephen Potter, p. 476). Political economists subvert language, as Blake also recognized. A few sentences later, Coleridge chides "a contemptible democratical oligarchy of glib economists" (p. 477).

41. Max Weber, *The Protestant Ethic and the Spirit of Capitalism*, trans. Talcott Parsons.

42. *The Illuminated Blake*, ed. and annot. David V. Erdman, p. 378.

Chapter V

1. Raymond Williams, *Marxism and Literature*, p. 150.

2. Karl Marx, *A Contribution to the Critique of Political Economy*, trans. N. I. Stone, pp. 11-12.

3. Claude Lévi-Strauss, *Les Structures elementaires de la parenté*, cited in Robert Scholes, *Structuralism in Literature*, p. 3.

4. Karl Marx and Frederick Engels, *Feuerbach*, p. 35.

5. In *The Crown of Wild Olive*, Ruskin raises the question of an effectual difference between the artist as player and the artist as worker, and then shirks it: "There's playing at literature, and playing at art;—very different, both, from working at literature, or working at art, but I've no time to speak of these" (*The Works of John Ruskin*, ed. E. T. Cook and Alexander Wedderburn, 18:408 [references in the text are to this edition]). Cf. Walter Benjamin, "Der Autor als Produzent," in *Gesammelte Schriften*, comp. Theodor W. Adorno and Gershom Scholem, ed. Rolf Tiedemann and Hermann Schweppenhäuser, II.2, 683-701.

6. John Dewey, *Art as Experience*, p. 54.

7. My description of the reading process is indebted to the theoretical descriptions in Roman Ingarden, *The Cognition of the Literary Work of Art*, trans. Ruth Ann Crowley and Kenneth R. Olson, and in Wolfgang Iser, *The Implied Reader: Patterns of Communication in Prose Fiction from Bunyan to Beckett*, esp. pp. 274-94.

8. Adam Smith, *An Inquiry into the Nature and Causes of the Wealth of Nations* (hereafter *WN*), ed. R. H. Campbell and A. S. Skinner, textual ed. W. B. Todd, bk. 1, chap. 8. References in the text are to this edition.

9. Karl Marx, *Capital*, ed. Frederick Engels, trans. Samuel Moore and Edward Aveling, 1:172. References in the text are to this edition.

10. Edwin Cannan, *A Review of Economic Theory*, pp. 191-92.
11. Smith, *WN*, bk. 1, chap. 10. For a further discussion of why labor was chosen by classical economists as the basis of value see Gunnar Myrdal, *The Political Element in the Development of Economic Theory*, trans. Paul Streeten, pp. 56 ff.
12. John Locke, *Of Civil Government*, p. 130.
13. David Hume, *Writings on Economics*, ed. Eugene Rotwein, p. 11.
14. Walter A. Weisskopf, *The Psychology of Economics*, p. 25.
15. See the whole of chapter 13 in E. A. J. Johnson, *Predecessors of Adam Smith*, pp. 259-77.
16. William Petty, *The Economic Writings of Sir William Petty*, ed. C. H. Hull, 1:182.
17. Malachy Postlethwayt, *Britain's Commercial Interest Explained and Improved*, 2:392.
18. Malachy Postlethwayt, *The Universal Dictionary of Trade and Commerce, translated from the French of . . . Savary*, 1:116.
19. Sir James Steuart, *An Inquiry into the Principles of Political Oeconomy*, I, 2.
20. John Neville Keynes, *The Scope and Method of Political Economy*, pp. 74-83.
21. Thomas Mun, *England's Treasure by Forraign Trade*, p. 12. References in the text are to the Blackwood edition.
22. Postlethwayt's volume *Britain's Commercial Interest Explained and Improved* is conceived on the same premise: to explain *is* to improve by adding art to nature. Thus, Postlethwayt contends that economics itself is productive knowledge:

    If our people of distinction . . . should . . . obtain a relish to pry deeply into the practical nature of the various manufactural and mechanic arts, *and, to this recreative knowledge and salubrious exercise, they should add the political study of the commercial and money affairs of the state;* is it not reasonable to conceive that the conjunctive wisdom of the representatives of the nation . . . could never be liable to deceit and imposition by any distinct order of manufacturers, in opposition to the interests of the whole?

    [*Universal Dictionary of Trade and Commerce*, 2:132; my italics] .
23. *"An* Horatian *Ode upon* Cromwel's *Return from* Ireland," ll. 119-20, in Andrew Marvell, *Complete Poetry*, ed. George de F. Lord (New York: Random House, 1968), p. 58.
24. Bishop Thomas Sprat, *History of the Royal Society (1667)*, ed. Jackson I. Cope and Harold Whitmore Jones, pp. 415-16.
25. See Dwight L. Durling, *Georgic Tradition in English Poetry*.
26. See appendix A in Johnson, *Predecessors of Adam Smith*, pp. 387-401, for a list of important economic articles published between 1665 and 1776.
27. Thomas Aquinas, *Summa Theologica secunda secundae*, Q. 77, Art. 4, trans. Dominican Fathers, p. 328. The Thomist defense of the ethical foundation of labor profit prompted R. H. Tawney to remark, "The true descendant of the doctrines of Aquinas is the labour theory of value.

The last of the Schoolmen was Karl Marx" (*Religion and the Rise of Capitalism*, p. 48).

28. David Ricardo, *The Principles of Political Economy and Taxation*, p. 6.

29. *The Letters of Hart Crane, 1916-1932*, ed. Brom Weber (Berkeley and Los Angeles: University of California Press, 1965), p. 309.

30. "Adam's Curse," in *The Collected Poems of William Butler Yeats*, p. 78. References in the text to the works of Yeats are to this edition.

31. *The Autobiography of William Butler Yeats*, p. 98.

32. William Morris, "Art and Socialism," in *Selected Writings*, ed. G. D. H. Cole, p. 636. References in the text are to this edition.

33. Morris thus follows and expands Ruskin, who wished to see political economy as "neither an art nor a science" but rather as "a system of conduct and legislature, founded on the sciences, directing the arts, and impossible, except under certain conditions of moral culture" (*Works*, 17: 147).

34. See specifically Leven Magruder Dawson, " 'Among School Children': ' Labour' and 'Play.' "

35. Yeats, *Collected Poems*, p. 242. For details of the poem's placement, see *The Variorum Edition of the Poems of W. B. Yeats*, ed. Peter Allt and Russell K. Alspach (New York: Macmillan, 1957), p. 495.

36. Archibald MacLeish, *The Collected Poems* (Boston: Houghton Mifflin, 1962), pp. 50-51.

37. W. H. Auden, "In Memory of W. B. Yeats," in *Collected Shorter Poems, 1927-1957* (New York: Random House, 1966), pp. 141-43.

Chapter VI

1. John Locke, *Of Civil Government*, p. 131. References in the text are to the Everyman's Library edition.

2. L. M. Fraser, *Economic Thought and Language*, p. 45 and 45n. Fraser attributes the invention of "catallactics" to Archbishop Whateley's *Introductory Lectures* (1831). See also John Laird, *The Idea of Value*, p. 11.

3. Adam Smith, *An Inquiry into the Nature and Causes of the Wealth of Nations* (hereafter *WN*), ed. R. H. Campbell and A. S. Skinner, textual ed. W. B. Todd, bk. 1, chap. 5. References in the text are to this edition.

4. See, for instance, A. L. Macfie, "The Invisible Hand in the 'Theory of Moral Sentiments,' " in his *The Individual in Society*, pp. 101-25.

5. Gary Snyder, *Six Sections from Mountains and Rivers without End Plus One* (San Francisco: Four Seasons, 1970), pp. 30-31.

6. Karl Marx, *Capital* (hereafter *C*), ed. Frederick Engels, trans. Samuel Moore and Edward Aveling, 1:130. References in the text are to this edition.

7. David Ricardo, *Principles of Political Economy and Taxation*, p. 30. References in the text are to the Everyman's Library edition.

8. Ricardo, p. 13 (subhead to section 3). Cf. J. R. McCulloch, *The Principles of Political Economy*, pp. 61-75.

9. Cf. Thomas Hobbes, *Leviathan*, ed. C. B. Macpherson, p. 151: "The

Value, or *worth* of a man, is as of all other things, his Price; that is to say, so much as would be given for the use of his Power. . . ." See also Jeremy Bentham, *An Introduction to the Principles of Morals and Legislation*, p. 179n: "It is a well-known adage, though it is to be hoped not a true one, that every man has his price. It is commonly meant of a man's virtue. This saying, though in a very different sense, was strictly verified by some of the Anglo-Saxon laws: by which a fixed price was set, not upon a man's virtue indeed, but upon his life. . . . For 200 shillings you might have killed a peasant. . . . A king in those days was worth exactly 7,200 shillings."

10. "Hence the identity of sale and purchase implies that the commodity is useless, if, on being thrown into the alchemical retort of circulation, it does not come out again in the shape of money . . ." (*C*, 1:113).

11. *C*, 1:112. Contrast the simpler semiotics of Malachy Postlethwayt (in *Great Britain's True System*): "Money being only the Sign of Commodities, the word *Circulation*, by which their Exchange is expressed, ought to be applied to the Commodities and not to the Money" (p. 333).

12. Karl Marx, *The Poverty of Philosophy*, p. 104.

13. Karl Marx and Frederick Engels, *Collected Works*, 3:323 (hereafter *Works*). References in the text are to this edition.

14. *Writings of the Young Marx on Philosophy and Society*, ed. and trans. Loyd D. Easton and Kurt H. Guddat, p. 268.

15. *Young Marx*, p. 266. For further analysis of the sacrality of the money form, see Norman O. Brown, *Life against Death*, p. 246.

16. Even David Hume agrees that the more artful our modes of production, the more prolific and inexpressible will be our desires (*Writings on Economics*, ed. David Rotwein, p. 14). For Hume, however, these new desires will evolve into a new humanism, allowing men to "enjoy the privilege of rational creatures, to think as well as to act, to cultivate the pleasures of the mind as well as those of the body" (p. 22). Significantly, Hume attempts to exclude the irrational element of money from his economic theory: "Money is not, properly speaking, one of the subjects of commerce . . ." (p. 33). Marx's point is that when money becomes the *principal* subject of commerce, it alters the way we must "properly" speak.

17. For further discussion of Marx as an imaginative writer see Stanley Edgar Hyman, *The Tangled Bank*, pp. 81–186. Edward W. Said's "On Repetition," in *The Literature of Fact: Selected Papers from the English Institute*, ed. Angus Fletcher (New York: Columbia University Press, 1976), pp. 135–58, also seeks to identify the poetics of Marx's own writing.

18. Noting that capitalist production also markets time, T. S. Ashton observed: "A new sense of time was one of the outstanding psychological features of the industrial revolution" (*The Industrial Revolution, 1760–1830*, p. 69).

19. For the further ramifications of this psychomachia, see Marx's anecdote of the aspiring capitalist who is frustrated by his own economics (*C*, 1:

192–93). The capitalist "assumes the modest demeanour of his own
workman, and exclaims, 'Have I myself not worked? Have I not per-
formed the labour of superintendence and of overlooking the spinner?
And does not this labour, too, create value?' " In wanting his work to be
counted as productive labor, the capitalist also becomes a victim of the
capitalist mode of production. Failing to define a satisfactory kind of
"labor" for himself, "the capitalist chanted to us the whole creed of the
economists," hoping to conjure up a meaningful sense of "value" that
would apply to him. Again he fails, and so, wishing to reject economics
in toto, he "would not give a brass farthing for it." Marx's ensuing joke
is particularly bitter because it reveals that the economists do not need
the capitalist's farthings: "He leaves this and all such like subterfuges and
juggling tricks to the professors of Political Economy, who are paid for
it" (*C*, 1:193). Their verbal juggling is the linguistic equivalent of money's apparitional powers in exchange. But, in being paid for it, economists
become not only valued laborers but also superior capitalists. Economic
theory emerges as the economists' surplus value, supplying the profit or
M' value for the original investment of their imaginations.

20. Raymond Williams, *Marxism and Literature,* p. 206.
21. *The Poetry of Robert Frost,* ed. Edward Connery Lathem, p. 530. Ref-
    erences in the text are to this edition.
22. John Dewey, *Art as Experience,* p. 54.

Chapter VII

1. See, for instance, V. G. Kiernan, "Wordsworth and the People," in *Marxists on Literature,* ed. David Craig, pp. 161–206; Wallace W. Douglas,
   "Wordsworth as Business Man"; and Mary Moorman, *William Wordsworth: A Biography (The Early Years, 1770–1803),* pp. 124, 166–69,
   212–13, 268–70, 297, 337–38, and passim.
2. Thomas Weiskel, *The Romantic Sublime,* p. 25.
3. Francis Ferguson, *Language as Counter-Spirit,* p. 240.
4. William Wordsworth, *The Prelude or Growth of a Poet's Mind,* ed.
   Ernest de Selincourt, rev. ed. Helen Darbishire, 14.354–69. References
   in the text (to book and line numbers) are to this edition and refer to the
   1850 version of the poem unless otherwise noted.
5. *Letters of William and Dorothy Wordsworth: The Early Years* (hereafter
   LEY), ed. Ernest de Selincourt, rev. ed. Chester L. Shaver, p. 59.
6. *The Excursion,* 8.391–95. All quotations of Wordsworth's poetry (ex-
   cepting *The Prelude*) are from *The Poetical Works of William Wordsworth,* ed. Ernest de Selincourt, rev. ed. Helen Darbishire.
7. *Prelude,* 10.190–92. The most immediate cause of Wordsworth's "absolute want" was the peculiar distribution of his family's funds following
   his father's death. See Moorman, pp. 71, 167–69.
8. Edward E. Bostetter, *The Romantic Ventriloquists,* p. 27.
9. That is, it is not enough to say that Wordsworth could sometimes keep a
   quite vigilant, even reactionary, watch over his labor's economic pros-

pects, as when he observed of *Salisbury Plain*, "I should certainly not publish it unless I hoped to derive from it some pecuniary recompense" (*LEY*, p. 120); or when, with a capitalist's élan, he told Joseph Cottle, "I have gone on very rapidly adding to my stock of poetry" (*LEY*, p. 215); or when he denounced Southey's unfavorable review of *Lyrical Ballads* as an economic betrayal of friendship ("He knew that I published those poems for money and money alone. He knew that money was of importance to me. If he could not conscientiously have spoken differently of the volume, he ought to have declined the task of reviewing it" [*LEY*, pp. 267–68]).

10. Kenneth MacLean's *Agrarian Age* surveys the agrarian character of Wordsworth's "poetic economics," a phrase which MacLean himself employs (see esp. pp. 87–103).
11. *The Prose Works of William Wordsworth*, ed. W. J. B. Owen and Jane Worthington Smyser, 3:241.
12. *Letters of William and Dorothy Wordsworth: The Middle Years (1806–1811)*, ed. Ernest de Selincourt, rev. ed. Mary Moorman, p. 195.
13. David Perkins, *Wordsworth and the Poetry of Sincerity*, p. 173.
14. See Harold Bloom, "Wordsworth and the Scene of Instruction," in his *Poetry and Repression*, pp. 52–82.
15. John Milton, *Paradise Lost* (hereafter *PL*), 1:17–19, in *Complete Poems and Major Prose*, ed. Merritt Y. Hughes. References (to book and line numbers) are to this edition.
16. Unless specifically noted (as here), the Preface to the *Lyrical Ballads* is quoted from the final text of 1850.
17. Karl Marx, *Capital*, ed. Frederick Engels, trans. Samuel Moore and Edward Aveling, 1:177. References in the text are to this edition.
18. From the context, Wordsworth clearly means "statist" not only in the sense of "a politician, statesman" (*OED* 1, which cites as example a Wordsworthian usage from 1799) but also in the sense of a political economist (which might include *OED* 2, "one who deals with statistics," the earliest usage of which is given as 1803).
19. Wordsworth's use of "power" in this communicative sense was first discussed by W. J. B. Owen in *Wordsworth as Critic*, pp. 191 ff.; see esp. pp. 210–22.
20. Adam Smith, *An Inquiry into the Nature and Causes of The Wealth of Nations* (hereafter *WN*), ed. R. H. Campbell and A. S. Skinner, textual ed. W. B. Todd, bk. 1, chap. 5. References in the text are to this edition.
21. For this particular sense of "homeostatic," see Weiskel, *The Romantic Sublime*, p. 25. In reading the lines from "Resolution and Independence," "As high as we have mounted in delight / In our dejection do we sink as low," Weiskel remarks: "Wordsworth's economics are here quite rigorous; delight and dejection are rendered quantitatively in terms that suggest the presence and absence of a fluctuating energy or 'might' that pushes the mind until it 'can no further go'" (p. 138). Weiskel is (again) using the word "economics" figuratively (and loosely) here to describe a psychological quandary; whereas Wordsworth's own economics (in re-

lation to labor, poverty, and life's business), as the critic properly observes, "are here quite rigorous." This is a classic example of how criticism unwittingly substitutes its own reductive and provocative metaphor for a poet's original, precise, and evocative metaphor.

22. Cf. Geoffrey H. Hartman, *Wordsworth's Poetry, 1787-1814* (New Haven: Yale University Press, 1964), pp. 268-69: "Though he [Wordsworth] begins with an emotion recollected in tranquillity, the tranquillity soon disappears and his mind not only recalls the past *but also responds once more to what it has recalled*" (my italics). This response to what the self has already created (through recollection) becomes, in "Resolution and Independence," the source of its comfort.

23. "And if, in what I am about to say, it shall appear to some that my labour is unnecessary, and that I am like a man fighting a battle without enemies, such persons may be reminded, that, whatever be the language outwardly holden by men, a practical faith in the opinions which I am wishing to establish is almost unknown" (*Prose*, 1:137).

24. In the 1815 Preface, Wordsworth cites ll. 57-65 and 75-77 of "Resolution and Independence" as evidence of "the conferring, the abstracting, and the modifying powers of the Imagination, immediately and mediately acting . . ."(*Prose*, 3:33). As immediate witness and mediating consciousness, Wordsworth enacts in this poem the roles of both reader and poet.

25. *The Poetry and Prose of William Blake,* ed. David V. Erdman, p. 655.

26. Wordsworth originally considered making "Michael" a jocular ballad in the manner of "The Idiot Boy" (see Stephen Parrish, *"Michael* and the Pastoral Ballad," in *Bicentenary Wordsworth Studies in Memory of John Alban Finch,* ed. Jonathan Wordsworth, pp. 50-75); jocular or not, Wordsworth felt that "Michael" contained some of his most important "views" (see Moorman, p. 506).

27. Hartman, p. 263. See also Lore Metzger, "Wordsworth's Pastoral Covenant."

28. Oliver Goldsmith, "The Deserted Village," ll. 275-78, in *The Complete Poetical Works,* ed. Austin Dobson (London and New York: H. Frowde, 1911), pp. 21-37. References in the text are to this edition.

29. Goldsmith was *in fact* dispossessed of his poem insofar as Dr. Johnson felt the need to rewrite its last four lines. Raymond Williams has observed that "what is strangest in the poem is its combination of protest and nostalgia, and the way these emotions are related, consciously and unconsciously, to the practice of poetry" (*The Country and the City,* p. 76). However, a central thesis of Thomas G. Rosenmeyer's *The Green Cabinet,* is that economic reality (the realm of *negotium*) always threatens to disrupt both the pastoral fiction of *otium* and the fiction-making practice of the artist.

30. See Wordsworth's letter of 14 January 1801 to the Whig M. P. Charles James Fox in *Wordsworth's Literary Criticism,* ed. W. J. B. Owen (London: Routledge and Kegan Paul, 1974), pp. 99-102.

31. Rosenmeyer also notes the intrusion of "georgic" elements upon "Mi-

chael" and judges this intrusion to be a flaw in Wordsworth's "pastoral" rather than a deliberate attempt to reimagine and to reconstitute the pastoral as a viable genre: "Wordsworth was foiled because he did not distinguish sufficiently between pastoral and Hesiodic [i.e., georgic] " (p. 24).

32. Virtually the only critical or analytical studies of "Home at Grasmere" are Muriel J. Mellown's "The Development of Imagery in 'Home at Grasmere' " and Karl Kroeber's " 'Home at Grasmere': Ecological Holiness." Kroeber's magisterial conclusion ("Of all Wordsworth's poems it is the one in which most explicitly and at greatest length he articulates his fundamental 'poetics' " [p. 140]) is severely compromised, however, by a series of rash premises ("He [the Wordsworthian poet] does not feel tied to an owned piece of property" [p. 134]) and unguarded assertions ("Like Cowper, Beattie, Collins, and Gray before him, Wordsworth celebrates a life of sensations and sensibility that exclude [sic] purposeful industry—bluntly, earning a living" [p. 137]). Michael Friedman's "Wordsworth's Grasmere: A Rentier's Vision," which came to my attention too late for consideration here, focuses more directly on Wordsworth's view of laborers.

33. John Milton, *Paradise Lost*, 1.21-22, in *Complete Poems and Major Prose*, ed. Merritt Y. Hughes.

34. This passage (see *Poetical Works*, 5:315-16) is from manuscript *B*, the first complete draft of the poem, which was, according to its editors, "probably written later in 1800" (*Poetical Works*, 5:475)—i.e., after March 1800, the date of the first incomplete text (manuscript *A*).

35. See *Poetical Works*, 5:339. These lines (and indeed the whole conclusion of manuscript *B*, of which they are part) were retrieved by Wordsworth and used as the "Prospectus" to *The Excursion*.

36. John Locke, *Of Civil Government* (Everyman's Library), p. 132.

37. See Stephen K. Land, "The Silent Poet," and Jonathan Ramsey, "Wordsworth's Silent Poet."

38. Percy Bysshe Shelley, *The Complete Poetical Works*, ed. Thomas Hutchinson (Oxford: Clarendon Press, 1904), p. 396: "To Peter's view, all seemed one hue; / He was no Whig, he was no Tory . . ." ("Peter Bell the Third," ll. 564-65).

39. George Gordon, Lord Byron, *Don Juan*, ed. Leslie A. Marchand (Boston: Houghton Mifflin, 1958), p. 7 ["Dedication," vi, 1-6].

40. J. S. Mill, "On the Words Productive and Unproductive," essay 3 in *Essays on Some Unsettled Questions of Political Economy*, p. 82.

Chapter VIII

1. Louis Zukofsky, *"A" 1-12* (Garden City, N. Y.: Doubleday, 1967), p. 67.

2. Ferdinand de Saussure, *Course in General Linguistics*, ed. Charles Bally and Albert Sechehaye, trans. Wade Baskin, p. 77.

3. George Thomson, "The Art of Poetry," in *Marxists on Literature*, ed. David Craig, p. 49. References in the text are to this edition.

4. From the manuscript in the Lockwood Collection, Library of the State University of New York at Buffalo. See William Carlos Williams, *Paterson* (hereafter *P*), pp. 214–18. I am extremely grateful to Paul Mariani for calling this manuscript page and Williams's unpublished letter to Munson (see n. 11) to my attention.

5. *Literary Essays of Ezra Pound,* ed. T. S. Eliot, p. 4.

6. Sigmund Freud, *Jokes and Their Relation to the Unconscious,* trans. James Strachey, p. 166. References in the text are to the Norton edition.

7. Ezra Pound, *Selected Prose, 1909–1965,* ed. William Cookson, p. 30.

8. T. S. Eliot, *The Sacred Wood,* p. 64. References in the text are to the Methuen edition.

9. Raymond Williams, *The Long Revolution,* p. 132.

10. *The Letters of Ezra Pound, 1907–1941,* ed. D. D. Paige, p. 260.

11. W. C. Williams to Gorham Munson, 5 March 1934, in the collection of the Center for Pound Studies, Yale University Library.

12. Randall Jarrell, "A View of Three Poets," in *William Carlos Williams,* ed. Charles Tomlinson, p. 174.

13. Randall Jarrell, *The Complete Poems* (New York: Farrar, Straus, and Giroux, 1969), pp. 117–19.

14. See Mike Weaver, *William Carlos Williams,* pp. 103–14.

15. Benjamin Sankey, *A Companion to William Carlos Williams's* Paterson, p. 190. See also Guy Davenport, "The Nuclear Venus: Dr. Williams' Attack on Usura."

16. Joseph N. Riddell, *The Inverted Bell,* p. 246.

17. *Time,* 13 February 1950, p. 38.

18. See Pound, *Prose,* pp. 354–55.

19. *Letters of Ezra Pound,* p. 8. For further discussion of the early poetic connection between Pound and Williams, see Geoffrey H. Movius, "Caviar and Bread: Ezra Pound and William Carlos Williams, 1902–1914."

20. Hugh Kenner, *The Pound Era,* p. 413.

21. *The Autobiography of William Carlos Williams,* p. 392.

22. William Carlos Williams, *Imaginations,* ed. Webster Schott, p. 22.

23. *The Cantos of Ezra Pound,* p. 51 (Canto 11).

24. William Carlos Williams, "The Desert Music," in *Pictures from Breughel and Other Poems* (New York: New Directions, 1962), p. 110.

25. See Sankey, p. 182, n. 17.

26. Sankey accurately notes that Williams's "verse on the subject of credit is a celebration rather than an argument" (p. 189), and one wishes that he had pursued that insight more vigilantly. Instead, in his next sentence, Sankey cites Augustus Edward Baker's "brief general account of 'social credit' " because it "may be of some use in following Williams's *argument*" (pp. 189–90; my italics).

27. H. Levy, *A Philosophy for a Modern Man,* p. 14.

28. See John C. Thirlwall, "William Carlos Williams' 'Paterson,' " p. 273.

29. Karl Marx, *Capital,* ed. Frederick Engels, trans. Samuel Moore and Edward Aveling, 1:178.

30. *A Defence of Poetry,* ed. John E. Jordan, p. 68.

31. *Opus Posthumous,* ed. Samuel French Morse (New York: Alfred A. Knopf, 1966), p. 240.

Afterword

1. See chapter three above, and especially pp. 101–8 and n. 55.
2. J. Huizinga, *Homo Ludens,* p. 51.
3. See L. M. Fraser's distinction in *Economic Thought and Language* between "embodied" cost, the work or labor put into something, and "displacement" cost, what is given up or sacrificed for something (p. 92).
4. *The Merchant of Venice,* 3.2.104–7. References in the text are to *William Shakespeare: The Complete Works,* gen. ed. Alfred Harbage. I have used the variant reading "plainness" for "paleness" in l. 106.
5. I have taken this last phrase from Edward W. Tayler's reading of *The Winter's Tale* in *Nature and Art in Renaissance Literature* (New York: Columbia University Press, 1964), p. 141.
6. They do not, that is, merely illustrate that commerce and business transactions are a kind of game (see Frank H. Knight, *The Ethics of Competition and Other Essays,* pp. 61–66).
7. Karl Marx, *Capital,* ed. Frederick Engels, trans. Samuel Moore and Edward Aveling, 1:72.
8. In "Venus and Adonis," Venus attempts to lure Adonis into bed with the advice, "Be prodigal" (l. 755): "Foul cank'ring rust the hidden treasure frets, / But gold that's put to use more gold begets" (ll. 767–68). Adonis replies,
   What have you urged that I cannot reprove?
   The path is smooth that leadeth on to danger.
   I hate not love, but your device in love,
   That lends embracements unto every stranger.
   You do it for increase. [Ll. 787–91]
   Venus's "device in love" is her monetary metaphor, her economic reasoning. In hinting that her sexuality is self-interested and usurious—a commercial "increase"—Adonis identifies Venus in her Venetian aspect as a love merchant, "lend[ing] embracements unto every stranger."

A SELECTED BIBLIOGRAPHY

Alanus de Insulis. *The Complaint of Nature*. Translated by Douglas M. Moffat. 1928. Reprint. Hamden, Conn.: Archon Books, 1972.

Aquinas, Thomas. *Introduction to Saint Thomas Aquinas*. Translated by Anton C. Pegis. New York: Random House, 1948.

——. *Summa Theologica secunda secundae*. Translated by Dominican Fathers. New York: Benziger Brothers, 1918.

Aristotle. *The Ethics of Aristotle*. Translated by J. A. K. Thomson. Baltimore: Penguin, 1955.

——. *The Politics*. Translated by T. A. Sinclair. Harmondsworth: Penguin, 1962.

——. *The Politics and Economics of Aristotle*. Translated by Edward Walford. London: George Bell, 1894.

——. *The Rhetoric and the Poetics of Aristotle*. Translated by W. Rhys Roberts and Ingram Bywater. New York: Modern Library, 1954.

Ashton, T. S. *The Industrial Revolution, 1760-1830*. New York: Oxford University Press, 1964.

Bagehot, Walter. *Economic Studies*. Edited by Richard Holt Hutton. 1880. Reprint. Stanford, Calif.: Academic Reprints, 1953.

Barker, Ernest. Introduction to *The Politics of Aristotle*. Oxford: Clarendon Press, 1946.

Bender, D. R. "A Refinement of the Concept of Household." *American Anthropologist* 69 (1967): 493-504.

Benjamin, Walter. *Gesammelte Schriften*. Compiled by Theodor W. Adorno and Gershom Scholem. Edited by Rolf Tiedemann and Hermann Schweppenhäuser. 4 vols. Frankfurt: Suhrkamp Verlag, 1972-77.

Bentham, Jeremy. *An Introduction to the Principles of Morals and Legislation*. New York: Hafner Press, 1948.

Berger, Harry. *The Allegorical Temper*. New Haven: Yale University Press, 1957.

Blackstone, Bernard. *English Blake.* 1949. Reprint. Hamden, Conn.: Archon Books, 1966.

Blake, William. *The Complete Writings of William Blake.* Edited by Geoffrey Keynes. London: Oxford University Press, 1966.

——. *The Illuminated Blake.* Edited and annotated by David V. Erdman. Garden City, N. Y.: Doubleday Anchor, 1974.

——. *The Notebook of William Blake: A Photographic and Typographic Facsimile.* Edited by David V. Erdman and Donald K. Moore. Oxford: Clarendon Press, 1973.

——. *The Poetry and Prose of William Blake.* Edited by David V. Erdman. Rev. ed. Garden City, N. Y.: Doubleday Anchor, 1970.

Blasing, Mutlu. "The Economies of *Walden.*" *Texas Studies in Language and Literature* 17 (1976): 159-75.

Bloom, Harold. *Poetry and Repression: Revisionism from Blake to Stevens.* New Haven: Yale University Press, 1976.

——. *The Visionary Company: A Reading of English Romantic Poetry.* Garden City, N. Y.: Doubleday Anchor, 1963.

Bonar, James. *Philosophy and Political Economy in Some of Their Historical Relations.* London: Swan Sonnenschein, 1893.

Bostetter, Edward E. *The Romantic Ventriloquists: Wordsworth, Coleridge, Keats, Shelley, Byron.* Seattle: University of Washington Press, 1963.

Breit, William, and Hochman, Harold M., eds. *Readings in Microeconomics.* 2nd ed. New York: Holt, Rinehart and Winston, 1971.

Bronowski, J. *William Blake and the Age of Revolution.* 2nd rev. ed. New York: Harper and Row, 1965.

Brown, Norman O. *Hermes the Thief.* Madison: University of Wisconsin Press, 1947.

——. *Life against Death.* New York: Random House, Vintage, 1959.

Brunner, O. "Das 'ganze Haus' und die alteuropäische Ökonomik." In his *Neue Wege der Socialgeschichte.* Göttingen, 1956, pp. 33-61.

Burke, Kenneth. *The Rhetoric of Motives.* Berkeley: University of California Press, 1969.

Cannan, Edwin. *A Review of Economic Theory.* London: P. S. King, 1929.

Cassirer, Ernst. *The Philosophy of Ernst Cassirer.* Edited by Paul Arthur Schlipp. Translated by Robert Walter Bretall and Paul Arthur Schlipp. Evanston: Northwestern University Press, 1949.

Coleridge, Samuel Taylor. *The Collected Works of Samuel Taylor Coleridge: The Friend.* Edited by Barbara E. Rooke. Bollingen Series 75. 2 vols. Princeton: Princeton University Press, 1969.

——. *Select Poetry & Prose.* Edited by Stephen Potter. London: Nonesuch Press, 1962.

Coquelin, Charles, et al., eds. *Dictionnaire de l'économie politique.* 2 vols. Paris: Librairie de Guillaumin, 1852.

Craig, David, ed. *Marxists on Literature: An Anthology.* Harmondsworth: Penguin, 1975.

Cullen, Patrick. "Guyon Microchristus: The Cave of Mammon Re-examined." *ELH* 37 (1970): 153-73.

Cunningham, William. *The Growth of English Industry and Commerce.* 3 vols. Cambridge: Cambridge University Press, 1896-1903.

Davenport, Guy. "The Nuclear Venus: Dr. Williams' Attack on Usura." *Perspective* 6 (Autumn 1953): 183-90.

Dawson, Leven Magruder. " 'Among School Children': 'Labour' and 'Play.' " *Philological Quarterly* 52 (1973): 286-95.

De Quincey, Thomas. *Letters on Self-Education, with Hints on Style and Dialogues on Political Economy.* London: James Hogg and Sons, n.d.

———. *The Logic of Political Economy.* Edinburgh and London: William Blackwood and Son, 1844.

Dewey, John. *Art as Experience.* London: George Allen and Unwin, 1934.

Douglas, Wallace W. "Wordsworth as Business Man." *PMLA* 63 (1948): 625-41.

Durling, Dwight L. *Georgic Tradition in English Poetry.* New York: Columbia University Press, 1935.

Eaves, Morris. "Blake and the Artistic Machine: An Essay in Decorum and Technology." *PMLA* 92 (1977): 903-27.

Edwards, Thomas R. *Imagination and Power: A Study of Poetry on Public Themes.* New York: Oxford University Press, 1971.

Ehrenberg, Richard. *Capital and Finance in the Age of the Renaissance.* Translated by H. M. Lucas. New York: A. M. Kelley, 1963.

Eliade, Mircea. *Rites and Symbols of Initiation: The Mysteries of Birth and Rebirth.* Translated by Willard R. Trask. New York: Harper Torchbooks, 1965.

Eliot, T. S. *The Sacred Wood: Essays on Poetry and Criticism.* 1920. Reprint. London: Methuen, 1960.

Engels, Frederick. *The Origin of the Family, Private Property and the State.* Edited by Eleanor Burke Leacock. New York: International Publishers, 1972.

Erdman, David V. *Blake: Prophet against Empire: A Poet's Interpretation of the History of His Own Times.* 2nd rev. ed. Garden City, N. Y.: Doubleday Anchor, 1969.

Evans, Maurice. "The Fall of Guyon." *ELH* 28 (1961): 215-24.

Feltes, N. N. "Community and the Limits of Liability in Two Mid-Victorian Novels." *Victorian Studies* 17 (1978): 355-69.

Ferguson, Francis. *Wordsworth: Language as Counter-Spirit.* New Haven: Yale University Press, 1977.

Fetter, Frank Whitson. *Development of British Monetary Orthodoxy, 1797-1875.* Cambridge, Mass.: Harvard University Press, 1965.

Finley, M. I. *The Ancient Economy.* Berkeley and Los Angeles: University of California Press, 1973.

Fleishman, Avrom. *Fiction and The Ways of Knowing: Essays on British Novels.* Austin: University of Texas Press, 1978.

Foucault, Michel. *The Archaeology of Knowledge.* Translated by A. M. Sheridan Smith. New York: Pantheon, 1972.

———. *Madness and Civilization: A History of Insanity in the Age of Reason.* Translated by Richard Howard. New York: Random House, Vintage, 1973.

——. *The Order of Things*. New York: Pantheon, 1970.

Fraser, L. M. *Economic Thought and Language*. London: Adam and Charles Black, 1947.

French A. *The Growth of the Athenian Economy*. New York: Barnes and Noble, 1964.

Freud, Sigmund. *Jokes and Their Relation to the Unconscious*. Translated by James Strachey. New York: W. W. Norton, 1963.

——. *The Standard Edition of the Complete Psychological Works of Sigmund Freud*. Translator and general editor, James Strachey with Anna Freud. 23 vols. London: Hogarth Press, 1953-66.

Friedman, Michael. "Wordsworth's Grasmere: A Rentier's Vision." *Polit: A Journal of Literature and Politics* 1, i (1977): 35-60.

Frost, Robert. *The Poetry of Robert Frost*. Edited by Edward Connery Lathem. New York: Holt, Rinehart and Winston, 1969.

Frye, Northrop. *Fearful Symmetry: A Study of William Blake*. 1947. Reprint. Boston: Beacon Press, 1962.

Godwin, William. *Enquiry Concerning Political Justice*. Edited by K. Codell Carter. Oxford: Clarendon Press, 1971.

Gordon, Barry. *Economic Analysis Before Adam Smith: Hesiod to Lessius*. London: Macmillan, 1975.

Hartman, Geoffrey H. *Wordsworth's Poetry, 1787-1814*. New Haven: Yale University Press, 1964.

Hauser, Arnold. *The Social History of Art*. Translated by Stanley Godman. 2 vols. New York: Random House, Vintage, 1951.

Heckscher, Eli F. *Mercantilism*. Translated by Mendel Shapiro. 2 vols. London: G. Allen and Unwin, 1935.

Heinzelman, Kurt. " 'Cold Consolation': The Art of Milton's Last Sonnet." In *Milton Studies X*, edited by James D. Simmonds. Pittsburgh: University of Pittsburgh Press, 1977, pp. 111-25.

Herskovits, Melville J. *Economic Anthropology: A Study in Comparative Economics*. 2nd rev. ed. New York: Alfred A. Knopf, 1952.

Hobbes, Thomas. *Leviathan*. Edited by C. B. Macpherson. Harmondsworth: Penguin, 1968.

Huizinga, J. *Homo Ludens: A Study of the Play-Element in Culture*. Boston: Beacon Press, 1955.

Hume, David. *Writings on Economics*. Edited by Eugene Rotwein. 1955. Reprint. Madison: University of Wisconsin Press, 1970.

Hutcheson, Frances. *A Short Introduction to Moral Philosophy, in three books; Containing the Elements of Ethicks and the Law of Nature*. Glasgow: R. Foulis, 1747.

Hyman, Stanley Edgar. *The Tangled Bank: Darwin, Marx, Frazer, and Freud as Imaginative Writers*. 1962. Reprint. New York: Grosset and Dunlap, 1966.

Ingarden, Roman. *The Cognition of the Literary Work of Art*. Translated by Ruth Ann Crowley and Kenneth R. Olson. Evanston: Northwestern University Press, 1973.

Iser, Wolfgang. *The Implied Reader: Patterns of Communication in Prose Fiction from Bunyan to Beckett*. Baltimore: Johns Hopkins Press, 1974.

Jarrell, Randall. "A View of Three Poets." *Partisan Review* 18 (1951): 691-700. Reprint. *William Carlos Williams: A Critical Anthology*, edited by Charles Tomlinson. Harmondsworth: Penguin, 1972, pp. 172-75.

Jevons, W. Stanley. *The Theory of Political Economy*. Edited by R. D. Collison Black. Harmondsworth: Penguin, 1970.

Johnson, E. A. J. *Predecessors of Adam Smith: The Growth of British Economic Thought*. New York: Prentice-Hall, 1937.

Jonson, Ben. *The Works of Ben Jonson*. Edited by C. H. Herford, P. Simpson, and E. M. Simpson. 11 vols. Oxford: Clarendon Press, 1925-52.

Kamen, Henry. "Golden Age, Iron Age: A Conflict of Concepts in the Renaissance." *Journal of Medieval and Renaissance Studies* 4 (1974): 135-55.

Kenner, Hugh. *The Pound Era*. Berkeley and Los Angeles: University of California Press, 1971.

Kermode, Frank. "The Cave of Mammon." In *Elizabethan Poetry*, edited by J. R. Brown and B. Harris. Stratford-Upon-Avon Studies No. 2. New York: St. Martin's Press, 1960, pp. 151-73.

Keynes, John Neville. *The Scope and Method of Political Economy*. 4th ed. London: Macmillan, 1917.

Knight, Frank H. *The Economic Organization*. Chicago: University of Chicago Press, 1933.

——. *The Ethics of Competition and Other Essays*. New York: Harper and Bros., 1935.

——. *On the History and Method of Economics: Selected Essays*. Chicago: University of Chicago Press, 1956.

Knight, L. C. *Drama and Society in the Age of Jonson*. London: Chatto and Windus, 1937.

Kroeber, Karl. " 'Home at Grasmere': Ecological Holiness." *PMLA* 89 (1974): 132-41.

Laird, John. *The Idea of Value*. Cambridge: Cambridge University Press, 1929.

Land, Stephen K. "The Silent Poet: An Aspect of Wordsworth's Semantic Theory." *University of Toronto Quarterly* 42 (1973): 157-69.

Lerner, Laurence. "Literature and Money." In *Essays and Studies, 1975*, edited by Robert Ellrodt, pp. 106-22. London: The English Association, 1975.

Levin, Harry. *The Myth of the Golden Age in the Renaissance*. London: Faber and Faber, 1969.

Lévi-Strauss, Claude. *Structural Anthropology*. Translated by Claire Jacobson and Brooke Grundfest Schoepf. New York: Basic Books, 1963.

Levy, H. *A Philosophy for a Modern Man*. New York: Alfred A. Knopf, 1938.

Locke, John. *Of Civil Government*. Everyman's Library. New York: E. P. Dutton; London: J. M. Dent, 1924.

McCulloch, J. R. *The Principles of Political Economy*. 4th ed. Edinburgh: Adam and Charles Black, 1849.

——, ed. *A Select Collection of Scarce and Valuable Tracts and Other Publications on Paper Currency and Banking*. London: Printed for the Political Economy Club by Lord Overstone, 1857.

Macfie, A. L. *An Essay on Economy and Value: Being an Enquiry into the Real Nature of Economy.* London: Macmillan, 1936.

——. "The Invisible Hand in the 'Theory of Moral Sentiments.' " In his *The Individual in Society: Papers on Adam Smith.* London: George Allen and Unwin, 1967, pp. 101-25.

Machlup, Fritz. *Essays on Economic Semantics.* Edited by Merton H. Miller. Englewood Cliffs, N. J.: Prentice-Hall, 1963.

MacLean, Kenneth. *Agrarian Age: A Background for Wordsworth.* New Haven: Yale University Press, 1950.

Malthus, Thomas R. *Definitions in Political Economy, Preceded by an Inquiry into the Rules Which Ought to Guide Political Economists in the Definition and Use of Their Terms; with Remarks on the Deviations from These Rules in Their Writings.* London, 1827.

——. *An Essay on the Principle of Population.* Edited by Anthony Flew. Harmondsworth: Penguin, 1970.

Marshall, Alfred. *Principles of Economics.* Edited by C. W. Guillebaud. 9th (Variorum) ed. London: Macmillan, 1961.

Martineau, Harriet. *Illustrations of Political Economy.* 9 vols. London: C. Fox, 1834.

Marx, Karl. *Capital: A Critique of Political Economy.* Edited by Frederick Engels. Translated by Samuel Moore and Edward Aveling from 3rd German ed. 3 vols. New York: International Publishers, 1967.

——. *A Contribution to the Critique of Political Economy.* Translated by N. I. Stone. 2nd rev. ed. Chicago: Charles H. Kerr, 1904.

——. *The Economic and Philosophic Manuscripts of 1844.* Edited by D. J. Struik. Translated by Martin Milligan. New York: International Publishers, 1964.

——. *Grundrisse: Foundations of the Critique of Political Economy.* Translated by Martin Nicolaus. New York: Random House, Vintage, 1973.

——. *The Poverty of Philosophy.* New York: International Publishers, 1963.

——. *Writings of the Young Marx on Philosophy and Society.* Edited and translated by Loyd D. Easton and Kurt H. Guddat. Garden City, N. Y.: Doubleday Anchor, 1967.

Marx, Karl, and Engels, Frederick. *Collected Works.* New York: International Publishers, 1975. Vol. 3.

——. *Feuerbach: Opposition of the Materialist and Idealist Outlooks (The First Part of "The German Ideology").* 1965. Reprint. London: Lawrence and Wishart, 1973.

Mauss, Marcel. *The Gift: Forms and Functions of Exchange in Archaic Societies.* Translated by Ian Cunnison. 1925. Reprint. New York: W. W. Norton, 1967.

Meek, Ronald L., ed. *Precursors of Adam Smith: Readings in Economic History and Theory.* London: J. M. Dent, 1973.

Mellown, Muriel J. "The Development of Imagery in 'Home at Grasmere.' " *Wordsworth's Circle* 5 (1974): 23-27.

Metzger, Lore. "Wordsworth's Pastoral Covenant." *Modern Language Quarterly* 37 (1976): 307-23.

Mill, John Stuart. *Autobiography*. Edited by Jack Stillinger. London: Oxford University Press, 1971.

——. *Essays on Some Unsettled Questions of Political Economy*. London, 1844. Reprint. Series of Scarce Works on Political Economy, No. 7. London: London School of Economics and Political Science, 1948.

——. *Principles of Political Economy with Some of Their Applications to Social Philosophy*. Edited by J. M. Robson. Vols. 2 and 3 in *Collected Works of John Stuart Mill*, general editor, F. E. L. Priestley. Toronto: University of Toronto Press, 1965.

Milton, John. *Complete Poems and Major Prose*. Edited by Merritt Y. Hughes. New York: Odyssey, 1957.

Moorman, Mary. *William Wordsworth: A Biography (The Early Years, 1770-1803)*. 1957. Reprint. London: Oxford University Press, 1968.

Morris, William. [*Selected Writings*] . Edited by G. D. H. Cole. London: Nonesuch Press, 1934.

Movius, Geoffrey H. "Caviar and Bread: Ezra Pound and William Carlos Williams, 1902-1914." *Journal of Modern Literature* 5 (1976): 383-406.

Mun, Thomas. *England's Treasure by Forraign Trade*. 1664. Reprint. Oxford: Basil Blackwood, 1967.

Myrdal, Gunnar. *The Political Element in the Development of Economic Theory*. Translated by Paul Streeten. Cambridge, Mass.: Harvard University Press, 1954.

Nussbaum, F. L. *A History of the Economic Institutions of Modern Europe*. New York: F. S. Crofts, 1933.

Ovid. *Metamorphoses*. Translated by Frank Justus Miller. 2 vols. Loeb Library. Cambridge, Mass.: Harvard University Press, 1959.

Owen, W. J. B. *Wordsworth as Critic*. Toronto: University of Toronto Press, 1969.

Palgrave, Sir Robert Harry Inglis. *Dictionary of Political Economy*. Edited by Henry Higgs. 3 vols. London: Macmillan, 1925-26.

Parrish, Stephen. "*Michael* and the Pastoral Ballad." In *Bicentenary Wordsworth Studies in Memory of John Alban Finch*, edited by Jonathan Wordsworth, pp. 50-75. Ithaca: Cornell University Press, 1970.

Peacock, Thomas Love. *The Works of Thomas Love Peacock*. Edited by Henry Cole. 2 vols. London: Richard Bentley and Son, 1875.

Perkins, David. *Wordsworth and the Poetry of Sincerity*. Cambridge, Mass.: Harvard University Press, Belknap Press, 1964.

Petty, William. *The Economic Writings of William Petty*. Edited by C. H. Hull. 2 vols. Cambridge: Cambridge University Press, 1899.

Plato. *The Republic of Plato*. Translated by F. M. Cornford. New York: Oxford University Press, 1941.

Polanyi, Karl. *The Great Transformation: The Political and Economic Origins of Our Time*. 1944. Reprint. Boston: Beacon Press, 1957.

——. *Primitive, Archaic and Modern Economies*. Edited by George Dalton. Boston: Beacon Press, 1971.

Postlethwayt, Malachy. *Britain's Commercial Interest Explained and Improved*. 2 vols. London, 1757.

——. *Great Britain's True System*. London, 1757.

——. *The Universal Dictionary of Trade and Commerce, Translated from the French of . . . Savary*. 2 vols. London, 1755.

Pound, Ezra. *The Cantos of Ezra Pound*. New York: New Directions, 1970.

——. *The Letters of Ezra Pound, 1907-1941*. Edited by D. D. Paige. New York: Harcourt, Brace and World, 1950.

——. *Literary Essays of Ezra Pound*. Edited by T. S. Eliot. New York: New Directions, 1968.

——. *Selected Prose, 1909-1965*. Edited by William Cookson. New York: New Directions, 1975.

Quesnay, F. *Oeuvres economiques et philosophiques de F. Quesnay*. Edited by Auguste Oncken. Frankfurt: Joseph Baer; Paris: Jules Peelman, 1888.

Quintilian. *The Institutio Oratoria of Quintilian*. Translated by H. E. Butler. 4 vols. Loeb Library. London: Heinemann, 1921.

Raine, Kathleen. *Blake and Tradition*. 2 vols. Princeton: Princeton University Press, 1968.

Ramsey, Jonathan. "Wordsworth's Silent Poet." *Modern Language Quarterly* 37 (1976): 260-80.

Redfield, R. "The Art of Social Science." *American Journal of Sociology* 54 (1948): 181-90.

Reisner, M. E. "The Wages of Art: Blake and His Public." *Culture* 31 (1970): 327-37.

Ricardo, David. *The Principles of Political Economy and Taxation*. Everyman's Library. New York: E. P. Dutton; London: J. M. Dent, 1973.

Riddell, Joseph N. *The Inverted Bell: Modernism and the Counterpoetics of William Carlos Williams*. Baton Rouge: Louisiana State University Press, 1974.

Robbins, Lionel, Lord. *An Essay on the Nature and Significance of Economic Science*. 2nd. ed. London: Macmillan, 1935.

——. *The Theory of Economic Policy in English Classical Political Economy*. London: Macmillan, 1952.

Rosenmeyer, Thomas G. *The Green Cabinet: Theocritus and the European Pastoral Lyric*. Berkeley and Los Angeles: University of California Press, 1969.

Rousseau, Jean-Jacques. *Discours sur l'origine et les fondements de l'inégalité parmi les hommes*. Edited by Henri François Muller and René E. G. Vaillant. New York: Oxford University Press, 1922.

Ruskin, John. *Fors Clavigera: Letters to the Workmen and Labourers of Great Britain*. New ed. 4 vols. London: George Allen, 1896.

——. *The Works of John Ruskin*. Edited by E. T. Cook and Alexander Wedderburn. 39 vols. London: G. Allen and Unwin, 1903-12.

Ruthven, K. K. "Keats and *Dea Moneta*." *Studies in Romanticism* 15(1975): 445-59.

Sankey, Benjamin. *A Companion to William Carlos Williams's* Paterson. Berkeley and Los Angeles: University of California Press, 1971.

Sanzo, Eileen. "William Blake and the Technological Age." *Thought* 46 (1971): 577-91.

Saussure, Ferdinand de. *Course in General Linguistics.* Edited by Charles Bally and Albert Sechehaye. Translated by Wade Baskin. 2nd rev. ed. Glasgow: Fontana-Collins, 1974.

Schneider, Harold K. *Economic Man: The Anthropology of Economics.* New York: Free Press, 1974.

Scholes, Robert. *Structuralism in Literature: An Introduction.* New Haven: Yale University Press, 1974.

Schumpeter, J. A. *History of Economic Analysis.* Edited by Elizabeth Boody Schumpeter. New York: Oxford University Press, 1954.

Shakespeare, William. *The Complete Works.* General editor, Alfred Harbage. Baltimore: Penguin, 1969.

Shakespeare's England: An Account of the Life and Manners of His Age. 2 vols. Oxford: Clarendon Press, 1916.

Shell, Marc. *The Economy of Literature.* Baltimore: Johns Hopkins Press, 1978.

Shorer, Mark. *William Blake: The Politics of Vision.* New York: Henry Holt, 1946.

Smith, Adam. *An Inquiry into the Nature and Causes of the Wealth of Nations.* Edited by R. H. Campbell and A. S. Skinner. Textual editor, W. B. Todd. 2 vols. Glasgow Edition of the Works and Correspondence of Adam Smith. Oxford: Clarendon Press, 1976.

———. *Lectures on Justice, Police, Revenue and Arms: Delivered in the University of Glasgow, Reported by a Student in 1763.* Edited by Edwin Cannan. Oxford: Clarendon Press, 1896.

———. *Lectures on Rhetoric and Belles Lettres: Delivered in the University of Glasgow by Adam Smith, Reported by a Student in 1762–63.* Edited by John M. Lothian. London: Thomas Nelson and Sons, 1963.

———. *The Theory of Moral Sentiments.* Edited by D. D. Raphael and A. L. Macfie. Glasgow Edition of the Works and Correspondence of Adam Smith. Oxford: Clarendon Press, 1976.

Sonn, Carl. "Sir Guyon in the Cave of Mammon." *Studies in English Literature* 1 (1961): 17–30.

Southall, Raymond. *Literature and the Rise of Capitalism.* London: Lawrence and Wishart, 1973.

Spengler, Joseph. "The Aesthetics of Population." *Population Bulletin* 13 (1957): 61–75.

Spenser, Edmund. *The Complete Poetical Works of Spenser.* Edited by R. E. N. Dodge. Boston: Houghton Mifflin, 1908.

Sprat, Bishop Thomas. *History of the Royal Society (1667).* Edited by Jackson I. Cope and Harold Whitmore Jones. Washington University Studies. St. Louis: Washington University Press, 1959.

Stambler, Peter D. "The Development of Guyon's Christian Temperance." *English Literary Renaissance* 7 (1977): 51–89.

Stamp, Sir Josiah. *Some Economic Factors in Modern Life.* London: P. S. King and Son, 1929.

Steuart, Sir James. *An Inquiry into the Principles of Political Oeconomy: Being an Essay on the Science of Domestic Policy in Free Nations.* 2 vols. London, 1767.

Stone, Lawrence. *The Crisis of the Aristocracy.* Oxford: Clarendon Press, 1965.

———. *Family and Fortune: Studies in Aristocratic Finance in the Sixteenth and Seventeenth Centuries.* Oxford: Clarendon Press, 1973.

Tawney, R. H. *The Agrarian Problem in the Sixteenth Century.* London: Longmans, Green, 1912.

———. *Religion and the Rise of Capitalism: A Historical Study.* 1926. Reprint. Harmondsworth: Penguin, 1975.

Taylor, Overton H. *A History of Economic Thought.* New York: McGraw-Hill, 1960.

Taylor, P. B. "Commerce and Comedy in *Sir Gawain.*" *Philological Quarterly* 50 (1971): 1-15.

Thirlwall, John C. "William Carlos Williams' 'Paterson': The Search for the Redeeming Language—A Personal Epic in Five Parts." *New Directions* 17 (1961): 252-310.

Thoreau, Henry David. *Walden and Civil Disobedience.* Edited by Sherman Paul. Boston: Houghton Mifflin, 1960.

Vogler, Thomas A. *Preludes to Vision: The Epic Venture in Blake, Wordsworth, Keats, and Hart Crane.* Berkeley and Los Angeles: University of California Press, 1971.

Weaver, Mike. *William Carlos Williams: The American Background.* Cambridge: Cambridge University Press, 1971.

Weber, Max. *The Protestant Ethic and the Spirit of Capitalism.* Translated by Talcott Parsons. New York: Charles Scribner's Sons, 1958.

Weiskel, Thomas. *The Romantic Sublime: Studies in the Structure and Psychology of Transcendence.* Baltimore: Johns Hopkins Press, 1976.

Weisskopf, Walter A. *The Psychology of Economics.* Chicago: University of Chicago Press, 1955.

Werge, Thomas. "The Idea and Significance of 'Economy' before *Walden.*" *Emerson Society Quarterly* 77 (1974): 270-74.

Williams, Harold R., and Huffnagle, John D., eds. *Macroeconomic Theory: Selected Readings.* New York: Appleton-Century-Crofts, 1969.

Williams, Raymond. *The Country and the City.* New York: Oxford University Press, 1973.

———. *Culture and Society, 1780-1950.* 1958. Reprint. Harmondsworth: Penguin, 1963.

———. *Keywords: A Vocabulary of Culture and Society.* New York: Oxford University Press, 1976.

———. *The Long Revolution.* 1961. Reprint. Harmondsworth: Pelican, 1965.

———. *Marxism and Literature.* New York: Oxford University Press, 1977.

Williams, William Carlos. *The Autobiography of William Carlos Williams.* New York: New Directions, 1967.

———. *Imaginations.* Edited by Webster Schott. New York: New Directions, 1970.

———. Letter to Gorham Munson, 5 March 1934. Center for Pound Studies, Yale University Library.

———. *Paterson.* New York: New Directions, 1963.

———. *Paterson* manuscript dated 3 August 1950. Lockwood Collection,

Library of the State University of New York at Buffalo.

Woodring, Carl. *Politics in English Romantic Poetry*. Cambridge, Mass.: Harvard University Press, 1970.

Wordsworth, William. *Letters of William and Dorothy Wordsworth: The Early Years.* Edited by Ernest de Selincourt. Rev. ed. by Chester L. Shaver. Oxford: Clarendon Press, 1967.

———. *Letters of William and Dorothy Wordsworth: The Middle Years. Part I* (1806-11) edited by Ernest de Selincourt; rev. ed. by Mary Moorman. *Part II* (1812-20) edited by Mary Moorman and Alan G. Hill. Oxford: Clarendon Press, 1969-70.

———. *The Poetical Works of William Wordsworth*. Edited by Ernest de Selincourt. Rev. ed. by Helen Darbishire. 5 vols. Oxford: Clarendon Press, 1952-59.

———. *The Prelude: Or, Growth of a Poet's Mind*. Edited by Ernest de Selincourt. Rev. ed. by Helen Darbishire. Oxford: Clarendon Press, 1959.

———. *The Prose Works of William Wordsworth*. Edited by W. J. B. Owen and Jane Worthington Smyser. 3 vols. Oxford: Clarendon Press, 1974.

———. *Wordsworth's Literary Criticism*. Edited by W. J. B. Owen. London: Routledge and Kegan Paul, 1974.

Yeats, William Butler. *The Autobiography of William Butler Yeats*. New York: Macmillan, 1965.

———. *The Collected Poems of William Butler Yeats*. 2nd ed. New York: Macmillan, 1956.

INDEX

Alanus de Insulis, 57–58

Aquinas, Thomas, 58, 152–53

Aristotle, 37, 42, 44, 45, 49, 71, 108; and pseudo-Aristotle, 46; and Spenser, 52, 54–56, 61–62, 63, 66. Works: *Ethics,* 38–40, 52, 55; *Poetics,* 99 n. 43; *Politics,* 40–42; *Rhetoric,* 42 n. 11, 115 n. 17

Arnaut, Daniel, 248, 249

Ashton, T. S., 117 n. 27, 303

Astor, John Jacob, 23, 286

Auden, W. H., 162–65

Avery, Samuel Putnam, 258–60

Bacon, Francis, 86

Bagehot, Walter, 16, 48, 50, 76, 83, 276

Barker, Ernest, 39, 41

Barnfield, Richard, 54 n. 34

Beaumont, John, 16–17, 22

Benjamin, Walter, 141 n. 5

Bentham, Jeremy, 303

Berger, Harry, 68, 291

Bible, quotations from, 43, 57, 65, 93, 95, 106–7, 118, 128, 129, 130, 143

Blackstone, Bernard, 298

Blake, William (economist), 117–18

Blake, William (poet), 90, 107, 108, 110–33, 195, 196, 215; and alchemy, 116, 118, 298; and Bullion Committee, 117–18; and economists, 114, 117–18, 120–21, 125–27, 129, 130–31; and labor value, 114, 125–28, 130–33; and Yeats, 164. Works: *America,* 125; "The countless gold of a merry heart," 119–20, 121–22; *Four Zoas,* 113, 124, 132; *Jerusalem,* 113, 114, 115, 116 n. 23, 127–33, 137, 200; "London," 122; *Marriage of Heaven and Hell,* 120–21; *Milton,* 113–14; *Notebook,* 114–19, 298; "Public Address," 122–23, 297–98; *Visions of the Daughters of Albion,* 121, 125; *Visions of the Last Judgment,* 120–21, 122, 123–24

Blasing, Mutlu, 24, 286

Bloom, Harold, 201, 298

Bostetter, E. E., 199

Breit, William, 294

Bronowski, J., 299

Brown, Norman O., 116 n. 24, 303

Burke, Kenneth, 284
Burns, Robert, 213
Byron, George Gordon, Lord, 232

Calvert, Raisley, 197–99, 224
Cannan, Edwin, 144 n. 10, 288
Cassirer, Ernst, 69
Claudel, Paul, 165
Coleridge, Samuel Taylor, 8, 13, 14, 20, 22, 34, 205, 300
Confucius, 248, 249
Cook, Louise, 283
Cottle, Joseph, 305
Crane, Hart, 155–56, 165, 237, 254
Cromwell, Oliver, 151
Curie, Madame, 266, 270

Dahlberg, Edward, 250
Darmesteter, Arsène, 43
Davenport, Guy, 247 n. 15
Dawson, Leven Magruder, 158 n. 34
Defoe, Daniel, 18, 22. Works: *Moll Flanders*, 18–19, 20; *Robinson Crusoe*, 18, 20, 285
De Quincey, Thomas, 36, 276; and Malthus, 89; and Ricardo, 89–90; and Ruskin, 104–5. Works: "Dialogues of Three Templars on Political Economy," 89–91
Derrida, Jacques, 284
Dewey, John, 142, 192
Dickens, Charles, 27
Donne, John, 16, 290–91
Douglas, C. H., 244, 246
Douglas, Norman, 270
Douglas, Wallace W., 196 n. 1
Dreiser, Theodore, 247
Du Cange, Domino, 43, 288
Duchamp, Marcel, 3–5, 13, 14, 23, 274
Durling, Dwight L., 152 n. 25
Dyer, George, 207

Eaves, Morris, 111 n. 4
Eliade, Mircea, 116 n. 21
Eliot, George, 20–22
Eliot, T. S., 13, 242–43, 248, 254, 271

Engels, Frederick, 98, 145, 147
Erdman, David V., 111, 112, 115 n. 15, 119, 132
Evans, Maurice, 291–92

Feltes, N. N., 284
Ferguson, Francis, 196 n. 3
Fetter, Frank Whitson, 119 n. 28
Finley, M. I., 41, 43 n. 15
Fleishman, Avrom, 284
Foucault, Michel, 10, 71–72, 73, 91–92, 289–90
Fox, Charles James, 220 n. 30
Franklin, Benjamin, 19–20, 22, 194
Fraser, L. M., 73, 168 n. 2, 278 n. 3
French, A., 287
Freud, Sigmund, 9, 73, 96, 238, 245, 255, 273; and jokes, 115–16, 239–41, 267, 272; and primal words, 73
Friedman, Michael, 307
Frost, Robert, 188–95. Works: *A Boy's Will*, 188; "The Most of It," 191; "Mowing," 188–92; "Provide, Provide," 188, 192–95
Frye, Northrop, 113

Gaskell, Elizabeth, 87–88
Gaudier-Brzeska, Henri, 244
Gilchrist, Alexander, 298
Ginsberg, Allen, 250, 269
Godwin, William, 93, 295
Goldsmith, Oliver, 219–20
Gonne, Maud, 163
Googe, Barnabe, 55
Gray, Thomas, 262–63, 264
Gresham, Thomas, 13
Gutenberg, Johann, 103–4

Hamilton, Alexander, 252–53
Hartman, Geoffrey, 218, 306
Hatzfeld, Adolphe, 243
Hauser, Arnold, 287
Hazlitt, William, 208
Heckscher, Eli F., 13 n. 13
Hegel, G. W. F., 284
Herskovits, Melville J., 36 n. 2, 294
Hobbes, Thomas, 302–3

Hochman, Harold M., 294
Horace, 16
Huffnagle, John D., 294
Huizinga, Johan, 277
Hume, David, 146-47, 152-53, 303
Hutcheson, Frances, 45-46
Hutchinson, Sara, 215
Hyman, Stanley Edgar, 181 n. 17

Ingarden, Roman, 142 n. 7
Iser, Wolfgang, 142 n. 7

Jarrell, Randall, 246, 251, 256-57
Jefferson, Thomas, 157, 248
Jevons, W. Stanley, 85-87, 88, 108
Johnson, E. A. J., 43 n. 18, 127
    n. 37, 148
Jonson, Ben, 14-17, 19, 22, 76,
    243, 290

Kahn, Otto, 155
Kamen, Henry, 69 n. 45
Keats, John, 105-6, 159, 248, 292,
    296
Kenner, Hugh, 251
Kermode, Frank, 291-92
Keynes, Geoffrey, 119
Keynes, John Maynard, 294
Keynes, John Neville, 149, 287
Kiernan, V. G., 196 n. 1
Knight, Frank H., 76, 96, 279 n. 6,
    293, 294
Knight, L. C., 13 n. 12
Kroeber, Karl, 307

Land, Stephen K., 228 n. 27
Langer, Suzanne K., 29-30
Lawrence, D. H., 20
L'Enfant, Pierre, 252
Lerner, Laurence, 286
Levin, Harry, 69 n. 45
Lévi-Strauss, Claude, 94, 96, 139
Levy, H., 269-70
Locke, John, 95-96, 146, 157, 167-
    69, 174, 178, 227, 230
Lyons, Bridget Gellert, 286

McCulloch, J. R., 173

Macfie, A. L., x, 171 n. 4, 289
MacLean, Kenneth, 200 n. 10
MacLeish, Archibald, 162
Malthus, Thomas, 92-94, 95, 102,
    108; and Godwin, 93, 295.
    Works: *Principle of Population*,
    92-94, 95
Mammon. *See* Spenser, Edmund
Mandeville, Bernard, 171
Marlowe, Christopher, 243
Marshall, Alfred, 37, 144, 289
Martineau, Harriet, 8-9, 12
Marvell, Andrew, 151, 190
Marx, Groucho, 238, 239, 240, 266
Marx, Karl, 30, 37, 87, 88, 99, 125,
    126, 129, 159, 162, 172, 173-
    88, 189, 190, 192, 194, 202, 209,
    222, 234, 246, 271, 279-80, 281,
    284; and division of labor, 138-
    42, 147, 148, 167, 187; and Marx-
    ism, 138-41, 186, 187; and Ri-
    cardo, 47, 173, 178, 187; and
    sexual symbolism, 96; and Smith,
    47-48, 143-45, 173, 178, 185,
    187; and structuralism, 138-41.
    Works: *Capital*, 173-88, 303-4;
    Critique of Political Economy,
    138; *The German Ideology*, 139-
    40; *Grundrisse*, 47. *See also* En-
    gels, Frederick
Mathews, William, 197
Mauss, Marcel, 36, 286
Mendelief, Dmitri Ivanovich, 266
Merwin, W. S., 162
Metzger, Lore, 222
Meun, Jean de, 290
Midas, 6, 99
Mill, John Stuart, 73, 108, 137, 276,
    281; and Jevons, 85-86; and
    Marx, 84; and Ruskin, 79-80,
    105, 281; and Harriet Taylor,
    82-83; and Wordsworth, 81-82,
    84, 209, 232. Works: *Autobi-
    ography*, 79-82, 85; *Essays on
    Some Unsettled Questions of Po-
    litical Economy*, 232, 294; *Princi-
    ples of Political Economy*, 76-85
Miller, Perry, 286

Milton, John, 113-14, 130, 165, 198; and Wordsworth, 198, 201, 225, 226, 227, 228
Mirabeau, Honoré Gabriel Riquetti, comte de, 48-49, 69
Moorman, Mary, 196 n. 1, 198 n. 7, 216 n. 26
Morris, William, 103, 156-59; and Ruskin, 103, 302
Mun, Thomas, 149-51, 152, 153
Munson, Gorham, 245, 246
Myrdal, Gunnar, 146 n. 11

Nardi, Marcia [Cress] , 250, 256-60, 264, 269

Orage, A. R., 246
Ovid, 113, 124
Owen, W. J. B., 208 n. 19

Parrish, Stephen, 216 n. 26
Paul, Sherman, 27 n. 35
Peacock, Thomas Love, 38, 120 n. 32
Perkins, David, 201 n. 13
Petty, William, 73, 74, 95, 148, 153
Plautus, 15
Polanyi, Karl, 36-37, 41, 45, 46, 48, 73, 74, 99-101, 287, 294; and Aristotle, 41; and economic language, 73, 74; and fictions, 99–101, 287; and physiocrats, 45, 46
Polybius, 287
Poole, Thomas, 216
Postlethwayt, Malachy, 148-49, 301, 303
Pound, Ezra, 123 n. 33, 237, 238, 246, 247-51, 253, 254, 269, 270, 271, 273; and economics, 243-45; and Gaudier-Brzeska, 244; and imagism, 238-39, 240, 241. *See also* Williams, William Carlos
Propertius, 249

Quesnay, F., 48
Quintilian, 43

Raine, Kathleen, 116
Ramsey, Jonathan, 228 n. 27
Reisner, M. E., 111 n. 4
Ricardo, David, 74, 95, 98 n. 39, 108, 162, 277; and bullion crisis, 117; and labor, 154, 173, 178; and Marx, 47; and Smith, 154, 173, 277; and Thoreau, 25, 26; and value, 88-89, 97. *See also* De Quincey, Thomas; Marx, Karl; Smith, Adam
Riddell, Joseph, 247
Robbins, Lionel, Lord, 73, 101
Rosenmeyer, Thomas G., 306, 307
Rousseau, Jean Jacques, 296
Ruskin, John, 6-7, 11, 13, 22, 50, 73, 101-8, 109, 130, 137, 209, 281; and De Quincey, 104-5; and Keats, 105-6; and labor, 154-55, 161; and Malthus, 102; and Marx, 105; and *Merchant of Venice*, 103, 108, 276-77; and Mill, 79-80, 105, 281; and Morris, 103, 302; and Yeats, 161. Works: *Crown of Wild Olives*, 300; *Fors Clavigera*, 103 n. 48; *Political Economy of Art*, 105-6; *Sesame and Lilies*, 103
Ruthven, K. K., 296

Said, Edward W., 181 n. 17
Sankey, Benjamin, 247, 308
Sanzo, Eileen, 111 n. 4
Sappho, 249
Saussure, Ferdinand de, 9-10, 235
Say, J. B., 25, 26, 88, 90
Scholes, Robert, 139
Schumpeter, J. A., 43 n. 18
Shakespeare, William, 242, 277, 279. Works: *As You Like It*, 25; *The Merchant of Venice*, 103, 108, 276-82; *Venus and Adonis*, 309
Shell, Marc, 10-11, 15 n. 18, 284, 287
Shelley, Percy Bysshe, 229, 275, 292
Smith, Adam, 23, 93, 161, 164, 176, 246, 277; and Bible, 143-44; and

Blake, 125-26; and *homo oeconomicus,* 37; and Invisible Hand, 171-72; and labor, 125-26, 143-46, 153-54, 163, 169-70; and Marx, 47-48, 143-45, 178, 185; and price, 97-98, 277; and Ricardo, 154, 277; and Thoreau, 25, 26; and Wordsworth, 200, 208, 220, 230. Works: *Lectures on Justice,* 74 n. 16; *Lectures on Rhetoric,* 74-76; *Theory of Moral Sentiments,* 74, 171; *Wealth of Nations,* 46-48, 74, 125-26, 143-45, 153-54, 163, 169-73, 185, 220, 288-89

Snorri Sturluson, 5-6, 7
Snyder, Gary, 171-72
Socrates, 25
Southall, Raymond, 14 n. 17
Southey, Robert, 305
Spenser, Edmund, 49-69, 71, 80, 94, 248; and Guyon, 38, 50, 51-67, 193; and House of Alma, 67-68; and Mammon, 38, 44, 49-69, 70, 94, 182, 193, 290
Sprat, Bishop Thomas, 151-52
Stambler, Peter, 68 n. 43
Stedman, J. G., 125
Steele, Robert, 116 n. 20
Steinberg, S. H., 104 n. 49
Steuart, Sir James, 44-45, 46, 73, 149
Stevens, Wallace, 8, 254, 275, 286
Stone, Lawrence, 13-14

Tawney, R. H., 301-2
Tayler, Edward W., 279 n. 5
Taylor, Overton H., 77 n. 21
Taylor, P. B., 286-87
Temple, W., 75
Terence, 15
Thirwall, John C., 270 n. 28
Thomson, George, 235-36, 238, 250, 274
Thoreau, Henry David, 23-24, 36, 40, 71, 275. Works: *Walden,* 23-34

Thucydides, 16
Trollope, Anthony, 88
Turgot, A. R. J., 74, 296
Tzanck, Daniel, 3

Unwin, George, 13 n. 11

Van Buren, Martin, 248
Veblen, Thorstein, 246
Vergil, 152
Vogler, Thomas A., 299-300

Wallace, Mike, 250
Weaver, Mike, 246
Weber, Max, 78, 95, 130, 144
Weiskel, Thomas, 196 n. 2, 305-6
Weisskopf, W. A., 94-96, 98, 99, 146-47, 279
Werge, Thomas, 24, 286
Whateley, Archbishop, 168 n. 2
Williams, Harold R., 294
Williams, Raymond, 14 n. 15, 104, 111, 137-38, 142, 186, 220 n. 29, 243, 295
Williams, William Carlos, 143, 234-38, 245-75; and Freud, 245, 267, and Paterson (city), 252-53, 260; and Pound, 237, 238, 245, 246, 247-51, 253, 269. Works: *Autobiography,* 252; "The Desert Music," 264 n. 24; *In the American Grain,* 253, 263; *Kora in Hell,* 253; *Paterson,* 236-38, 245-75; *Spring and All,* 270
Wordsworth, Dorothy, 223, 224
Wordsworth, William, 90, 111, 142, 195, 196-233, 234, 270; and Calvert, 197-99, 201, 224; and Coleridge, 205; and Cottle, 305; and Dorothy, 223, 224; and Dyer, 207; and the georgic, 207, 222, 229, 231, 307; and Goldsmith, 219-20, 221; and Sara Hutchinson, 215; and Locke, 227, 230; and Marx, 202, 209, 222-23; and William Mathews, 197; and Mill, 81-82, 84, 209, 232; and Milton,

198, 201, 225, 226, 227, 228; and the pastoral, 216, 218-20, 221-22, 229, 231, 306, 307; and Thomas Poole, 216; and Smith, 200, 208, 220, 230; and Southey, 305. Works: *The Excursion,* 205, 206-7, 220, 233; "Home at Grasmere," 223-32; *Lyrical Ballads,* 216, 224, 305; "Michael," 215-23, 227; Preface to the *Lyrical Ballads,* 201, 202, 207-8; *The Prelude,* 197-99, 201, 205-6, 223, 224, 228, 272; *The Recluse,* 223; "Resolution and Independence,"

212-15; *Salisbury Plain,* 304

Xenophon, 75, 287

Yeats, William Butler, 156-65, 237; and Auden, 162-65; and Morris, 156-59; and Ruskin, 161. Works: "Adam's Curse," 156; "Among School Children," 157-59; *Autobiography,* 156; "The Choice," 159-61; "Coole Park and Ballylee, 1931," 159; *The Winding Stair,* 159

Zukofsky, Louis, 234

English Language Notes, for material from Kurt Heinzelman, "Blake's Golden Word," *English Language Notes* 15, no. 1 (September 1977).

Metheun & Co. Ltd., for material from T. S. Eliot, *The Sacred Wood*. Reprinted by permission of Metheun & Co. Ltd.

Modern Language Quarterly, for material from Kurt Heinzelman, "William Blake and the Economics of the Imagination," *Modern Language Quarterly* 39, no. 2 (June 1978).

Random House, Inc., for material from W. H. Auden, "In Memory of W. B. Yeats," in *Collected Shorter Poems, 1927-1957* (Random House, 1964). Copyright © 1961, 1964 by W. H. Auden. Reprinted by permission of Random House, Inc.

The Estate of Louis Zukofsky, for material from " 'A'-8," in *'A' 1-12*. Reprinted by permission of Jonathan Cape Ltd.

Gary Snyder, for material from "The Market," in *Mountains and Rivers without End,* copyright 1970 by Gary Snyder. Reprinted by permission of the author.

Holt, Rinehart and Winston, and the Estate of Robert Frost, for material from *The Poetry of Robert Frost,* edited by Edward Connery Lathem. Copyright 1934, © 1969 by Holt, Rinehart and Winston. Copyright 1936, 1942, © 1962 by Robert Frost. Copyright © 1964, 1970 by Lesley Frost Ballantine. Reprinted by permission of Holt,Rinehart and Winston, Publishers, and Jonathan Cape Ltd.

Houghton Mifflin Company, for material from Archibald MacLeish, *New and Collected Poems, 1917-1976,* copyright 1976 by Archibald MacLeish. Reprinted by permission of Houghton Mifflin Company.

Macmillan Publishing Co., Inc., and A. P. Watt Ltd., for material from "The Choice," in *Collected Poems,* by William Butler Yeats. Copyright 1933 by Macmillan Publishing Co., Inc., renewed 1961 by Bertha Georgie Yeats; for material from "Among School Children," in *Collected Poems,* by William Butler Yeats. Copyright 1928 by Macmillan Publishing Co., Inc., renewed 1956 by Georgie Yeats; and for material from *Autobiography,* by William Butler Yeats. Copyright 1916, 1935 by Macmillan Publishing Co., Inc., renewed 1944, 1963 by Bertha Georgie Yeats. Reprinted with permission of Macmillan Publishing Co., Inc.

W. W. Norton & Company, Inc., for material from Sigmund Freud, *Jokes and Their Relation to the Unconscious,* translated by James Strachey. Reprinted by permission of W. W. Norton & Company, Inc.

Library of Congress Cataloging in Publication Data
Heinzelman, Kurt.
The economics of the imagination.
Bibliography: p.
Includes index.
1. English literature—History and criticism.
2. American literature—History and criticism.
3. Economics in literature.   4. Economics—History.
I. Title.
PR409.E37H4   820'.9'31   79-4019
ISBN 0-87023-274-6